Displacing Jesus

Displacing Jesus

An Immanent Reading of Jefferson's *The Life and Morals of Jesus of Nazareth*

CHARLES A. WILSON

CASCADE *Books* • Eugene, Oregon

DISPLACING JESUS
An Immanent Reading of Jefferson's *The Life and Morals of Jesus of Nazareth*

Copyright © 2024 Charles A. Wilson. All rights reserved. Except for brief quotations in critical publications or reviews, no part of this book may be reproduced in any manner without prior written permission from the publisher. Write: Permissions, Wipf and Stock Publishers, 199 W. 8th Ave., Suite 3, Eugene, OR 97401.

Cascade Books
An Imprint of Wipf and Stock Publishers
199 W. 8th Ave., Suite 3
Eugene, OR 97401

www.wipfandstock.com

PAPERBACK ISBN: 978-1-6667-6376-8
HARDCOVER ISBN: 978-1-6667-6377-5
EBOOK ISBN: 978-1-6667-6378-2

Cataloguing-in-Publication data:

Names: Wilson, Charles A. (Charles Alan), 1947–, author.

Title: Displacing Jesus : an immanent reading of Jefferson's "The Life and Morals of Jesus of Nazareth" / Charles A. Wilson.

Description: Eugene, OR: Cascade Books, 2024. | Includes bibliographical references.

Identifiers: ISBN 978-1-6667-6376-8 (paperback). | ISBN 978-1-6667-6377-5 (hardcover). | ISBN 978-1-6667-6378-2 (ebook).

Subjects: LSCH: Jefferson, Thomas, 1743–1826. | Jesus Christ. | Bible—Gospels—Criticism, interpretation, etc. | Theology.

Classification: E322 W55 2024 (print). | E322 (ebook).

VERSION NUMBER 011524

Contents

Acknowledgments | vii

1 Introduction | 1
2 Beginnings | 6
3 The Teacher of Wisdom | 21
4 The Ethic | 31
5 Lukan Additions to the Sermon | 44
6 Parabolic Discourse | 56
7 Performing the Wisdom I | 64
8 Performing the Wisdom II | 75
9 Final Affairs | 83
10 The Displacement of Jesus: A Cataphatic Account | 109
11 Methodological Considerations | 118
12 Immanent Theological Conversations | 140
13 Jefferson and Religion | 181
14 Contributions of the *LMJN* to the Understanding of Religion in Jefferson | 222

Bibliography | 237

Acknowledgments

I wish to thank Barbara S. Wilson for hours and hours of careful, wifely editing; students Melody H. Suite and Lukas S. Lindgren for Jeffersonian insights; Prof. Steven Greiert for locating Jefferson for me; colleagues Martin, Schweiker, Miller, and Ottati for years of drafts at the Theology and Ethics Colloquies; and Anderson, Cooper, Anderson-Hermann, and Peterson for the June seminars.

1

Introduction

At least since the 1800 presidential election, people have puzzled over Thomas Jefferson's elusive and secretive views on religion and Christianity. Some wonder why he says so little in public about his views. Is he a church person of some kind? Others suspect his Enlightenment views are dangerous. Does he even believe in God, and if so, in what kind of God? Is he one of those deists, like other founding fathers of the republic? Much rests on these and related questions, and they come up time and again. People are curious what the presidential giant thinks, and especially so, since he works to hide his views on religion. Jefferson even turns his secrecy into a general principle: humans are to keep their beliefs to themselves and not bother with others' views, as religion is a private business before one's deity. To this very day, people have picked up multifarious and enigmatic signals, mostly from Jefferson's private letters, and construed them like the duck-rabbit of psychology.[1] One day Jefferson is a pillar of the Christian nation;

---

1. See Vicchio, *Jefferson's Religion*, 2. Current Jefferson research swings back and forth, whether researchers and others see a duck or a rabbit, more of a religious man, maybe even a Christian, or more of a secular figure. Venerable efforts (i.e., Sanford's and Gaustad's) to correct older, more secular interpretations of Jefferson have accented his consistent pattern of concern for religion and Christianity amid his intense criticisms of the two. And recently the duck has turned into the rabbit: where newer critics (like Scherr and Holowchak) have dismantled the religious portrait of Jefferson by accenting the intense critical record about religion in his corpus. On a wider canvas, Jefferson himself has become as much a mirror to the unfolding American character as Jesus has been to the Christian world. His image is re-created over and over as a portrait of what the Americans want to be. See Ellis, *American Sphinx*, 291–302, for a history of the American struggle with the character of Jefferson, a struggle in which he can be all things to all people. The theme of mirroring in Jefferson research is deep and complex. We will see Jefferson mirroring himself in the image of Jesus he constructs,

the next he is a dangerous modern pagan. His views have been subject to mythicizing, to debunking critiques, and to religious and political attempts to co-opt him.[2] Indeed, in popular discussions, in amateurish research, and even among critical scholars, Jefferson's views on religion have become fodder for defining an evolving national identity. Undoubtedly, Jefferson's complex, elusive, and secretive views on religion open him to wild and diverging interpretations.

Fortunately, in the last years, Jefferson scholars have worked to clarify many of the issues concerning his views on religion.[3] Here we cannot work through all of this territory. Instead, we will pursue one specific issue: How does the image of Jesus emerge in Jefferson's much-discussed *The Life and Morals of Jesus of Nazareth* (abbreviated as the *LMJN*)? We speak indirectly of the issue in an indirect and impersonal way because of the complexity of identifying Jefferson's Jesus. First, we indicate that because of the peculiar manner by which Jefferson assembled his Jesus book, that is, through a literal cut-and-paste method, we are unable to determine absolutely which details in the book represent his plans and intentions, and which things remain as a residue of the biblical gospels. Thus, we cannot be exact in specifying how many of the details of Jefferson's text belong to the shape

---

and, to add a double reflection, research on Jefferson tends to mirror the values of the researcher and of the values of America in a particular age. Note that Burstein speaks of Jefferson as a "lightening rod" for researchers' views of religion. Each of them tends to find in Jefferson their own views of religion, and Jefferson researchers follow Jefferson's own temptation to confess his religious views to others in order to validate themselves. Burstein, *Inner Jefferson*, 246–47.

2. See Foote, *Religion*, 2–8. For an extensive bibliography of early assessments of Jefferson and religion, see Peterson, *Jefferson Image*, 499–500.

3. As I see it, modern critical scholars of Jefferson's religion have developed substantial agreement or, at least, predictably different views on these major themes in the Jefferson corpus, namely, (1) the origins of Jefferson's religious views, (2) his materialist metaphysical orientation, (3) his critique of supernaturalism, (4) his willingness to judge things religious by reason, (5) his dislike of the "platonic mysticism" of the traditional metaphysical and theological traditions, (6) his critique of the incoherence of most (Christian) doctrines, (7) his theory that priests and others have corrupted the earnest heart of religion, (8) his insistence that religion is finally a private affair of the human subject, (9) his valuing of the moral heart of religion and the power of the moral sense, (10) his understanding of God, (11) his rejection of atheism, (12) his turn to a deistic style of belief in God, (13) his struggle to make sense of evil, (14) his complex and murky attitude toward eschatological themes, (15) his freedom in relation to sacred Scripture, (16) his affection toward but critique of Greek ethical recourses, (17) his critique of Jewish religion, (18) his theory that Jesus is fundamentally a religious/moral reformer, (19) his gradual warming to Christian religion, (20) his theory about the simplicity of Christian religion, and (21) his sense of the usefulness of Christian religion for the founding of the Republic. See the discussion of these points in chapters 12–14 where I summarize some of the main issues of these twenty-one points.

of his gospel narrative or how many to his peculiar method of cutting away objectionable material. Second, we have to insist that even with an exacting reconstruction of Jefferson's intentions for the text, such a reconstruction, however speculative, should not norm, much less exhaust, the meaning of the text, since the text always has autonomy independent of the intention of the author.[4] In this writing we attempt to *let the text offer its world independent of Jefferson's possible intentions.*

Jefferson, of course, is famously private about his views of religion, but he does speak of Jesus in a handful of letters to his closest friends. These remarks are important and tend to make general observations about Jesus as a moralist and the tragic fate of his message at the hands of his followers. They locate Jesus in the larger themes of Jefferson's view of religion and Jewish and Christian religion. Indeed, the figure of Jesus embodies many of Jefferson's mature views on religion. In his correspondence Jefferson makes Jesus a moral hero. When Jefferson scholars consider his Jesus books, the temptation has been to read his cut-and-paste Jesus through the lens of Jefferson's few comments about Jesus in the letters. *That is, they find in the Jesus books an enactment and a confirmation of the themes about Jesus from his letters.*

In this book we reject this interpretive approach for the same reason that we reject the intentional orientation: it sets up a procedure, slightly better than intention-guessing, that turns away from the autonomous imaging of Jesus in the *LMJN* book itself. In this writing, we let the *Life and Morals* piece speak with its own voice first, and only then do we turn back to the comments on Jesus from the letters.[5] When we, thus, swim against the interpretive stream, we notice that the book's Jesus is richer and more subtle than that of many studies.

Unlike the private and rare comments about Jesus in the letters, the *LMJN* speaks volumes, but it does so in an odd way. First, we have to note that the text is meant to be a *private volume*. Whatever we judge as other, possible uses of the text, we know that the text is fundamentally a private document for Jefferson's meditative purposes.[6] Second, we know that he

---

4. See this approach for interpreting a text in Ricoeur, *Conflict*.

5. Bryan, "Reauthorizing," 20. Bryan also thinks that the *LMJN* needs an "independent" and "complex" analysis. Her work parallels this study. She fears that the interpretation of the *LMJN* will be dominated by warhorse themes like the antisupernatural and anticlerical themes as well as by Jefferson's political struggles. Therefore, the *LMJN* should be seen not simply as a "companion piece" to *The Philosophy of Jesus*. I share her concern that the early material in the corpus can shape the interpretation of the *LMJN* too much, but I also worry that the themes of the letters will dominate the interpretation of the *LMJN*.

6. We have to say emphatically that the *LMJN* belongs among Jefferson's private

opted for a daring method to construct an image of Jesus by cutting out and reassembling the words of the evangelists. *What is odd about our most extensive source for Jefferson's Jesus is that he constructs a Jesus by cutting away what he does not want to say about Jesus from the biblical gospels.* What he leaves in of the evangelists' words in his own account may match Jefferson's intentions (as reconstructed from the historical sources). But even here we will have to qualify the claim, because Jefferson is working with four unwieldy sources that do not agree with each other. What Jefferson leaves out of his gospel from the four biblical gospels probably represents things he does not like. The qualification goes further, since we readers get the impression that he leaves out items for different reasons and that some of the reasons may represent no actual hostility to the content. For instance, Jefferson may want to eliminate repetitions, or he may want to simplify a presentation from one of the gospels, or perhaps he cuts when he simply does not understand the meaning of a pericope.

Thus, our chief source of Jefferson's Jesus in the *LMJN* comes to us in the actual words of the New Testament gospels, appears in a document that selects some of the gospel words and deselects other words, and requires us to reconstruct the unspoken values and themes operative in the selections. Even more outrageously, it dares us to guess immanently what the absence of a theme or instance means.[7] Obviously, the interpretation of Jefferson's Jesus-book Jesus is inherently difficult and open to various construals, ones as divergent as those making sense of his views of religion.

Now the interpreter may be squeamish about guessing the meaning embedded in a recast Jesus story or in removing something from the gospel picture, and rightly so. There are dangers afoot in any attempt to interpret Jefferson's Jesus. The chief danger is inherent in the project itself. Namely, his Jesus is constructed by pulling out certain things from an already set narrative. Stephen J. Prothero names his method as "scripture by subtraction."[8] We may assume that what is pulled out has meaning, but, ironically, we are then applying meaning to what is not there! Odd indeed. Even odder, we cannot know for sure whether what Jefferson leaves in means that an item

---

documents and is not at all one of his public pieces. It pertains to his private understanding of religion that Jefferson so values and protects. We also have to say that possibly the private status may not exhaust the uses of the text, intended or not.

7. The letters are particularly useful as a corroborating standard when we face explaining what is absent from or unclear about the Jesus book.

8. Stephen Prothero's phrase is insightful and witty, but, as we argue in our method section, there is more deliberation operative in Jefferson's actual treatment of the life and message of Jesus than simple subtraction. Prothero is quoted in Edwards, "How Thomas Jefferson Created His Own Bible."

has a ringing endorsement from him or that he simply finds insufficient reason to eliminate it. The latter could be only a lukewarm affirmation, and on that basis we would not want to build a great castle of meaning. Perhaps he does not remove an item because removing it would be too difficult for his razor technique of editing. Moreover, as we have noted, many things Jefferson does with religion and with Jesus are enigmatic, and Jefferson does not bother to clarify his scheme. These items tempt researchers to interpret them according to their wider construals of Jefferson's political and religious views. We attempt to avoid these standards until our immanent analysis is done.

How do we protect against capricious and/or manipulative interpretations, particularly since in some sense we must guess what Jefferson means? Too often Jefferson scholars peer into his Jesus book and find the themes they already know about from his general views of religion. That is, they *use the Jesus book to confirm the already known.* While this approach does much to secure a Jesus that matches his already expressed views of religion, the time has come to become more methodologically exacting in discerning what happens in his Jesus book itself. We propose, then, a new approach to Jefferson's Jesus-book Jesus, with three aspects: First, we will conduct an immanent analysis of the patterns of Jefferson's selections and arrangements of the gospel material. The method will bracket as much knowledge of Jefferson as humanly possible. Second, from his patterns of inclusion and exclusion we will offer criteria for discerning the values and themes that underlie his choices; and third, only then will we match the patterns and genuine values of the book against Jefferson's comments about Jesus and his general view of religion from his letters and other documents.[9]

---

9. This third step, admittedly, depends on the work of professional Jefferson scholars, and the hope that there can be a developing consensus on his views.

2

Beginnings

Precis

In a combination of Matthew's and Luke's accounts, the *LMJN*'s story of Jesus begins without genealogy; without divine descent; without accolades and titles; without shepherds, angels, or magi; without a connectedness to John the Baptist; without prophecy fulfilled; and without the flight into Egypt. Basically, Jesus is born on a taxation trip! Things that hint of divine origin, like the Virgin Birth and the fulfillment of prophecy, the *LMJN* omits. The text includes the story of the twelve-year-old Jesus impressing the doctors of the Law in the temple, and we can imagine why: a central theme ahead is that the *LMJN* will want to predate Jesus' teaching wisdom in his youth.

Jesus begins his adult ministry by being baptized by John. The *LMJN* has the baptism launch the ministry but does not allow us to infer that Jesus is a disciple of John. Immediately after the baptism, Jesus assembles his own disciples and followers, including his mother, and heads for a short visit to Capernaum in northern Galilee. Here again, Jesus inspires with his own, underived teaching, since his disciples, not the healers or exorcists of the synoptic accounts, are essentially a class of students. The author immediately wanders away from the Galilee beginning and restarts the public ministry, remarkably, with a trip to Jerusalem for Passover. Jesus' first act of ministry (not his last act, as is common in the synoptic gospels and in contemporary Jesus research) is the famous temple cleansing, and the *LMJN*'s cut of the text focuses Jesus' attack on the money dealings in the holy place, as if

God's house should not be for merchandising. Importantly, by cutting and pasting, the author dissociates the temple story from the conflict traditions of the synoptic account and from the trouble in Jerusalem with both the Jewish authorities and the Roman occupiers. Then, following the narrative of the gospel of John, the *LMJN* locates the second start of Jesus' ministry in Judea, not in Galilee. Jesus might have remained in Judea, had John not gotten jailed and the Judeans not gotten mad at Jesus. The *LMJN* allows the Herod/Salome story, blames Salome for the beheading of John, and absolves Herod (as does Mark's gospel).

Exposition of Beginnings of the Ministry

While John loses his head, Jesus restarts his ministry in Capernaum, in the synagogue, and with astonishing authority "unlike the scribes." The *LMJN* then jumps ten chapters in Mark to locate the inaugural act of the Galilean teacher: the story of picking corn on the Sabbath. Immediately, the author's scissors set the proper problematic for Jesus' ministry: his authority allows him to bypass the niceties of the Law and simultaneously to get into trouble with the Pharisees. Interestingly, the problematic is neither of John the Baptist (the repentance theme) nor of John's preparation for and deference to the messiah; and certainly it is not the temptation of Jesus, as the Synoptics present it. Recall that the Synoptics first have Jesus preaching in Galilee a message of repentance, and then they set the theme of the ministry as the rejection of Jesus in Nazareth, his hometown. From there, once Jesus dusts off Nazareth, he goes on the road and calls his disciples. The *LMJN* ignores all of these themes and turns directly to the challenge of the Pharisees. The issue is how properly to interpret the Law, exemplified in the controversies over what a Jew can do on the Sabbath. More exactly, the issue is not a midrashic debate on the best way to interpret Torah, but on who can speak authoritatively in matters of Law. Tellingly, the next issue the *LMJN*'s Jesus faces is the issue of healing a man with a withered hand on the Sabbath. Actually, we do not see the man being healed in the *LMJN*'s version; instead, the text turns to Jesus' debate with the Pharisees. They are angered by Jesus' saying concerning Sabbath law and they seek to destroy him. The conflict the author frames in a surprisingly hypothetical way; we see that the Pharisees are actually ready to kill Jesus on the basis of his answers in this "academic" discussion!

The Sources of Jefferson's Jesus-Book Jesus

Apart from scattered general references to Jesus in his letters, Jefferson treats the figure of Jesus in three places: First, in an early *Syllabus* of a book he wants to write, attached to a letter to Benjamin Rush and written during two weeks in 1803.[1] This piece sets in place a comparative format for much of Jefferson's interest in Jesus, namely, by asking how Jesus compares with "the philosophers" (Greek Epicureans and Stoics mostly) and with sources from the Jews.[2] Second is the 1803 compilation from the gospels of his favorite Jesus sayings, which he called *The Philosophy of Jesus*.[3] Third is Jefferson's painstaking, cut-and-paste piece, *The Life and Morals of Jesus of Nazareth*,[4] produced in the 1819–20 period and intended primarily for his own meditative enjoyment.[5] In a letter to F. A. Van der Kemp Jefferson

---

1. We know that Jefferson was curious, seriously studying, and writing about the figure of Jesus already in the 1790s (Samuelson, "Jefferson and Religion," 143). Jefferson's kind of critical work on Jesus, sorting the good stuff from the bad, emerged soon after Reimarus's so-called *Fragments* appeared between 1774 and 1778. Reimarus, *Fragments*. Jefferson sent an epitome of his views on Christianity to Benjamin Rush as early as his April 21, 1803, letter (Jefferson, *Writings* [Peterson, ed.], 1123). There he hoped to reveal his views in such a way that rationalist Christians and deists both could embrace them. Jefferson used this little *Syllabus* to defend himself to his friends, after years in which Benjamin Rush pressed him for such a defense. Indeed, Rush felt that Jefferson needed to see that Christian faith and his own Republicanism would be partners (Burstein, *Inner Jefferson*, 185). Originally the *Syllabus* went only to six friends.

2. See the early comparativist interest in the letter to Priestley, April 9, 1803 (Jefferson, *Writings* [Peterson, ed.], 1121).

3. Jefferson began this piece during his first term as president. The manuscript has been lost, but cut fragments from his preparations of the piece remain and have been minutely reconstructed in Adams and Lester, *Jefferson's Extracts*. For a text-historical introduction to *The Philosophy of Jesus*, see Adams and Lester, *Jefferson's Extracts*, 45–53.

4. Planned and prepared for years, the work was assembled in 1819 or 1820 by cutting from Greek, Latin, French, and English Bibles. It is this source that is known popularly as The Jefferson Bible. The term "Bible" is a misnomer, however, as Jefferson does not attempt to rework the whole Bible, but only four small pieces of it, the canonical gospels. Even the term "gospel" is problematic, though I will use it occasionally to represent the project of the *LMJN* that assembles its own version of the Jesus stories comparable to the noncanonical gospels. The matter depends on how we define "gospel." If a gospel is a saving narrative of the savior according to the Christians, a mixture of myth, saga, and history in an exhortative form, Jefferson's effort is on the edge of being a gospel. He expels the mythic from his gospel but does not seem to recognize the mythic character of the metahistorical materials he presupposes. He does not seem to have a sense for saga, but he routinely makes historical judgments on elements of saga. In the final chapters of the *LMJN* Jefferson's deep sense for the moral crisis of the day and his account of the shepherd who gives his life for his sheep counts as a gospel, a modest saving narrative.

5. Jefferson scholars debate the use of his commonplace book on Jesus, since his

speaks of this work as an attempt "to restore Scriptures to their original purity."[6] In his letter to William Short of August 4, 1820, he speaks of wanting the "vindication of Jesus."[7]

The *Syllabus* is a formal outline of what should be integral to any good treatment of Jesus' message in a comparative mode. Jefferson hopes that someone with more skill and time will execute the outline completely.[8] *The Philosophy of Jesus* consists only of the message of Jesus as Jefferson assembles it. Jefferson, apparently, never shows the text to anyone and it no longer exists.[9] The longer, third source, *The Life and Morals of Jesus of Nazareth*, adds to the message of Jesus much of the familiar narrative plot of the canonical gospels.[10] He wrote this piece under the gentle prodding of John Adams's letters after a delay of fifteen years.

---

evident private use and hopes for the piece are qualified by his occasional sharing of the text (and the *Syllabus*) with his closest confidantes (like Rush and Priestley), all to clarify his real religious views in times of controversy. There is also the bizarre and puzzling cover note to *The Philosophy of Jesus* suggesting Jefferson writes it for "the Indians." This notion seems to be something of a throwaway, though it could be tied to Jefferson's fascination with Native Americans and his belief that as natural humans, they would find Christianity appealing, were it pared back to its natural form. Forrester Church provides the interesting speculation that "the Indians" reference is an allegory for the Federalists with whom Jefferson fights. Such a view coheres with a political reading that suggests his Jesus is a moral inspiration for a republican nation (see Church, Introduction, 19–20; and Holowchak, *Bible*, 19). Note that the differences between the private and the public uses often divide how scholars interpret the *LMJN*, with some emphasizing the private, devotional use of the constructed text and some advocating more for the public, republican values and even, as we see above, Jefferson's claim to want to vindicate Jesus as the great moralist. In point of fact, Jefferson sends out several signals concerning the use of the *LMJN*. These three ideas seem to be the most important: his private devotional use, his concern to vindicate Jesus, and his concern for Jesus as a model of the republicanism Jefferson envisions.

6. Letter to Van der Kemp, April 25, 1816 (Adams and Lester, *Extracts*, 368–69).

7. The question is, in the face of what does Jesus need vindication? In some respect *Jefferson comes to vindicate Jesus against his own dismissive, early judgments about him.* Thus, vindication fits in the period after he discovers Priestley's theory of the corruption of Christianity at the hands of the early followers and priests. See Letter to Short, August 4, 1820 (Jefferson, *Writings* [Peterson, ed.], 1436).

8. Letter to Rush, April 21, 1803, in Jefferson, *Writings* [Peterson, ed.], 1123.

9. The Jefferson scholar Dickenson Adams has reconstructed this document from the "holes" cut into copies of the gospels Jefferson used to produce his pamphlet (Adams and Lester, *Extracts*, 45–53).

10. A good text-historical summary of *LMJN* can be found in Adams, *Extracts*, 125–26. Sanford argues that the differences in value and theme between Jefferson's two cut-and-paste Jesus books is minimal (Sanford, *Religious Life*, 104). In light of Adams's reconstruction of the former book and the analysis of the latter book below, scholars may have to revisit this claim when the reconstruction has been fully digested.

Jefferson's Jesus project, then, spans much of his mature years of public service and office, and it becomes something of a lifelong obsession of his to condense his larger views on religion. The obsession begins in his letters to Benjamin Rush and their conversations to the effect that Jefferson should write down his views on Christian religion. It gets stronger through years of political conflict and suspicion about his religious views, particularly in the conflicted election of 1800. And in his correspondence with Joseph Priestley Jefferson comes to see that a cleaned-up picture of Christian origins would be a support for "reasonable republicans" founding a nation. His method from the start: figure out the genuine message of Jesus to clarify true Christian religion (and simultaneously recognize where it has gone wrong). It is an admittedly *reductive method*, aimed at recovery of a "rational Christianity" that could persuade many who are perplexed when they read about the Jesus of the gospels.

Jefferson's treatments of Jesus take the form of typical eighteenth-century "commonplace books," in which intellectuals would assemble insightful passages found in their favorite books for personal reflection.[11] Consequently, the cut-and-paste method, harsh to modern sensibilities, fits nicely within Jefferson's era, and once he learns from Bolingbroke that Jesus is a moral fragmentist (like Epictetus), he no longer worries about disconnecting the moral nuggets from their narrative frame.[12] While Jefferson's freedom to reshape the narratives presupposes Enlightenment critical methods, his novel, cut-and-paste assembly of the texts into his own single narrative has a crucial limit: it is blind to the redaction of the Jesus story at the hands of the different evangelists.[13]

---

11. Crews, "Jefferson's Secret Bible," 39. In fact, Jefferson assembled another commonplace book, called the "Literary Bible," that included the mostly religious ideas of Bolingbroke (Church, Introduction, 4).

12. Church, Introduction, 4.

13. Sanford notes that Jefferson's method does not have the benefit of the gospel harmonies that appear after his work and help in the creation of redaction criticism. That he rests his work on a single Jesus narrative ignores the tradition-historical value of what he cuts away. With a good protestant and Enlightened mindset, he wants only one uncorrupted Jesus and views what he cuts away as dross. See Sanford, *Religious Life*, 109–10. (By "protestant" with a lowercase *p* here and throughout, I refer to a general attitude and cultural orientation, which is distinct from the Reformation tradition called "Protestant" with a capital *P*.) So, the writing shows dependence on the old gospel harmonies compiled by scholars contemporary to him, such as Charles Thomson and Joseph Priestley. In that harmonizing approach authors would weave together a comprehensive account of the Jesus story from the four canonical gospels. By the time Jefferson takes up the task, his old style of harmonizing has taken on two new developments: first, some materials from the gospels are disposed of, and, second, the harmony is constructed from the best words and stories from all four gospels. Then

Such a commonplace of Jesus functions for Jefferson's personal use and meditation,[14] and also to inform a few selected, close friends what he really believes in times of criticism. Jefferson's Jesus-book Jesus, then, is not intended for public consumption.[15] By the time that Jefferson has incorporated the corruption theory into his ideas, he is able to recover wisdom from Jesus that he admires and on which he wishes to meditate daily. If the works are primarily for private use, do they also have a direct public and political use? Many scholars turn to his comments on the vindication of Jesus, to his attempt to clarify for others his own religious views, and to documents where he claims a public political use for the text.[16] Likely then we have four distinct functions for the Jesus project in the corpus,[17] with the lead use his own meditative enjoyment.[18]

We begin our immanent study of *The Life and Morals of Jesus of Nazareth* with eight chapters of exposition and analysis.

Exposition: The Origins of Jesus

The Life and Morals of Jesus of Nazareth begins with, "And it came to pass in those days," and moves to the story of Joseph and Mary heading to Bethlehem. It uses the familiar Lukan story of Jesus' birth, but importantly without Luke's (and Matthew's) genealogies. Instead, the *LMJN* chooses a seven-verse block from chapter 2 of Luke that goes from the tax census to the no-room-in-the-inn episode. Missing are the birth story in Matthew, including

---

the disposed-of materials are rejected by the author under Priestley's corruption theory. See Sanford, *Religious Life*, 109.

14. See the discussion of Jefferson's devotional life in Sanford, *Religious Life*, 92. Jefferson scholarship is often shaped by researchers who downplay or ignore the importance of religion in interpreting Jefferson. Sanford was one of the important scholars who tried to correct secular readings of Jefferson (Sanford, *Religious Life*, 135).

15. See Sheridan, *Jefferson and Religion*, 64: "There can be no doubt that Jefferson compiled it strictly for his own moral and religious instruction." But nonetheless, a few scholars debate with Sheridan's sweeping judgments. See the discussion in Holowchak, *American Messiah*, 82–84. Holowchak's recent book moves toward the public, republican use of the text and de-emphasizes the personal devotional use. The private use can be found in many places and is implied in Jefferson's repeated pleas for secrecy about his religious views. The justification of the character of Jesus can be found in the Letter to Short, August 4, 1820 (Adams and Lester, *Extracts*, 395).

16. Holowchak, for instance, thinks our author "considers Jeffersonianism to be the political embodiment of Jesus' true teaching" (Holowchak, *American Messiah*, 13, 84).

17. The four are *a private, meditative use, a semipublic explanation to friends of Jefferson's views on religion, a vindication of Jesus, and the value of the study for the republic*.

18. Though some scholars hear tones of several of Jefferson's projects and controversies in the book.

the role of Joseph and his dream, the "virgin shall conceive" prophecy, the wise men's visit to and adoration of Jesus, the prophecy from Micah about Bethlehem as the messiah's birthplace, Herod's involvement and jealousy, the flight into Egypt, the slaughter of the innocents, the prophetic lament from Jeremiah, and the second dream of Joseph to return to Nazareth.[19]

The *LMJN* removes Luke's prologue to the gospel and the entire saga of Jesus' relation to John the Baptist before Jesus' public ministry, including the childlessness of Elizabeth and Zechariah, the appearance of the angel Gabriel, the celebrative quote from Num 6:3, the birth of John, the annunciation of Gabriel to Mary, the prophetic use of Isa 9, Mary's visit to Elizabeth, and the Magnificat. The text picks up the seven verses of 2:1–7 from the famous opening of the Christmas story down to the manger scene, but then drops the shepherds and their adoration, with the praise of Jesus from the angel chorus. It completes the Christmas story with two verses (Luke 2:21 and 2:39) from the circumcision of Jesus. The text, then, omits the entire story of the purification and presentation of Jesus at the temple in Jerusalem, the sacrifice, and Simeon's "Nunc Dimittis" quote from Second Isaiah; it also omits Anna's prophecy of the redemption of Jerusalem.[20]

Analysis: The Origins of Jesus

Presumably, the *LMJN* does not want to associate Jesus with the two neatly contrived genealogies that take Jesus' lineage back to David and Abraham. Presumably also, the *LMJN* ignores the lineages because they put Jesus into an implicit prophecy/fulfillment scheme. This omission represents the *first instance of the* LMJN's *rejection of the prophecy/fulfillment pattern*. Notice the extent to which the meaning of the *LMJN* depends on what is not there, since the production of the text is an exercise in an editorial removing of meaning units. Interestingly, Peter Manseau notes that the *LMJN* begins by rejecting the beginnings of all four gospels of the New Testament. That is, *LMJN* starts with a giant NO to the ways that biblical gospels begin the Jesus

---

19. Biblical references will be included within the exposition and analysis of the *LMJN*. I will locate the original texts in two ways: first, I will use a recent, available, modern printing of the English text: Thomas Jefferson, *The Jefferson Bible. The Life and Morals of Jesus*, in the Jefferson, *Bible* (Beacon ed.). Second, I will use the photographic version of the folios of the *LMJN* from Dickenson W. Adams and Ruth W. Lester, *Extracts*, hereafter designated by "folio" number and the page number in the Adams and Lester edition. The content of our first paragraph is thus: Jefferson, *Bible* (Beacon ed.), 37; folio 1:135. Notes concerning materials removed from the four canonical gospels to produce the *LMJN* will be located with the same double notation.

20. Jefferson, *Bible* (Beacon ed.), 37–38; folio 1:135.

story. We can only speculate why, of course, but for sure the text emphatically rejects the canonical beginnings to the Jesus story.[21]

Analysis: The Block Editing

The *LMJN* typically quotes blocks of narrative that are acceptable to the author based on his standards of selection from the stories of the origin of Jesus. Initially, the style is blocky, as the author cuts out whole passages, full sentences, full verses, and sometimes whole paragraphs, rather than remove individual words or phrases from a larger block. However, toward the end of the book, the text becomes less blocky, since the author appears willing to make smaller cuts and make more complex constructions. There he does a few single-verse cuts and even a couple half-verse cuts. Still, *the LMJN never adds or removes individual words or phrases.* The blocky approach to editing brings with it certain consequences for content: a block may say more than the author strictly wants. Because he usually cuts blocks in straight-line cuts, he takes the cut of the passage to the end of a line. Therefore, at times he may enter a block that has a little more content than what he may like, or he may cut off materials that are not that bad by his values. The risk of block editing becomes evident when we face seams between two passages.

If our author's editing is blocky, it is also "pagey." That is, he has a medium-sized folio page on which he pastes two columns parallel to another folio page with two more columns. The four columns on two facing pages consist of the four languages he uses to construct his gospel: Greek, Latin, French, and English in that order from left to right. The author constructs eighty-two folios. Of his chosen passages for each double page, he must fit the passage in each of the four languages into the same two-page columns.[22] Often it is the English version of the passage that is wordy and barely fits the page spread. In any case, part of the author's blocky editing includes making each passage fit a page. The passages must fit; in only two exceptions in the entire book does he squeeze a verse or a few words into the margin of the English version after he has filled in its column. Since most passages start a topic at the top of the page, and since usually the passage or assembled passages end a topic at the bottom of the page, we know the author works at

---

21. The insight comes from Manseau, *Jefferson Bible*, 65. Manseau speculates that the author of the *LMJN* must think the actual beginnings of the biblical story already reflect the corruption of the pure message of Jesus.

22. And a chosen block may overlap onto the next page, onto the back side of the print of the first page; consequently, Jefferson had to have two copies of each of his four language versions so that he could catch the continuation of a block on a separate page of the second copy (Sheridan, Introduction, 30).

filling the page, page by page and rounding out an episode or topic, before he quits the page. His manner of composition, thus, is episodic, even more so than that of the biblical gospels. He thinks of filling a page, so to speak. Of course, some of his topics do not finish neatly at the bottom of a page and they wrap around onto the next folio. One suspects the pagey character of the folio explains why so many passages from the gospels simply disappear without obvious explanation: they do not fit the page, if not the topic. Of course, they also might be redundant, or offensive, or their ideas or plots are simply too long to fit the blocky manner of composition.

Analysis: The Reduction of the Birth Account

Some themes are emerging already. The *LMJN* has *no interest in prophecy* fulfilled in the appearance of Jesus, nor in anticipatory praise or meta-praise of Jesus, whether from the angels, the wise men, the shepherds, or the evangelists. We will have to figure out why. Also, *the text eliminates supernatural phenomena* (i.e., the Bethlehem star, the appearances of remarkable dream-predictions, and the angels). Next, it shows no interest in the primal, familial connection of Jesus to John the Baptist; but how will this lack of interest relate to the mature encounters of Jesus and John? Perhaps, the rejection of the early encounter of Jesus and John fits with the *LMJN*'s disinterest in prophecy-and-fulfillment patterns. Clearly, the *LMJN* suppresses the theologically charged notion that John anticipates the importance of Jesus and will act as a forerunner who happily defers to Jesus. And, too, the *LMJN* finds *no christological surplus of meaning in the wonders of Jesus' birth or in the family connection to John the Baptist*.

Exposition: The Young Jesus

Surprisingly, the *LMJN* does include the brief gospel story of the twelve-year-old Jesus debating the teachers with a telling clue to the meaning of the story. Instead of putting the "filled with wisdom" claim of Luke at the end of the origin stories, the *LMJN* uses it to introduce Jesus' questioning the "doctors of the Law" in the single verse (Luke 2:40).[23] From the start of the public ministry, Jesus is already remarkable for *his precocious wisdom*.

---

23. Jefferson, *Bible* (Beacon ed.), 38; folio 2:137.

Analysis: The Remarkable Young Jesus

The relocating of the "filled with wisdom" passage is striking; it does not sum up Jesus' genesis or his childhood, as it does in Luke, but it introduces Jesus' youthful encounter with the rabbis and, thus, shows *Jesus already as a teacher and dialectician*. What the *LMJN* omits from the Christmas story, shows that the real genesis of Jesus happens in his gift for moral dialectic: *the prescient wisdom of Jesus, thus, substitutes for his remarkable birth*. Surely his primal wisdom replaces all the gospel features of the origin of Jesus that the *LMJN* leaves out.

Exposition: The Ministry Begins

Jesus' adult ministry in the *LMJN* begins with Luke's locating that ministry within the reigns of all the major figures of authority. John is in the wilderness preaching a baptism of repentance. Then the text shifts to three verses of Matthew (3:4–6) that describe John physically, his wide popularity, and his baptism of crowds of people.[24] In the *LMJN*'s account Jesus himself is in Galilee by now and must zip across the country from Galilee back to the Jordan River in Judea to be baptized by John (Matt 3:13).[25] The baptism of Jesus itself is exceedingly brief and understated. The text declares Jesus to be about thirty years of age, but, interestingly, *the text tolerates none of the familial connection between Jesus and John, permits no supernatural phenomena, and allows no hints of prophecy/fulfillment*. Immediately, the *LMJN* gets Jesus to Jerusalem and the temple event (John 2:12). We will hear no more of John until Herod executes him.[26]

Analysis: The *LMJN*-Abbreviated Relationship between Jesus and John

The *LMJN* shows no interest in the connection of John and Jesus as infants, and it ignores the prophetic connection of the two. Against the Synoptics, Jesus and John are not relatives. We will hear more of the adult encounters

---

24. Notably the *LMJN* omits use of the prophecy of Second Isaiah (Isa 40:3: "Prepare the way of the Lord") in Matthew and Mark. Again, our text does not want prophecy/fulfillment schemes, nor does it allow John as the forerunner of Jesus.

25. We note how the *LMJN* continues to scramble the synoptic geography. *He does not know where things are in Palestine, nor does he consider the time and distance involved in having Jesus go to Galilee and back to Judea*. His displacement of the story indicates just how significant it is for the author to begin the ministry in Judea, not in Galilee, with the temple event in Jerusalem.

26. Jefferson, *Bible* (Beacon ed.), 38–39; folio 2:137.

of the two soon, but for now we notice how much the *LMJN* deletes from the Jesus/John relationship. Mark, of course, does not have a Christmas story, but instead starts his story at Jesus' first meeting with John the Baptist. The *LMJN* leaves out the prophecy of the voice crying in the wilderness. It also omits John's denunciation of the Pharisees and Sadducees who come for baptism (from the Q source in Matt 2:7–10 and Luke 3:7–9).[27] Indeed, John calls them a "brood of vipers" who "flee from the wrath to come" and will soon be cut-down trees. The *LMJN* also omits John's message to the multitudes, the tax collectors, and the soldiers, to all of whom John urges fair dealings in their public actions (only in Luke 3:10–14). *The first conflict with Jewish authorities happens in Jerusalem,* and John anticipates what becomes the main theme in the *LMJN* before Jesus finds it: *John's criticism of the Pharisees and the Sadducees for their hypocrisy leads into Jesus' own critique of the Jews.* More significantly, the *LMJN* omits the apocalyptic aspects of John's ministry with its grim judgment and the warning not to bear bad fruit.[28] Moreover, the *LMJN* ignores Luke's simple moral lesson on fairness to the three groups of pilgrims at John's place of baptism.

Important themes we must watch so far include *the conflict with the Jewish authorities, predated, as it were, in John's ministry; the elimination of supernaturalistic features of the story; the muting of the apocalyptic; and the reduction of Jesus' relationship to John the Baptist.*

The text then skips over the crowd's pondering John's message and whether he might be the Christ (Luke 3:15–18). Next it leaves out John's famous placing of his baptism with water in relation to the coming baptism of the Holy Spirit from the one "mightier" than John (in Matthew, Mark, and Luke) and the coming judgment and fire (in Matthew and Luke). Once again, we find the *LMJN* is uncomfortable with the biblical Jesus/John relationship, presumably because it presents so powerfully John's deferring accolade of Jesus and it hints of prophecy fulfilled. The *LMJN* does not mention that John has been arrested for preaching against Herod's marriage to his brother's wife (Luke 3:19–20), probably because the author wants no distraction from John's role as the baptizer and as the harsh critic of the Herodians.[29] We also need to hold open the idea that the *LMJN* limits the role of John because his grim preaching of judgment is too judgmental for the author.

---

27. Later we will figure out why the *LMJN* omits mention of the Pharisees and Sadducees: it cannot entertain the idea that the enemies of Jesus are repenting and getting baptized by John, since the whole point of the author's gospel is Jesus' conflict with Jewish authorities.

28. Once again, we note how the *LMJN* is fascinated by the tree/fruit images.

29. The author continues to jumble the geography of Palestine.

The baptism itself lacks all detail in the *LMJN*: our author omits Matthew's prophetic justification for Jesus' baptism (Matt 3:13–15); he omits the heavens opening with the Spirit/dove descending and the voice from heaven (quoting Ps 2:7): "This is my beloved Son." Again, the text rejects prophecy-fulfillment and a heavenly prodigy similar to those in the Christmas stories. *The pattern is well set already: Jesus is not christic, neither in fulfilling prophecy, nor as the subject of the supernatural.* Already, then, we have in place two enduring themes of the *LMJN*'s gospel. We will have to watch whether the values embedded in these themes are absolute or subject to qualification. So far, we recognize that the *LMJN* "creates" its story of Jesus "by extraction."[30]

Exposition: The Temple Event

In the story of Jesus according to the *LMJN*, Jesus' first public act of ministry is not the temptation stories as in the synoptic gospels, but the temple fracas.[31] In so locating the temple event, the *LMJN* follows the gospel of John, not the synoptic accounts, even as it vaults over the miracle at Cana in John. Though the *LMJN* puts the temple event at the beginning of Jesus' ministry, it omits all of the four gospels' rich interpretations of the event. The event is not prophecy fulfilled; it is not Jesus' promise to rebuild the temple (John 2:17); it is not a debate with "the Jews" (John 2:20); and it is not a postfactum memory of the disciples (John 2:22). Rather, it is simply anger with the Jewish sellout of the holy place to filthy lucre.[32]

After the temple event, Jesus baptizes in Judea. He then learns of John's fate at the hands of Herod and Salome. For some reason the *LMJN* reports

---

30. To use Holowchak's repeated phrase, *Bible*. Extraction language, of course, overlooks the reconfiguration and displacement of themes.

31. Importantly, the event that modern scholarship on Jesus regards as the last of his life is his first act in the *LMJN*. Of course, the author of the *LMJN* does not benefit from modern gospel research; his choice for John's account means that he is *rejecting the temple fracas as the exact cause of Jesus' death at the end of his life*, as it might be for a contemporary Jesus researcher. Rather, he picks up John's account and its location in the story of Jesus as a simple option between two accounts, the temple fracas at the beginning of Jesus' ministry according to John vs. the same at the end of his ministry, according to the Synoptics. Eventually we see that *the* LMJN *sets the temple event up front to establish definitively and early Jesus' conflict with Jewish authorities.* To compensate for the early relocation of the temple event, the author will repeat the event at the end of his gospel! Thus, Jesus' ministry of conflict with the authorities becomes sandwiched between two temple explosions.

32. Jefferson, *Bible* (Beacon ed.), 39–40; folio 3:139.

the entire Salome story from Mark 6.[33] When Jesus returns to Capernaum to teach in the synagogue, nameless people are "astonished at his doctrine," for he has "authority" unlike that of the scribes (Mark 1:21–22).[34] *The LMJN thereby gives us the first view of its major theme: Jesus' authoritative teachings stand in opposition to that of the Jewish authorities.* Here the Mark passage serves as an introduction to a section of the text on moral education and the Sermon on the Mount.[35]

Analysis: The Lost Antecedent

Readers of the gospels sometimes struggle with imprecise referents for certain pronouns. Because the author of the *LMJN* shuffles the order of the pericopes, we find the *problem of the lost antecedent exaggerated*. It is not simply the patterns that some pronouns have been taken out of context that disrupts their natural antecedents; it is that the blocky editing has scrambled the location of many pronouns. The author must piece together blocks in such a way that the beginning of a block does not leave too many pronouns dangling. Remember that his razor and his decisions in his mode of editing do not allow him to snip out a word here or there, nor can he add a random word to clarify the meaning of an ambiguous pronoun. Usually we can figure out who "he" or "him" is, but we readers are often confused who the "they" are. There are two formal principles operative in the editing: first, since the author cannot add or subtract individual words, he must seek out two passages, one already chosen and a new passage to which it can be attached smoothly and without too many pronoun problems. Often the new passage continues the old one, say, more of the same chapter of Matthew he has been quoting. The narration, once started, usually continues with his main favorites, Matthew and Luke, until something offends him or becomes repetitive. Recall that the author repeats only a handful of episodes in his entire gospel. Some new passages continue the theme into the next step or the plot already established. We can recognize part of the logic of what will be next in the exposition: for all of the author's bold reconfiguring of the gospel, *he still presupposes many of the main lines of the synoptic*

---

33. Likely to demonstrate how decadent life is among the Jews; we note that the *LMJN* makes no distinction between the Herodians and the Jews.

34. In the English-language columns of the *LMJN* Jefferson quotes a local English printing of the King James Version (KJV) now over two hundred years old. Adams and Lester, *Extracts*, the definitive version of the *LMJN*, have the following note about Jefferson's KJV on page 299: "The English NTs were both editions of the King James Version printed in Philadelphia in 1804 by Jacob Johnson & Co."

35. Jefferson, *Bible* (Beacon ed.), 40–41; folio 3–4:137, 139.

narrative, which, as we know today, has been constructed by Mark. And the author unfolds the account of Jesus mostly by following the synoptic story, except where he runs into things offensive, which he deletes, and except where his basic thesis about the life and message of Jesus requires his own amplification, modification, or intensification.[36] We arrive at the first editing principle, which we will call the *principle of contiguity*. That is, a good next pericope must be contiguous in one or more points of plot, theme, chronology, or in gospel sequence. And the best next passage will not leave too many pronouns without antecedents.

Second, in addition to the above formal point of contiguity, we offer a material point: namely, *the author of the* LMJN *simply does not bother to understand the geography of Palestine*. He routinely has Jesus zip between Galilee and Judea and back as if the gang of disciples were walking around the block. Moreover, *our author does not distinguish the story and plot associated with the largely Galilean Pharisees tied to the synagogues from stories of the aristocratic, priestly families of Sadducees, based in the temple in Jerusalem.* He misses the distinctions that the gospels themselves show, and much less, of course, does he know what modern historians know about these different groups. Where do the scribes fit for the author? Who are the crowds, and are they all the same? How do the Pharisees relate to the Sadducees? Who are the elders of the people? Without modern historical knowledge, he seems not to be interested in distinctions among Jewish leaders. Instead, he constructs a *novel theory that all Jewish authorities oppose Jesus,* and for our author there are no important religious differences among their views, nor are there significant differences among Jewish groups. In fact, many of the floating "theys" are generic crowds, adoring or scorning Jesus, and many other "theys" refer to generic Jewish authorities.

Analysis: Conflict at the Center of Jesus' Ministry

We have seen that the *LMJN* begins Jesus' ministry with the temple fit. So to locate the fracas at the beginning of the ministry, the text rushes Jesus north to Capernaum in one verse and then to the Passover in Jerusalem in the next. The author of the *LMJN* thereby affects *an unwitting, double displacement: of location and of the Jewish "authorities."* He relocates the temple event away from the end of Jesus' ministry and relocates the conflict traditions with Pharisees from Galilee to Jerusalem, where Jesus' opponents are Sadducees. The *LMJN* thus follows the gospel of John's account of the temple event and emphasizes that the temple has become a place of

---

36. As we will see gradually.

merchandising. To get Jesus to the temple, so to speak, the *LMJN* omits the famous sign/wonder at the wedding at Cana (also in Galilee). By now we are not surprised that the author drops out a supernatural-looking event. More importantly, however, *conceiving the launch of Jesus' ministry through the decisive temple event secures the conflict theme as the* LMJN's *major theme of Jesus' entire ministry.*[37] In this conception, *the* LMJN *clumps the Sadducees of Jerusalem and the Pharisees of the countryside into generic Jewish authorities who oppose Jesus from the start of his ministry.* We will have to see where this theory goes. Note that the conflict is about Jesus' teaching, where he brings to light the comparison between his kind of wisdom and the foolishness, or worse, of the religious authorities. Nonetheless, in this distinctive reconstruction of the synoptic account Jesus makes *instant enemies in Jerusalem*, not Galilee, at the very beginning of his ministry. And the rest of the life and ministry of Jesus becomes preoccupied entirely with his clash with the Jewish authorities. *The* LMJN *will tolerate no other campaign, cause, or theme to the ministry of Jesus.*

---

37. Unfortunately, Jefferson interpreters typically miss the dramatic displacement of the temple fracas and its consequence in reorienting the ministry of Jesus toward an intra-Jewish conflict story. For instance, Manseau's recent rereading of the *LMJN* misses that the text follows John's chronology and thereby reorients the entire gospel story (Manseau, *Jefferson Bible*, 67).

3

The Teacher of Wisdom

Precis

Once the Pharisees turn on Jesus, he withdraws to the mountains, calls his disciples, and has to deal with great crowds following him. We are left wondering why the crowds follow him, though we know from Mark, they follow him because of the healing ministry, information absent in the *LMJN*. The *LMJN* has Jesus turn immediately to the Sermon on the Mount, from Matthew's gospel. Significantly, the author has Jesus teach his disciples, not the crowds, the ethic of the Sermon, and the teaching happens "up" on the mountain, away from the crowds. It is a *message for the insider students*. The Sermon begins with the familiar beatitudes and then with woes drawn from Luke. The author does little to resolve the tension between permission and high demand, characteristics of Jesus' ethic, but his change of the audience for the Sermon makes it clear that the disciples, not the people, must outdo the scribes and Pharisees in minute acts of righteousness. As the *LMJN* quotes Matt 5–7 almost completely and without significant modification, it draws in Matt 12, and then shifts to sizeable portions of Luke's so-called Sermon on the Plain. For instance, it places the woes of Luke (6:20–21) after the Matthean beatitudes (5:3–11) and before Matthew's "salt of the earth" passage (5:13) and the powerful, generalized Lukan passage (6:34–36) that points to a rewardless divine mercy, even for enemies.

Exposition: The Great Teacher

The Life and Morals of Jesus of Nazareth begins to depart from the unfolding Jesus story we recognize today in the earliest gospel from Mark; the author of the *LMJN* appears to be looking for passages rich in ethical value from the Jesus story wherever they can be found. The first choice appears when Jesus lectures the Pharisees on the proper meaning of the Sabbath on the Sabbath itself. Following Matt 12, the *LMJN* quotes the debate in two blocks of text but presents a significant reconfiguration of the text. The text preserves King David's hungry courage to eat the "bread of the Presence" and Jesus' praise of the "blameless" priests who follow David's pattern. Therefore, we have a text *affirming both the general observance of the Sabbath and occasional suspension of obedience for a cause: both observance and suspension of Torah.*[1]

The story in the *LMJN* then shifts. The text jumps over Matthew's sermon (Matt 12:5–8) in which Jesus hints that something greater than the temple is among them, that Jesus desires mercy not sacrifice, that the Pharisees should not condemn the innocent, and (significantly) that the "Son of Man is the lord of the Sabbath" (v. 8). Apparently, the *LMJN* does not value these aspects of Matthew's sermon, for they reveal Jesus' command on the issue of Sabbath-keeping and Jesus' self-suggestion that he is in charge of Sabbath ritual. Clearly the christology of Matthew here is too high for the *LMJN*, and possibly too tied to ritual observance.

The text continues with Matt 12:9–12, a passage in which Jesus uses the case of the man with the withered hand to ask if it is lawful to heal on the Sabbath. Actually, the biblical passage continues in Matthew with Jesus' healing of the man, but the *LMJN* omits Jesus' actual act of healing and turns it and the hand into a teaching opportunity. This Jesus continues the lesson of the Sabbath, only now it is the instance of rescuing a fallen sheep on the Sabbath.[2] The point is the same as with the man with the withered hand: on the Sabbath sometimes *more pressing needs than holiness intrude upon the day*. The pericope ends with the Pharisees plotting to destroy Jesus, while he and the crowds withdraw (Matt 12:14–15).[3]

The *LMJN* concludes its prolegomena with the call of the disciples from Luke 6:12–17. While we wait for the huge treatment of the Sermon on the Mount, the *LMJN* chooses the Lukan account of the call of the disciples and goes into the "Plain" sermon of Luke as a transition to Matthew's Sermon on the Mount. After naming the twelve apostles, the text says that the

---

1. Jefferson, *Bible* (Beacon ed.), 42; folio 5:143.

2. The passage is the first instance of what becomes the central christological image of the end of the *LMJN*'s gospel, the shepherd tending his flock.

3. Jefferson, *Bible* (Beacon ed.), 42–53, folio 5:143.

crowd comes to hear Jesus and to be "healed of their diseases" (Luke 6:17). But in the next passage our text omits the description of those troubled with unclean spirits and of the crowd wanting to touch Jesus and receive his power.[4] What elements of the early synoptic account are not in the *LMJN*? *The text omits the entire temptation story from Matthew, Mark, and Luke: thus, it omits the lead-in to the public ministry with its epitome of Jesus' message of repentance and of the coming of the Kingdom* (Mark 1:14–15 and parallels); *and it lacks the theme of the rejection at Nazareth.*[5]

In Mark this theme begins as Jesus amazes the crowds with wise teaching at the local synagogue. Mark reports that the amazement is actually jealous resentment of the carpenter-made-good (Mark 6:3). In response, Jesus notes that prophets always have trouble in their hometowns, and he discovers that he cannot do wonders there. He explains the deep unbelief of the people in Nazareth. Matthew follows with the same story (13:16–30), while Luke amplifies it with Jesus' first sermon from Isa 61, in which Jesus suggests that the liberation hoped for "this day is . . . fulfilled in your ears" (4:21). The sermon appears in Luke as the beginning of Jesus' ministry. Luke adds a challenge to Jesus' prophecy and a long passage in which Jesus draws a parallel between his prophetic circumstance and that of Elijah. Note that the *LMJN* leaves out the call of the disciples connected with the work of fishing. Matthew's Jesus calls the fishermen, who immediately follow him and abandon their work in order to become "fishers of men" (Matt 4:19). Mark's version is similar. We may not know why Matthew and Mark omit the story, but Luke's version may be omitted because it contains an unacceptable story of the miraculous catch of fish (Luke 5:1–11).[6]

Readers may be surprised that the *LMJN* eliminates the episode in Mark 1:21–28, Jesus' "astonishing" teaching in the synagogue in Capernaum. Actually, the *LMJN* uses the introduction to the pericope (Mark 1:21–22) much earlier, before the Sabbath debate, to get Jesus to Galilee, since the *LMJN*, following John's gospel, has Jesus begin his ministry in

---

4. Jefferson, *Bible* (Beacon ed.), 43; folio 5:143.

5. Note that the rejection-at-Nazareth passage will return toward the end of the saga of the *LMJN*'s Jesus. We know then that the author of the *LMJN* does not reject the idea of the rejection of Nazareth itself, but, rather, that *he cannot accept the rejection at Nazareth so early in the Jesus story because he starts the Jesus story in Judea, and Jesus could not have evoked hostility in Nazareth in Galilee so early in the gospel.* The deletion of the rejection story is required because of the original displacement of the temple event.

6. The call of the disciples returns later when the *LMJN* enters a long thematic cluster on the nature of discipleship. Likely, *Jesus does not call his fishermen-disciples early in the narrative because the author of the* LMJN *locates much of the early ministry in Judea, not near the Sea of Galilee as Mark's chronology has it.* Again, we see *the geographical displacement in the* LMJN.

Judea, not Galilee. Interestingly, the pericope praises the authoritative teaching of Jesus, which is unlike that of the scribes: in case the interpreter wonders why such praise would be eliminated from the *LMJN*, read further in Mark, where the teaching in the synagogue turns into the first exorcism and launches Jesus' reputation as an exorcist. Also, the *LMJN* bypasses the next story in Mark (1:29–31 and parallels), the healing of Simon's mother-in-law. Thereafter, the text omits the events of Mark 1:32–34, healings and exorcisms, and Jesus' growing fame (Mark 1:35–38, 39 and parallels). We have already noted that our text omits the miraculous catch of fish. With those deletions the *LMJN* is finally ready to take on the Sermon on the Mount.

Analysis: The Great Teacher

Establishing Jesus as the great teacher becomes a major achievement of the LMJN. What the author has ruled out so far in the gospel story tells us much about his christology but primarily in a negative way. We will not find the preexistent Logos who enters human life, nor the wonder-working exorcist and healer, nor the one in a hostage negotiation with the devil, nor the "gnostic" revealer of the secrets of salvation. For the author of the *LMJN* everything depends on uncovering Jesus' "astonishing" teaching role. So, the central sections of the *LMJN* establish all the elements of his teaching. Where is it from? Why does it arise from Nazareth? What are its main themes? How does the teaching differ from that of the Jewish authorities? What prompts them to object and with such anger? And what is Jesus' critique of their positions?

The inaugural story of Jesus' great teaching is of the Pharisee and the sinful woman in Luke 7. The author puts it into his gospel without editing, except that at the end the *LMJN* cuts off both the tale of the sinful woman and the parable/allegory of the two debtors in favor of a critique of the Pharisee's thin love in light of the sinful woman's lavish love. The author of the *LMJN* probably enjoys both the Pharisee's failure and the surprising love of a fallen woman. We have seen that the supposedly righteous Jewish authorities have been set up to receive the blame for Jesus' death, and now we get to see that the person with a history of evil actions and a bad reputation is really the acceptable one. *Therefore, we are to enjoy the theme of inversion or of reversals and recognize it as a major theme in the teaching of the* LMJN's *Jesus.* But we are not allowed to savor Luke's spin on the story via the parable/allegory. Indeed, we do not know how the story ends once we learn of the inversion of loves. The *LMJN* suppresses the entire Jesus coda on forgiveness, and for a second time the text drops explicit discussions of forgiveness. *We must keep track of the theme of forgiveness. What is the LMJN doing with the theme? Is the deletion incidental or rich with meaning?*

Luke's text makes the issue that Jesus, not God, is forgiving sin, and that some raise eyebrows about such a presumptuous human act. Not only does Jesus forgive, but he declares that the woman's faith saves her. Perhaps we have a clue why the author of the *LMJN* has some issue with forgiveness. Does he assume that Jesus makes a point of accepting the significant sins of the woman as readily as the few sins of the Pharisee? Or is equating "salvation" with simple forgiveness too cosmic an idea for the *LMJN*? Likely, Luke's coda to the story identifies Jesus as the focus of faith and of God's action, and surely this position is a christological bridge too far for the values of the *LMJN*.

By starting the Galilean ministry with the Pharisee and the sinful woman, the *LMJN* erases major themes from that ministry: the healing of Peter's mother-in-law (Mark 1:29–31 and parallels), the healings and exorcisms on the same evening (Mark 1:32–34 and parallels), the healing of the leper and the miraculous catch of fish (only in Luke 5:1–11), the first synoptic story in the Galilean ministry section, and the question whether healing on the Sabbath violates Mosaic Law (Mark 1:40–45 and parallels). As is evident, *the* LMJN's *Jesus is not a healer.*

An evening of healings and exorcisms scares the author of the *LMJN*, since the passage ends in Luke with the demons crying, "You are the Son of God," because "they knew that he was the Christ" (Luke 4:41). We also miss the synoptic beginning to the ministry in Galilee with Jesus and his entourage leaving Capernaum for Galilee, where Jesus preaches in the synagogues, casts out demons, heals many, and attracts great crowds. The author of the *LMJN* would not approve of such stories.

Once again, *the* LMJN *locates what is christologically interesting about Jesus in his teachings, not in his wondrous acts.* Here the contrast is between Jesus and Jewish authorities, this time in a synagogue. The people proclaim Jesus' authoritative teaching as different from the teaching of the Jewish authorities. Interestingly, Jesus' first lesson has him instructing the Pharisees on the meaning of the Sabbath, after his disciples have picked corn on the holy day. Jesus criticizes the Pharisees for missing the example of David, who eats the "shew-bread," and of the priests who follow his daring act (Matt 12:5–8). But the *LMJN* drops Matthew's explanation of the corn-picking event as having value greater than the Sabbath, greater than the temple, that is, to honor mercy over sacrifice and to name the Son of Man as the lord of the Sabbath. These are crucial omissions.

We can now underline the central theme of the *LMJN*'s portrait of Jesus so far: *the teaching and the wisdom of Jesus play the leading role in his conflict with Jewish authorities. Indeed, the conflict with the authorities is the mode by which the sage becomes christic. Jesus must earn his glory in his dialectical confrontations*, as it is not conferred on him from birth, from the prophets, from his lineage, or from wonders.

The *LMJN* transforms Matthew's Sabbath text in a remarkable way. A point of debate about the nature of the Sabbath piles on three lessons (David and the priests, the man with the withered hand, and the lost sheep) to bring us to the punch line: "the Sabbath is made for man, and not man for the Sabbath" (Mark 2:27). But the *LMJN* will not allow Jesus to act out the point by healing the man: the lesson without the action. The lesson resorts to historical and hypothetical cases to perform the point, ones presumably familiar to educated Jews. And yet the Pharisees, in the *LMJN*, are ready to destroy Jesus, entirely on the basis of rather mild, midrashic debates. Of course, if we were allowed to hear about Jesus' miracles, we might understand the Pharisaic anger. But since the miracles are banned by the *LMJN*, the anger against Jesus seems almost inconceivable. *How can the Pharisees get so mad so early from midrashic debates?*[7]

According to its deep values, the *LMJN* must purge the healing stories and turn the entire Sabbath debate into a didactic point, but not a performance. In Matthew, the Sabbath debate ends with "he healed them all" (Matt 12:15) and that reference the *LMJN* omits, too, even though in the very next pericope, the call of the disciples, the *LMJN* declares that the crowd comes to him to be "healed" of their diseases![8] *We have to wonder why the* LMJN

7. Manseau notes that the *LMJN* builds up Jesus' authority without the healing stories, without the actual occasion of an episode, without Jesus flexing any muscle, without an actual clash with authorities (*Jefferson Bible*, 45, 68–69). Manseau also finds support for his questions in the Letter to Charles Clay, December 20, 1814 (Adams and Lester, *Extracts*, 361–63). Our questions, however, ask *whether Jesus' wisdom is sufficient to establish his authority, and, by extension, whether a morality can be extracted from the rejected supernatural.*

8. The obvious inconsistency in the *LMJN* should be noted: in a text allergic to supernaturalism we find the author willing to allow Jesus to be *known as a wonder-worker*. It may be premature to note that the author frequently allows Jesus to be considered as a healer or exorcist, even as he will never show Jesus' healings. The simplest interpretation of this inconsistency is that it arises from the difficult task of cleaning all references to the supernatural in a narrative so saturated with it. A more complex suggestion considers that the author may think of the residue of the miraculous as an instance of the corruption of the pure Jesus story. Or possibly the author wants to have Jesus known as a wonder-worker even if he is not one for some narrative point: to show the enthusiasm for Jesus among the people, even if it is misguided, or to show the way that the people constantly misread the charisma of Jesus out of their naivete, not corruption. We will have to pay attention to this theme.

flirts with the miraculous and presupposes it at times, without allowing us to see it. Perhaps this oddity is a function of the author's blocky mode of editing: the wonders are so embedded in the traditions that he cannot extricate valued materials without reference to the very wonders themselves.[9]

According to the LMJN, *the conflict over Jesus' teaching generates serious anger and hostility from the Jewish authorities. Apparently, the* LMJN *allows Jesus to be known as a healer, to be sought out as a healer, without showing Jesus actually healing anyone.* Instead, the *LMJN* directs us to the real charisma of his ethical brilliance. Obviously, the *LMJN* continues to suppress supernatural phenomena, and so far as it does, *the suppression makes the hostility of the Pharisees and other Jewish groups more incredible.* The logic of the hostility requires what we call the miracles, but the logic of the *LMJN*'s selection scheme requires that miracles must be suppressed. Therefore, we see that *the* LMJN *uses the expectations of and rumors about healing as a way to legitimate the growing hostility of Jewish authorities.* The text allows us to understand that the people stir up talk of wonders when they think of Jesus and, consequently, that the authorities are terrified of a charismatic wonder-worker. That the *LMJN* dabbles in suggestions of miracles also supports the rather flimsy rationale for the eventual execution of Jesus, an event so far grounded only in moral controversy with the Jewish authorities. At this point, we do not know clearly why they are afraid, but we have seen two hints revealed in the temple event: *Jesus' anger against the authorities rests on his sense that they pollute the sacred space with commerce; and at the same time, Jesus challenges certain interpretations of Sabbath law that misunderstand acting with moral urgency on that day.*

Before we turn to the Sermon on the Mount, the great teacher's greatest teaching, we need to identify what is missing from the account in the *LMJN*. We have already considered what is missing about the origins of Jesus; now we need to identify what is missing in the materials up to Matthew's Sermon block and match them with "early" items in Mark's account of the early preaching in Galilee (where there is no use of the Q source). The most significant missing item is the temptation story that leads Jesus into his adult ministry according to the synoptic accounts. Recall that the *LMJN* substitutes the temple fit and the Sabbath controversy for the temptation, as the lead-in to the adult ministry. Consequently, in the *LMJN Jesus is instantly critical of the conduct of the two main religious institutions of the Jews (the temple and the Sabbath), and he is already angry.* However, in the synoptic accounts Jesus must hone his vocational sense through the

---

9. Eventually we will have to face why the plain gospel of Jesus got supernaturalized; the author will have to propose a theory to address this matter, but it will not appear directly in the text of the *LMJN*.

temptation and an extensive ministry in Galilee healing and exorcising. In Mark's brief account the Spirit leads Jesus to forty days of temptation by Satan and the angels who tend him: that is it! Jesus immediately begins to preach in Galilee, not in Judea, that the time is fulfilled and the Kingdom is at hand.[10] Possibly, this short version that the *LMJN* deletes is too full of apocalyptic.

If we add the accounts of Matthew and Luke to that of Mark, we have the familiar three-part temptation scene in which the "tempter" bargains with Jesus. After each temptation, Jesus levels an elegant rebuke of the tempter and then the devil disappears and Jesus begins his ministry in Galilee. Why does the *LMJN* ignore this story? We do not know, but probably its conversations with the devil make it too mythological for the *LMJN*. In any case, the *LMJN* has already launched the ministry of Jesus (and in Judea, not Galilee) with the instantly angry Jesus. The text may not need the temptation story, as Jesus' moral sense already shines in his youthful encounter with the rabbis in the synagogue and in the temple fracas. Also note that, for some reason, the *LMJN* does not include the famous announcement of the theme of Jesus' gospel (according to Mark 1:14 and Matt 4:17).[11] We may guess that the passage also appears too apocalyptic for the *LMJN*'s taste.

We may speculate why the *LMJN* ignores the temptation story and the announcement of ministry. It is, however, more difficult to figure out why the rejection at Nazareth would not be included early in the *LMJN*. Would not our author enjoy Jesus as the local guy who wows people in the synagogue? Possibly the jealousy experienced by the people of Nazareth distracts from the *LMJN*'s values, as does Jesus' rebuke of Nazareth. We shall see. But clearly, we expect that the *LMJN* would flee from the prophecy identifying Jesus as a prophet, a text in which Jesus compares himself to the great Elijah. We must also consider that the rejection in Nazareth adds a different and possibly distracting source of conflict for the controversy tradition and the passion of Jesus. *After all, having Jesus' neighbors resentful may not directly advance the theory that Jesus' conflict rests in his critique of the religious establishment.* More will be said on this issue later. The simplest explanation for our author's cutting out the rejection at Nazareth may be that his Jesus has not been in Galilee long enough to arouse hostility yet.

The *LMJN* omits the call of the disciples who work as fishermen. Those accounts in Matthew and Mark seem harmless and, thus, their absence is

---

10. Again, we see the *LMJN*'s displacement of the story of Jesus, where *the mostly Galilean story of the Synoptics becomes the mostly Judean story of the* LMJN.

11. Mark has Jesus "proclaiming the good news of God," saying, "The time is fulfilled, and the kingdom of God has come near; repent, and believe in the good news." Mark 1:14–15.

inscrutable, since we can easily imagine the author of the *LMJN* embracing the idea of being "fishers of men." Of course, the Lukan text with its miraculous catch must be eliminated from a gospel that has already eliminated all traces of the supernatural in the birth of Jesus.[12] On the same theme, we find *the text omits the entire exorcist ministry so central to Mark*. By now we are not surprised. The *LMJN* next selects the first nine verses of Luke 13, a pericope from the L1 source. The passage starts with a story of certain Galileans who are persecuted by Pilate: Should their extreme suffering mean that they are more sinful than others? Are we to believe that those killed in a tower accident are more sinful than others in Jerusalem (13:1–2)? Jesus says no, but turns the story into a warning about repentance. Then the text picks up the fig-tree story, the version in which the man allows the tree one more year to produce fruit (vv. 6–9). Significantly, the *LMJN* ignores the story from Matt 21:19 in which Jesus zaps a fig tree and it dies immediately. Evidently, *the* LMJN *is quite interested in the fig tree as a story or a symbol but not as a wonder*. So, too, the text ignores the healing of an infirm woman in the synagogue. This event gets Jesus in trouble with authorities for healing on the Sabbath, and he calls the ruler of the synagogue a hypocrite (vv. 13–17). One assumes the *LMJN* would love this useful story, were it not tied to a healing.

In order to get to another critique of the Pharisees, the *LMJN* abandons most of Luke 11. The Pharisaic misdeeds are many, but the author's favorite term for them is "hypocrisy." The strange feature of the *LMJN*'s text, a feature of Luke and the other Synoptics as well, is that debate, criticism, name-calling, and judgments generate such a violent response: deep anger from Jesus and serious plots of violence from the Pharisees. *The hostility does not fit its cause*. Modern scholars know that the disjuncture between this cause and its effect arises from the fact that the synoptic tradition uses the Pharisees as post-factum foils to explain why so many Jews of the second and third generation do not respond positively to the notion of Jesus as the Jewish messiah. So, the disjuncture between causes and violent results cannot be blamed on the *LMJN*: the synoptic tradition invents it. Still, the *LMJN* widens the disjuncture. *How can debates over Jewish belief and practice generate so much hostility to Jesus?* Christian readers of the gospels, of course, hardly ever digest how much disjunction there is in the Galilean controversy traditions. As we learn more, we will have to work out how the *LMJN* abstracts from the controversy traditions and converts them into a generic opposition from the religious authorities of Second Temple Judaism.

---

12. The call of the disciples will return quite late in the gospel.

We see, therefore, that the *LMJN* is achieving a distinctive rationale for the passion of Jesus by highlighting his struggle with the Pharisees. We have noticed the way in which *the text draws out and clusters various religious groups and shapes them into a generic and unified opposition to Jesus on the part of Jewish religious authorities.* Usually, it is a Pharisee or a group of Pharisees who debate with Jesus. They get more and more angry with him. The clusters of Jewish opponents can include the Sadducees, the lawyers, and the scribes. The *LMJN* does not distinguish among the many, and indeed does not bother with distinctions among "officials," as does the gospel tradition. *We notice, for instance, that the* LMJN *does not distinguish clearly between the synagogue and the temple, the Galileans and the Judeans, the Pharisees and the Sadducees, the rabbis and the scribes.*

4

The Ethic

Precis

Obviously, the author of *The Life and Morals of Jesus of Nazareth* does not invent Jesus' ethical sayings; he takes what is in front of him, mostly from the synoptic Q accounts. And he does not put interpretive spins on the message of Jesus to explain what this or that means in the texts. Rather, his only tools of interpretation are the cutting and relocating of materials. Matt 12, usually considered beyond the Sermon on the Mount, becomes a part of the Sermon with the same audience, the disciples, not the crowds. Within the *LMJN*, the complete Sermon now includes conflict traditions with the Pharisees over the Sabbath (Matt 12:1–12), which are underlined by the "Sabbath made for man" logion of Mark 2:27. The effect is that *Jesus gives his main moral teaching to the disciples, not the public, and he does so before they are called and amid the growing threat of the Pharisees.* Again, we see the intimate, even gnostic, character of Jesus' teaching of his students; they get the best moral learning. The *LMJN* draws the call of the disciples from Luke 6, and then it returns to the familiar items of Matthew's Sermon on the Mount.

In all of these moves the author's hand shows in his selecting and locating of materials; he vaults over details in each gospel narrative, scrambles the narrative order, and, of course, does not recognize the manner in which the locations of material in the narrative signal important points for the redaction of the Jesus story. The irony in his treatment of the main moral teaching of Jesus rests in *his unforeseen intention to make the Sermon an address to the in-crowd, the disciples,* while the multitudes throng to Jesus and the Pharisees become more hostile toward him. Once he comes down from the gnostic instruction, the crowds follow him, and he begins his itinerant ministry. Oddly, in our author's gospel, the crowds neither get to hear Jesus' main message nor see his wondrous acts. But yet they get excited about him, and the controversy about him grows!

In the first act of his village ministry Jesus eats with a Pharisee (Luke 7:36). Then he meets his mother and brothers and uses them to make a generalized point that all who do the will of God are his family. Significantly, the *LMJN* omits Jesus' caustic repudiation of his family, the famous "hate" logion that has troubled gospel critics for generations. We do not know why the author leaves it out, but we notice that typically our text flattens the sting of some of Jesus' moral injunctions. We know that by the time the author writes the *LMJN*, Jesus is a moral hero to our author. Conceivably, he leaves out the sharpest moments of the sayings tradition because he feels he has gotten the point of Jesus without using his "eastern hyperbole" remark or without any corruption under his followers' hands. For instance, the *LMJN* ignores Jesus' prohibition against divorce and only focuses on a man's need to give the divorced wife "a writing of divorcement." Then he turns the issue of divorce toward the moral problems for man and woman when the woman remarries.[1] Here is another example of the *LMJN*'s temptation to flatten some of the strident moral injunctions of Jesus.

Exposition: The Sermon on the Mount

From the first page of the *LMJN* we have been prepared to recognize that Jesus would be a great teacher. Here in the Sermon we find the core of his teaching. Obviously, the *LMJN* uses the Matthew text as the basis of Jesus' ethic, and it quotes the entire three chapters almost verbatim (chapters 5–7). There is nothing distinctive in the way that the author quotes the Beatitudes. Indeed, since he includes the entire sermon, we realize the extent to which we depend on the author's removal of materials to get a clue what he thinks about an episode. Will we be able to discern how the text intends us to understand the Sermon when he simply dumps the whole thing in our laps, and will that discovery match any of the traditional modes of interpreting the Sermon? Further, we have no idea how the author reacts to some of the radicality of Jesus' sermon. What must our author think about selling all property or of the extreme advice about sexuality and marriage? *It is striking that the author who puts all value in the ethic of Jesus seems to reveal no hint*

---

1. Jefferson, *Bible* (Beacon ed.), 47; folio 8.

of how we should interpret Jesus' core moral advice, except that he wants the whole Sermon in his book.

How would he want us to take a particular injunction, or the aim of the whole Sermon? Of course, we know that he endorses the whole Sermon to some degree, or it would not have appeared in the *LMJN*. What eludes the reader is some hint whether he prefers certain material in the Sermon over other themes and how he interprets the extreme demands of the texts. The only clue we have comes from evoking a *double-coherence criterion:* what enters the *LMJN* from Matthew's version of the Sermon can be judged against what the author saves from Luke's Sermon on the Plain. An inclusion of similar material from both Matthew and Luke (that is, *double attestation*) would be quite convincing of high value for the *LMJN* author.[2] Note that we say "saves" because what the *LMJN* leaves out of Luke's account could be missing for no other reason than that the author was concerned to reduce redundancy.

While there is nothing exceptional about the quotes from the Sermon in Matthew, we do notice that the *LMJN* does not quote the Q parallels from Luke's Sermon on the Plain. Luke, we remember, has "the poor" blessed, period, while the *LMJN* affirms that the real Jesus thinks of Matthew's "poor in spirit." While Matthew has the blessed as those who "hunger and thirst for righteousness," the *LMJN* opts simply for "the hungry" from Luke. If the author really means the poor in spirit and not the poor, the really hungry and not the hungry for righteousness, we need to know why our author softens the one injunction and not the other. Interestingly, Matt 5:12 claims the poor and so on will be rewarded in heaven like those persecuted prophets of the past.[3] At the end of the Beatitudes, the *LMJN* inserts Luke's list of woes: to the rich, to the full of food, to those laughing, to those about whom people say good things (from Luke 6:24–26),[4] all in such a way that we think that the "poor in spirit" from Matthew is an editorial confusion or mistake on the author's part.[5] His additions from Luke confirm that the author values many of Luke's feistier forms of the Jesus sayings and particularly Luke's critique of the wealthy.

---

2. Note that the author of the *LMJN* must consider Matthew's Sermon before Luke's, since he takes the whole sermon from Matthew early in the text and does not do what he usually does, pick and choose among four gospels.

3. We note an affirmation of the prophets of the past, even as the *LMJN* runs away from the fulfillment of prophecy. We will want to think through what kind of eschatology is embedded in the text of the *LMJN*.

4. Jefferson, *Bible* (Beacon ed.), 43–44; folio 6:145.

5. Or that the author had cut for use the Matthew version before he noticed the sharper form from Luke.

After the Lukan "woes" interrupt the *LMJN*'s use of Matthew's Sermon, the text returns to Matthew's copy with the salt-and-light pericopes (Matt 5:13–16), and they end with an injunction to do good works.[6] Then, the *LMJN* quotes Matthew's own source material completely (Matt 5:17 from the M1 source, not Q), which affirms three notions of importance for the interpretation of the Sermon: first, that Jesus comes to fulfill, not abolish, the law; second, that the audience (i.e., the disciples, to be consistent with the initial choice of audience for the Sermon) must not relax any of the laws in order to be great in the Kingdom of heaven; and third, that the audience's righteousness must exceed that of the scribes and Pharisees. We note, therefore, the earnest rigor of the *LMJN*'s Jesus' demand, even if we are now more puzzled why the author softens some of the rigor.[7] We note also that the audience presumably continues to be the disciples, not people in general.

The *LMJN* starts the well-known "But I say to you" series with the saying that equates hate and murder, and quotes the entire Matthew passage (5:21–26), including the saying that equates lust and adultery (5:27–30). The text even includes the entire prohibition against divorce from Matthew (5:31–32), with Matthew's famous qualification of the prohibition under the condition of the wife's unchastity. So, too, our author includes the "But I say to you" on swearing (Matt 5:33–37). In all of these, the three injunctions from the distinctive source M1, the *LMJN* takes them verbatim.[8] The "But-I-say-to-you" quoting turns to the Q materials in Matthew concerning the Exod 21:24 lex talionis, to the striking of the cheek, the suing for the coat, the going of the second mile, and the refusal of no one who begs. Again, Luke's version, not substantially different from Matthew's, is simply redundant for the advance of the *LMJN*'s purpose.[9]

The *LMJN*'s Matthew continues through the entire pronouncement about loving one's enemies: another "But I say to you" where Jesus heightens the demand of the law as the new Moses. Such love is like God's love where the sun shines on both good and evil (5:43–45). Jesus explains that it is easy to love the lovable and that even the "publicans" so love.[10] At this point we arrive at a value-rich editing choice. The next verse (5:48) in Matthew

---

6. Jefferson, *Bible* (Beacon ed.), 44; folio 6:145.
7. Jefferson, *Bible* (Beacon ed.), 45; folio 6—7:145, 147.
8. Jefferson, *Bible* (Beacon ed.), 45–47; folio 7—9:147, 149, 151.
9. Jefferson, *Bible* (Beacon ed.), 45–46; folio 7—8:148, 149.
10. The *LMJN* follows the Latin term "publican" twice in Matt 5:46–47. The Greek is *telonai*, often "tax collector." Newer interpretations take the meaning to be "Gentiles." Without debating the proper sense of the term here, we can see that the choice of the *LMJN* affirms the charged and compromised reputation of the tax collector (Jefferson, *Bible* [Beacon ed.], 48; folio 9:151).

THE ETHIC   35

is the powerful "You, therefore, must be perfect, as your heavenly Father is perfect." Shockingly, the *LMJN* omits this one verse from Matthew after following exactly the whole of Matthew's Sermon on the Mount (except for adding the woes from Luke). Apparently, *the author dislikes the comparison of serious human morality to the perfection of God*. Instead, he shifts to the Lukan five-verse midrash on the love-for-the-enemy: yes, we are to do good to the enemy without concern for a reward, but then in a dramatic moment, *the* LMJN *substitutes Luke's version ("Be merciful, even as your Father is merciful" in Luke 6:36)*[11] *for the perfection analogy of Matthew. Here we get a glimpse of our author's sense that the genuine rigor of the Sermon is not fanatical or extreme; it is aimed at mercy, not at some unattainable divine perfection.* Keep track of this preference for mercy, not perfection, as it will grow into one of the text's major themes.

Our text returns to Matthew's account of the instruction on almsgiving from the M1 source. The *LMJN* quotes the entire pericope, which emphasizes being modest about one's charity, and continues, word for word, with the M1 source from Matthew on praying and public shows of piety (Matt 6:5–8). Then our text quotes Matthew's version of the Lord's Prayer but adds the common "For thine is the Kingdom, and the power, and the glory, forever. Amen" from the Gospel to the Hebrews, and finishes Matthew's meditation on forgiveness (Matt 6:14).[12] We notice that the *LMJN* does virtually no editing in this section of the Sermon. Thus, the text quotes the entire M1 source from Matthew on fasting (6:16–18) and continues with the Q text in Matthew's version of the "treasures in heaven" pericope (6:19–21) and of the eye and the lamp (6:22–23). Significantly, the *LMJN* does not use Luke's version of "Do not lay up for yourselves treasures on earth" to make a sharper point, a move typical of Luke: "Sell your possessions and give alms" (Luke 12:33). Thus, to summarize, *the* LMJN *once again moderates some of the extreme injunctions in parts of Matthew's Sermon (and Luke's version).* We wonder about the meaning of such moderation. Is it that certain views in Jesus' instructions simply fall off the morally reasonable map?

At this point the *LMJN* prepares to bring the Sermon to an end. It follows Matthew by rejecting the service of both God and mammon (6:24), by quoting verbatim the entire section on anxiety (6:25–34),[13] by starting with Matthew's "judge not" (7:1), and by shifting quickly to one verse from Luke (6:38) that develops the "measure you give, measure you get" logic of

---

11. Jefferson, *Bible* (Beacon ed.), 49; folio 10:153.

12. Jefferson, *Bible* (Beacon ed.), 50; folio 11:155.

13. Luke's version of the anxiety discourse (12:22–31) does not differ from Matthew's in significant ways (Jefferson, *Bible* [Beacon ed.], 51; folio 12:157).

Matt 7:2. But before it quotes Luke instead of Matthew, the *LMJN* omits a powerful phrase from Luke: "forgive and you will be forgiven" (Luke 6:37).[14] Earlier we sensed the author has some issue with the theme of forgiveness. Now we get a hint that the *LMJN* may be *making the case that Jesus must offer some kind of a limit to forgiveness.*

The *LMJN* continues with the "log in the eye" pericope, Jesus' condemnation of hypocrisy from Mark 7, the "holy to the dog" logion from M1 in 7:6, the ask/seek discourse (Matt 7:7–11), the Golden Rule (7:12), the "narrow gate" saying (7:13–14), and the teaching on false prophets and good fruit (7:15–20).[15] The author of the *LMJN* must have remembered that Matthew and Luke also continue with the good tree/good fruit theme in 12:35–37, since he uses it as a meditation on the good man who brings forth good things and the evil one who will be condemned.[16] Finally, the *LMJN* leaps over Matt 7:21–23 and ends the Sermon with 7:24–29.

This final pericope warns that people should hear and do the words of Jesus; those who hear and do are wise ones who build their houses on rock. What the *LMJN* leaves out of the account is 7:21–23, a passage in which Jesus hypothesizes that not everyone who calls him "Lord, Lord" will enter the Kingdom of heaven. Only those who do the will of the Father will make it into heaven. So, many of those who say "Lord, Lord" and who prophesy, exorcise, and do wonders in his name will not be recognized "on that day."[17] At the end of the Sermon the people are astonished at Jesus' teaching, which comes with "authority" unlike that of the scribes (Matt 7:29).[18] By the end of

---

14. Jefferson, *Bible* (Beacon ed.), 52–53; folio 13:159.
15. Jefferson, *Bible* (Beacon ed.), 53–54; folio 13:159, 161.
16. Jefferson, *Bible* (Beacon ed.), 54; folio 14:161.
17. Here we have another example of the extreme apocalyptic that the *LMJN* rejects.
18. Jefferson, *Bible* (Beacon ed.), 55; folio 15:163. To pull off the inversion of the messianic secret, the *LMJN* gathers in the middle of the book an assemblage of all the acceptable texts that show Jesus' teachings, his informing and training of his disciples, the revelation of truths long lost, the warning of those who do not listen or catch on, and so forth. One mystery that we have not unraveled yet is the identity of the Son of Man, one of the *LMJN*'s favorite christological categories. Recall that in certain settings the text erases passages with the title, while in others it allows the title emphatically. We see no trace of incidental or inattentive patterns of use and nonuse. Rather, *the rejected Son of Man tends to be in the obviously apocalyptic passages.* If there is a pattern to the accepted Son of Man, then we have a further secret to uncover: the Danielic Son of Man may not be the real one. Also, the *LMJN* sometimes avoids the Kingdom-of-God language and sometimes embraces it. The *LMJN* always removes the title Son of God. *We sense the instances definitely avoided are ones sounding clearly apocalyptic.* Could the rejection of an apocalyptic Son of Man and of the Kingdom be of a piece? *The interpretive issue will be to explain why the* LMJN *rejects obviously apocalyptic materials and why it uses some apocalyptic-sounding materials, materials we recognize as apocalyptic.*

the Sermon we readers realize that *the LMJN's Sermon contains the repository of the astonishing wisdom already evident in the prescient twelve-year-old in the temple.*

Analysis: The Sermon on the Mount

Perhaps the most important thing to remember is that *the LMJN is serious about using Matthew's Sermon as the centerpiece of Jesus' ethic.* The Sermon is the full-grown wisdom of the once twelve-year-old lad debating the rabbis at the temple. The *LMJN* text includes basically the entire Sermon and places it at the beginning of the account of the life and message of Jesus. But, of course, so positioning the Sermon does not by itself solve how the author intends to convey the meaning of the Sermon. As we know, the Sermon as a whole has received a myriad of different types of interpretations, as have the injunctions in it. How does the author find the Sermon to have meaning? We already know that the sayings of Jesus dominate the *LMJN*'s stage at the expense of the wondrous actions of Jesus. We already know too that the *LMJN* aims the whole Sermon at the disciples, not the crowd. There is, of course, a great difference in meaning if the audience is supposed to be the disciples only, if it is for the crowd of listeners interested in his message, or if it really is for all humans.

Why would the LMJN's *Jesus speak the greatest ethic only to the disciples?* Does the author want to set up the disciples for the failure that will come to them later in the story? And what good would it be to convey a universalized ethic if the crowd of people do not get in on the wisdom? Is this Jesus keeping secrets? Is he acting tribally in the Sermon? Possibly the aiming of the Sermon is no more than an accident of the author's byzantine method of editing the original texts.[19] We must ponder these issues as we consider the Sermon in the context of the entire teachings of Jesus. We must figure out how a decision about the Sermon's audience shapes its meaning and use, and we must solve how an intimate audience for the Sermon affects the theme of secret wisdom. *So far, readers already sense that the* LMJN's

---

Is it that the author does not recognize them as apocalyptic, or is he adapting apocalyptic for, say, a moral point? Further, the absence of the "Son of God" term and the occasional inclusion of the "Son of Man," sometimes in coordination, suggests that *the author thinks of "Son of God" as an unacceptable divine term, while "Son of Man" refers to something in the human world.* More on this matter later! Sanford suggests "Son of God" evokes an arrogance of status and thus is improper for Jesus (Sanford, *Religious Life*, 114).

19. Church notices this strange internal tension within the project of the *LMJN* (Jefferson, *Jefferson Bible* [1989], 43).

Jesus is christic because of his wisdom, and that Jefferson's christology will be a sophiological one. The LMJN's *Jesus is essentially the extraordinary sage.*

The use of Matthew's "poor in spirit" (against Luke's message of blessings to "the poor") alerts us to the notion that we must watch what the *LMJN* does with the Sermon's asceticism from the Q source. Is it hunger for righteousness or simple hunger? Will the poor be rewarded in this life or only in heaven? Should they expect deliverance here and now? *The bold introduction of Luke's woes into the world of Matthean beatitude may suggest that the* LMJN *wants to hold to a powerful moment of justice against what might seem like the "cheap grace" of Matthew's Beatitudes.* Perhaps, justice simply needs to be asserted. The *LMJN* does allow Luke to express his special anger against the rich.

In some sense, the *LMJN* must affirm the radical sayings of the Sermon. The four "But I say to you" logia pose strenuous demands.[20] What is remarkable is that the author does nothing with the three in which Jesus appears to qualify or extend or intensify Mosaic law. Remarkably, even though we have seen that the *LMJN* moderates some radicality of the Sermon, *it does nothing to tone down the core demands of the Sermonic Jesus.* Why? Perhaps the full analysis of the gospel will give us a clue how we should take what the text means to mean. Here we only know that the *LMJN* does not soften these essential Jesus demands, though the author does prefer Matthew's qualified version of the divorce injunction, since he rejects the Mark 10:12 and Luke 16:18 versions, which forbid divorce. *Therefore, we see both rigor and a softening in the* LMJN's *selections from Matthew's account of the Sermon. The rigor is affirmed even as it is not allowed to be unreasonably extreme.* How shall we understand the two tendencies in an interpretation?[21]

We return to the Q source of the Sermon and of the versions of the higher righteousness demanded by Matthew's Jesus. The *LMJN* ignores the abbreviated versions of the logia in Luke's Sermon; indeed, Matthew is the *LMJN*'s go-to gospel. Again, note that our text accepts the radicality of Matthew's Jesus to the point that it quotes the entire M1 logia and Matthew's version of the Q material. And again, we do not yet know how to construe the *LMJN*'s acceptance of the radical Jesus. Possibly, given how much of Matthew he quotes in total, the author thinks that it is simply more convenient to go with Matthew's account, and that there is no great value in the choice of Matthew, since his sermon is so much more developed than Luke's.

---

20. Plus, the "But I say to you" instances later in the Sermon.

21. Perhaps, the position on the rigor with the occasional softening of the Second Mile Ethic matches two other moments in the exposition of the *LMJN*'s gospel: the notion that the law requires obedience but tolerates occasional suspension, and the idea that ritual holiness is acceptable so far as it rests in the moral.

But in some sense the author of the *LMJN* allows, even enjoys, the austere demands of the Second Mile Ethic in that he opts not to drop them. What are we to make of the "But I say to you" theme of Matthew's Jesus, affirmed by the *LMJN*? Does the text endorse the ascetic-sounding injunctions of Matthew's Jesus? Perhaps we will discover further clues. For instance, does our author's use of "publicans" suggest that the *LMJN* via Luke is particularly concerned with the crimes of money and wealth?

The *LMJN* does little editing of all the moral, pious injunctions of the Sermon. It simply quotes Matthew. At one point, in the use of Matthew's "laying up treasures" logion, the *LMJN* rejects Luke's command to "sell your possessions." The choice seems surprising but cannot be accidental. We have already seen the *LMJN*'s endorsement of Luke's tough woes on wealth. We must assume the author's endorsement includes a softening of some of the radical ascetic expectations of Jesus' Sermon. When the *LMJN* follows Matthew's Sermon word for word, we have to assume the author affirms the ideas, however much he may spin an interpretive approach. When the author adds material from Luke, we face a significant inclusion, since the *LMJN* lets the Matthew text dominate; but when on rare occasions the author omits something from Matthew's Sermon, we sense a major theme. So far, *we have discovered a noticeable softening of the ascetic Jesus themes, and so far, we see the author substitute God's mercy as a model for the human moral life, instead of God's perfection. Jesus' Sermon poses a rigorous moral life but not one unreasonable in its denials; the human ideal is divine mercy, not perfection.*[22]

Both of these moves suggest that the *LMJN* intends to show that Jesus' ethic is not as impossible as it appears to many readers. Indeed, the fact that the author, on occasion, will soften the demand suggests that he thinks *the Second Mile Ethic is livable by humans*. It is not ascetic denial, but also not simply an ideal to inspire us, and certainly it is not a demand meant to crush us into relying on the grace of God. Further, we have seen a couple of hints that the author wishes to direct the give/get logic of the Sermon almost into

---

22. *The shift in attributes for God, from perfection to mercy, is profound for our author's view of God and his understanding of the moral life.* Recall how often early in his life the author would name the attributes of God as good and perfect: see the Letter to Ezra Stiles Ely, June 25, 1819 (see it on the *Founders Online* website from the US National Archives, listed in the bibliography; or Adams and Lester, *Extracts*, 386–87). More remarkably, even when our author is in an apophatic mode and he despairs of knowing anything of God, he still mentions that Jesus knows God is good and perfect. Consequently, when the *LMJN* ignores the perfection of God and replaces it with mercy, we are at a decisive moment in the theology of the text. See also the Letter to Benjamin Waterhouse, June 20, 1822 (Adams and Lester, *Extracts*, 325–26) for the theme of the perfection of God.

a Deuteronomic "if *p*, then *q*" morality.[23] Here, the "if *p*, then *q*" is forward-looking and not a retrospective moral reading of the past. It is framed as the *LMJN*'s favorite image, *that the good tree brings forth good fruit*.[24] Good fruit means doing actual good, not simply talking about it. It means being modest and not showy, humble and not seeking reward. The contrary is true, too, and the *LMJN* does not hide that there will be judgment for not doing the good.

We need to pause and think about the significance that the text substitutes mercy for perfection. *We have already seen that the substitution of mercy seems to fit with other re-aimings of the extreme rigors of the Sermon*; our author sides with Luke, not Matthew, on this matter and indeed eliminates the more daunting Jesus sayings. And we have speculated that the tacit assumption he makes is that the Sermon's ethic is livable, perhaps for all people. Recall that the *LMJN*'s Jesus aims the Sermon at the disciples. Recall also that the author does not want a gnostic gospel for the elite. Now we have to face the notion that *the mercy of God, not God's perfection, provides the analogy and inspiration for disciples in the moral life*.[25] Instantly, the author of the *LMJN* makes mercy, not perfection, not mimicking the perfection of God, the point of judgment of the moral life. Not only is the Second Mile Ethic livable for humans, in this understanding, but the main moral teaching of Jesus is no ascetic denial: it is not the way of the saint, not advice for moral giants, and certainly not a demand meant to crush humans so that they turn to the grace of God. It is a working ethic; it is doable by the ones who have freed themselves from blindness and vain foolishness.

---

23. Recall that the Mosaic sermon in Deuteronomy proposes the moral logic that obedience brings blessing and disobedience brings curse. The logic works in an "if *p*, then *q*" format. In the *LMJN* we may be discovering another moment of moderation within Jesus' judgments, that there can be apocalyptic themes without the apocalyptic extremes.

24. The letters confirm the importance of the images of tree and fruit for the moral life. Letter to Miles King, September 26, 1814 (Jefferson, *Writings* [Lipscomb and Bergh, eds.], 14:109).

25. Does he really mean disciples or the many or all humans? One cannot avoid the suspicion that the author means the Sermon's injunctions are for all people and not just the disciples. One wonders if his introductory aiming of the Sermon to the disciples is simply a mistake on the author's part. The audience, of course, makes a world of difference in the meaning of a law, but the author may not have noticed the issue in his editing and in his obsession to uncover in the Sermon Jesus' contribution to universal, natural law. It is almost impossible to believe that the author imagined Jesus' sublime ethic only for the gang of the disciples or only for the Christians, for that matter. Indeed, why would he parochialize Jesus' ethic, given his tendency to universalize every hint of the Israelite moral tradition? *The issue of the audience of the Sermon, then, continues to bedevil the interpretation of Jesus' ethic.*

The *LMJN* has been influenced by Matthew's higher moral righteousness, but in one important way is different from Matthew. In the hands of our author, Matthew's Sermon stands on its own as the whole ethic of the sage. *It no longer stands on the words of Moses*; it no longer is a midrashic comment on the Law, as it is in Matthew's gospel; it is no longer an extension or an intensification of the Law, since *our author cuts the gospel from its Jewishness. Indeed, the new wisdom of the* LMJN's *Jesus has been assembled against the whole of Second Temple Judaism*, from all the different Jewish officials to the jeering crowds demanding his death. The new wisdom, without the Torah, without the functioning purification and ritual frame, without the holiness codes, has left Judaism behind, more so than even Matthew has.

While the author of the *LMJN* may seem unaware of the implications when he selects some moral nuggets of Jesus and disregards others, he does take the moral advice of Jesus in a serious but curious way. The author is fixed on the question: How many times? How many times can Jesus forgive? How many times can we forgive? We have seen the *LMJN*'s tepid relation to the theme of forgiveness in the ministry of Jesus. The compilation both affirms forgiveness and allows Jesus to demand so many times of forgiveness that we get lost in the count, but it also struggles to find a limit. We have supposed that the *author plays the card of justice against an unlimited forgiveness*. In the most recent selections, he drops some references to forgiveness from Jesus, or suggests that *forgiveness ends when the forgiven do not forgive*. We have, then, hints that the author wishes to accent the *give/get logic* in the Sermon in order to match the earlier Deuteronomic "if p, then q" moral logic. That is, he affirms the Lukan sense that people get according to what they give. If so, the "if p, then q" morality is forward-looking, as it is in the book of Deuteronomy,[26] and not a retrospective moral reading of the past, as it is for the Deuteronomistic Historian overall. The logic is framed simply that a *good tree brings forth good fruit*. The *LMJN* likes to emphasize that bringing forth good fruit means actually doing the good, not simply talking about it. And it means doing the good while being modest and not showy, humble, and not seeking reward. The contrary is true, too, and the *LMJN* does not hide that there will be judgment on the evil. *The point for the issue of forgiveness is that forgiveness and times of forgiveness cannot undermine the justice embodied in the forward-looking use of the good-tree/good-fruit connection.*[27]

---

26. As in Deut 8:18.

27. John C. Kilgo recognized Jefferson's struggle with forgiveness as early as the beginning of the 1900s ("Religious Belief," 7). The connection to bearing good fruit is revelatory, in that *the fruit Jefferson demands of the faithful is active good works*. Salvation is insufficient or incomplete so long as we do not act for the good and do so in our

The challenge for the writer of the LMJN is to affirm judgment to support the moral life without falling into the extremes of the apocalyptic in the gospels. The ones who bring forth bad fruit will be judged, but it seems likely from what we have seen that the apocalyptic model of judgment looks too supernaturalist for our author. Thus, we know why the *LMJN* rejects the final pericope in Matthew: it oozes of apocalyptic, even under the typical Matthean effort to tone down the apocalyptic. The related point is this: *Jesus must have "authority," but it must be an authority founded in his teaching. The authority in question rejects those who speak of "Lord, Lord" in a showy way.* It certainly cannot be an authority founded in prophecy, exorcisms, and wonders. It must be a teaching authority but unlike that of the scribes. Here we see *the* LMJN *works to create a consistent theory for the opposition to Jesus: the writer proposes teachings that unnerve the officials of Second Temple Judaism.*

We return to the question of whether the *LMJN*'s Jesus' Sermon fits, overlaps with, or endorses any of the standard patterns of interpreting the Sermon ethic.[28] Notice the components of the judgment: First, in a work that interprets through omission, we find evidence that the author of the *LMJN* is serious about the Second Mile Ethic of Jesus. He quotes nearly everything in the Sermon, when he might have suppressed its rigorous moral ideas. Second, our author seems to assume that the teachings in the Sermon are a moral blueprint for ordinary humans in this world and not simply for the disciples. This observation contradicts the *LMJN*'s repeated announcement earlier when the text set up the Sermon.[29] There is no trace that he thinks of the ethic as for another world, no hint that the ethic is a qualified ethic (say, just for believers, just for the disciples, or just for the end-time of history). There is no hint of an "interim ethic," as New Testament scholars have called it. The ethic is public and enduring for all. Perhaps the author comes to the public and enduring character of the ethic by way of his deep rejection of extreme apocalypticism. He has already established that Jesus is

---

power. While Jefferson would not care how his claim plays in the court of traditional theology, it is likely that Jefferson is some kind of a Pelagian heretic on this point. See the Letter to Thomas B. Parker, May 15, 1819 (Adams and Lester, *Extracts*, 385–86). He is quite far from the Augustinian model when he claims the faithful ones must finish faith's salvation entirely on their own power. The Letter to Miles King, September 26, 1814, secures the centrality of good works for quality religion: "I must ever believe that religion substantially good which produces an honest life" (Jefferson Letter to Miles King).

28. Here we can identify another moment of moderation within the *LMJN*'s Jesus: *judgment may use some apocalyptic themes, but without the apocalyptic extremes.*

29. This change confirms that earlier the author inadvertently understood the audience of the Sermon to be the disciples, not the crowds.

a prescient sage who teaches a wisdom beyond the wisdom from teachers of the law. Therefore, *the LMJN's Jesus is not an apocalyptic prophet.*

Apparently, then, *our author is not unnerved by the rigor of Jesus' ethic.* In addition to removing Jesus' ethic from the apocalyptic, he often does select already softened versions (usually from Matthew) of some of the most aggressive injunctions of the Sermon (i.e., the poverty of the blessed; the possibility of divorce when faced with unchastity; the rejection of Luke's "sell your possessions"; and the rejection of moral perfection as a yardstick, in favor of divine mercy; and so forth). Still, the author also allows Jesus' heightening of basic moral commands. Not killing is too easy, since the highest demand is not to hate. The expectation is that *Jesus fulfills the law by raising its aim to the interior of the heart and to the universal.*[30] Recall that the *LMJN* quotes the entire, riddling passage from M1 that the faithful must exceed the righteousness of the scribes and Pharisees and that not one dot of the law can be relaxed (Matt 5:17–20). We interpreters would wonder how to make sense of the author's approval of this passage, had we not already established that *outdoing the Pharisees, for our author, means to be faithful without hypocrisy and pride.* In fact, one suspects that he does not have a clue to the meaning of this striking text, which says that Jesus' people must outdo the Pharisees in the minute details of the moral life. Likely the only thing our author hears in this passage is outdoing the Pharisees, and he has already determined that the Pharisees are wicked, like all the Jewish authorities.

Therefore, we may conclude that our author is close to interpretations that see the *LMJN's Jesus' demanding ethic rooted in inner humility and expressed in acts that aim at the ideals set out in the Sermon.* The new righteousness informed by Matthew inspires the ethic of the *LMJN's* Jesus: a heightened moral effort beyond mechanical marching to recipe laws. It ends in justice, is enacted by moral exemplification, and moves beyond simple consolation. It might be close to what we call *the counsels of perfection tradition,* but the ethic of the *LMJN* perhaps means to inspire ordinary people, not simply moral giants.[31] The ethic certainly would be far removed from the two-Kingdoms notion of Luther or from a holiness ethic.

---

30. In the moral heart, good people act with good motives, with intentions that flow from the developing moral sense; the heart poses duty to them as an expression of the intuitive feeling: see the Letter to Thomas Law, June 13, 1814 (Jefferson, *Writings* [Peterson, ed.], 1335–39).

31. By this time in our analysis we are convinced that the author of the *LMJN* has not thought through to whom the Sermon is addressed. He indicates through his editing that Jesus aims the Second Mile Ethic in all its rigor to the twelve disciples; but surely he thinks of the ethic as appropriate and livable by all humans. It is likely the next thing to natural law, we bet, and therefore his aiming the Sermon at the disciples

5

Lukan Additions to the Sermon

Precis

After the author completes the Sermon on the Mount from the hands of Matthew (chapters 5–7) with only a few interruptions, he turns to Luke's Sermon on the Plain (chapters 6–9). Once again, a crowd assembles about Jesus after episodes involving eating and about Jesus' mother, and once again, Jesus turns to his disciples to instruct them. The message is dark and ominous. The hypocrisy of the Pharisee looms. Jesus talks of secrets to be made known, of fears and threats and dangers, of greed and of hoarding wealth. To these he contrasts the life of faith, an existence similar to the carefree life of birds and lilies. These characteristically Lukan themes of wealth and carefree treasure appear in Luke 12, and by the end of the discourse Jesus is speaking of the coming of the Son of Man in foreboding ways full of judgment. Surprisingly, our author does not shy away from a modest use of apocalyptic language here, even if he gives no clue whether he is reading it as end-of-the-world material.

---

severely undercuts the universality of the ethic and, indeed, of all ethics. *It is hard to reconcile his choice of audience for Jesus with the author's often expressed critique of moral tribalism.*

Exposition: Teaching in Luke's Sermon on the Plain I

The story of Jesus now turns to the what-next after the focus on the origins of Jesus and the great Sermon of Matthew. The storyline has been developing, more or less, via the synoptic narrative and has been dominated by Matthew. Now the *LMJN* gathers the wisdom of Jesus from the three synoptic accounts, and Luke comes to be a major player. To synoptic readers the text seems to be random at times, because it collects fragments from the three gospels, and because it carefully tiptoes around the passages in which Jesus begins his healing and exorcising ministry, according to Mark's narration. We know we are in Galilee and that Jesus is teaching in "the villages" at the start of his itinerant ministry. Interestingly, the *LMJN* selects a single verse from the rarely used Mark (6:6) to give us the village location for this post-Sermon ministry. According to the *LMJN* Jesus simply starts talking of comfort to the heavy laden (in an M1 passage from Matt 11: 28–30) and invites others to share in his yoke and to find rest in it. The shift to a long passage in Luke (7:36–46 from the L1 source, without synoptic parallels) introduces the first parable and the first plot confrontation. *We need to be alert to the conflict accounts as the mode through which the* LMJN *establishes the authority of Jesus*. The conflicts develop the plot of our author's gospel as they do in portions of the canonical gospels, but here they do so without their partners, the signs, wonders, and exorcisms of those gospels.

The first confrontation account shows Jesus' encounter with a Pharisee who wishes to eat with him and invite him to his home. Meanwhile, a woman known as a sinner comes into the house and begins to wash and anoint Jesus' feet. The Pharisee is upset and suggests Jesus should have known better than to have allowed such behavior, if he were a real prophet. Jesus tells his first parable, about the creditor who forgives two debtors' debts of fifty and five hundred pence respectively. Jesus then turns the story into a question for the Pharisee: which of the two debtors would be more grateful? At this point we see that the story is really an allegory of the Pharisee of the small debt and the sinful woman of the large. Jesus ends the conversation by criticizing the Pharisee for an unwelcoming welcome and praising the woman for her lavish attention.[1] Curiously, *our author lets Jesus have the reputation of a prophet even as the* LMJN *typically purges any hint of prophecy*. That the *LMJN* allows the rumor of Jesus as prophet oddly matches its willingness to let Jesus be known as a healer. We wonder why.[2]

---

1. Jefferson, *Bible* (Beacon ed.), 56–57; folio 16:165.
2. Our author must enjoy that Jesus creates a hubbub among the common people, even if their enthusiasm is misidentified. The people seem to get excited by Jesus' genuine moral charisma but in folkways that may anticipate the corruption of Jesus' message.

The story of the woman kissing Jesus' feet and wiping them with her hair is familiar, but the *LMJN* omits Luke's conclusion: Jesus forgives the woman's many sins because of her generous love while the "one who is forgiven little, loves little" (7:48): allegorically, this one is the Pharisee. Then the people at the table wonder who dares to forgive sin, but Jesus says the woman's faith has saved her and has given her peace (v. 49). *Again, we get a hint that the author of the* LMJN *tones down the stories of unlimited forgiveness. Again, we see the author tease his readers with suggestions about Jesus that he will not allow directly in this text: the hint that Jesus is regarded as a prophet, this time not a healer, in a text that banishes both prophecy and healing!*

We miss these insights about what our author leaves out if we read only the *LMJN*'s version of the gospel. From here the *LMJN* goes immediately to the story of Jesus' mother and brothers visiting him, which the *LMJN* takes from Mark 3:31–35, quoted without change. The *LMJN* does not elect the shorter and softer account in Luke, which omits Jesus' pointed question "Who are my mother and my brothers?" included in both Matthew's and Mark's accounts.[3] *Again, we notice that the author of the LMJN softens slightly one of the most brutal of Jesus' sayings.*[4]

What would be next in the *LMJN* account? Since the story of Jesus' mother and brothers visiting is now floating rather freely from the synoptic account, the next could be almost anything. The author chooses to repeat material, now from the entire chapter 12 of Luke. Once we dive into that chapter, we see the scheme: the *LMJN* focuses on Luke 12 to develop the growing hostility between the Pharisees and Jesus. Recall that Jesus addresses the multitude with a warning against the hypocrisy of the Pharisees (12:1).[5] Then Jesus goes into the most transcendental sermon in the synoptic tradition, a sermon full of dark insights and warnings. Here are some of its main topics or themes: the revelation of secrets; not to fear those who "kill the body" but rather to fear him who can cast one to hell; the comfort of God that watches over all; the critique of judgment (perhaps); a first parable against foolishness; a warning about covetousness; a saying about the foolishness of storing up earthly treasures; a reminder to look beyond the body and material things, followed by the sayings "Consider the ravens . . . consider the lilies"; promise of comfort in the Kingdom; a command to sell one's goods (a repeated theme); the recommendation to be watchful and

---

3. Jefferson, *Bible* (Beacon ed.), 57; folio 16:165.

4. The real tension between permission and demand in the ethic of the *LMJN*'s Jesus is real and will be unwoven in subsequent chapters.

5. Jefferson, *Bible* (Beacon ed.), 57; folio 17:167.

prepared, "waiting for the Lord" to come; a similar warning to be ready, "for the Son of Man cometh at an hour when ye think not" (12:40); again, a command to become a prepared servant of the Lord, who "will come in a day when he looketh not for him" (12:46); signs of the times; and a final criticism of hypocrites, and their hypocrisy, for not discerning the time (12:56).[6]

Analysis: Teaching in Luke's Sermon on the Plain I

Luke's version of the Q material we call the Sermon on the Plain is short, and it consists of much of the material in Luke chapters 6–9. Since the author of the *LMJN* starts with nearly the whole of Matthew's Sermon, Luke's contribution to the moral legacy of the *LMJN*'s Jesus is necessarily scant. Typically, our author goes with Matthew's longer version and usually omits Luke's similar content. The reader is pretty clear that the author of the *LMJN* identifies most with Matthew's Sermonic Jesus, since he quotes virtually the whole Sermon and he could easily have suppressed things in Matthew if he had wanted to show his disapproval. But it is much more difficult to judge what we are to make of the *LMJN*'s use of Luke's Sermonic Jesus. We begin with the assumption that *when the* LMJN *provides small bits of Luke's Sermon to Matthew's huge array, he highlights a value he affirms*. For instance, when the *LMJN* adds Luke's woes to Matthew's Beatitudes, we see a valued, darkened sense of judgment that is the inverse of the announcement of blessing on the poor and the miserable. In fact, *judgment and reversals of status begin to play a major role in the message of the* LMJN's *Jesus*.

The text picks up Luke's favorite word to supplement the blessings of the Beatitudes ("woe") and puts it to work for Jesus' wisdom that has been assembled from the four gospels. Woe is no longer Luke's special theme, but an aspect of the composite gospel emerging in the *LMJN*.[7] Indeed, *woe is the comprehensive judgment on the morality of those who oppose Jesus and his wisdom*. For instance, the composite Jesus suggests that there will be judgment on those who are already full and consoled, those who are having too much fun, and those who are too proud of their reputations. The negative and inverse of Jesus' well-known blessings have been thematized and integrated into the whole of his ministry. *Woe brings the reversals that enrich the*

---

6. Jefferson, *Bible* (Beacon ed.), 58–62; folio 18, 19, 20:169, 171, 173.

7. When we say "composite," we note that the *LMJN* has done what Christians have done for centuries: assemble a Jesus from the four gospels. The text is a new version of the old gospel harmonies. We have to see that the Jesus he assembles is indeed a composite picture that does not appreciate the modern sense of the discrete Jesuses. Obviously, creating a harmonized Jesus leaps over the distinctive character of each evangelist's account.

LMJN's picture of Jesus: Woe energizes the campaign of Jesus against the Jewish authorities, and woe sets wisdom against the foolishness of his opponents. That is, woe is not a little add-on from Luke, but it grows into judgment on the entire opposition to Jesus in the *LMJN*. Naturally, to put wisdom and foolishness next to each other invites controversy, and the *LMJN*'s woes up the ante on the conflicts with the authorities already woven into the gospels. Jesus uses occasions to confront the religious leaders, and since each episode of Jesus' ministry has been cut from the context in its home gospel, Jesus' confrontations leap out as opportunities for him to attack his opponents. So, many of the ministry episodes start with Jesus baiting the authorities; after all, he is the sage who starts his campaign against hypocrisy by overturning the tables in the temple. And, of course, the authorities respond by baiting Jesus.

But remember also that in the midst of the conflict sections where the moral teaching of Jesus unfolds, the conflict is all verbal; it's all talk. No one does any violence until the end, though the authorities certainly plot in threatening ways. The pattern of conflict becomes fairly predictable: it starts with an incident or occasion that becomes bait for one side or the other. Very often, like a good dialectician, Jesus asks a leading question. The question unnerves the opponent, maybe even subverts someone with authority. Jesus then traps the discussant in his foolishness.[8] The scheme moves from the objection of one side to something the other side does or says. Of course, in the canonical gospels, the instigation is often a healing or an exorcism, but those occasions are completely purged in the *LMJN* or are kept below the surface of the narrative of the confrontation. As we have seen, many of Jesus' confrontations with the authorities presuppose a sign or a wonder that we are not permitted to see, since the author of the *LMJN* carefully steers the narration instead to a point of debate. Often, as in the canonical gospels, the position of the authorities is not explicit but is more implied by the question they pose to Jesus. In all cases we can predict how Jesus will react: we will hear his critique in no uncertain terms. His opponents get angry, and often they begin to plot to get rid of this sage, and then they disappear.

Meanwhile, in Jesus' response to his opponents we find a striking transformation of the issue that launches the confrontation. What starts as a violation of holiness codes, a ritual disruption of law, or a break in accepted practice (like handwashing) becomes a moral issue, not an issue of purity: Jesus reveals the reality of the conflict as a deep divide between the superficial grasp of some rite by the authorities and the moral heart of the

---

8. See Susan Bryan's analysis of the dialectical engagement ("Reauthorizing," 23, 28).

matter that Jesus discovers.[9] The scribes and the Pharisees routinely miss the point and do not understand its profound moral importance. Every issue of conflict in the *LMJN* becomes a moral one and a profoundly moral one at that. The conflicts are not about issues of "religion," of holiness, of ritual observance, of rival visions of Israel, or of being a Jew in a colonial age. In other words, the Jesus of the *LMJN* moralizes every issue of law, custom, and observance and leads it away from the particularities of Judaism.

Of course, *ritual practice is about the moral life in worlds where it lives naturally. But viewed from a distance and under critique, ritual practice looks superficial and mechanical to the protestant soul.* The ally of this criticism, undoubtedly, is the intensification of law in Matthew's Sermon, in certain readings, where prohibiting killing alone, where going only one mile, or where simply keeping Sabbath is insufficient for the moral life. The deeper moral life requires the "second mile." Once we have associated the moral with the second mile, with an extra expectation, with a broadened concern, and with its intentionalized and internalized demands, suddenly keeping holiness codes, being observant, looks less than moral. Thus, we can imagine how the protestant Jesus of the *LMJN* comes to the judgment of hypocrisy against his enemies. The author of the *LMJN* takes a big step. Having a tin ear for holiness, he treats every conflict in a moralized way. Basically, if our author cannot moralize an issue of ritual, he will drop it. And usually, the foolish way is captured by the word "hypocrisy."

We have seen Matthew's contribution to the wisdom that opposes hypocrisy: the privilege of the poor, the virtue of humility, the calmness and the comfort, the attention to the other, the embrace of the enemy, the high honoring of commitments, the self-expenditure, the rightly aimed priorities, the special calling of the higher righteousness, and so on. Those values have already been claimed by the *LMJN*. But with Luke's Sermon we encounter added themes that we know are valued enough to be included beyond Matthew's list. They fill out what is in Matthew and take us to new emphases, not foreign to Jesus of the gospels but accented via Luke in the *LMJN*'s gospel, nonetheless. For instance, *the* LMJN *clearly wants a woe-filled counterpoise to the lavish blessings on the unfortunates in the Beatitudes.* We may need some more data to help us with the meaning of the woes, but clearly *the author of the* LMJN *must be reminding us of the issue of fairness, of justice in an ethic overflowing with blessing.*

The *LMJN* enjoys sharing Jesus' message of comfort to the miserable, but our author is just as *eager to remind people of the requirements of justice.*

9. We note again that the text regards holiness and issues of ritual as superficial at best. And the author consistently moralizes about or dispenses with the holy and with ritual.

Jesus ministers to the sinful woman and sides with her, yes, but he does so against the Pharisee who gets stuck in the notion that the woman is sinful and nothing else. The Pharisee is stubborn, shortsighted, blind in his moral vision. The *LMJN*'s version, however, cuts off after the woman anoints and kisses Jesus' feet. *We do not get to hear Jesus' forgiveness* and his suggestion that since the woman has sinned much, she will be forgiven much (Luke 7:47). We wonder why we do not hear this theme in the *LMJN*. Could the author think Jesus' lavish announcement of repeated forgiveness to the many-sinned woman needs a correction that reminds us of justice? We do not know, since the forgiveness passage has been deleted. But it is a tough sell that Jesus' treatment of a sinner would stop short of forgiveness. We need to unpack more to help us interpret the *LMJN*'s understanding of forgiveness, since the encounter with the sinful woman is the third time the *LMJN* takes a swipe at forgiveness.

Here is a final point of analysis: in the *LMJN*'s selection from Luke's Sermon we continue to discover a theme that may be connected to the judgment issue above: the way that the *LMJN* circles around apocalyptic materials in the synoptic Jesus story. As we have seen, *the first reaction of the* LMJN *author is to throw out anything that smells of apocalyptic*. The most extreme, cosmic moments of apocalyptic (the battles, signs of the times, the tribulations, and so forth) are the first to go. Yet, as we have seen, on occasion he allows softer apocalyptic moments. These are recognizable to us in the twenty-first century; were they evidently apocalyptic for our author? Does he recognize how apocalyptic they are? Does he find an alternative use for apocalyptic passages, perhaps, under a theory to discover the essence of an apocalyptic passage? Or does he work with a view that some things in the gospels have been distorted with apocalyptic?

Most bewildering is *the author's pattern of using apocalyptic-seeming passages after he has rejected apocalyptic extremes.*[10] Will we be able to solve the mystery? One example is his use of "Son of Man." We have seen examples of his deleting powerfully apocalyptic passages with "the Son of Man" in a Danielic sense. But we have noted several others where the Son is not riding the clouds to bring in the Kingdom of God: in these passages the category of "the Son" seems to take some other meaning, or the context seems apocalyptic and yet the author includes the Son, or Jesus himself seems to be the Son. We need to see if we can figure out the pattern. Perhaps the author of the *LMJN* has no theory about the meaning of the Son and includes and excludes reference to the figure according to other values in

---

10. Just as he hints at prophecy and wonders without showing them directly in his text.

the story rather than whether the Son is an apocalyptic figure. Perhaps our author has metaphorized the figure. Consequently, as we develop a holistic view of the *LMJN*, we wonder whether it works with a single, coherent view of apocalyptic and of the Son of Man.

Exposition: Teaching in Luke's Sermon on the Plain II

Oddly, the *LMJN* turns back from chapters 12 and 13 in Luke to chapter 11 and rejects the entire chapter until v. 37. Only the Lord's Prayer comes from Matthew's version. Our text, then, rejects a lot of the L1 source material and both Matthew's and Luke's parallels from Q. Of course, the Prayer could be rejected because it is redundant at this point in the Jesus account. The friend-at-midnight passage (11:5–8) is simply obscure, and the prayer passage (11:9–13) is ignored, perhaps, because its punch line in Luke (11:13) is about the coming of the Holy Spirit. But the Matthew version (7:11) is inoffensive, and its exclusion is puzzling. It is easy to see that the two passages on exorcism and the status of exorcisms (11:14–26) would be omitted in the *LMJN* and that the author would reject the apocalyptic, evil-generation passage (11:29–32). But it is less easy to figure out why the "light under the bushel" passage (11:33–36) would not appeal, especially since we have already noticed that the author favors the revelation of all secrets. We will have to return to the theme of secrets when we know more.

What is clear is that the author of the *LMJN* clips his way through Luke's chapter 11 to find the sought-after gem: something to develop the very theme of conflict we have seen since the beginning of our analysis. He turns to the handwashing controversy between Jesus and a Pharisee with whom he dines. When the Pharisee objects that Jesus' disciples do not wash their hands before the food arrives,[11] Jesus explodes in a stinging critique to the effect that the Pharisees tend to address outward purity but do not understand the wickedness within themselves (11:39 with parallel from Matt 23). He calls them "fools" and levels three woes on them for their superficial giving that ignores the big issues of justice and the love of God. Jesus' charge aims at the Pharisaic tendency to miss the important and moral thing in an issue.[12] Indeed, in order to return to his favorite criticism of the Pharisees,

---

11. New Testament scholars and historians know the issue is the status of the oral Torah, which the Pharisees endorse, and which Jesus rejects for the more conservative position of honoring only the written Torah. See Jefferson, *Bible* (Beacon ed.), 64–65; folio 21, 22:175.

12. We see another example of *the LMJN's theory that a focus on ritual blocks the moral issue.*

52 DISPLACING JESUS

the author of the *LMJN* uses texts (Greek, Latin, French and English) in which the word *"hypocrisy" names the failure of the Pharisees* (Luke 11:44), though the term is not in modern translations of Luke.[13] However our author gets ahold of the term, its use matches the other woes on the Pharisees and supports the denunciation of the Pharisaic prideful, but ignorant, focus on themselves.[14] Suddenly, a lawyer takes offense at the criticism, and Jesus blasts him with two more woes: that the lawyers burden people and do not help them handle their own burdens.[15]

Then the text backs up and turns again to chapter 11, starting at v. 37 (the handwashing episode). But before we get to v. 37, the *LMJN* author removes Luke's version of the Lord's Prayer (vv. 1–4, already mentioned above) and a fistful of passages: a puzzling parable of hospitality in the middle of the night (vv. 5–8); the "ask-given, seek-find" discussion on prayer, which ends with the Father who gives the Holy Spirit (vv. 9–13 from Q, also omitted from Matthew); the long Beelzebub controversy about the spiritual foundation of casting out demons (vv. 14–23); the return of an evil spirit (vv. 24–36 from Q, omitted from Matthew also); the blessedness of Jesus' mother (vv. 27–28 from L1); the evil-generation and the signs-of-the-times, apocalyptic passage (vv. 29–32, with Matthew's Q version also deleted); and finally vv. 33–36, the "light under the bushel" pericope (from Q with Matthew's version deleted also).[16] At this point we should not be surprised at any of these deletions.

Analysis: Teaching in Luke's Sermon on the Plain II

Luke 11:37 begins the discourse against the Pharisees. In a sense, we readers have been prepared for this work since the first confrontations, the first action of Jesus' ministry, the temple fit, the first teaching, and Jesus' lecturing the Pharisees on the proper meaning of the Sabbath. This time it is handwashing at the dinner of a Pharisee. Jesus opposes it and the Pharisees favor it.[17] While to us the difference may seem slight, it is a big issue for Jesus in

---

13. Jefferson, *Bible* (Beacon ed.), 64; folio 22:177.

14. The term "hypocrites" (in Luke 11:44) is not in modern translations, but it is in Matthew's version (18:27), and it is in all four of the texts that the author uses in preparing the text (Adams and Lester, *Extracts*, 177). Many Jefferson scholars have missed that Jefferson's text does not match modern translations of Luke. See Jefferson, *Bible* (Beacon ed.), 64.

15. Jefferson, *Bible* (Beacon ed.), 64–65; folio 22:177.

16. Jefferson, *Bible* (Beacon ed.), 64–65; folio 22:177.

17. Of course, this encounter has nothing to do with a modern germ theory. Rather we must think of it as ritual purity before eating. And modern historians know that the

relation to the Pharisees. But in any case, the handwashing issue is a major issue for the synoptic tradition and especially for Q. In these sources Jesus' criticism of the Pharisees on this issue is of a piece with the battles over healing on the Sabbath, picking corn on the Sabbath, violating kosher, and the like. The synoptic trajectory of *confrontation attempts to explain why the Jewish messiah is killed with the help of Jewish authorities. We have seen that the* LMJN *supports this trajectory and even enhances it by frontloading the opposition to Jesus (via the Johannine location of the temple event), by abstracting the confrontation from other causes* (i.e., role of the Romans, the controversies over the interpretation of Torah, and so forth), *by unifying all the leaders of Second Temple Judaism into a generic cluster of Jewish authorities, and by collapsing ritual holiness into morality.*

When the *LMJN* faces the handwashing issue in Luke 11:37, it does not worry about oral Torah or about keeping kosher. In both Luke and the *LMJN* Jesus takes the issue to be that handwashing fixes on externals, cleaning the outside, when the real issue is deep, inner wickedness. Jesus' opponents are "fools" and "hypocrites" who miss that "all things are clean unto you" (Luke 11:41). They fix on superficial things and miss the issue of judgment and love of God (v. 42) and are under God's woes, three of them, actually. When "one of the lawyers" suddenly asks why Jesus is so tough on "us" (v. 45), we do not know how he connects to the one Pharisee who complains about no handwashing, nor do we know whether he is among the group of Pharisees Jesus condemns. In any case, he pops up and complains about Jesus' criticism. Immediately, Jesus hits all the lawyers (and by extension, all Jewish authorities) with a woe (v. 46) for burdening the people with foolishness without alleviating their real burdens. The lawyers have kept the key to knowledge to themselves; *they keep secrets, and the* LMJN's *Jesus will not tolerate secrecy* (v. 52).

At this point the Pharisees, not the lawyers, begin to provoke Jesus "vehemently" and wait to catch him in his own words. We note that we seem to have in v. 52 the added *theme that the Pharisees hide saving knowledge from the people.* If so, we may have found other instances of a grand theme: *that in the presence of Jesus all secrets must be revealed.* The woes include another one on the lawyers for celebrating the tombs of the prophets that their fathers killed years ago (vv. 47–48). The criticism continues: the Wisdom of God indicts the same lawyers (presumably the very ones who persecute and kill the prophets); the saying insists that this generation will pay for the blood of earlier generations (vv. 50–51), but perhaps these passages are

---

real issue is that handwashing is not in the written Torah, while the oral Torah requires it and the Pharisees favor it.

omitted in the *LMJN* because they are pretty obscure. Or possibly, they hint at a corporate notion of sin, perhaps of the sort that generates the doctrine of original sin.[18] In any case, they could support the text's critique of hypocrisy had other values of the author not collided with the themes of the above passages.

The long quotation from Luke 12 presents quite an interpretive nightmare. Mostly it is Luke's fault for stuffing together bits of moral wisdom. Behind the diffuse themes is a message of exhortation and warning meant as a reminder, a caution, and a comfort in a time of urgency. The growing urgency of the chapter intrigues. It sounds as if the theme is moral urgency and yet more than moral urgency. It sounds like apocalyptic urgency: discerning the times, being ready for the coming of the Lord, being prepared. Is the passage really apocalyptic for an author who usually purges his gospel of traces of apocalyptic? Perhaps the Jesus materials are genuinely apocalyptic or have been edited to become apocalyptic, and the *LMJN* repurposes them into a simpler urgency. *We do notice that the apocalyptic materials advance the theme of judgment that emerges as we move toward the end of Jesus' story.* Perhaps, independent of the apocalyptic judgment in Luke chapter 12, we have the powerful evocation of the coming of the Son of Man, which appears to evoke the original Danielic sense of the term. We know, of course, that the term has many uses in Jesus' time, but this one looks very apocalyptic. Why would the *LMJN* not purge the "Son of Man" reference from Luke? Again, is the *LMJN* re-aiming the "Son of Man" image?

The apocalyptic question is even more troubling when we realize that in the midst of the *LMJN*'s quoting nearly the whole of Luke 12, the text omits vv. 49–53, some of the most dramatic material in the synoptic tradition. Right in the midst of the apocalyptic-sounding urgency, the *LMJN* drops the Jesus who is eager to cast fire on the earth (v. 49), who denies he will bring peace on earth (v. 51), who will bring divisions on earth, especially within families. We probably cannot solve the tension in the apocalyptic issue at the end of Luke 12. However, we can recognize materials that seem to be apocalyptic, and we note that in the *LMJN*'s version of Luke these materials seem muted and far from hard-core apocalypticism. Perhaps, then, the author is using apocalyptic simply to heighten moral urgency.

This interpretation coheres with earlier suppressions of apocalyptic materials we have seen and helps explain why our author rejects some apocalyptic passages and allows others to enter the new gospel. It offers a plausible explanation why the *LMJN* rejects the extreme apocalyptic passages such the fire-and-division Jesus (Luke 12:49–53), where the author

---

18. And would undermine individual autonomy our author so values.

can see no moral value in the materials. Meanwhile, we may have a clue that he sees moral value in certain apocalyptic-sounding passages and finds a useful sense of moral urgency in an apocalyptic passage. This nonapocalyptic use of apocalyptic may explain why the author makes peace with such an apocalyptic category as "Son of Man." Here we may have a muted christological use of apocalyptic.[19] In any case, *we do know that the author of the LMJN will have nothing to do with extreme apocalypticism.*

The *LMJN* next selects the first nine verses of Luke 13, a pericope from L1. The passage starts with a story of certain Galileans who are persecuted by Pilate: Does their extreme suffering mean that they are more sinful than others? Likewise, are we to believe that those killed in a tower accident also are more sinful than others in Jerusalem (13:1–2)? Jesus says no, but turns the story into a warning about repentance. Then the text turns to the fig-tree story in which the tree is allowed one more year to produce fruit (vv. 6–9). Significantly, the text ignores the fig-tree story in which Jesus zaps the tree and it dies (Matt 21:19). Evidently, the *LMJN* is quite interested in the fig tree *as a story or a symbol* but not as a wonder. So, too, the text ignores Jesus' healing of an infirm woman in the synagogue. This event gets him in trouble with authorities for healing on the Sabbath, and he calls the ruler of the synagogue a hypocrite (13:19–17). One assumes the *LMJN* would take up this story, were it not tied to a healing.[20]

---

19. Of course, it is possible that the author does not recognize just how apocalyptic is "Son of Man."

20. Again, we see how intertwined are the things the author likes and the things he does not.

6

Parabolic Discourse

Precis

The transition out of the Sermon on the Mount consists of two episodes from Luke 13: one pericope in which Jesus, discussing some unfortunate Galileans, seems to break the "if p then q" connection between sin and misfortune from the Deuteronomic tradition, and another episode in which a Pharisee wishes to eat with Jesus (Luke 11). The first parable, about the fig tree that does not bear fruit, leads to the eating scene. The Pharisee notes that Jesus does not wash his hands before dinner, and Jesus launches a heavy critique of the superficiality and hypocrisy of the Pharisees. The woes bring the Pharisees to hostility. Soon, back to Matthew (with supplement from Mark), the *LMJN* has Jesus preaching parables to the multitudes by the sea. Here is the famous Parable of the Sower. But Jesus sends the crowd away and continues his explanation of the sower to the disciples only. The parable leads into the dark and judgmental wisdom of Matthew's apocalyptic discourse. The interpretation of the Sower Parable and of several subsequent parables (Tares, Net, Pearls) emphasizes understanding the real meaning of the Kingdom of heaven, and judgment on those who do not. The parables turn into an occasion for a Pharisee to criticize Jesus about handwashing and for Jesus to unleash a scathing set of woes on and criticisms of the Pharisees, who are already angry and plotting to accuse him of sins/crimes deserving death.

Exposition: The Parabler without Secrets

We are now by the Sea of Galilee with Matt 13 and the Parable of the Sower. Jesus preaches from a boat to the crowds on the shore. After the main parable the *LMJN* follows in Matthew's version (13:1-9), Mark's version,[1] and cuts in with one verse (Mark 4:10) to relocate the explanation of the parable to the disciples alone, who ask him its meaning. Importantly, the *LMJN* omits Matthew's long quotation of Isa 6, with its "hardening of hearts" theme (13:10-15), and the interrupting passage from Q in Matthew, a passage that tells the disciples how lucky they are to be hearing the message from Jesus that "prophets and righteous men" have long sought (Matt 13:16). The *LMJN* takes the interpretation of the parable from Matt 13:18-23 and ignores both Mark's longer allegorical decoding and Luke's briefer text. Then it fixes on Matthew's version of the interpretation (Matt 13:24-52).[2] Between these two long passages the *LMJN* again puts in a telling transition from Mark 4:21-23: it is the light under the bushel passage, the meaning of which emphasizes the now-familiar *LMJN* theme, *the hidden must be made manifest and all secrets known*. The pericope ends with a reminder, perhaps a warning, that those who can must listen.[3] Pointedly, the *LMJN* removes the more intense warning found in all three Synoptics: that the measure you give will be the measure you get; "For to he that hath, to him shall be given: and he that hath not, from him shall be taken even that which he hath" (Mark 4:25). Though this grim warning is eliminated, we do not know why. Perhaps it is too judgmental; more likely, it is a rhetorical flourish that makes a point but undermines the sense of justice.

Next, the *LMJN*'s parabler does not follow the basic synoptic chronology by following the sower parable with some of the most famous seed parables. Indeed, the *LMJN* deletes the Parable of the Seed Growing Secretly (Mark 4:26-29), Matthew's Parable of the Weeds (M1 in 13:24-30), the Parable of the Mustard Seed (Mark 4:30-32 and parallels from Q),[4] the Parable

---

1. Recall that Mark is the one who invents the messianic secret and uses the Parable of the Sower to establish *the theory that parables hide truths*. Both Matthew and Luke depend on Mark's theory but to a lesser extent. That the author of the *LMJN* goes to Matthew for the Parable of the Sower, then, is intriguing, since he has been developing the notion that there should be no secrets in the revelation. Perhaps the author senses Matthew's movement away from secrecy, since Mark never explains the messianic secret and Matthew has to defend the secret with the "hardness of heart" passage from Isa 6. But, of course, the author of the *LMJN* could not defend the meaning of the Sower by an appeal to prophecy, so he must delete that passage altogether.

2. Jefferson, *Bible* (Beacon ed.), 65-66; folios 22, 23, 177, 179.

3. Jefferson, *Bible* (Beacon ed.), 67; folio 24, 181.

4. Note that this parable appears later in the *LMJN*.

of the Leaven (Matt 13:33 and Luke 13:20–21 in Q), and finally an important rationale for Jesus' use of parables (Matt 13:34–35 and Mark 4:36–34). In Matthew, the theory is that Jesus offers parables to fulfill prophecy in which Jesus reveals things hidden since the beginning of the world. All these items the *LMJN* drops. Then, oddly, the *LMJN* continues with the *interpretation* of the Parable of the Weeds, but not with the just-eliminated parable itself! The interpretation in Matt 12:36–43 comes from M1 and is without parallel. Since the interpretation is cut off from its specific parable, it acts as the meaning for all the seed parables, most of which have been deleted. It is an allegory in which the sower of good soil is the Son of Man (13:37),[5] while the good seeds are the "sons of the Kingdom" and the weeds are evil and under the devil. The harvest is the "close of the age" when weeds will be burned and angels will gather the good into "the Kingdom of their Father" (13:43). Anyone reading our analysis of the *LMJN* would wonder why on earth the author of our text would exclude the revelatory seed parables and yet include the harsh interpretive allegory. The seeds are so morally useful, while the interpretation is so, well, apocalyptic, and probably would scare away our author.

The *LMJN* continues with the text in Matt 13:44–46, the Parables of the Hidden Treasure and of the Pearl, both of which speak of a found, valuable thing that requires a heavy cost to keep. In the following parable, of the Net (Matt 13:47–50 in M1), we find a parable that becomes an allegory of a catch of fish so great that it needs to be sorted on the shore. Angels will separate the evil fish from the righteous, and the evil will be burned. Thereafter follows the Parable of the Householder (also M1 in Matt 13:51–52), which seems to be a summation of all the parables quoted and omitted. Jesus compares a good scribe trained for the Kingdom of heaven to a householder who brings out his treasure.[6] We must attempt to unravel the logic of the editorial decisions of the post-Sower selections.

Analysis: The Parabler without Secrets

We notice first that the *LMJN* author makes two significant alterations to the Sower Parable. First, he eliminates the entire segment in which the disciples

---

5. Jefferson, *Bible* (Beacon ed.), 67–68; folio 24:181. We note the affirmed use of "Son of Man" and the allegorical use of the image for the one who sows. It is followed by another use with a more apocalyptic-sounding meaning for the term immediately after the use in the interpretation of the seed parables (Jefferson, *Bible* [Beacon ed.], 68; folio 25:183).

6. Jefferson, *Bible* (Beacon ed.), 68–69; folio 25:183.

ask Jesus what the parable means, along with the segment in which Jesus reacts with surprise or worse that the disciples have been given the secrets of the Kingdom and yet seem not to know the parable's meaning. Obviously, the disciples should know what it means even if the crowd does not. Then in Matt 13:12 we have a cryptic saying suggesting that those who understand will receive even more, while from those who do not have, even that will be taken away. Once again, *the author of the* LMJN *suppresses the idea of secrecy surrounding the message of Jesus. He even suppresses the idea that people will be judged according to their understanding of secrets.*

Second, we see that the *LMJN* suppresses one of the certifiably hard sayings of the gospel. Here in Matt 13:13, the synoptic Jesus explains his method: *the parables are for the outsiders, not the instructed disciples, and the parables hide everything in secrets so that the outsiders do not understand Jesus' meaning. Parables do intend to hide meaning,* according to Mark. But the *LMJN*'s *Jesus will have none of this hiding the message from the crowd*; much less will our author have Mark's earlier version, where the meaning is hidden from the outsiders so that they will not turn and be forgiven (Mark 4:12)! Here the *LMJN*'s Jesus will not stand against forgiveness (even as he struggles with the theme).[7]

Our text also drops the Isa 6 hardening-of-the-hearts motif found only in Matthew. Presumably, Matthew quotes Isaiah because he, too, is overwhelmed by Jesus' claim that he wants neither understanding nor forgiveness, and Matthew turns to the hardening-of-the-hearts motif to soften and explain the Jesus saying. Of course, we already know that the *LMJN* eliminates as many of the prophecy/fulfillment passages as possible. Again, *the LMJN will not support claims for Jesus based on prophetic fulfillment.*

But here, the elimination is more dramatic, as the hardening-of-the-hearts motif anchors the messianic secret in Mark, and in Matthew and Luke to a lesser degree. Of course, we live after William Wrede's study[8] and know that the messianic secret likely emerges in the second or third generation after Jesus as the community's way to deal with observant Jews who are unimpressed that Jesus could be the messiah of Israel. But *the author of the LMJN knows nothing of this theory and can only react to the messianic secret as nonsense put onto Jesus. In addition, he would likely reject the notion as immoral that judgment would be tied to knowing the obscure secrets of the Kingdom of God.* So, we have another, grand transformation of the biblical Jesus story: *the Jesus of the* LMJN *holds and tells no secrets while the* LMJN

---

7. Note that we are still not able to unravel the *LMJN*'s complex relationship with the idea of forgiveness.

8. Wrede, *Messianic Secret*.

overturns the synoptic gospels' dependence on the messianic secret.[9] Consequently, there is no hidden light of wisdom; much less is there a judgmental test for those fit for the Kingdom of God.

So far as the author omits the secret, he creates a simpler reading of Jesus' ministry, since Jesus does not need to veil everything he says and does. At the same time, we have a coherent explanation why his opponents go after him and eventually kill him. They see and hear him say offensive things and do so at the beginning of his ministry. Of course, the *LMJN* must have Jesus deliver offense to the authorities via his teaching, since the wonders will not work in our author's gospel. But we note that the *LMJN* does not endorse everything offensive from the narrative.[10]

Modern historians of Jesus, of course, do not frame the issue of secrecy as either the synoptic tradition or the *LMJN* does, because they think the messianic secret is an artificial construct put onto the Jesus tradition, one meant to answer problems in the second and third generation of the Jesus movement. Those historians pose a simpler story without the secrets of Mark. What is remarkable is that the author of the *LMJN* also moves toward a plainer and more plausible story without the help of modern research on Jesus. We will have to continue to seek his rationale. We note also that with his abandoning of the messianic secret, *the* LMJN *author will also have nothing to do with the "hardening of the hearts" motif.* Such an idea gives a rationale for the ultimate secret about Jesus and thus is unacceptable. Perhaps there is more. We have to keep track of the theme of revelation of all secrets. We sense that we are on the trail of a major theme. *According to the values of the* LMJN *Jesus will be the revealer of wisdom, not its disguiser.*

To pull off the inversion of the messianic secret in the middle of the book, the *LMJN* sets out to assemble all the acceptable texts that reveal Jesus' teachings: his training of his disciples, the revelation of truths long lost, the warning to those who do not listen or catch on, and so forth. One riddle that we have not solved yet is the identity of the "Son of Man," a favorite christological category of *LMJN*. Recall that sometimes the text erases whole passages with the category, while at other times it allows it emphatically. We see no trace of an incidental or inattentive pattern of use or nonuse. Rather, the Son of Man rejected by the *LMJN* tends to be from the obviously extreme apocalyptic passages. If there is a pattern to the accepted Son of Man, then we have a further secret to reveal: *the apocalyptic Son of Man likely is not the*

---

9. Interestingly, the author of the *LMJN* discovers the no-secret theme in Jesus as early as 1813. Letter to William Canby, September 18, 1813 (Adams and Lester, *Extracts,* 350).

10. As we have seen in the *LMJN*'s softening or removal of Jesus' edgier sayings in Luke 12 and 13.

real Son for the LMJN. Also, the *LMJN* sometimes avoids "Kingdom of God" language and other times embraces it. The instances clearly avoided are ones that sound clearly apocalyptic. Possibly the rejection of both an apocalyptic Son of Man and of a coming Kingdom of God may be intertwined. The interpretive issue will be to explain why the *LMJN* rejects some obviously apocalyptic materials and yet uses other apocalyptic sounding materials, we usually recognize as apocalyptic.[11] Is it that the author does not recognize them as apocalyptic, or is he adapting apocalyptic for, say, moral urgency? In any case, we face another major transformation of Jesus' ministry: *the Jesus of the* LMJN *tells no secrets, and he is an enemy of secrecy*. The Pharisees, on the contrary, employ secrets, since *for the* LMJN, *they can maintain their moral superiority only through gnosis, through secret knowledge.*[12] There is no hidden light, much less is there a judgmental test for those fit for the Kingdom of God, since *all secrets are to be known and the* LMJN's *Jesus reveals these cheerfully and without guile*. After all, we can note an obvious logic to the author's plan: were Jesus to keep all things secret, why then would the Jewish authorities get so upset with him so early, at the beginning of his ministry? Remember, the author cannot allow the opposition to arise from the work of the wonder-worker. Therefore, the *LMJN* attempts to clean up the tension inserted into the synoptic tradition via Mark's messianic secret. He opts for a simpler Jesus story, rather as modern scholars of the gospel do. But the author's motive is different from that of the modern critics: he aims to assemble a coherent explanation for why Jesus' opponents go after him and eventually kill him. They see and hear him do offensive things. And they see him offend on the first pages of his story, as it were, with the temple event moved by the author to be the first act of Jesus' ministry.

We can now name *two consequences of the author's attack on secrets*. First, since the Jewish authorities figure out the moral danger of Jesus in the first inning of the game, they are instantly mad at Jesus and instantly plotting to get rid of him. They have the entire ministry of Jesus for increasing anger and to be confirmed in their view of his danger. He continues to offend them. *But there is no growth in their opinion of Jesus: he is instantly a danger and instantly they plan to kill him.* The only drama is to figure out how and when to do the act. We find no gradual recognition of his danger. But we do find that *Jesus' goading of the Pharisees reveals their gnostic-like dependence on secret knowledge.* Second, the danger is an odd one, since all

---

11. Though it is fully conceivable that Jefferson does not hear "Kingdom of God" as an apocalyptic concept in the way that modern scholars do.

12. Today, Jesus researchers are apt to say that the Pharisees are into secrets because they value the oral Torah and Jesus does not. However, Sanford recognizes the importance of the critique of the secrecy theme in the *LMJN* (Sanford, *Religious Life*, 116).

the anger against the *LMJN*'s Jesus turns on his confronting authorities because of their foolishness. Unlike the canonical accounts, where Jesus' healing and exorcism ministry develops a growing reputation, notice, and threat to order, the *LMJN*'s Jesus evokes hostility immediately and completely on the basis of his counterwisdom. His great teaching, not the wonders, bears all the weight of all his acclaim and opposition. Consequently, *the* LMJN*'s selections exaggerate both the enthusiasm and the hostility for Jesus' moral wisdom. The shouting for and against Jesus remains the same in the* LMJN *as in the canonical gospels, but the reaction is aimed exclusively at his teaching.* How can his wisdom generate such anger so quickly? We will have to look for Jesus' techniques in roiling up the controversy.

At this point the author of the *LMJN* seems to be hunting for agreeable teachings of Jesus that he has not already included. In Mark 4:26–29 he goes back to reclaim the seed parables he has ignored earlier and finds the one-sourced Parable of the Seed Growing Secretly, a parable that marvels at the silent growth of the grain to harvest independently of the understanding of the farmer. Then he includes Mark's version of the Parable of the Mustard Seed, previously deleted from the seed cluster (Mark 4:30–32 and parallels) but he skips over to the discipleship aphorisms in Luke 9:57–62 (parallel in Matt 8:19–22): the foxes-have-holes, bury-my-father, and hand-to-the-plow sayings. Apparently, the idea is to generalize the daunting character of following Jesus, but the logic here is difficult to see. Is there a unity to these jumps? We do not know where we are going until we read the next passage.

The reason for following Jesus into the seeds is clarified by the next choice of text: the call of Levi, the tax collector, in Luke 5:27–29 (with synoptic parallels). We hear of Levi's great feast for Jesus in Luke but without the most powerful aspect of the pericope: that Jesus is hanging out with "tax collectors and sinners." The author of the *LMJN* turns to the parallel text in Mark 2:15–17. Here Mark gets to show the Pharisees and scribes criticizing Jesus' conduct and his comeback to them, "Those who are well have no need of a physician," and "I came not to call the righteous, but sinners" (v. 17). We note, therefore, that *the* LMJN *continues to develop the earlier reversals theme by introducing the synoptic point that Jesus hangs out with the wrong people.* He actually enacts the reversal, and, indeed, since the *LMJN*'s Jesus is not permitted to do wonders, the performance of his message of reversals, instead, happens as he meets ordinary people. *Stories of reversals, of the "wrong" people being drawn into Jesus' company, even God's company, replace the miracles.* Such stories are highly valued by the *LMJN* author. But, we must add, those wrong people cannot be blind or leprous, sick or dying, even if they would have been commonly counted as the wrong people, since the author of our text is allergic to healing stories. Evidently, the wonder of the Jesus story rests in the transformation of humans, some drawn into the human story for the first time and others facing correction and judgment because of their narrow sense of the human: clearly *the wonder is not in the miraculous, but in moral transformation.*

The text shifts to another new topic, this time from Luke 5:36 (with parallels), the Parables of the Garment and the Wineskin. The *LMJN* quotes the parables fully from Luke's version (except Luke's confusing v. 39). Perhaps to find meaning in these cryptic parables, the *LMJN* author turns to Jesus' rejection in Nazareth in Matt 13:53–57.[13] We wonder why the author includes the rejection here when he has ignored the theme earlier. Perhaps, he intends to make the case that Jesus rejects his hometown only upon the development of the controversies with the authorities and wants to disconnect Jesus from the post-factum prophecy that no prophet can arise from Nazareth. Recall that Jesus is done with his parables and returns to his home country; he teaches in the synagogue and astonishes the people who wonder whose kid he is. When the crowd identifies him by his family, the people are offended at him and Jesus levels them with the famous, "A prophet is not without honor save in his own country" (v. 57). Clearly the connection is that the controversial parabler could stir up resentment among his old neighbors. There is a darkness in the reversals theme: to be confronted with reversals brings out opposition. This opposition, of course, is different from that of the religious authorities, but it also arises out of a reverse hypocrisy: it is resentment that Jesus has "made it big" and therefore must have a swelled head. In a sense the Nazarenes assume that Jesus thinks of himself as a haughty religious authority, maybe a prophet; indeed, they assume that Jesus has othered them, and they resent his ministry. Notably, the *LMJN* omits the final verse of the pericope, v. 58, which observes that Jesus did not do mighty works there because of their unbelief. Would the *LMJN* permit Jesus to do such works, had they believed in him? Once again, the *LMJN* teases the reader with hints of the miracles and shows how much the wonders shape the whole story of Jesus, even when they are removed from the story. Once again, *the* LMJN *implies that miracle happens in the eye of the beholder.*[14]

---

13. A rejection ignored earlier when the *LMJN* wants Jesus in Judea.

14. This perspectival approach to miracle suggests that the author is close to a theory about the genesis of religious error.

7

Performing the Wisdom I

Precis

Jesus heads to Nazareth where the hometown boy faces disbelief and criticizes the people. The crowds gather and they are hungry; Jesus has compassion, but does nothing. He calls his disciples and sends them (again) on their itinerant mission with comforting advice and premonitions that they will be persecuted. To accent how powerfully the opposition grows, Jefferson drops in a rare transition from John 7:1: Jesus retreats to Galilee, as he is unable to travel in Judea where "the Jews" seek to kill him. In Galilee scribes and Pharisees note that Jesus' people are not handwashers, and Jesus responds with his well-known comments about what defiles a human. Then Jesus gives a long discourse (Matt 18) to his disciples, who are jockeying for position and do not understand humility, forgiveness, and compassion.

Again, Jesus sends out his disciples, this time the seventy, in the Lukan version, to be begging itinerants, and again, the ministry goes badly with them. Here, too, our author uses John's gospel to bring Jesus to Jerusalem for feast days. There are crowds and people murmuring, although the author does not show us why: Jesus' great "one work" (John 7:21) we never hear about. The Pharisees seek out the high priests and together they intend to arrest him. At this point, the author's account becomes increasingly chaotic: he suppresses all things supernatural, and he relies on John's narrative to carry the story beyond the synoptic account. Jesus enters Jerusalem, but without the hoopla of Palm Sunday, and teaches at the temple about mercy to the adulterer (a message unlike the message of the Pharisees), attends to a blind man (without an actual healing), and delivers some of the I AM discourses of John without the attending miracles.

Exposition: Performing the Wisdom[1]

Out of the blue the *LMJN* turns to Luke 10 and a lawyer who "stood up" with a tempting question: "Master, what shall I do to inherit eternal life?" The question seems midrashic and generically theological, but it helps develop the conflict theme running through the entire middle section of the *LMJN*. Recall how Luke 10 unfolds: Jesus responds to the lawyer, here a virtual symbol of Jewish authority, with the words of the *Shema'* in Deut 6:4. However, when the lawyer asks, "Who is my neighbor?" we realize that he means to confound Jesus. At this point Jesus tells the famous Parable of the Good Samaritan. *Since the* LMJN *configures the use of the parable within the growing conflict narrative, the parable takes on a political-religious edge.* It is not a pleasant example story about being a nice person, but an edgy answer to the who-is-my-neighbor question. Here the *LMJN*, perhaps by happenstance of editing decisions, comes upon an interpretive frame for the Samaritan Parable that is closer to modern interpretations. The author of our text must see the parable as a stinging critique of the priest and Levite, who, like the lawyer, represent the Jewish establishment. The neighbor is the hated, biracial, "heretical" Samaritan, who shockingly comes through with a pledge to cover the cost "whatsoever thou spendest more" (10:35).

1. The *LMJN* makes a major issue of Jesus insisting that the moral life cannot be simply spoken, but it must be done. Yet, the text refuses to allow Jesus to be a wonderworker or exorcist. Consequently, *the options for action are limited.* Instead of wonders, the *LMJN*'s *Jesus embarks on a series of parables, example stories, hypothetical scenes that "perform" the moral insights, all oddly spoken acts and hardly actions!* These language forms function to act out and to draw listeners and readers into the world of new moral possibility. The message of Jesus is no longer simply didactic in the old sense of learning new ideas, *but performative of the reality to which the language form points.* The language of performance here is drawn from contemporary parable research. The meaning of a parable is not a lesson really, and certainly not a rationalist, moralistic, allegorical meaning but an entrance into a new way of being, into a new world. Parables arise from the productive imagination, not the reproductive, in that they get people to taste a world never known before. So many of Jesus' final stories in the *LMJN* work as performances. See Crossan, for instance, for a performative model (Crossan, *In Parables*). The intriguing thing about the author of the *LMJN* is that he anticipates modern developments in parable research. But he backs into these interpretive moves because he must purge the account of Jesus of its supernaturalism and must account for the lacuna left without the miracles. Perhaps we think of the wonderful liberation from the mythic world, and the author does, but he has to face a separate problem: Where will he find the materials to enact the moral life, on the one hand, and to account for the execution of Jesus, on the other?

66 DISPLACING JESUS

The account performs the moral reversal of the religious authorities and the outcast Samaritan, and we readers are told to "Go and do thou likewise" (v. 37).[2] Here we have the perfect example of a performative story, a narrative that enacts a moral change. By implication it is the Sage, unlike the Jewish leaders, who plays the role of the Samaritan pledging to cover an unlimited cost of the care of the injured man.

In the rest of the Luke 11 block Jesus instructs his disciples how to pray: ask and receive, seek and find, knock and open. The logic poses a pretty simple understanding of prayer. The disciples wish to know how to pray, and Jesus gives them the Lord's Prayer,[3] but the prayer, linked to the Parable of the Friend's Midnight Request that follows it, melts into a discussion of the meaning of serving the other. *In this model, prayer is not a private conversation with God, but a performative act that launches the life of service.*

When a friend comes to one with a need, respond, not because the person is a friend, but because the person is in need (Luke 11:5–8 from L1). Then with vv. 9–13 (from Q) the *LMJN* and Luke continue the prayer theme with the well-known ask-seek-find and knock-open ideas, which seem fairly mechanical. But then the *LMJN* introduces the idea that the giver may aim the giving specifically to the needs of the receiver. And in a remarkable passage, our author allows a daring saying of Jesus: even evil parents give good gifts to children; "how much more will the heavenly Father give the Holy Spirit to them that ask him?" Note that the saying includes the second quoted and the first clearly favorable reference to the work of the Holy Spirit.[4]

The next, new block is a heavy use of Luke 14. Once again, the theme chosen by our author is the growing conflict with Jewish authorities. Jesus is eating bread on the Sabbath at the house of one of the "chief Pharisees." A man with "the dropsy" appears, and Jesus poses the question to the lawyers and Pharisees whether it is lawful to heal on the Sabbath. The officials are unable to answer. Jesus responds with another example of work on the Sabbath: saving a fallen ox. Again, they do not reply. What Luke adds in v. 4 is a brief report that Jesus heals the man with dropsy, but the *LMJN* author removes this half verse. Again, *we have the drama and theological debate of a healing that we cannot see.* Next the *LMJN* goes directly to Luke 14:4–14, where Jesus offers a parable of guests choosing their places at a banquet.

Who selects the most honored place, and who goes to the lowest place? The right thing to do is to go to the lowest place and be called up as

---

2. Jefferson, *Bible* (Beacon ed.), 85–87: folio 38:209.
3. In our second hearing of the Prayer, now tied to the theme of service.
4. Jefferson, *Bible* (Beacon ed.), 87–88; folio 39:211.

appropriate (v. 10). Jesus lets the parable grow into a lesson on humility and the reversal of the expected order. Naturally, Luke thinks the feast should go to the lowly, the poor, and that the host will be rewarded, not by the poor, who cannot respond, but in the "resurrection of the just." Here we have a second evocation of the resurrection and it is tied to the issue of justice. However, the *LMJN*'s main point in including this parable is not about the resurrection; rather the parable takes us back to the Jewish authorities, who need the lesson of the reversal of high and low. Recall, too, that we have just finished hearing the Parable of the Good Samaritan. Therefore, here we find a *diagnosis of the failure of the Jewish establishment: it is not their doctrinal purity at issue but their haughty pride and position*.[5] Indeed, it is not what they say and think; it is what they do, or actually what they do not do. They must perform the moral life.

Luke moves to the next parable, that of the Great Supper (4:15–24 from Q), but without the opening verse, 15. That verse is a blessing on those who "eat bread in the Kingdom of God." Apparently, the passage sounds too eucharistic and too apocalyptic for the *LMJN*. The Great Supper is the story of a man who gives a great banquet and invites many guests; the guests, however, come up with one excuse after another not to come. In response to that rejection, the angry host orders that the poor and the disabled be brought to the feast, and the parable finally ends with the host "compelling" strangers on the road to attend (Luke 14:23).

The parable speaks of grace and judgment and the resulting exclusion of the privileged. Before we get the explanation for the reversal, the *LMJN* author has to censor vv. 25–27 for reasons that are predictable to us by now. To the crowd, Jesus demands his followers must hate their families and their own lives (v. 26) and must bear their own crosses to be disciples (v. 27). Our author has already deleted one chance to put in the hate-your-family text (from Matthew), probably as it seems misunderstandable and morally questionable. He would certainly not like a hint-prediction of the cross awaiting Jesus. Both the Lukan Jesus and the *LMJN*'s Jesus finish the thought with an analogy of building a tower; no one builds without planning for the cost (v. 28), and no one begins a war without adequate preparations (v. 28). Those who are not prepared will be mocked (v. 30).[6]

Next the *LMJN* employs the entirety of Luke 15 (from Q). Here the publicans and the sinners draw near to Jesus, and the Pharisees and scribes grumble about Jesus' receiving and eating with them. Instead of a confrontation or a comeback, Jesus delivers the Parables of the Lost Sheep and the

---

5. Jefferson, *Bible* (Beacon ed.), 87–88; folio 39:211.
6. Jefferson, *Bible* (Beacon ed.), 88–90; folio 40:213.

Lost Coin. Each one who has lost something drops everything to find the lost. The meaning underlines the joy in heaven over each single repentant person; the joy touches even the "angels of God" (v. 10).[7] Then following the theme of the lost and returned, both Luke and the *LMJN* tell the Parable of the Prodigal Son (15:11–32 from L1). The *LMJN* quotes the entire Parable without editorial comment.[8]

The author of the *LMJN* employs the whole of Luke 16 next. He quotes vv. 1–13, the Parable of the Unjust Steward from L1. Recall that the passage tells of the rich man whose steward wastes his money and gets fired. But the steward decides to make it right by calling in all the rich man's debtors and reducing the amounts on all their bills. His master praises him for this move, "for," Jesus comments, "the children of this world are wiser in their generation than the children of light," and then he commands, "make to yourselves friends by means of the mammon of unrighteousness; that, when ye fail, they may receive you into the everlasting habitations" (vv. 8–9). Does the *LMJN* mean to criticize Israel? Whatever the meaning of these cryptic phrases, at least we are clear that Luke continues to criticize money/wealth and that the *LMJN* goes along with him. The passage continues with the dangers of wealth and the word that people cannot serve two masters (v. 13). Meanwhile the Pharisees, "who were covetous," deride Jesus (v. 14), but he goes after them for prioritizing earthly values rather than those of God. As we wait for an explanation, we realize that the *LMJN* omits vv. 16–17, presumably because Luke's text offends, with its theory that the era of the law and the prophets ended with John the Baptist and that now is the era of the direct proclamation of the Kingdom of God, though many try to enter the Kingdom by force. Jesus declares that not one letter of the law can be dropped (v. 17).[9]

With that declaration, Luke is allowed to become specific: no divorce, since divorce is adultery (v. 18 from Q). Then the Parable of the Rich Man and Lazarus appears with no transition. Indeed, the parable makes little sense without the deleted vv. 16–17, since the parable presupposes the continuing power of the law and prophets, and judgment on those who ignore their demands. The parable presents a rich man who has every advantage and poor Lazarus with his sores. The poor one dies and goes to heaven, and the rich one goes to hell. The rich man asks Abraham to get Lazarus to bring him cool water, but Abraham reminds him that he had his cool water, so to

---

7. A random remnant of a supernaturalist world construction.

8. Jefferson, *Bible* (Beacon ed.), 90–91; folio 41:215. For the Prodigal Son see Jefferson, *Bible* (Beacon ed.), 92–94; folio 43—44:219, 221.

9. Jefferson, *Bible* (Beacon ed.), 95–96; folio 44:219.

speak, in his earthy life while Lazarus now lives in comfort. When the rich man learns that there is a chasm between heaven and hell not to be crossed, he wants Lazarus to warn his five brothers to repent. But Abraham tells him that, if they have ignored the law and the prophets, they will never listen to one raised from the dead (v. 31).

We report in detail on this long story because it raises the tricky themes of forgiveness and judgment that we have watched developing in the *LMJN*.[10] Luke 17 takes us directly to the next treatment of forgiveness. The *LMJN* quotes much of the chapter. It begins with a typical Lukan woe, this time on those who bring offense to "one of these little ones." Is the *LMJN* author thinking again about the special protection and privilege of children? Concerning one's brother Jesus suggests that if someone trespasses against a brother, then rebuke the trespasser, and if he repents, then forgive him (v. 3). And if he trespasses seven times in a day and repents, then forgive him each time (v. 4). The *LMJN* omits vv. 5–6, probably because they make little sense[11] and its editing returns in vv. 7–10 with an obscure passage on the proper wages for a servant. *The point seems to be that obedience (allegorically to God) is a duty independent of the promise of reward.*[12]

We readers are not surprised when the *LMJN* leaps over the next text (the healing of the ten lepers, including the account of the only one who returns to say thank you, a Samaritan). The passage should be a great resource for the *LMJN* author, so soon after we have heard of the Good Samaritan, but the healing of the lepers breaks the value code for our author. Instead, we have Jesus demanding of the Pharisees when the Kingdom of God would come. But without waiting for a reply, he dives in with the claim that the Kingdom comes without observation (v. 20) and thereby aligns with the gospel traditions of a muted, not catastrophic, apocalyptic.[13] Then, the *LMJN* omits the next verse, that the Kingdom is among us (17:21 from L1); in fact, it drops all of vv. 22–25, which speak of signs of the coming Son of Man and the suffering of this generation. When the text returns to chapter 17, it rehearses the whole story of Noah and his people and the destruction of the world, and of Lot's sin and punishment but as an analogy to the coming days when the Son of Man is revealed (v. 30). The apocalyptic

---

10. Jefferson, *Bible* (Beacon ed.), 98; folio 47:227.

11. The disciples ask for help with faith, and Jesus tells them if they had faith like a tiny mustard seed, you could say to a great tree to be uprooted and planted in the sea, and it would obey you.

12. Jefferson, *Bible* (Beacon ed.), 98–99; folio 47:227.

13. We think of the passages in which there will be neither signs nor sign-seeking for the Kingdom, and of passages that bring out Jesus' theme that the Kingdom is within us or already present.

passage turns into the reversal of losing and gaining one's life, and the *LMJN* includes even the grim "in that night there will be two men in one bed; one will be taken and the other left" (v. 34). Surely, readers are surprised. Why would the author of the *LMJN*, so allergic to apocalyptic, quote one of the most clearly apocalyptic passages of the Bible?[14]

Analysis: Performing the Message

Where are we in the text of the *LMJN* at this point? Readers may be confused and tired out, as the text has become a series of episodes, mostly from Luke, without an evident plot. Indeed, the *LMJN*'s whole story of Jesus is light on plot. But now, the author of the *LMJN* has nothing left in Jesus' life to cover but his death. He has exposited the main themes of his version of Jesus' ministry. Indeed, the ideas he presents vividly have begun to repeat. And even when we are not quite clear about the meaning of his chosen selections, we are familiar with the themes he likes and the things he rejects. We have only two more steps left, setting out the plot by which Jesus comes to his arrest and considering the account of his execution. So then, what does our author accomplish in the catchall final pericopes? The clue seems to be in the Good Samaritan Parable. Not only is this one an essential Jesus parable, but also it fits into the major theme of conflict with Jewish authorities, who are discredited by the power of the parable. The parable draws the readers into the story, we criticize the authorities, and we reverse who is a hero and who is a scoundrel. And when the parable comes with the "Who is my neighbor?" question and the final comment from Jesus, "Go and do likewise," we realize we have been drawn into a moral performance. *This great parable brings us into a transformation as convincing and self-engaging as wonders ever could be. And for the author of the* LMJN *the moral performance actuates the teaching of Jesus in a way that does not distract or embarrass, as the miracles do.* When Luke couples the parable itself with the question and the command of the sage, we readers step into the primal choice: *foolishness or wisdom. The final performance stories actuate the teaching wisdom of Jesus for the* LMJN *in much the same way that the miracles actuate the Kingdom of God in the synoptic gospels or the signs concretize the I AM sayings in John.*

We see the editorial hand of the author of the *LMJN* once again as he works through the Luke stories. Just as he did with the sections of John above, so he lets Luke pose the new issue and then selects acceptable passages from a given chapter. He will not stick with Luke 11, because of its exorcism episodes, and because he has raided favored passages from his last

14. Jefferson, *Bible* (Beacon ed.), 99–100; folio 48:227.

scan through the chapter. But we now are able to see how the author chooses the order of and approach toward the content in the middle of the story of Jesus' ministry: *after he establishes the beginnings of Jesus' life and ministry, our author discovers a theme in one of the gospels, goes with it as long and as far as he can countenance its content, and then sorts through the other gospels for thematically related material.*

Roughly, Matthew dominates his first pass through the Jesus material and tends to provide the first issues; Luke is his second choice to pose new issues and to exposit acceptable materials. Recall that a large block of John interrupts his use of Luke. Mark gets less attention than Matthew and Luke but often provides the transitions and place markers, probably since Mark creates the synoptic chronology. Mark also is of less of interest because he presents Jesus primarily as an exorcist-healer who speaks in parables, not aphorisms, and does so under the presentation of the messianic secret and the theory that parables are encoded secrets. All of these themes, of course, are unacceptable to our author.

We may wonder why the *LMJN* returns to Luke after the John interlude. Undoubtedly, Luke has lots of material not in the other gospels with favorable themes that the *LMJN* can endorse. Obviously, *Luke provides plenty of support for the conflict theme*, the dominant theme in the *LMJN*'s reconstruction of the Jesus story. In fact, by the time we are done with the added Luke passages, we come to think of *the* LMJN's *gospel as a presentation of the tale of the official Jewish opposition to Jesus of Nazareth*. Yet Luke also develops other, favorite themes such as the moral reversals that accompany Jesus' ethic, the theme of judgment and forgiveness, and the theme of the privilege of children.

As readers, we are aware that the *use of Luke underscores clearly the editorial weakness of the* LMJN's *entire project to demythologize or naturalize the saga of Jesus without destabilizing the ethic of Jesus.* That is, the author of our text tries to extricate the ethic of Jesus by suppressing most of the hints of the supernatural world of the texts. The author excises offensive ideas and phrases from a text saturated in supernatural framing and presuppositions. But too often *the residue of the supernaturalism remains as we focus on worldly and ethical lessons, and too often the lessons are flattened, generalized, or made incoherent, once the offensive has been purged. In other words, the moral lessons the* LMJN *would highlight cannot be cleanly extricated from the whole frame and system of presuppositions.*

Consequently, we start noticing that the author of the *LMJN* handles the de-supernaturalizing in an uneven way; perhaps he has no choice, given the parameters he set for himself. For instance, he is embarrassed by the apocalyptic frame of Jesus' ministry and yet has to use it at times and even allow some sense for the Son of Man, the Kingdom of God, the urgency of a world headed to a cataclysmic end. In another example, on a related theme, he draws back from the Day of Judgment and cosmic battles of the apocalyptic worldview, even as he insists that there has to be real judgment of evil and recompense for those who suffer. In light of the above set of themes, how should one play justice in relation to mercy and forgiveness? Or, how does one extract an ethic from the scene of a healing without presupposing a world in which there can be supernatural healings?[15] *The chief means by which the author of the* LMJN *adapts to the loss of the miracles is to replace them, as it were, with the performance story.*

As we would expect, especially as we move toward the death of Jesus, *the performance consistently addresses the conflicts with the authorities.* Early on in the *LMJN* the pattern has been that some Jewish official would draw Jesus into a conflict. Now toward the end of the story often the pattern is that Jesus initiates the confrontation with one or more official. Sometimes he condemns them directly, or he presents them with a parable that embarrasses, confounds, or undermines them. They are often reduced to silence. *We get from Jesus a sharpened diagnosis of their hostility: it arises from their arrogance and pride (Luke 14:4–14). Their pride is expressed in failed understanding of the law; exclusive, privileged behavior; and downright greed.*

Luke brings out the theme of greedy wealth and the dangers of mammon, as hinted earlier in the *LMJN*'s woes relocated in the midst of Matthew's Beatitudes. Clearly *the author's voice can be heard in the critique of wealth*, and undoubtedly the author enjoys the theme of reversals in the gospels, whether or not they are apocalyptic reversals. Usually, he puts moral urgency at stake in the reversals, but the reversals can also involve a group and center on station and money as well. Whatever the topic, the conflict theme develops into dark anger toward Jesus and increasingly feisty or maddening debates. Therefore, we get an inkling how Jesus' message could evoke a deathly hostility: If the values behind Jesus' message of reversals were actuated, the authorities would lose their wealth and privilege. Their anger is intelligible.

Jesus' performances may not provoke only embarrassment among and harsh criticism from the authorities. The opposite is possible, especially where we learn of Jesus teaching his disciples about discipleship. *Jesus aims the learning about prayer (Luke 11) to bring the disciples to service of the neighbor.* The story of the man with dropsy creates a world in which healing is actually possible on the Sabbath (even if the *LMJN* will not let us see the

---

15. Holowchak notes that Jefferson's challenge is to establish a notion of judgment without supernature and apocalypse (Holowchak, *Bible*, 46).

actual healing from Luke 14:1–6). Jesus shows the Pharisees that they themselves would save their own oxen on the Sabbath! In the story of the proper seating at the banquet (14:7–14), Jesus traps the Pharisees into the logic of moral reversals by reminding them of their own doctrine of resurrection where, surely, the lowly will be seated among the honored. In the Parable of the Great Supper (14:15–24) the *LMJN*'s Jesus takes the reversed reward of the poor even further: there will be judgment on those guests who come up with lame refusals to the gracious invitation. We recognize the reversals when we see the grumbling brother of the Prodigal Son and the running father so overjoyed by the Son's return. The list could go on.

Perhaps without a crisp resolution, *the performance story daringly gets us inside the tension between justice and mercy in the* LMJN, a tension that may well live in the gospels and in Jesus himself. We have already seen that the *LMJN* emphatically asserts the Jesus message of the endless mercy of God and the expectation of limitless forgiveness. Yet the *LMJN* often returns to these endless and limitless aspects to remind the readers of the just judgment of God. Will we discover a resolution to this noticeable tension? The Parable of the Unjust Steward (Luke 16:1–13) presses us to sense a divine world in which justice and mercy are in sync. That is, *it invites us into a possibility of limitless forgiveness that does not undercut justice*. In the Parable of the Rich Man and Lazarus (Luke 16:19–30) we learn that such a possibility requires the reversal about which we have been hearing and may require the resurrection.[16] The *LMJN* will soon quote the quintessential performative parable on mercy and justice, the Laborers in the Vineyard (Matt 20:1–16). We and the early workers grudgingly learn the lesson of grace within a system of justice.

We are getting to the end of Jesus' ministry according to the *LMJN*. We have one complex, clustered chapter in Luke 18, and then the text turns back to Matthew to get us on the journey to Jerusalem and the passion week. Two final parables and the Mary/Martha scene from L1 prepare the *LMJN* for the journey to Judea. In the Parable of the Unjust Judge (Luke 18:1–8) we hear of a heedless judge who is pestered by an aggrieved widow. Though the judge "feared not God, neither regarded man," he gives in to her cause because she wears him down. God hears the judge, and Jesus announces that God will vindicate his elect who long cry out. But, says Jesus, "Nevertheless, when the Son of Man cometh, shall he find faith on earth?" (v. 8). Here we find the theme of vindication and the on-again, off-again coming of the Son of Man in the *LMJN*. The final question gives it an ominous urgency.

---

16. Again, Jesus uses the Pharisaic doctrine of resurrection to entrap them. We also note that the *LMJN* enters into apocalyptic-like talk and talk about resurrection.

Thereafter, we face the Parable of the Pharisee and the Publican (Luke 18:9–14) where the smug Pharisee is pleased that he is not like the sinners, and the humble tax collector begs God for mercy. Jesus declares the latter as the one justified before God; indeed, the one who humbles himself will be exalted (v. 14). The parable, therefore, continues the critique of the Pharisees and their blind pride; we get another shot of the themes of humility and the moral reversal of one's position. Then the *LMJN* will not touch the rest of chapter 18. Oddly, the author ignores another passage where Jesus welcomes children into the Kingdom (Luke 18:15–17) and the long passage where the ruler asks him what he could do to inherit eternal life. Recall this passage as the one where the ruler calls Jesus "Good Teacher." Jesus turns the ruler's question into a sermon on the "one thing" the ruler has not done: to sell his property, to give to the poor, and to follow Jesus (18:24). The sermon includes the saying about the camel and the needle's eye and ends with the note that only God can save a person. The end of chapter 18 takes us to Luke 19:38–42 (from the L1 source) for the Mary/Martha story. Of course, we do not deal with the raising of Lazarus, since this occasion seems to be the first time Jesus has met the two. It is the famous story where Martha does the kitchen work while her sister enjoys listening to Jesus.

We have no idea why the author puts the Mary/Martha story here, though it shows Jesus approving of someone listening to his teaching. Possibly he thinks Martha, like a Pharisee, focuses on superficial things. Once again, the geography of the *LMJN* is all messed up. According to the canonical gospels, Mary and Martha live in Bethany (close to Jerusalem), but if we follow Mark's geography, then at this point in the *LMJN* Jesus must leave Galilee soon for Jerusalem. Therefore, we know the Mary/Martha story has been selected for its content, not its location. Is it that Mary focuses on the urgent lesson of the day, while Martha is busy with the details of the kitchen?

8

Performing the Wisdom II

Precis of the Lukan Interlude

The author of the *LMJN* turns to Luke to fill the space before the endgame. He incorporates large portions of Luke 10–19 without many interruptions from other gospels. The contents of these chapters include teachings on prayer (11:1–13); several debates with Pharisees (i.e., over healing on the Sabbath! [11:37—12:3; 14:1–6]); the Parables of the Good Samaritan (10:25–37), the Great Supper (14:15–24), the Sheep (15:3–7), the Coin (15:8–10), the Prodigal Son (15:11–32), the Unjust Steward (16:1–9), and the Rich Man and Lazarus (16:19–31); injunctions on humility (17:1–10) and on wealth and discipleship (18:18–30); and even comments on the dark age of the Son of Man (17:22–37). (After selecting from this material, our author uses Matt 19 to restart the conflict with the Pharisees.) Naturally, the *LMJN* leaves out the exorcism and the sign-seeking in Luke 11 and notably eliminates the healing of the leper in chapter 17, presumably because it seems to affirm both the supernatural and the role of the priestly/ritual theme.

The next episode is from Luke 10, the sending out of the seventy followers. The start of the itinerant ministry, however, becomes the occasion for the *LMJN* to pack the Jesus story with favorite texts from John. Before those texts we find twelve verses of Luke 10 in which the *LMJN* warns that the itineracy of the disciples will be daunting and dangerous. Jesus gives them rules of the road, of visits, and of eating with the people in their homes. They are to announce, "Peace be to this house" (10:5) and to move on when they have overstayed and when they meet hostility (Luke 10:5–12). Then, out of the blue, the *LMJN* omits one verse (10:9), the command to "heal the sick that are therein [in a town], and say unto them, 'The Kingdom of God has come near to you.'" The disciples are to dust themselves off and leave when not welcomed, with a warning that "the Kingdom of God is come nigh unto you" (10:11). Jesus leaves unwelcoming towns with a judgment worse than that on Sodom (10:12). This episode contains some surprises we will have to make sense of, but the most startling feature of the *LMJN*'s version is that without v. 9 *the disciples have no real purpose to their ministry. Apparently, they are only to warn of the nearness of the Kingdom.*[1]

Exposition: The Mission of the Twelve

The *LMJN* launches a new theme with a passage from the gospel of John.[2] The text uses 7:1 to orient us: Jesus has been in Galilee, not Judea, because "the Jews" sought to kill him in Judea. Then a shift back to the primary synoptic story takes us to Mark 7 (from the underused gospel) and to a rare *LMJN* repetition: to the handwashing incident again. The text artificially gathers Pharisees from Galilee and scribes largely from Jerusalem to challenge Jesus for his disciples' unwashed behavior. The account then deletes Mark 7:9–13, a passage that includes a prophecy from Isa 29 that criticizes people for hypocrisy, for following human law, and for introducing new law.[3] Jesus then gathers the people and begins a new sermon: Mark 7:14–24 with Matt 15 parallels.[4] *The sermon argues that all defilement of the human comes from the inside of the person.* Jesus has to interpret the saying for the disciples by emphasizing the notion that evil comes from the heart. It turns out that to make the point that evil comes from within is the reason the *LMJN* repeats the handwashing account. Actually, the point is a double one: *that evil is deep within the person, and that it is rooted in human will.* Both points are crucial: the former distinguishes evil from things the *LMJN* regards as superficial and unimportant, while the latter affirms powerfully that evil lives in the free choice of the will.

The repetition of the handwashing scene also underscores the phenomenon of hypocrisy, since the Pharisees think the crucial issue is doing the ritual, while Jesus tweaks them with the idea that the real issue,

1. Jefferson, *Bible* (Beacon ed.), 79–80; folio 33:199.
2. We have not heard from the gospel of John for thirty pages of text. See Jefferson, *Bible* (Beacon ed.), 74; folio 29:191.
3. Perhaps referring to the Pharisees' support for an oral Torah.
4. Jefferson, *Bible* (Beacon ed.), 74–75; folio 29, 30:191, 193.

defilement, is in the depth of the human. That the Pharisees confuse the surface and the depth of the matter makes manifest their actual wickedness. Of course, while they miss their own evil, they charge the disciples with evil.[5] Thereafter, Jesus leaves for the area of Tyre and Sidon (Mark 7:24).

The discussion develops as the disciples pose the question of who of them will be the greatest in heaven. (The *LMJN* turns to the abbreviated Matt 18:1 from among the synoptic options.) Our text makes Jesus' point by focusing on the child as the greatest in the Kingdom of heaven, without judging among the disciples (Mark 9:35). Recall the earlier attention of the *LMJN* to children. Here we get a clue why the author of the *LMJN* shows such affection for Jesus' honoring of children. *Children exemplify the humble reversal of wisdom in the* LMJN's *entire picture of Jesus.* After the appeal to the example of children the *LMJN* jumps over parallel texts discussing the inversion of high and low in the Kingdom, and, significantly, drops only vv. 5 and 6 from the whole of Matt 15. Those verses emphasize that *anyone who receives a child in Jesus' name receives Jesus* (v. 5) and the reverse, whoever causes a child who believes in Jesus to sin will be drowned in the sea (v. 6). We would have to guess why the text drops those two verses.

Once the *LMJN* has purged Jesus' two emphatic self-references from Matt 15:5–6, it returns to Matt 18:7 to quote most of that chapter. We get a "woe" to those who live for temptations, and especially for the ones who bring temptations (v. 7); we hear of the hand that offends and should be cut off and the eye that sins and should be plucked out (18:8–9). However, we are not allowed to hear about the despised children who become angels and always get to see the Father in heaven, nor do we encounter the disputed text from Matthew, "For the Son of Man came to save the lost" (18:11). We do hear of the lost sheep (from Q) or of the shepherd's celebration after finding that sheep.[6] Apparently, *the author of the* LMJN *wants the theme of children reserved for his theme of reversals, but not when the evangelists let it get caught up in syrupy theological themes.*[7]

The *LMJN* continues with more of Matt 18, now including advice from the Q source about confronting one's "brother" who sins against oneself and who may need the intervention of the church (v. 17). The uncorrected brother should be regarded as one regards a heathen or a tax collector (v.

---

5. Jefferson, *Bible* (Beacon ed.), 75–76; folio 30:193.

6. The manuscript in English that the *LMJN* uses writes v. 14 as "Even so it is not the will of *your* Father which is in heaven, that one of these little ones should perish." In many manuscripts the "your" is a "my." We assume the author of the *LMJN* goes with the "your" by simply following his printed version. But we do know that "your" rather than "my" fits nicely with the values of the *LMJN*.

7. Jefferson, *Bible* (Beacon ed.), 76–77; folio 31:195.

17). The daring rules for church involvement get cut off, however, when the *LMJN* omits vv. 18–20. Here Matthew gets to his famous "bind-on-earth, bind-in-heaven" saying: the two asking on earth being bound in heaven, and two who come to an agreement on earth having it done for them by the Father in heaven. Note that these heavy ideas are omitted in the *LMJN*. The text's story returns in Peter's question to Jesus about how many times to forgive; *Jesus' response, of course, blows apart the idea of counting times of forgiveness* (vv. 21–22 from Q). Then, to complete the chapter, the *LMJN* employs the Parable of the Unmerciful Servant (vv. 23–34) with the same editorial connection as Matthew himself used: the continuity of the theme of forgiveness. But the parable shows a limit to forgiveness not found in vv. 21–22: the endless repetition of forgiveness stops where one, the forgiven, does not forgive another (vv. 34–35). We note, again, that the *LMJN* sets a limit to forgiveness, and the limit rests where forgiveness does not meet forgiveness.[8]

Analysis: The Mission of the Twelve

The case of handwashing is worth repetition within the *LMJN*, as it may represent the perfect example of the author's protestant attitude toward ritual and holiness codes. Keep in mind, again, that for the *LMJN* the ritual has nothing to do with germs or the status of the oral Torah. The *LMJN* lets us see only the Pharisees' fixation on a fussy ritual while they miss the grave moral point: the genesis of evil in humans. Evil comes from the heart, from the free choice of the will within the person. Thus, such evil presents the perfect example of what our author takes to be hypocrisy. For the Pharisees of the *LMJN* to grasp Jesus' point, their values would have to be flipped over, to value exactly what they hate. Thus, we see why the *LMJN* turns to the pericope about children next. *Children exemplify the humble option in the drama of the reversal of high and low in the discipleship of Jesus.* As much as Jesus points to their presence in his ministry, children exemplify humble discipleship. In the *LMJN*, when Jesus points to children, he evokes the qualities of discipleship and does not make christological or eschatological points.

We should note how much the author of the *LMJN* dislikes the rare moments in which Jesus allows titles and honors to himself. These moments sometimes come from Jesus himself, especially in the gospel of John. More often they are suggested or implied by others; and of course, they appear also in the synoptic tradition where the revelation of Jesus' status and titles

---

8. Jefferson, *Bible* (Beacon ed.), 77–79; folio 32:197.

happens in spite of Mark's messianic secret. Even as the author of the *LMJN* eschews accolades for Jesus, he seems to make peace with the term "Son of Man," if we do not get caught up in a heightened apocalyptic sense. It is, in fact, our author's favorite christological category so far for Jesus. We know that the term does not mean the Danielic rider on the apocalyptic cloud. *The author of the* LMJN *warms up to claims and names for Jesus as the reconstruction of the Jesus story continues; early in the texts, the author purges every honor for Jesus, while by the end of the text, he will allow selected texts to call him Son of Man, Christ, or Messiah, in increasingly apocalyptic-sounding contexts.*[9]

The theme of forgiveness continues to haunt the text; it recurs in selected passages and in some deletions. So far, we have our hunches about forgiveness, and we know for sure the author of the *LMJN* endorses the many times when Jesus speaks to the plenteous character of God's and humans' forgiveness. The theme above in Matt 18:21–32 suggests that *we cannot and should not count the number of times we need to forgive.* Yet we know that by careful selection *the author uncovers what may be a problem with unlimited forgiveness.* We have seen hints that he may be raising *the concern about fairness*; and here, in Matt 18:34–35, *the* LMJN *may be setting a limit to forgiveness when the forgiven refuses to forgive.*

Exposition: The Return to the Gospel of John

The *LMJN* now is ready to bring John's gospel into the story and dives in with much of chapter 7–9 before he returns to chapters in Luke. The *LMJN* deletes John 7:1, probably because it has "the Jews" *of Galilee, not of Jerusalem*, looking to kill Jesus. John's theory of the geography of Jesus' ministry requires Jesus to travel to Judea for the Feast of Booths, but, as we know, the *LMJN* displaces the Jesus story mainly to Jerusalem, and thus the author rejects John 7:1. In any case the rationale for the visit to Jerusalem supports a familiar theme: to make known widely what has been secret (v. 4). But Jesus' time has not yet come, though the world already hates him (v. 8).

People look for Jesus and some complain about him: "the Jews" also look for him and are frightened by the crowds. Jesus goes into the temple to teach in the midst of festival time. The people are astonished; how can he have such learning without being taught (v. 15)? John's Jesus gets to answer the question: his teaching is not his "but his that sent me" (v. 16). He explains that those who do the will of God will recognize whether his teaching

---

9. Of course, toward the end of the Jesus story, the author must work his way around and through the synoptic apocalypse.

is from God (v. 17). Jesus will be one who seeks "his glory that sent him" (v. 18). The *LMJN*'s Jesus returns in v. 19 with a disquisition on keeping the law. He notes that though Moses has given the law to "you," yet "you" have planned to kill "me," that is, Jesus himself (v. 19). Then Jesus defends himself for healing on the Sabbath; he points to the law of circumcision and asks whether the crowd would be mad about circumcising on the Sabbath. How can they be mad if Jesus has "made a man every whit whole on the Sabbath-day?" (v. 23). The expression implies that the *healing* makes a human whole, but the *LMJN*'s translation makes it hazy. The punch line of the entire episode is to "Judge not according to the appearance, but judge righteous judgment" (v. 24).[10]

The tension builds. The crowds in Jerusalem discuss whether Jesus is the one whom they want to kill. How can he still be preaching? Is he really Christ/Messiah (vv. 25–26)? The *LMJN* omits five verses (vv. 27–31) that show the Messiah should not be known as Jesus is, where Jesus preaches to them that he comes from the true one whom they do not know (v. 28), and that he knows the Father because God sent him. Many believe in him but think the Messiah should do more signs (v. 31). Instead, the *LMJN* wants to get to the Pharisees' "murmuring" (vv. 12, 32); indeed, the Pharisees actually send officers to take him while the crowd debates whether arresting him is a good thing (v. 32)! When the officers fail to bring him in, they explain that no one has ever spoken like Jesus, but the Pharisees think the officers have been deceived, as none of the authorities and no Pharisees believe in Jesus (vv. 46–48). The chapter ends with a judgment from John himself: *this people does not know the law and are cursed* (v. 49).[11] The coda to the chapter is the story of Nicodemus, the one who meets with Jesus at night. Nicodemus asks if it is fair to judge Jesus before he is heard from, while the rest wonder if Nicodemus is also from Galilee, from which no prophet can arise (v. 52).

Chapter 8 in John offers the *LMJN* the first eleven verses, but the rest of the chapter is cut. What the author of the *LMJN* likes in chapter 8 is the scene where Jesus teaches at the temple and the Pharisees confront him with a known adulterer to test him (vv. 1–11). Jesus tries to ignore them and finally says that the one without sin should throw the first stone. When his opponents leave him, Jesus wonders if anyone has condemned her and says he will not condemn her either. She should sin no more (v. 11).[12] As we read

---

10. Jefferson, *Bible* (Beacon ed.), 80–81; folio 34:201.

11. Jefferson, *Bible* (Beacon ed.), 81–83; folio 35:203.

12. This story does not have secure status in the best manuscripts. See Jefferson, *Bible* (Beacon ed.), 83–84; folio 36:205.

on, we know immediately why the *LMJN* rejects the rest of chapter 8: Jesus begins to give one of his intense, self-referential sermons with "I am the light of the world." True, the Pharisees show up and debate with him, but the premise of the discussion scares the author of the *LMJN*: Jesus testifies and judges not by human standards (v. 16). In fact, he testifies on his own behalf, and the Father testifies on his behalf also (v. 18). The disquisition takes a transcendental turn: Jesus is going off to heaven and identifies himself as the Son of Man who speaks from the Father (v. 29). The turn moves to the issue of truth, true freedom, and a critique of the Jews for failed obedience to the model of faith, Abraham. The pericope ends with the Jews discussing whether Jesus is possessed by a demon and Jesus' indirect answer identifying the dialectic of glory in which he and the Father live. Of course, the whole passage is too transcendentally christological for the *LMJN*'s Jesus![13]

The *LMJN* author continues by following the same pattern he has in the two previous chapters in John: He lets John set out an issue but then omits the resolution John presents for the issue. Here in chapter 9 the *LMJN* claims only the first three verses, another amusing passage where the gospel launches a healing of a blind man, but the *LMJN* takes the account only far enough to propose a discussion. Jesus rejects the notion that the man's blindness is tied to his sin or that of his parents. Rather, the blindness is to make manifest the works of God (v. 3). The *LMJN*, of course, will not let us see the healing of the man, nor the disquisition from Jesus as the "light of the world," nor the interrogation of the man by the Pharisees. We are not surprised that the *LMJN* omits these topics since they do not match the catalog of values we have developed in our rereading of the selections. The wonder is that the *LMJN* uses any of John, since so much of it wanders into dangers. But the *LMJN* finds one safe passage in John 10, the first sixteen verses of allegorical meditation on the safety of the sheep and the attentive care of the shepherd. The passage leads to several I AM sayings of Jesus and the "I am come that they might have life . . ." but the *LMJN* censors vv. 6–10 to avoid the most dramatic self-references. The selections return in v. 11 with the simpler, less metaphysical, "I am the Good Shepherd." This shepherd is moved to die for his sheep, though the text eliminates the powerful v. 15: "As the Father knoweth me, even so know I the Father: and I lay down my life for the sheep" as well as the entirety of vv. 17–18 where John's Jesus notes that it *is the love from the Father that prompts him to lay down his own life*. Again, we see one-sentence excising of John to save the *LMJN* from an intimate Jesus-Father relationship and from the hint of resurrection (v.

---

13. Jefferson, *Bible* (Beacon ed.), 84; folio 36:205.

18).[14] *The author of the LMJN seems unable to warm up to John's portrait of the intimacy of Jesus with the God whom he calls Father.* He must cut his way through John's transcendental meditation on this intimacy. *But the LMJN does turn to a more promising but metaphysically lower doctrine, a shepherd christology.*

---

14. Jefferson, *Bible* (Beacon ed.), 84–85, folio 37:207.

9

Final Affairs

The Turn to the Passion

The author of *LMJN* turns to Luke to fill the space before the endgame. He incorporates large portions of Luke 10–19 without many interruptions from other gospels. The topics include teachings on prayer, several debates with Pharisees (i.e., over healing on the Sabbath!), the Parables of the Good Samaritan, the Supper, the Sheep and the Coin, the Prodigal Son, the Steward, the Rich Man and Lazarus, portions of the Sermon, injunctions on humility, wealth and discipleship, even the dark age of the Son of Man. He uses Matt 19 to restart the conflict with the Pharisees. Naturally, Jefferson leaves out the exorcism and the sign-seeking in Luke 11 and notably eliminates the healing of the leper in chapter 17, presumably because it seems to affirm both the supernatural and the role of the priestly/ritual theme.

The crowds follow Jesus to Judea and the Pharisees pick a fight with him about marriage and divorce (Matt 19:1–12). They ask him if divorce is lawful for any cause. In typical fashion, Jesus says no by appealing to the Genesis expectation of a permanent, single union of the two. Matthew's Jesus goes on to explain that Moses allowed men to divorce their wives because of the hardness of the hearts (v. 8), while Jesus allows it in the case of unchastity (v. 9). When the disciples wonder if marriage is not the best, Jesus suggests that the better state is to be a eunuch for the Kingdom (v. 12).

We do not know what the author of the *LMJN* thinks about these radical views, since he leaves a major portion of v. 12 out in his cutting and pasting. Leaving out more than half of a verse could be an editorial leap, but it is unprecedented in the *LMJN*, and the passage in question stops midsentence. The critical opinion is that this deletion was a mistake and not a deliberate editing of the verse.[1] On the larger issue, our author's editing signals that he does not think the radical ethic of Jesus to be problematic.

Luke and the *LMJN* move from marriage and being a eunuch to children in the next episode (Matt 19:13–15). This episode shows people bringing children to be touched by Jesus and the disciples trying to block them. But Jesus permits the children to approach him[2] with his famous dictum: "Suffer little children come to me, and forbid them not, to come to me: for of such is the Kingdom of heaven" (v. 14). The saying is powerful but becomes more so when Matthew's Jesus says to his disciples and the people that they must turn and become children to enter the Kingdom of heaven (v. 15). The passage is indeed powerful, but it is particularly interesting because the *LMJN* often includes texts that pertain to children.[3]

Then the *LMJN* author repeats from Matthew what he has already quoted from Luke: Matt 19:16–26 from a larger pericope that spans to v. 30. It is the story of the rich young man who asks Jesus what he must do to have eternal life. Again, Jesus objects to being called "good," as no one but God is good; then Jesus gives a string of commandments and tells the young man that if he wants to be perfect to go and sell what he possesses. The generalized claims follow: that rich people "hardly ever" enter into the Kingdom of heaven, that rich "camels" cannot fit through the eye of the needle, and that with God all things are possible. We need to consider why the *LMJN* repeats these powerful ideas. We do notice that after the episode with the rich inquirer Jesus changes the subject and speaks of the new world when the Son of Man will sit on his throne and judge the tribes of Israel (vv. 28–29), but of course the *LMJN* must drop these ideas.[4]

Instead, the text heads to Matt 20, one of the remaining large blocks the author has not mined, and he works through the first 16 verses. Then he moves on. The text in question is the Parable of the Laborers in the Vineyard which the *LMJN* quotes verbatim. Remember that it is the story of the Kingdom of heaven and it compares the Kingdom to the situation of a householder who hires laborers for a day of work in the vineyard by adding more workers as the day goes on. When he pays them all the same wage, the early shift grumbles that the arrangements are unfair. The householder defends

---

1. Jefferson, *Bible* (Beacon ed.), 102–3; folio 50:233.

2. Mark's parallel account has Jesus becoming "indignant" with his disciples (Mark 10:14).

3. Jefferson, *Bible* (Beacon ed.), 103; folio 51:235.

4. Jefferson, *Bible* (Beacon ed.), 103–4; folio 51:235.

his scheme by pointing to his free generosity. The coda is, the last will be first, and the first last; many are called, but few chosen (20:16).[5] While the coda purports to round out the parable in a denotative meaning, in fact, it misses the point of the parable. Rather, *the performance of the parable leads people to enter a world where mercy and justice are not in conflict.*

Jesus is traveling toward Jerusalem from Jericho when the chief publican Zacchaeus invites him to eat at his house (Luke 19:1-10 from L1). "They" see Jesus as Zacchaeus' guest and "murmur" that he is eating with sinners (v. 7). Zacchaeus defends himself by his extraordinary generosity. Jesus declares that salvation has come to the house of this son of Abraham (v. 9) and states that the Son of Man is come to seek and to save those lost. Again, we see a positive use of the Son of Man title (v. 10).[6] Then Jesus delivers his Parable of the Pounds (Luke 19:11-23), a strange parable in which a king leaves his kingdom to claim new territory and entrusts his servants with different amounts of money to tend wisely while he is gone. Some of the servants make wise investments with good and decent returns while one hides his one pound to return to the king without any interest. The king calls the latter wicked, takes the single pound from him, and gives it to the servant who makes the most profit. Then the king generalizes the point: the ones who have more will get more, while the ones who have little, that little will be taken away. And the king demands that his enemies in the city be brought in and executed (v. 28). The *LMJN* cuts out the final two verses of Luke 19:29-30, in which Luke, via Q, levels some strident extensions of two ideas offered at the end of the parable: that those with more get more and those with less lose even that, and that the too-cautious servant will receive a painful and vivid punishment (v. 30).[7] Even toned down by the *LMJN*, the passage seems to say that among the faithful, those who invest well and return their loans with interest are the blessed, and those who do not will suffer. Do we dare interpret the piece a step further? Perhaps the author of the *LMJN* connects the passage with the issue of forgiveness we have already seen: if so, *the allegorical parable may suggest that we cannot expect cheap grace but must participate in the work of the Kingdom.*

Performing the Final Wisdom

The case of handwashing is worth the *LMJN*'s repetition, as it may represent the perfect example of the author's protestant attitude toward ritual

---

5. Jefferson, *Bible* (Beacon ed.), 105-6; folio 52:237.
6. Jefferson, *Bible* (Beacon ed.), 106-7; folio 53:239.
7. Jefferson, *Bible* (Beacon ed.), 107-9; folio 53—54:239, 241.

and holiness codes. Keep in mind, again, that for the *LMJN* the ritual has nothing to do with germs or the status of the oral Torah. The *LMJN* lets us see only the Pharisees' fixation on a fussy ritual while they miss the grave moral point: the genesis of evil in humans. Evil comes from the heart, from the free choice of the will within the person. Thus, such evil presents the perfect example of what the author takes to be hypocrisy. For the Pharisees to grasp the point that the *LMJN*'s Jesus is making, their values would have to be flipped over: they would have to value exactly what they hate. Thus, we see why the *LMJN* turns to the pericope about children. *Children exemplify the humble option in the drama of the reversal of high and low in the discipleship of Jesus.* That message is the point of children in Jesus' ministry, not the flowery theological points the *LMJN* suppresses.

We should note how much the author of the *LMJN* dislikes the rare moments in which Jesus allows titles and honors to himself. These moments sometimes come from Jesus himself, especially in the gospel of John. More often they are suggested or implied by others; and of course, they appear even in the synoptic tradition where the revelation of Jesus' status and titles happens in spite of Mark's messianic secret. Even as the author of the *LMJN* eschews accolades for Jesus, he seems to make peace with the term "Son of Man," if we do not get caught up in a heightened apocalyptic sense. It is, in fact, a favorite christological category for Jesus. So far, we know that the term does not mean the Danielic rider on the apocalyptic cloud. *The author of the* LMJN *warms up to claims and names for Jesus as the reconstruction of the Jesus story continues; early in the texts, the author purges every honor for Jesus, while by the end of the text, he will allow selected texts to call him Son of Man, Christ, and Messiah, in increasingly apocalyptic-sounding contexts.*[8]

The theme of forgiveness continues to haunt the text; it recurs in selected passages and in some deletions. So far, we have our hunches, and we know the author of the *LMJN* endorses the many times when Jesus speaks to the plenteous character of God's and humans' forgiveness. The theme above, from Matt 18:21–12, suggests that *we cannot and should not count the number of times we need to forgive.* Yet we know that by careful selection *the author uncovers what may be a problem with unlimited forgiveness.* We have seen hints that he may be raising *the concern about fairness;* and here, in Matt 18:34–35, the *LMJN* may be setting a *limit to forgiveness when the forgiven refuses to forgive.*

---

8. Of course, toward the end of the Jesus story, the author must also work his way around and through the synoptic apocalypse.

Precis of the Execution of Jesus

In the *LMJN*, Jesus is condemned to death according to Mark 14, but thereafter John takes over for the trial by Pilate (chapter 18) while Luke gets Herod's story and Matthew gets Pilate's release of Barabbas, the final decision to crucify Jesus, and Judas' remorse. Jefferson uses Luke for the story of Simon of Cyrene and for Jesus' comforting of the women; our author calls on John's account of the actual crucifixion, on Matthew for the taunting at the cross, on Luke's account of the forgiveness of the one robber and of the crowd, and for the arrival and departure of Jesus' mother. Matthew gets the cry of dereliction and the death. John completes the story with the burial, the help of Joseph of Arimathea, and the garden tomb. Matthew closes the door on the tomb with a great stone, and with that the *LMJN*'s story is done.

Exposition: The Jerusalem Finale

The *LMJN* starts us through Jesus' final week by using Matthew's account packed with highly edited side comments from the other evangelists. It begins with an edited Matt 21:1–10 in which Jesus commissions two disciples to find his entry mount. The text omits vv. 4–5 that connect the event to Zechariah's prophecy. Meanwhile the crowd assembles with tree branches, though in the *LMJN* they are not allowed to sing their hosannas (v. 9). Still, the whole of Jerusalem wonders who he is (v. 10). The *LMJN* then jumps to John 12:19–24 to bring us back to the main theme: *the conflict with the Pharisees, who now fear the crowds.* They direct the disciples to contact Jesus, who answers them with a spacey comment about the way that *seed dies to bring forth much fruit* (John 12:24). That single, important verse[9] substitutes for a suppressed passage in John, one of John's meditations on the glory of the Father as Jesus ponders his impending death. Next is one verse, Matt 21:17, where Jesus goes to Bethany while we go back to Mark 11:12 to be assured that he got to Bethany. Then we leap over to the fig-tree cursing (Mark 11:13–14) *for a second temple event,* this one from Mark 11:15–19.[10] Likely the *LMJN* repeats this important event because, for the author of the *LMJN, the temple fracas marks both the beginning and end of the conflict with the Jews.*

Mark's version of the temple uproar emphasizes Jesus' teaching aspect of his action. The temple should be a house of prayer "for all the nations"

---

9. As we will see, the images of the seed and the tree bringing forth much fruit are central to Jefferson's christology.

10. Jefferson, *Bible* (Beacon ed.), 109–11; folio 55—56:243, 245.

(v. 17). But more importantly, the passage expresses for the *LMJN*, not only the astonishment of the crowds at his teaching, but also the decision of the scribes and chief priests to destroy Jesus, a decision which we have been anticipating since the beginning of the *LMJN*. Our text turns to one final verse from Mark 11, in which Jesus says to "the priests and the scribes and the elders" (v. 27) who question his authority, "Neither will I tell you by what authority I do" my work (v. 33). It is an odd verse, since Jesus is already returning to Jerusalem and immediately baits the priests, scribes, and elders of the people with a parable about two sons, one obedient and one disobedient (Matt 21:28–31). But before we get to the parable, after the *LMJN* omits the heated debate, the text has the priests and elders inquire about the authority by which Jesus teaches. Jesus traps them with a question about the authority of John's teaching. The authorities would not answer the trapping question, and Jesus evades their question.[11] Again, we see that the *LMJN* consistently omits or minimizes Jesus' connection to John.

Instead, in the Parable of the Two Sons (Matt 21:28–32), one refuses to work in the vineyard but later changes his mind while the other promises to work but does not actually do the work. Jesus asks the leaders which son does his father's will. The leaders choose the first and Jesus declares: "Truly, I say to you, the tax collectors and the harlots go into the Kingdom of God before you" (v. 31). The *LMJN* stops the story at this point and we realize that Jesus has just given *the decisive critique of the Jewish establishment*. Unfortunately, it is not as powerful as it could be, because the text deletes the final reference to John the Baptist: "For John came to you in the way of righteousness, and you did not believe him, but the tax collectors and the harlots believed him; and even when you saw it, you did not afterward repent and believe him" (v. 32).[12]

The *LMJN* adds a parable from Mark 12:1–9, the next story in the synoptic account; here the author shifts from the usual Matthew to the account from Mark. It is the story of a vintner who establishes a fine vineyard but then leaves the country; he sends a servant back to the vineyard for some of the harvest. The workers at the vineyard abuse the servant, then another, and finally they kill a third. Finally, he sends his "well-beloved" son, who also is killed. The story ends with a question: what should the vintner do?

---

11. Jefferson, *Bible* (Beacon ed.), 110–12; folio 56:245. The folio 56 is one of the two pages on which the author notes a sidebar indicating he wants Mark 11:27 added to the main English column. The afterthought locates the return of Jesus and disciples to Jerusalem and to the temple where he meets the chief priests, scribes, and elders. In fact, the added verse reminds us that *Jesus is about to take on the temple for a second time* (according to the *LMJN*). See Jefferson, *Bible* (Beacon ed.), 111.

12. Jefferson, *Bible* (Beacon ed.), 10–12; folio 56:247.

He resolves to destroy the manager and give the vineyard away. The *LMJN* copy of the story ends with the question and shifts to Matt 21:45, to one thin verse in which the point of the whole story comes to be clear: *the chief priests and the Pharisees understand that Jesus is talking about them* (Matt 21:45). By implication, *they are the ones who will kill the beloved son, and who will themselves be destroyed by their crime. The Jewish authorities are guilty of the death of the beloved son.* The author of the *LMJN* finds one verse out of context that says bluntly the intention of his version of the gospel, and at the same time allows him to avoid quoting the prophetic Ps 118. The coda to the episode is found in v. 45 of Matt 21: the Jewish authorities seek to arrest this prophet because they fear the crowd.[13]

The *LMJN*'s Jesus tells one last parable before he is arrested. It is the Parable of the Wedding Banquet (Matt 22:1–14 from Q), a Kingdom parable. The feast is ready and the king sends out messengers. Of course, we have already heard Luke's version in 14:16–24 from Q. The *LMJN* repeats the basic story but in the much edgier version of Matthew. Some of the servants actually are killed when the king sends his troops to shame and kill them. The parable ends with the wedding full of random people drawn in. The king spots one who is not dressed for the occasion and orders the man tied up and thrown into the outer darkness where there will be gnashing of teeth (v. 13). The *LMJN* ends with "For many are called, but few are chosen" (v. 14).[14] Again, the end of Jesus' ministry comes with both violence and grim judgment.

The *LMJN* gives the Pharisees their last chance to trap Jesus with a leading question whether or not it is lawful to give tribute to Caesar (Matt 22:15–22). Knowing their motive and the test, Jesus gives his famous answer. He calls them the *LMJN*'s favorite term for Pharisees, hypocrites, and they marvel at his answer (v. 22). Suddenly the Sadducees try to trick Jesus with another hypothetical case: if a woman marries seven brothers one at a time at the death of each brother, and then she dies, whose wife will she be in the resurrection? Of course, the question is a setup, especially since the Sadducees do not even believe in the resurrection! Jesus reminds them that the God of Abraham is the God of the living not the dead (v. 32). Nonetheless the crowd is "astonished at his doctrine" (Matt 22:33).[15] The text then completes the chapter with a section from Mark 12:28–33, a passage where one of the scribes, impressed with Jesus, asks him which is the greatest of

---

13. Jefferson, *Bible* (Beacon ed.), 112–13; folio 57:247.

14. Jefferson, *Bible* (Beacon ed.), 113–14; folio 57—58:247, 249. The theme of judgment appears again.

15. Jefferson, *Bible* (Beacon ed.), 114–16; folio 58—59:249, 251.

the commandments. He answers quoting the *Shema'* with the heart, soul, mind, and strength specification (vv. 29–30) and adds the "neighbor as thyself" (v. 31). This passage, we note, is the third evocation in the *LMJN* of this synoptic idea. If we have not yet gotten how important this commandment is, the author of the *LMJN* throws in one verse, Matt 22:40, to say that these two commandments are the foundation of both the law and the prophets. The good scribe is allowed to say that Jesus has spoken the truth: to love God thus and the neighbor as oneself is greater than all burnt offerings and sacrifices (Mark 12:33).[16]

We now see the plot of the *LMJN*'s helter-skelter assemblage of final dialogues with the Jewish authorities. Jesus is in Jerusalem. He has already disrupted life in the temple and, according to the *LMJN*, will do so a second time! In these final encounters the *LMJN* shows the rationales for the upcoming death of Jesus: Jesus' growing criticism of the religious establishment and the determination of the authorities to be rid of him. Our next episode comes as a direct criticism of the scribes and Pharisees: they do not do what they say (Matt 23:3 with parallels); they pile burdens on people but do not themselves do any actual work; they want to be seen in their extravagant worship; and they want the best seats, the most honors, and the title rabbi. But Jesus says his disciples are not rabbis but brothers to each other with one master, Christ, and only God as Father (v. 10). A criticism follows of the pride and predictable reversals of the religious elite (v. 12) and then a woe on the "hypocrites": they devour widows' houses and worry about showy prayer (a switch to Mark 12:40 or Luke 20:47, hitherto unrecognized in the 1989 Beacon Press edition), followed by another woe on the "hypocrites" for drawing in proselytes who are turned to evil (Matt 23:15). Another woe on the "blind guides" follows: the Pharisees say that swearing by the temple means nothing, but by the gold of the temple, well, that is everything (v. 16). The *LMJN* even includes Matthew's long exposition of the critique of swearing (vv. 19–22).[17]

When we reach the fifth woe in a row and face several ahead of us, we realize we are at the culmination point of the entire presentation of the life and ministry of Jesus. *The LMJN's gospel is the story of a good man with an unmatched ethic who falls into conflict with groups who represent petty and hypocritical forces of evil.* They object to Jesus, begin to criticize him, and plan to destroy him. The fifth woe accuses the scribes and Pharisees of offering spices when they ignore justice, mercy, and faith. "You blind guides, which

---

16. Jefferson, *Bible* (Beacon ed.), 116–17; folio 60:253. Once again, the *LMJN* emphasizes the sometime gospel theme that the ritual must bow to the moral.

17. Jefferson, *Bible* (Beacon ed.), 117–19; folio 61—62: 255, 256.

strain at a gnat and swallow a camel" (Matt 23:23).[18] The sixth woe hits the blind hypocrites for cleaning the outside of the cup and plate and ignoring the inside (23:25). The seventh attacks the hypocrites for fancy tombs with dead bones; that is, they appear as righteous but are full of iniquity (23:28). The meaning repeats in the eighth woe: they build lavish monuments for the prophets and the righteous yet pretend they would not have murdered the same ones (23:30). For such charges Jesus says these serpents can expect to be punished in hell (23:33). Just when we are on a roll with the woes, the author of the *LMJN* cuts Jesus' continuing critique in Matt 23:34–36, where Jesus seems to rise in authority and claims that he will send more prophets, wise men, and scribes which the Pharisee-hypocrites will probably "kill and crucify" so that all the righteous will be persecuted by the same people.[19] The omitted passage (v. 36) ends with "all this will come upon this generation." But, the *LMJN* ends the chapter with Jesus watching the people cast money into the temple treasury and his commenting on the poor widow who offers two mites: her offering is more than all the others have offered (Mark 12:43).[20]

A new lesson comes from the visit to the temple (a selective reading of Matt 24). Before this episode we do not get to hear of Jesus' lament for Jerusalem (Matt 23:37–39 from Q), but now the *LMJN* lets us see Jesus' prediction that "there shall not be left here one stone upon another" (Matt 24:2). Then the *LMJN* skips content: v. 3 and the signs of the close of the age; vv. 4–8, the signs of the parousia with the rumors of war and famines, and the beginning of the sufferings. There will be a tribulation when Jesus' people will be persecuted, but there is also an admonition not to worry, as the Spirit of the Father will give people the right words (v. 20). The passage predicts that people will attack and kill family members (v. 21); there will be all sorts of betrayal and hate, false prophets and a growing wickedness (v. 12). Those who "endure to the end" will be saved (v. 13), and the gospel of the Kingdom will be preached over the whole world, after which the end will come (v. 14). Despite the heavy apocalyptic imagery here, nonetheless, we do not hear of the desolating sacrilege from Daniel (v. 15).[21] The *LMJN* returns with v. 16 of Matt 24: a passage that speaks of the fears of the end time in Matthew. *The* LMJN *obviously re-aims the apocalyptic fear, however,*

---

18. Again, the ritual masks the ethical issue unrecognized by the Pharisees.

19. We should note that the scribes were part of the objectionable cluster of Jewish authorities early in the *LMJN*, but now at the end of the story the *LMJN* redeems them.

20. Jefferson, *Bible* (Beacon ed.), 119–20; folio 62:257.

21. Jefferson, *Bible* (Beacon ed.), 120–21; folio 63:259.

for the time of Jewish wickedness. The author, therefore, effectively remakes a cosmic-historical apocalypse into a local, moral apocalypse.

The people of Judea should flee to the mountains without clothes or possessions. Woe to those who are pregnant, or who must flee in winter or on the Sabbath. The tribulation will be the greatest ever (v. 21), and the sun will be darkened and the whole heavens upset (v. 29). Meanwhile, the *LMJN* omits vv. 23–28. Verses 23–24 of Matt 24 speak of the time of the false Christs and prophets; meanwhile, neither do we do hear of the signs of the times and the coming of the Son of Man (vv. 26–28). The *LMJN* returns with a wildly apocalyptic passage (v. 29) of a period after tribulation when the heavenly bodies are all disrupted. Then the text removes vv. 30–31 with its vivid apocalyptic imagery of the angels gathering the elect "from one end of heaven to the other."[22]

Matt 24 continues with the Parable of the Fig Tree, in which the tree's budding leaves anticipate the coming of summer (24:32): so "you" will know that "it" or "he" is near.[23] But the *LMJN* omits three pronouncedly apocalyptic verses: this generation will not pass away until all of these things have happened (v. 34); heaven and earth will pass, but not "my words" (v. 35); and no one knows when these things happen, not even the Son but only the Father (v. 36). Interestingly, this "fig tree" story, as it appears in Matt 24, has no connection to the destruction of the temple.[24]

Then we have Jesus' comparison of the days of Noah to those of the coming of the Son of Man (Matt 24:37). He explains that before the flood people in Noah's time live lives of eating and drinking; but all good things have been taken from them. All should be watchful, as one will be taken, one not. We know not the hour that the Lord comes (24:42). Bless the faithful servant who tends the house, and beware of the evil servant: the lord will come when he is not expected and will cut down the wicked one (v. 43). The apocalyptic-like passage ends, as we expect, "Therefore you also must be ready," except that the *LMJN* omits the final clause of the verse: "for the Son of Man is coming at an hour you do not expect" (v. 44). Here we see one of the "Son of Man" passages that the *LMJN* omits from an apocalyptic context.[25] The *LMJN* moves right into the final passage of chapter 24 in

---

22. Jefferson, *Bible* (Beacon ed.), 120–21; folio 63:259.

23. The author's English version has "it" and probably means the destruction of Jerusalem, while modern versions usually use "he" to name the Son of Man figure mentioned in v. 37.

24. Jefferson, *Bible* (Beacon ed.), 121–22; folio 64:261.

25. And the author's blocky form of editing allows him to cut the end of the verse, when he never cuts only a word or phrase! Since the "Son of Man" phrase was printed as a single line, the author could not edit the line as he did. That is, it is for him always

Matthew with a summary saying that captures the entire content of the final passages: Jesus contrasts the faithful and wise servant who will be honored for doing his duties, and the wicked one who wanders off away from his duties. The former will be showered with the master's possessions, while the latter will be punished and "put with the hypocrites" where "men will weep and gnash their teeth" (v. 51). We know the author of the *LMJN* is obsessed with hypocrisy, and that the charge becomes a badge for his and Jesus' criticism of the Pharisees and the scribes. Here again, we see how emphatically *the* LMJN's *Jesus declares extreme judgment on what he calls their hypocrisy.*[26]

The new chapter follows Matt 25 nearly word for word. It begins with the familiar parable, likening the Kingdom of heaven to the case of the ten virgins (Matt 15:1–13 from M1). It is, of course, the tale of the wise and prepared virgins against the foolish ones. When the bridegroom suddenly arrives, the foolish ones are unprepared and are excluded from the marriage (v. 10) by the groom, who does not recognize them. The message is to watch and be prepared, but the *LMJN* cuts out the final, apocalyptic-sounding phrase: "for you know neither the day nor the hour" (v. 13).[27]

Our text next follows Matthew's version of the Q Parable of the Talents (Matt 25:14–30). It is the familiar one, a Kingdom parable, of a rich man who plans to leave the country and entrusts his wealth to his servants according to their ability. We notice that the *LMJN* has quoted the Lukan version (19:12–27) already; that the author repeats this long parable suggests its importance for the *LMJN*'s reconstruction of the gospels. We get a message from the parable that repeats similar values: *attentive and courageous risk pays off and is rewarded, while timid handling of the money gets punished.* The moral appears in the repeated coda: the one who has will get more, and the one who has little will have even that taken from him. Indeed, the "unprofitable" servant will be cast into the outer darkness where people weep and gnash their teeth (25:30). Again, there are two sorts of people with two reactions, two behaviors, and one is celebrated and one judged and punished in the most extreme terms. The *LMJN* rounds out the long parable with Luke's conclusion to the Synoptic Apocalypse (Luke 21:34–36

---

much easier to cut a whole line than a particular word or phrase. Thus, we have a clue that sometimes the convenience of knife-cut editing determines what he will or will not cut out. We have to extend the observation that some items not valued by the author, i.e., some "Son of Man" phrases, may be kept in a passage, not because he is enthusiastic about the ideas, but because cutting them out is too difficult, given his editing technology. *In other words, he may tolerate certain ideas because they are so embedded in a block of material acceptable for other reasons* (Adams and Lester, *Extracts*, 263).

26. Jefferson, *Bible* (Beacon ed.), 121–22; folio 64:261.

27. Jefferson, *Bible* (Beacon ed.), 123–24; folio 65:263.

from L1): do not give in to evil or to the cares of the world so you will not be snared on "that day"; watch and pray for strength to stand before the Son of Man (v. 36).[28] We note here another remarkable reference to the Son of Man.[29]

Even more remarkably, the *LMJN* employs Matthew's entire treatment of the last judgment (Matt 25:31–46 from the M1 source). Once again, our author daringly dives into the passage about the coming of the Son of Man in his glory. The Son will gather the nations and separate the good from the evil, and the King will welcome the good into the Kingdom prepared from the foundations of the world (vv. 33–34). The passage includes a poetic set of declarations from the poor and the needy whose situations have been addressed by the righteous; their care for the poor is actually care for the King. The evil ones, however, will be cursed for ignoring the needs of the poor, and they will be given over to eternal punishment (v. 46). Once again, *the LMJN sets righteous persons next to wicked ones, and praises and rewards the former and condemns the latter to the darkest fates.* The text offers the ultimate moral either/or that has been building since the first day of Jesus' public ministry. With that either/or before us, the *LMJN* takes us to the passion story.[30] Again we see *that the LMJN author is willing to incorporate passages at the end of his story that are wildly apocalyptic, after having removed all traces of apocalyptic from the first half of his account.*

Analysis: The Jerusalem Finale

The *LMJN* troops us through a long narrative that gets Jesus into Jerusalem and ready to die. The narrative retells the biblical gospels, part a digestion and part a selection of acceptable passages. The themes repeat and require less comment, except that *the tone is darkening as the conflict turns into the passion story.* Indeed, the story gets judgmental as it falls into the declaration of the eight final woes. Conflict now hints at upcoming persecution and death. A second temple event, or a repeat of the first one originally located in John at the front of the public ministry, becomes the final straw for the authorities. *We notice how the temple events become the bookends for the whole narrative on conflict with Jewish authorities; the first bookend launches the story of conflict long before the synoptic gospels get there, and the second one, via Mark, turns the temple into the center of teaching on wisdom and prayer, not the locus of animal sacrifice for human atonement with God.*

28. Jefferson, *Bible* (Beacon ed.), 124–25; folio 66:265.
29. Jefferson, *Bible* (Beacon ed.), 126–27; folio 67—68:267, 269.
30. Jefferson, *Bible* (Beacon ed.), 126–27; folio 67—68:267, 269.

Apparently, we are no longer to think of the temple as the center of the sacrificial system and its atonement ritual. Sure enough, the officials ask about Jesus' authority, and Jesus traps them with an evasive question about the authority of John the Baptist. They are reduced to silence and Jesus remains silent. Then Jesus baits the "priests and scribes and elders"[31] with the Parable of the Two Sons and forces the authorities to judge who is the good son and who is not. Who wins? The tax collectors and the harlots, not the officials. The conflict and challenge have gotten so bad between the two parties that we readers can understand why the authorities will execute Jesus.

The tragic-comic pattern of conflict repeats throughout the entire gospel of the *LMJN*. Jesus does or says something offensive and the authorities get mad, always mad. For the whole gospel the Jewish authorities are getting mad and actually plot to put Jesus away. Now in the finale of the story they are really mad and they are really taking steps to arrest him and charge him. By carefully selecting of the acceptable pericopes, *the author of the* LMJN *has subtly reshaped the conflict traditions of all the canonical gospels: the move to anger from unspecified religious authorities toward Jesus is instant and up front in the story, rather than building over the entire narrative; the anger aims entirely at Jesus' message and performative speech, instead of emerging as a reaction to his exorcisms and healings; the anger comes from the generic collection of authorities, without acknowledging that different groups attack Jesus with different agendas, and without a sense that angers might differ had the gospel been assembled with a more nuanced and critically informed treatment of Jewish life. Indeed, the new gospel evokes no serious Roman anger.* We are therefore ready to name the reshaping of the conflict traditions this way: *The third great transformation of the gospels in the gospel according to the* LMJN *names Jesus' conflict with Jewish leaders as the immediate and dominant theme of the entire the* LMJN. *Jesus' ministry is a fight against the foolishness of the authorities of Second Temple Judaism. To establish this theme the author must abstract from various, plausible causes and complications (i.e., the crowds and various issues) in the gospel texts and distill the story into one theme: the conflict with Jewish authorities. In so abstracting and distilling, the* LMJN *exaggerates the conflict tradition, even though the conflict does indeed follow Jesus' canonical career. And, at the same time, other major themes of the canonical gospels shrink, such as Jesus' message of the coming of the Kingdom of God, Jesus' distinctive Galilean conflict with the Pharisees over holiness and the interpretation of Torah, and,*

---

31. Again, we see how the author of the *LMJN* clumps all the officials of Second Temple Judaism into a cluster of opponents.

of course, Jesus' healing and exorcising ministry. Even the ministry to include the marginalized gets set onto the back burner in the LMJN.

The teaching opportunities in the finale of Jesus' story reveal the risks of abstracting and distilling the canonical pictures of Jesus. In the passages we have just explored, the author's prime values so blind him that he has to reject materials that could be used for his favorite themes. Consider the way that the *LMJN*'s Jesus cannot enjoy the reversals of the Pharisees for the tax collectors and harlots (Matt 21:32) because Jesus' condemnation comes with a reference to John the Baptist (Matt 21:32). *Here, as in so many excised miracles, the author guts the inherent logic of the story, since his allergy to John blinds him from appreciating the faith of the tax collectors and the failures of the Pharisees.* So allergic to John is the author of the *LMJN* that he chooses to suppress the reference to John even at the cost of affirming his favorite theme of reversal.

Now, at the end of the references to John, are we able to pin down a rationale for the *LMJN*'s rejecting Jesus' connection to John the Baptist? We know our author hates prophecy-and-fulfillment schemes; we know that he cannot tolerate the heavens opening and speaking at the baptism; we know also that he would not like Jesus declared by God to be Son of God; and we know he would not like the saving-historical schema culminating in John and then Jesus. But are these factors enough to explain Jesus' odd dissociation from John in the *LMJN*? Perhaps a fuller explanation proposes that the *author's own christology cannot buy the idea that John was Jesus' mentor* who would have taught Jesus the themes of his own ministry, a sage who would have instructed him in wisdom. Thus, we can finally claim that in the *LMJN: to reduce John from Jesus' ministry actually makes Jesus' wisdom even more remarkable; according to the* LMJN *Jesus is no one's student. In fact, the genesis of his wisdom is as miraculous on the* LMJN*'s turf as the exorcisms and healings are in the synoptic gospels. It is in the interest of the* LMJN*'s christology that Jesus' wisdom is immaculately conceived.* "How can such a man have such wisdom?" The logic of the passage selection in the *LMJN* requires that the wisdom of Jesus does not derive from the historical continuum, as it were, for it to have the moral power the author wants. And certainly, *the author thinks of Jesus' moral power as the functional equivalent of that of the wonder-worker. Surely, Jesus' wisdom must be on a direct line to natural reason, a line that bypasses the entire legacy of Israel.*

Not surprisingly, *the author of the* LMJN *becomes more daring in his naming of Jesus as he comes to the end of the story.* For instance, in the performance Parable of the Two Sons (Matt 21:28–32) Jesus gets the chief priests, the scribes, and the elders to admit that the "first son" of the parable is the good son and, when they so admit, Jesus zaps them with the idea that the publicans and the harlots enter the Kingdom of God before they do (Matt 21:31). The author of the *LMJN* would love Jesus' reversal and condemnation of the Jewish authorities. But they do not come logically from the texts that the author selects, since he leaves out the reference to John the Baptist; that is, Jesus reminds the Pharisees that they are the very authorities who rejected John while the publicans and the harlots believed him. Our author cannot bear that John would be included in the story; therefore, the Pharisees choose the right son, the beloved son, but they are not allowed to apply the Matthean allegory in order to identify explicitly that Jesus is the beloved son (Ps 118). Therefore, *we have an incomplete performance parable blocked from designating Jesus as the good son, because of our author's blindness to anything associated with John the Baptist and by extension anything associated with the life of Israel, while the incomplete parable implies that Jesus is intuitively the autodidact, the good son.*

Each story chosen among the final ones before the arrest of Jesus bristles with *ominous suggestions of judgment.* In the Parable of the Wedding Banquet (Matt 22:1–14), the host not only struggles to find guests and not only has to receive the unworthy, but banishes a ruffian who is poorly dressed "into the outer darkness where there will be gnashing of teeth" (v. 13). The final comment on this story (v. 14) speaks of the many called, but few chosen. Meanwhile, Jesus inverts the expectations of the feigning Sadducees who needle him with a hypothetical question about a woman who has outlived seven husbands: whose wife will she be? *Jesus affirms the very doctrine that the Sadducees reject: the resurrection.* Of course, the crowd marvels at his wisdom. A random scribe then asks Jesus what is the greatest commandment. Jesus answers with the *Shema'* and with the loving the "neighbor as thyself" phrase (Mark 12:31). The dual love of God and neighbor is greater than all burnt offerings and sacrifices (Mark 12:23): *a final reminder of the primacy of the moral over the ritual.*

If we readers have not gotten the sense of doom yet, the *LMJN*'s list of eight woes secures the point, once and for all. The authorities are prideful, hypocritical, blind to moral crises of justice and mercy, with misplaced attention to superficial concerns like offerings. Jesus says they will persecute and crucify the prophets and sages, but they will be sent to hell (Matt 23). The woes morph into the (second) attack on the temple and the prediction of its destruction. They slide into the *LMJN*'s version of apocalypse, a muted one, to be sure, but nonetheless amazing. We have seen the author of the *LMJN* flirt with apocalyptic earlier, and we know he does not like apocalyptic extremes, but at this point the *LMJN* joins much of Matt 24 with its apocalyptic description of the coming tribulation, the darkened sun, the false Christ, the coming of the Son of Man, and so on. We are now prepared to declare that *the LMJN comes to affirm apocalyptic images and framing in order to express in some way the coming darkness of the persecution and crucifixion of the noble Sage, even though early in the volume, the author banishes virtually all hints of apocalyptic.* The change in the author's attitude toward apocalyptic is gradual, from an early hostility to a considerable embrace of the elements of the synoptic apocalypse. Still, he continues to reject extreme, cosmic signs of the apocalypse, such as battles of the children of light against children of darkness and of angels fetching the elect for heaven (Matt 24:30–31). We cannot know for sure why our author warms up to apocalyptic, but we can assume that he finds in apocalyptic something beyond simple moral urgency, namely, the language to express the appalling execution of the great Sage, who dies for his wisdom. By the criterion of coherence, we see that his considerable embrace of the apocalyptic comes within Jesus' maximal criticism of the authorities' actions and within the deepest premonition of persecution. *We probably cannot tell how much our author metaphorizes apocalyptic imagery, even if we can suppose causes for his including some elements of the apocalyptic.*

To underscore the apocalyptic turn, we need to be reminded that the author's choices can be irritatingly erratic. He throws out Daniel's Son of Man, but accepts some other sense of the "Son of Man" category; and as he is reading the synoptic apocalypse, he seems to adopt the notion that the Son of Man is coming in a time of tribulation (i.e., he accepts the comparison between the time predicted by Jesus and the time of Noah's flood, in Matt 24:37). Our author emphasizes that all must watch for the hour when the Lord comes (Matt 24:42) and that he will cut down the wicked and honor the wise for doing their duties. Where our author consistently suppresses something from apocalyptic passages, such as from the synoptic apocalypse, is in pericopes that presuppose a clear and immediate timing of the apocalypse and the coming of the Son (i.e., Matt 25:13).

Exposition: The Execution

The story of the death of Jesus in the *LMJN* begins with a chapter that draws upon all four gospels. We start in Mark 14 by learning that it is Passover and the feast of the Unleavened Bread, and that the priests and the scribes are figuring out how to kill Jesus. In Bethany a woman anoints Jesus with expensive oil, and when some complain about the waste, Jesus tells them to back off: "The poor will be with you always." Jesus approves her act of anointing his body before burial (Mark 14:3–9). But as is typical, the *LMJN* removes the generalizing and dramatic final verse or two from the story, the commentary. Here we do not get to read that her action will be saved in memory as the gospel is preached to the whole world (v. 9).[32]

Next in the story, from Matt 26:14–16, we have Judas going to the chief priests and bargaining to deliver Jesus. Then in vv. 17–20 we have the preparation for the Passover where Jesus is called "Master," then the seating for the meal (v. 20). The *LMJN* immediately shifts to Luke 22:24–27, not to the meal itself, but to the dispute among the disciples concerning who would be the greatest among them. Jesus tells them that only the gentiles jockey for greatness, and that they must reverse their thinking; and then the meal is over (v. 27). To finish dinner that quickly, the *LMJN* has to jump over lots of material. From Matthew (with parallels in Mark and Luke) the list of eliminated material includes Jesus' pause in eating to announce that one of the group will betray him (26:21); the indirect identification of the betrayer (v. 23); a prophetic indication from Jesus that the Son of Man will be betrayed; a woe to the betrayer of the Son; and Judas' question whether he is the one, including Jesus' direct identification of him in answer to his question (v. 25). Also omitted is the entire institution and theology of the Eucharist (vv. 26–29 with parallels) and Luke's suggestion that the betrayal has been foretold and a woe on the betrayer (22:21–23). While the *LMJN* does show the disciples' debate about who is greatest, it rejects the application of status reversal to the Son of Man, who is to serve and give his life as a "ransom for many" (in Mark 10:45).[33]

Once the *LMJN* closes off the meal, with its rich theology and ritual in the Synoptics, it turns to a fragment in John to declare the supper over (13:2). But our author tiptoes over John's declaration that Jesus knows his time to leave this world has come, that his love for "his own" is over, that the devil has gotten Judas to betray him, that Jesus himself is from God and (knowing that the Father has given all things to him) is ready to "go to God" (13:1–4). These heavy theological ideas find no role in the *LMJN* but the foot washing account does. Jesus sermonizes on cleanness and uncleanness after the act that embarrasses the disciples. When Peter objects that he needs his whole body washed (v. 9), Jesus says they are all clean by the washing of the feet except for one, Judas (v. 10). In the next two verses (11–12) Jesus sits down and asks his disciples if they know what he has done for them. Jesus notes they call him Lord and Master, yet he washes their feet. Jesus says they are right to call him by these terms (v. 12) and that they must follow his example. These daring and atypical words from him have a point: to illustrate that the servant is not greater than the lord, nor is he that is sent

---

32. Jefferson, *Bible* (Beacon ed.), 127–28; folio 68—69:269, 271.
33. Jefferson, *Bible* (Beacon ed.), 128–29: folio 68—69:269, 271.

greater than he who sends him (v. 16). Here we find the reversal theme, but now a reversal with emphasis on humility: everyone, lord and servant both, must be humble, and all must be humble before God. Do these things, and be happy (v. 17).[34]

The *LMJN*'s use of John in a mainly synoptic story jumps over 13:18–20, a passage in which Jesus explains in good Johannine lilt that he is not speaking the above words on reversals and humility to everyone, only to those he has chosen (v. 18). And Jesus aims at the chosen "to fulfill the scripture" (possibly, Ps 41:9), though the one who eats bread with him will turn "his heel against me" (v. 18). The reference is to Judas, of course. Then Jesus delivers one of his introspective observations: that the one who receives one he has sent receives him also and so, the one who receives him receives him who sent him" (v. 20). But *such a prophetic and cozy relationship between Jesus and God does not fit the* LMJN's *plan for the end of Jesus*. We return to the *LMJN*'s account with vs. 21–35 the text omits vv. 27–30. Jesus announces that one of his disciples will betray him. He signals that the betrayer is Judas (v. 26), and then the author cuts away when Satan enters Judas and Jesus tells Judas to act quickly (v. 27). Our text uses the beginning of v. 31, Jesus going out of the room, but drops the rest of it and all of vs. 32–33: "[N]ow the Son of Man has been glorified, and God has been glorified in him. If God has been glorified in him, God will also glorify him in himself and will glorify him at once." Interestingly, the author of the *LMJN* wants nothing to do with John's theology of glory. He also rejects Jesus' introspective warning to "little children," that he will not be with them very long, and that his message to his disciples is what he has told the Jews already, namely, that where he goes, they cannot follow (v. 33).[35]

Rather, the *LMJN* heads to the famous new commandment, that the disciples should love one another, as Jesus has done (v. 34), and that by so doing they will be known as disciples (v. 36). Then the *LMJN* omits Simon Peter's discussion of where Jesus will go and whether Peter can follow. Jesus says no, not now. Peter then promises he will lay down his life, but Jesus proposes that he will soon deny him (v. 38). The *LMJN* leaves John for Matt 26, goes to Luke 22, and returns to Matt 26 to finish the jumpy chapter.

The reader wonders why at the end of Jesus' story the *LMJN* employs all four gospels in increasingly smaller blocks. In any case, in the first verses from Matt 26 our text saves Jesus' prediction (!) that all will be offended because of him this night, but removes the prediction from Zech 13:7 that some "I" will strike the shepherd and the sheep will scatter (26:31). It also

---

34. Jefferson, *Bible* (Beacon ed.), 130–31; folio 70:273.
35. Jefferson, *Bible* (Beacon ed.), 131; folio 71:275.

rejects Jesus' claim that he will be "raised up" and "will go before you to Galilee" (v. 32), predictions of the resurrection, it seems. Back to Peter, the next saved passage has him admitting that "all men shall be offended because of thee," yet he will not be offended (26:33). We next switch quickly to Luke 22:33–34, where Jesus says simply that he is ready for prison and death, and then warns Peter that he will deny him: another iteration of the denial theme.[36]

The rest of the chapter continues with a block from Matt 26:35–45. Peter and the disciples deny that they will deny Jesus (v. 35) and the gang heads to Gethsemane. We have the familiar story of Jesus praying while the disciples fall asleep, much to his irritation. Jesus is troubled and in sorrow. Knowing what is ahead of him, he tells his "Father," "Thy will be done" (v. 42) and lets the disciples sleep. After omitting Matthew's Jesus saying that the hour is at hand for the Son of Man to be betrayed into the hands of sinners, and after the arrival of the betrayer (half of vv. 45 and 46),[37] the *LMJN* author shifts to John 18:1–3. This is the account of Jesus going to the garden and of Judas' arrival with the police from the chief priests and the Pharisees.[38] Quickly, our author shifts back to Matt 26:48–50 where we hear of Judas's kiss and Jesus' "Friend, why are you here?" (v. 50). But immediately, our author takes us back to John, after omitting Matthew's account of the actual arrest (which includes Jesus' restoring an ear and his bragging that he could call in twelve legions of angels [vv. 26:51–52, 55–56, omitting vv. 53–54]). Jesus here muses that he must be arrested to fulfill the Scriptures; meanwhile the disciples flee. But the *LMJN* provides a different account from that of Matthew, one actually out of chronology, derived from John 18. Jesus asks whom the group (Judas and the police) seeks, and then Jesus identifies himself. A certain number of the group falls to the ground and Jesus dismisses them (vv. 6–8).[39]

We bounce back to Matthew's chronology with chapter 26 again for seven verses (50–56), according to the plot above, except that the *LMJN* omits Jesus' bragging about the angels and the two references to the fulfillment of Scriptures (vv. 54, 56). Then the *LMJN* inserts the bizarre interlude about the naked young man who flees the scene (Mark 14:52–53) and one verse from Matt 26:27, which brings us to Caiaphas's house. Following them with several verses from John 18, the *LMJN* traces Jesus and Peter to

36. Jefferson, *Bible* (Beacon ed.), 131–32; folio 71:275.

37. Another rare moment when the author takes away half of a verse to build his account. See Jefferson, *Bible* (Beacon ed.), 131–33; folio 71–72:275, 277.

38. We note that the priests and the Pharisees are effectively one unit as Jewish authorities in Jerusalem, both in John and in the *LMJN*.

39. Jefferson, *Bible* (Beacon ed.), 133; folio 72:277.

Caiaphas where the "damsel" who manages to prompt Peter to deny Jesus confronts him. The story is in place, except that the *LMJN* inverts vv. 17 and 18 and leaps over vv. 19–25: Jesus' intense defense of himself before Caiaphas where he explains that he has never kept his message in secret, his first beating, and the demand for testimony from him about his wrongs (v. 23). Surprisingly, next, the *LMJN* repeats Peter's denial and we wonder why (v. 27). We whip our heads back to Matt 26:75, one verse that shows Peter coming to grips with his denial. Even stranger, the *LMJN* turns to John 18:19–23 for Jesus' testimony that he has never taught in secrecy and wishes real testimony against him (compare the omitted version above).[40]

The author of the *LMJN* employs Mark 14 to get Jesus to the high priest's (v. 53). The council finds no capital crime (v. 55).[41] Some bear false witness against Jesus and repeat his promise to destroy and rebuild the temple (v. 58). The witnesses cannot agree and the high priest asks Jesus to respond. He refuses and the priest then asks him if he is the "Christ the Son of the Blessed," to which Jesus says, "If I tell you, ye will not believe" (Luke 22:67). Obviously, we have shifted to Luke 22 to hear more of the trial. In Luke, the priest then asks him if he is the Son of God; Jesus responds, "Ye say that I am" (v. 70). Once again, we shift, this time back to Mark 14. After Jesus' last comment, the chief priest explodes that he is a blasphemer and no more witnesses are required (vv. 63–64). The priests condemn Jesus. Some spit on him and jeer him for his prophecy (v. 65). Back in John 18, they take Jesus from Caiaphas's place to the hall of judgment to face Pilate, who thinks the Jews must judge Jesus according to Jewish law (v. 31). The Jews point out that they cannot deal with capital crimes, and Pilate then asks Jesus if he is the king of the Jews. Jesus evades the question. Pilate points out that he raises the question only because Jews have brought Jesus to him.

Pilate asks, "What hast thou done?" (v. 35).

Jesus then says his Kingdom is not of this world, and thus the priests do not have an issue with him (v. 36).

"Art thou a king then?"

Again, Jesus says that Pilate has said so, but more: "To this end was I born, and for this cause came I into the world, that I should bear witness unto the truth" (v. 37).

Pilate delivers his famous comeback: "What is truth?" (v. 38) and then tells the Jews he finds no fault in Jesus (v. 38).[42]

---

40. Again, we get suggestions that Jesus never keeps secrets. See Jefferson, *Bible* (Beacon ed.), 134–36; folio 73—75:279, 281, 283.

41. The *LMJN* omits a verse about Peter sitting in the courtyard (Mark 14:54).

42. Jefferson, *Bible* (Beacon ed.), 136–39; folio 75—76:283, 285.

FINAL AFFAIRS   103

In another rough transition, the author brings us back to Luke 23 for one verse about the anger of the Jews (v. 5) and one verse that brings up Pilate again to note the many Jewish accusations (Matt 27:13). Finally, we are back to Luke for a sizable block (23:6-16 from L1). Pilate learns that Jesus is from Galilee and decides to send him to Herod (v. 7); Herod is pleased to see Jesus finally and wants him to do a miracle (v. 8);[43] he questions Jesus but, again, Jesus says nothing. The priests and scribes accuse him and Herod's people mock him (v. 11). They put a robe on him and return him to Pilate. Again, Pilate says he can find no fault in him (v. 14), nor can Herod; therefore, Pilate plans to chastise and release him (v. 16).[44]

The story turns to the Barabbas account in Matt 27. The crowd demands that Barabbas be released and that Jesus should be crucified (v. 22). Then the text leaps over two powerful verses, 24-25, in which Pilate (again) confesses that he finds no guilt, washes his hands, and declares he is innocent of Jesus' blood (v. 24).[45] Indeed, Pilate puts the blood on the Jewish people and their children (v. 25). Pilate's struggle with conscience may be too much for the *LMJN*, and so the text returns to releasing Barabbas, scourging Jesus, and sending him to be crucified (v. 27). The soldiers gather, but the *LMJN* skips v. 28 where we learn that Jesus is stripped and robed in scarlet. Our text has him dressed as a would-be king and named as the King of the Jews (v. 29). He is beaten and mocked, disrobed and sent to the cross. In Matt 27:3-8, a passage relocated after nearly all of chapter 27 has been used,[46] the story shifts to Judas, who repents his crime and tries to return the thirty pieces of silver to the Jewish authorities (v. 3). He realizes he has betrayed "innocent blood," but the priests reject him. Judas throws the money in the temple and goes and hangs himself (v. 5) while the priests bury the "price of blood" in the field of blood (v. 8).[47]

The *LMJN* shifts the story to Luke 23:26-32 where we hear of Simon Cyrene helping Jesus carry the cross. Jesus comforts the wailing women of Jerusalem: "Weep for yourselves, and for your children" (v. 28). Then Jesus

---

43. Once again, the *LMJN* allows Jesus to be known as a wonder-worker even as it suppresses the miracle.

44. Jefferson, *Bible* (Beacon ed.), 139. *We note that it is the Roman and the mixed-race Herod who absolve Jesus, and by implication the* LMJN *blames the Jews for his execution.*

45. Within the larger theme of the absence of the Romans in Jesus' story, we note that Pilate protests his inability to find any guilt in Jesus, a theme clearly established in the synoptic gospels, especially in Luke.

46. One of the very few times the author of the *LMJN* scrambles the synoptic chronology.

47. Jefferson, *Bible* (Beacon ed.), 140-42; folio 78—79:289, 291.

speaks in an apocalyptic voice about the coming days in which the childless will be the fortunate ones, when people will beg for the mountains to crush them[48] (vv. 29–30). The narrator of Luke announces that two other "malefactors" will be executed with Jesus (v. 32) and a shift back to John 19:17–24 takes us to Golgotha where the crucifixion is reported without gruesome detail. Pilate orders a "King of the Jews" sign in three languages (vv. 19–20) against the protest of the chief priests (v. 21). The soldiers draw lots for Jesus' garments. A second shift takes us back to Matt 27:39–43 where we hear that passersby mock him by repeating his promise to destroy the temple and by pointing out his inability to save himself: after all, the Son of God should come down from the cross (v. 40). Even the Jewish authorities mock him: he saves others but not himself; if he comes down from the cross, they will believe in him (v. 42). "He trusted in God; let him deliver him now, if he will have him: for he said, I am the Son of God" (v. 43 KJV).[49]

The third shift in the crucifixion account returns us to the three verses of Luke 23:39–41. Here we have the story of the one malefactor who ridicules Jesus about saving himself, while the other rejects his view with a "Dost not thou fear God?" (v. 40 KJV) and claims Jesus has done no wrong (v. 41). The Luke passage includes Jesus forgiving "them," for they do not know what they are doing (v. 34). The fourth shift returns us to John 19:25–27 with the arrival of the women. Jesus gives over his mother to his beloved disciple (v. 26). Then, in the fifth shift, a selective use of Matt 27:46–56, we hear Jesus cry out, "My God. My God, why hast thou forsaken me?" (v. 46); we then hear the bystanders respond that he is calling for Elias and that Jesus is "yielding up the ghost" (v. 50 KJV). The women begin to minister to him (vv. 55–56), and the passage that the *LMJN* skips consists of vv. 51–54, from right after Jesus' death. It is the famous passage about the tearing of the temple curtain and the earthquake, about tombs opening and the dead rising, about the dead appearing to the living in Jerusalem, and about the watch centurion declaring, "Truly this was the Son of God" (vv. 52–54).[50]

The *LMJN*'s final word on the life and ministry of Jesus comes from John 19:31–42. The painful end to his story includes "the Jews" realizing that the dead Jesus cannot hang on the cross as the Sabbath arrives; they ask Pilate to order the soldiers to break Jesus' legs, but the soldiers realize he is dead already and they do not break them. One soldier does, however, throw a spear into his side (v. 34). We have a gap in the John account from v. 35 though v. 37. Here John claims that an eyewitness to the spearing has

---

48. The voice is not clear in the *LMJN*.
49. Jefferson, *Bible* (Beacon ed.), 142–44; folio 79—80:291, 293.
50. Jefferson, *Bible* (Beacon ed.), 144–45; folio 81—82:295, 297.

reported the account. All of these events happen to fulfill Scripture from the Passover instruction for the *seder* lamb. Exodus 12:46 reads, "None of his bones shall be broken" (v. 36). Then Joseph of Arimathea, a secret Jewish disciple of Jesus, appears and persuades Pilate to let him bury Jesus (v. 38). Nicodemus brings myrrh and aloe and the two of them take Jesus' body, wrap it in linen and spices in the Jewish custom, and bring it to a new tomb in a garden (vv. 39–41). They roll a great stone to the door of the tomb and leave (v. 42).[51]

Analysis: The Execution

When the *LMJN* gets to the death of Jesus, the gospel turns primarily to narration of the steps of the event; it requires less analysis than the teaching parts. We notice that *the account of the end of Jesus consistently allows more honors for Jesus than were permitted in the beginning of the text*, though we recognize that the author continues to remove lavish and theologically dense claims for Jesus. We wonder why. For instance, the account begins with the woman who anoints Jesus with expensive oil as an anointing before his burial (Mark 14:8). Allowing this passage in the gospel may be dramatic for the *LMJN* when we remember that the word "anoint" is the English translation of the Hebrew "messiah" and realize that Jesus predicts his own death. In this predictive sense, we realize that the author of the *LMJN* has presupposed that his much-emphasized conflict theme ends in Jesus' persecution and death. In so presupposing, he has internalized the after-the-fact predictions of Jesus' persecution and death from the synoptic traditions.[52] *In the canonical gospels there is virtually no surprise that Jesus will die, as there is no surprise in the* LMJN. *However, in the canonical gospels his inexorable march to death is largely a function of the will of God; but in the* LMJN *Jesus' movement toward death is the inexorable consequence of the hostility of the Jewish authorities to his wisdom, a very earthy causality.* Jesus is anointed to die, yes, but the *LMJN* puts a check on the enthusiasm to come by refusing to include Mark's comment that the anointing will be remembered worldwide (14:9).

In the same vein of honor but not over-the-top honor, *we find Jesus as "Master" who conducts a completely ritual-free final dinner* where the theme is, who is the greatest disciple. Jesus reminds the disciples that they are thinking like Gentiles and need to invert their values. The lesson is a familiar and good one, but the dinner contains no hint of Passover or Eucharist.

---

51. Jefferson, *Bible* (Beacon ed.), 146–47; folio 82:297.
52. Here the *LMJN* author seems to violate his own hostility to prophecy/fulfillment.

Interestingly, in a book determined to purge other people's prophetic moments, Jesus is accorded the privilege of prophecy at the end of his life: he predicts the betrayal and the denial. In fact, the *LMJN* even prevents the idea that Judas's betrayal has been predicted in Hebrew Scriptures.[53] Oddly, the *LMJN* allows a generic predictive interpretation of foot washing and of Judas's betrayal of Jesus as fulfilling Scriptures (John 13:18).[54] Therefore we see that *the* LMJN*'s Jesus can use prophecy in a modest way when it is forbidden for others and for the evangelists.* This allowance represents a development away from the early part of the text, where all prophecy is forbidden. *The* LMJN *allows Jesus to use prophetic passages about himself especially concerning moral points (e.g., the foot washing's lesson of humility).*

As we expect, the *LMJN* holds to *no fulsome atonement theory.* For instance, it purges "ransom" language (Mark 10:45); the intense, intimate Jesus-Father discussion on his time to go to the Father; and the intervention of the devil (John 13:1–4). There is no transfer of the glory of the Father to the Son, as in John. We have already seen that our author rejects the ritual participation in the eating of the body and the drinking of the blood of the martyred Jesus. Yet even as our author trims down the theological weight of Jesus' death, he *throws in a final performance deed: foot washing.* Of course, he does not want anything that looks like a sacrament here, but makes it a simple enactment of humility, where the Master does the task of the servant and everyone learns to be humble. The one who is humbled is the one who undergoes the reversal and who expects his people to understand the lesson and to follow in the performed reversal.

The last episodes before the execution are Jesus' attempts to get the disciples to recognize the seriousness of the impending death of the Sage. Jesus shoots down Peter's pledge that he will "lay down his life" for Jesus; Peter will deny him (Matt 26:26), and the disciples will be offended because of Jesus (v. 31). Because of the disciples' failure, Jesus grasps what will happen to him and relents to the Father's will. Is he still free? How does he know the future? Of course, the *LMJN*'s Jesus does not brag about the angels he can command, nor does he magically fix the ear of the slave, but he does have time for the final lesson: love one another, as I have loved you, the new commandment by which the disciples are to be known (John 13:34).

---

53. Exod 24:8, Jer 31:31, and Zech 9:11.

54. The *LMJN* is actually inconsistent in predicting Judas' betrayal. The author omits the prediction from Matt 26:23, while the use of John 13:18 points to a prophesied betrayal. Consequently, the former may be simply a choice to eliminate an entire block from Matthew, while the inclusion of prophetic prediction of Judas' betrayal is significant in John, because it violates the pattern of hostility to prophecy/fulfillment in the *LMJN*.

Seemingly, the author has saved this sermonic summary of the sage's message as a reminder to his wayward disciples. The commandment matches his Socratic defense of himself before Caiaphas and his demand for real testimony against him (John 18:23).

In the same context Jesus returns to one of the *LMJN*'s favorite themes: his denial that he ever teaches in secrecy (John 18:20). Indeed, the main steps in each episode of the trial sequence consist of dialectical revelations of the last things about Jesus. Of course, Jesus does not simply blurt out his identity. When the high priest cannot get him to confess to the destruction of the temple, the *LMJN*'s Jesus also refuses to answer whether he is the Christ, the Son of the Blessed, because if Jesus answered truthfully, he would not be believed (Mark 14:61). Almost immediately, the *LMJN* shifts to Luke 22 with another discussion before the priest: is Jesus the Son of God? Jesus responds like a teacher, "Ye say that I am" (v. 70).[55]

What are we to make of Jesus' dialectical sparring with the dreaded authorities? Previously we have noted that the *LMJN*'s account of the execution is a patchwork of selections, some very small, from all four gospels. Even Mark and John play a role. Such a mosaic implies that what gets into the *LMJN*'s gospel has serious value. When *the author of the* LMJN *selects particular aspects of the canonical death narrative to create a talking, teaching, dialectically charged death of the sage*, we know we are dealing with his core values. Perhaps we should capitalize "sage," since our author shows Jesus as the greatest *Sage, who is prepared to lay down his life for his wisdom*.[56] Jesus also evades Pilate's question "What hast thou done?" (John 18:35). The remarkable feature of the constructed death scene is that the *Sage, who keeps no secrets, uses secrecy effectively in his final teaching episodes to flummox the fools*. It is Jesus' *final reversal*: the enemy of secrets pulling out a secret in his last moments.

Interestingly, the Roman leader, Pilate, upon his exchange with Jesus on truth, is unable to find fault in Jesus. Naturally, the guy who has not participated in the grim debate with the Jewish authorities finds Jesus innocent. Indeed, the *dynamic of the gospel's conflict has nothing to do with*

---

55. All of these final touches suggest that the author is teasing us with a Jesus who is conscious of and deliberate about his status at the end of his life; we make this claim without slipping into a lavish christology of any kind. Whether this speculation is fair or not we probably will not know from the basis of the *LMJN*. But the teasing seems to stretch beyond the modest christological signals of the letters. In any case we probably can claim that *the author at the end of the* LMJN *is close to the position of Priestley that he rejected early in his life: that Jesus thinks he has a divine mission*. See Letter from Priestley, May 7, 1803 (Adams and Lester, *Extracts*, 342).

56. Again, one thinks of the comparison to Socrates so important to Jefferson's development and his debt to Bolingbroke.

the Romans. Of course, Jesus' final silence offends. Herod wants a miracle and thereby shows he does not have a clue about Jesus' actual identity. The crowds prefer an old criminal to Jesus. The Roman soldiers recognize the real status of Jesus, but in an inverted, macabre honoring of him as the real "King of the Jews." Even the priests hide Judas's blood money.

As Jesus heads to his cross, he concludes his teaching by comforting the women; he worries about the children and childlessness in an incredibly apocalyptic passage (Luke 23:28–30) which the *LMJN* allows. Perhaps we have a clue that for our author, *apocalyptic works well to express the catastrophic*. The Roman hero of the execution, Pilate, gets to perform the ultimate reversal toward which the entire gospel is directed: he gets to label the Sage dying on the cross as "King of the Jews" over the objections of, yes, the chief priests. *The reversal of wisdom and foolishness is complete, and it is the Roman prefect who undercuts the foolish Jewish authorities* (John 19:19–20) at the same time that they continue to mock Jesus on the cross (Matt 27:43). Both the crowds and the priests mock Jesus with phrases and titles of praise. Is the mockery simple irony, or do we have the last reversal set up by the *LMJN* author? Even on the cross Jesus continues to teach the two criminals, one of whom represents foolishness, and the other, the wisdom of Jesus. Jesus forgives both (Luke 23:34)! And with the same irony, virtually the last act of the death scene, the breaking of Jesus' legs, to kill him quickly, is not needed. The author of the *LMJN* allows a singular prophecy from Exod 12:46 to affirm that the seder lamb cannot have any of its bones broken. How ironic is that? The final, fulfilled prophecy hints that *the Sage who lays down his life is the paschal lamb. Thus, we see that the author of the* LMJN *is prepared to break many of his editorial rules in order to articulate the death of the great Sage.*

10

The Displacement of Jesus: A Cataphatic Account

In this chapter we gather the main themes of the immanent analysis we have just completed. That is, we set aside all the apophatic comments on aspects of Jesus not in the *LMJN* and focus only on what the text affirms. We call it a cataphatic summary, because it picks up on positive claims for Jesus without all the items that have been erased under the apophatic method. The task is not easy, since the materials left out are so intimately entwined in the items saved. We proceed under *the image of displacement*. The image, initially inspired by the way the *LMJN* relocates the temple event, becomes a metaphor to name the considerable transformation of the Jesus Sage in the *LMJN*. Displacement starts literally with a scrambling of the geography and chronology of the biblical Jesus particularly in the synoptic gospels. But it develops into *a metaphor for the complicated reorientation of the content of the biblical Jesus story in the* LMJN. Of course, there is irony to speak of a transformation of the story that proceeds only by quoting the founding stories of Jesus, and only the words of Jesus at that. But we know that a change of context reshapes meaning, and the disappearance of about 60 percent of the content of the biblical gospels is fruit-basket upset. Here we will not replay the analysis but simply identify and explain the large themes.

Foundational Displacement

Displacement is a moving from one place to another. The displacement of Jesus in the *LMJN* begins with a theory that Jesus does not come from Nazareth via Bethlehem. He does not come from the place of Christmas, from the Abrahamic and Davidic lineage, from prophecy fulfilled, not from the place of his relative John the Baptist and certainly not from the world of shepherds, Magi, angels, and the virginal conception. And while critical gospel scholars have no problem recognizing the mythic and sagaistic character of the origin stories, *the LMJN launches the story of Jesus in an atopic way.* With the exception of the story of the smart-aleck preteen who wows the rabbis in the temple with his prevenient wisdom, Jesus simply appears *from no place to throw a fit in the temple.* And as we have emphasized, the *LMJN*'s Jesus story emerges in conflict with his relationship to the leaders of the Jerusalem temple. It has nothing to do with Galilee and the Pharisees (who were quite capable of cooking up their own and different conflict with Jesus). So, we have a displacement of Jesus' ministry in the *LMJN* from which the entire story of Jesus never recovers. Jesus will battle with generic Jewish leaders up to the day of his death. And note, the physical displacement and confusion is not simply a geographical confusion but a symbol of a massive transformation of what Jesus is about: *the entire cause of his ministry is to fight with Jewish leaders over pressing, eternal moral issues.*

The *LMJN* takes us immediately to the foundational event of Jesus' ministry: *the temple fracas. Locating this event at the beginning of the ministry determines the course of the whole ministry.* For Jesus the money changers in the temple present a moral violation, not a violation of holiness, in which *leaders of the Jewish nation sell out the moral for profit.* The Jewish leaders, unnerved and threatened by Jesus' behavior, read the fracas as an affront to their position and begin immediately to plot his execution. Recall that the *LMJN* displaces the temple event according to the gospel of John against the pattern of the synoptic tradition wherein Jesus' one trip to Jerusalem brings an end to his life. Of course, Jesus is an observant Jew and in the *LMJN*'s vision his temple fit has nothing to do with observance of Torah. It becomes the primal explosion of Jesus' righteous anger in which he strikes against the Jewish guardians of the holy in Jerusalem, who have sold out the holiness of the temple for profit.

Displacement at the Launch of the Ministry

The early temple event disrupts the synoptic chronology and geography and, as a consequence, reshapes the entire ministry of Jesus. No longer is Jesus the Galilean peasant dominated by the coming of the Kingdom of God, who leads a campaign to redefine the identity of Israel in a time of colonialism. Or, if one prefers a more theological portrait, no longer is it the story of the preacher of the intensification of Torah, or of the suffering messiah, or of the world-class charismatic, or the incarnate Word. Jesus is no longer the disciple of John the Baptist, his relative, and his wisdom is not learned from the prophet but is a natural gift. That is, *the LMJN gives us a Jesus from nowhere*, unlike anything in the biblical gospels, even as it uses only words and events from the Jesuses of the gospel accounts! The displacement launches a fundamental rearrangement of the familiar synoptic narrative. Now Jesus emerges instantly as *a moral reformer of Second Temple Judaism who cannot hide his anger at the hypocrisy of the Jewish leaders*. The displaced gospel story becomes *a conflict story over the nature of the moral life*; it ends badly.

In order to pull off the displacement of the mission of Jesus, as we know, the *LMJN* collapses the Pharisees into generic Jewish leaders, and Jesus' encounters with these synagogue-Galilean, Pharisaic rabbis become a grand conflict with the Jerusalem Jewish authorities over his strike on the temple. Meanwhile, *the* LMJN's *Jesus focuses exclusively on a reformation of the Judaism ruled by evil leaders;* other possible missions drop aside as *he becomes a combatant with the leaders of Judaism*. Jesus is not busy with the lives of the people; with ritual purity; with holiness codes; or with a ministry to the blind, leprous, and otherwise marginalized, unclean Jews. There is no ministry of the coming of the Kingdom of God. The Romans play no serious role, and their colonial rule of the Jewish people is almost invisible. Indeed, *the* LMJN's *Jesus moves away from very things that make Judaism a* religion, as we moderns call it.

The new Jesus is atopic as a figure. His wisdom comes from nowhere, and when it flies into the face of the Jewish authorities, he instantly becomes a moral warrior against the Jews' wicked leadership. He needles them; he reverses things on them; he criticizes them, and exposes their foolishness; he traps them in their logic and leads them by parables to invert their values. After the first temple event the authorities immediately seek to set Jesus up to be killed, and eventually he begins to bait them in response. Meanwhile, he offers samples of the new righteousness that blow away both peasants and leaders in their unheard-of insight. He zips back and forth between Judea and Galilee with a teaching ministry like an itinerant Cynic; he is baptized—sort of—by John the Baptist; he assembles disciples. As we have seen, he formulates a comprehensive case against the Jewish authorities: they are hypocrites who say fine things but do not live by them. Actually, they come from a long line of leaders who persecute the prophets and sages.

Moral Displacement

Jesus' ethic consists of wisdom set against foolishness in the manner of the wisdom tradition of the Israelites, though in the case of Jesus the wisdom is radical wisdom. The threat is not simply foolishness but foolishness that masks deep and deathly wickedness on the part of the Jewish authorities. When Jesus uncovers their foolishness, he lets fly a woe-filled judgment on their behavior. The message of Jesus is heavy on judgment, but nonetheless the urgency of justice is not fanatical or legalistic. Sensibly, the demanding ethic of Jesus struggles both with justice and forgiveness. Justice cannot become mechanical or brutal, while forgiveness has some limits or it undermines justice. The demand of justice stretches beyond the tribal feud and can never turn into revenge. Justice, like love, extends beyond the obvious and easy objects and worries about those who are excluded, different, even enemies. Genuine forgiveness expects repeat offenders and offers them mercy over and over, but there *is a limit to forgiveness: where the forgiven will not be forgiven.* So, too, the ethic expects to *live up to the mercy of God, but not the perfection of God*, a standard that would actually turn rigor into fanaticism.

Though Jesus puts himself in the center of a reform that would clean Second Temple Judaism, he remains a remarkably modest and understated sage. He heightens moral expectations at times but moderates some extremes. Generally, *the LMJN's Jesus tends to soften words or actions that seem ascetic and fanatical in the Sermon on the Mount, while he ups the ante on words or actions measured by the mercy of God*. And typically, Jesus puts value on people who do rather than say the righteousness required and do it without ostentation. Jesus is obsessed with the quality of the fruit of the tree. *Both the softening and the intensification of the law in the Sermon ethic makes the Jewish and Mosaic character of the ethic rather muted*. His teaching meets opposition on the first pages of his ministry: Jesus is angry about the commercialization of the temple, and the Sadducees are angry with Jesus, who threatens their position and profits. *The primal conflict between Jesus and the Jewish authorities shapes the entire gospel.* No other themes of the biblical story matter.

Jesus becomes a skilled dialectician in the face of challenges; he becomes a moral exposer of the authorities' showy emptiness, of their greed and corruption. His ministry then consists of challenges posed to him by various Jewish leaders, and Jesus' responses, which include debates, exposés of hypocrisy, and reversals. Jesus becomes obsessed with the constant needling of the Jewish leaders and soon the conflict takes over his entire mission. He announces that the Jews will have to do better than their leaders, the Sadducees, the Pharisees, the scribes, and the lawyers. He emphasizes that they must become humble and renounce their obsession with wealth and position underneath their showy piety. Indeed, he reverses the privilege they enjoy and makes the marginalized people and the children the ones favored by God.

To begin with, Jesus is indifferent to the apocalyptic currents of Second Temple Judaism, and he aims his ministry at teaching the disciples first and the crowds next. The disciples are impressed with his moral vision. They spread rumors that he is a prophet and a wonder-worker. His disciples, however, prove to be disappointments and play little role in the ministry. As teacher, Jesus is the great revealer of the intense and demanding wisdom and the enemy of any religious secrets. His job is to shed moral light in plain, moralized parables and aphorisms. His teaching is demanding, rigorous, for the most part, but not so extreme that ordinary people are left out. It represents a reasonable vision of the highest righteousness, marked by *the model of the mercy of God*. It stretches common moral prohibitions to go after the *intentional heart of morality, to demand the purity of heart*. It is mindful of judgment and forgiveness but only so far as the two do not fall into legalism, on the one hand, or cheap grace, on the other.

Jesus' message comes packaged with little context and moves toward universal claims. The rationale for the universal rests on *his powerful critique of a tribal vision for the moral life*. He astonishes and offends with universal demands and his rhetorical gift. His most striking points criticize showy, instrumental, and superficial pieties. He has a sharp antenna for insincerity in the moral life, and he leads every story from an outward focus to the higher, inner morality. Ritual gives way to morality. Moral fakes are exposed. Moral surface gives way to depth. Jesus loves inversions of common thinking; he exposes foolishness with striking wisdom and becomes a Sage of unheard-of wisdom in the tradition of the radical sages of Hebrew Scripture. His moral base is that of Torah, to be sure, and he is an observant Jew who affirms Mosaic law. But sometimes he intensifies Mosaic law and suggests that there are times *when law and ritual and holiness get in the way of the moral*. Basically, he sees *need for moral urgency, and this need becomes more urgent as we move to the end of the story*. Jesus' great Sermon on the Mount sets out the urgency in rigor without establishing it as ascetical, fanatical, or cultishly irrational. The *LMJN*'s Jesus ethic of the Second Mile has a demanding tone but pitches to all people, not only to moral giants.

Once we get clear about Jesus' ministry, we watch Jesus sending out his disciples to continue his moral campaign for repentance, though they will be sheep among wolves out there in the Galilean villages. Persecution at the hands of authorities will be likely. In fact, the ministry goes badly, Jesus is rejected in his hometown, and "the Jews" seek to kill him. One important battleground Jesus opens up with his insistence that *evil comes from within one*; the critique contrasts with the showy and superficial attentions (e.g., handwashing) of the Pharisees. The disciples get distracted while Jesus suggests that God favors children, not adults, for their humble simplicity. We get one of the basic images: Jesus, full of forgiveness, is like a shepherd for lost sheep, wayward sheep. Indeed, *this shepherd will die for his sheep*. Still, Jesus limits forgiveness, not by setting a boundary on times forgiven, but by refusing forgiveness to those who will not forgive.

The middle of the gospel account engages *Jesus as a parabler who reveals his wisdom without any secrets:* the revealer's parables are the light of truth that comes from the very foundations of the world. The parables speak plainly and even the leaders recognize their meaning. They, however, like their secrets and hence they are angry with Jesus. The parables also confront the foolish with terrible wisdom; Jesus has nothing to hide and is confrontational and direct with fools. Roughly, *the chosen parables evoke personal-moral qualities and add allegorical meanings focused on the personal moral life rather than on cosmic meanings about the coming of the Kingdom of God*. The fact that Jesus hangs out with the wrong people and declares them acceptable to God turns Jewish anger into rage. Jesus seeks out the wrong people and invites them to beatitude and moral transformation. Part of his message effects a reversal of the high and the lowly.

Displaced Apocalyptic

The *LMJN*'s Jesus is skeptical of apocalyptic in the beginning of the gospel: perhaps it is too supernaturalistic, too "judgy," too tied to revenge. But by the end of his life, he begins to employ apocalyptic images, likely for their moral urgency and, perhaps, to locate *the passion of the Sage within a larger struggle for justice*. In between his two views the author sets out a series of confrontational accounts in which Jesus does something or says something that prompts an angry response from Jewish leaders. Early on, they track his moves after the temple event, and toward the end of the story Jesus starts to bait them with ideas and reactions that will set off their urge to kill him, already anchored in the temple event at the start of his ministry. When the authorities object to something, *Jesus is unsparing in his criticism*. The *LMJN* builds the plausibility for his execution through such episodes of confrontation. At each point, the Jewish leaders look worse—woe to them—and Jesus seems doomed. In fact, *the woe, a special condemnation from Luke, becomes the property of the whole record of Jesus' judgment on the immorality of the*

Jewish leadership. The woes bring judgment to the front in the narrative as it plays out as Jesus' wisdom against the deadly foolishness of the leaders.

Jesus says and does many things that offend the leaders. He begins a campaign *to reveal all the secrets of salvation and to confront the Jewish authorities with their gnostic secrets, secrets that protect their power and prestige.*[1] He hangs around with the disreputable and marginalized and thereby enacts the open tent of God toward all people. He even breaks with his family and hometown to enact his atopic ministry in an itinerant campaign that challenges the authorities. He trains his disciples in the politics of challenge.

In each confrontation Jesus sees the moral heart of the issue while the officials protect their territory, react superficially, and miss the moral crisis of the day, whatever that is. The moral crisis seems to be recognized in the way the leaders cannot recognize where God's mercy and beatitude shine. They look to the so-called better people, indeed to themselves, and cannot recognize the moral reversals with which Jesus hits them. The leaders can be judged for their superficiality, for ripping off the people, for their distractions and failure to understand the moral crises of the day, for their showy love of being onstage, for their history of killing God's good agents, and, interestingly, for their penchant to keep religious secrets.

In response, Jesus sets up *rhetorical situations and discussions with the leaders that aim to press them into moral transformation.* He uses parables, example stories, aphorisms, and dialectical debates all to get people to see first and then sample next a different way of being in the world. In these language forms the hearers have to confront something reviled or different and try it on with an application: Who is my neighbor? Who is the forgiven son? Who got a fair wage? Who was forgotten and who was found? *The stories are performative and aim to unmask fools and make them enter an alternative wisdom.* Of course, the foolish often resist and get all the angrier, and the resistance to Jesus grows into actual plans for his murder. The story of Jesus darkens and heads to its end.

Moral urgency morphs into an apocalyptic urgency, without the outlandish phenomena associated with Jewish apocalyptic. The gospel hints at the death of Jesus and the possibility of a Son of Man involved in a coming time of justice, who seems to be identified somehow with Jesus as we move to the end of the story. At times Jesus seems to use "Son of Man" as an indirect self-reference, and at other times he seems to identify himself with the Son of Man, who undergoes persecution. In any case, persecution is upon him and he tells the Parable of the Wicked Tenants (the Parable of the Murdered

---

1. Here we see the logic for *LMJN*'s rejection of the important messianic secrecy motif of Mark. *Secrets are under control of the elitist clergy class.*

"Beloved Son"). The apocalyptic heats up as the execution nears, and in a rare moment *Jesus prophesies his own death*. We cannot determine how literally he takes the apocalyptic and how much it is metamorphosed; however, we are clear that Jesus wants judgment but not with a cosmic catastrophe.

Displacement in the Execution

As Jesus moves toward the end of his story, the *LMJN* becomes more comfortable with calling him Son of Man or Christ/Messiah, if we do not think of an apocalyptic figure of the end of times. One senses that the permission to use these categories may pertain to the darkening of the story with the threat of persecution. And its use hints of a truce with the materials from the end of the gospels, which are so christologically dense that the *LMJN* may be unable to purge all the author might like to get rid of. Jesus "returns" to Jerusalem and cleans house on the temple *for a second time!* The gospel of John helps the author focus the blame on "the Jews," and the *LMJN*'s gospel hints that the *dying Shepherd will bring a wholeness to his followers like that of a healing*. He will be for them the Good Samaritan who pledges to provide whatever help they need. The sheep will continue his ministry of service, while the Jewish authorities will walk by on the other side of the road.

Embedded in the call to service is the great reversal of who is wise and who is foolish; Jesus' ministry enacts the plot of the reversal of the Parable of the Great Banquet and other such parables. The marginalized and the children understand the determinative questions from the good-Samaritan parable: Who is the true neighbor? Who acts as the hero? Who is the scoundrel? In fact, Jesus does not simply teach the reversal; *his parables enact them for the marginalized*. And of course, the scoundrels hear them loudly and clearly. *The parables perform the reversal.* The parables also mediate the rocky relationship between justice and mercy by allowing people to imagine a world in which the two are consonant. The Pharisees simply do not get it: they are the rich young rulers who balk at selling their property.

Soon Jesus and his company head to Jerusalem and their voyage is full of stops and starts. The Pharisees try to trap him; he has to prepare for Passover; he creates a stir that frightens the Jewish authorities, especially after his *second* attack on the temple. Jesus continues to astonish the crowds. He takes on the priests and elders, and in the Parable of the Two Sons he devastates the Jewish establishment by tracing its failure to follow the "Father's" will; he does the same with the Parable of the Vintner whose "well-beloved" son is killed. *Apparently, Jesus is talking of himself facing the hatred of the Jewish authorities.* He faces several final dialogues and challenges that set up his impending death: Jesus delivers the final eight woes on the authorities and increasingly evokes apocalyptic images. Likely, he uses the apocalyptic, not in its cosmic, end-of-the-world sense but as a way to show the power and tribulation of Pharisaic wickedness. He suggests the generation will not pass away "until all these things occur." We are not certain which things he means, but surely *he must be thinking of the death of the Shepherd for the sheep, a death he associates with the mysterious "Son of Man."* The verses speak of not knowing the day and the hour, presumably for the great event, but there will be judgment on that day.

The rest of the story follows with a selection of passages from all four gospels consisting of the steps the authorities take to get rid of Jesus. At this point *the reversal theme turns on the tension between those who believe in the beloved son and those who would put him to death.* Each group will be judged accordingly. The trip to Jesus' death is very familiar; it is put together from all four gospels. We have the betrayal, a final meal (without anything ritualized), and a trimming down of the considerable theologizing from the biblical gospels. The Master washes the disciples' feet in an identifiable act of humility and service. Peter promises to follow Jesus, but Jesus says he will deny him. They all go to the garden and Jesus does his praying and troubling; the disciples disappoint; Peter is crushed by his actions. Jesus is evasive before the high priests, and his avoiding the "Son of God" question causes an explosion; the priests condemn him. Jesus is then sent to Pilate, since the charge against him is a capital one. Significantly, *the Romans are nearly invisible in this story; Pilate can find no fault in Jesus. This action secures the notion the whole* LMJN *gospel blames the Jews, not just the Jewish leaders, for the death of the beloved son.*

Before Pilate again, the crowds prefer Barabbas be spared crucifixion, and Pilate asserts his innocence in Jesus' death. Jesus is on the cross; Judas hangs himself for the guilt against "innocent blood." The death scene is muted and abbreviated. Pilate gets the last word; he says the words that the Jewish authorities must have feared the most: Jesus is the "King of the Jews." All the while, the Jewish authorities mock the dying Jesus. The dying Jesus receives more honors in the *LMJN*'s account than in those of the gospels, though the text is cautious about dramatic christological claims. *Jesus becomes the only prophet in the* LMJN *gospel: he predicts his own death. And in the final reversal, Jesus, the enemy of secrets, keeps his own status a secret.* According to Torah, the *seder* lamb dies with its legs being broken: Jesus, who dies on the cross without his legs having to be broken, thereby mimics the paschal lamb. Surprisingly, the *LMJN* turns to the dreaded prophecy-fulfillment frame to speak of the Sage who lays down his life as the paschal lamb. How ironic is it that our author turns to Jesus' death as a fulfilment of biblical prophecy.

11

Methodological Considerations

General Remarks about Method

So far, the study of Jefferson's Jesus book has been dominated by text- and source-critical concerns. One main concern is to position the book in Jefferson's intellectual history. No one has studied these texts with the eyes of so-called higher criticism and with an attention to literary and theological themes. If the era of text-historical criticism is largely over,[1] scholars need to turn to the next interpretive task: what is the inherent meaning of the text itself, and what is the theological significance of Jefferson's Jesus book? Typically, scholars find great themes of Jefferson's thought confirmed indirectly in the picture of Jesus.[2] The confirming approach has some merit, to be sure. For instance, Dickenson W. Adams's argument finds in the *LMJN* Jefferson's route to a demythologized focus on the moral life.[3] And Charles Mabee finds Jefferson's anticlericalism enacted in his treatment of Jesus.[4] These and

---

1. Culminating perhaps in Adams and Lester's reconstruction of the lost *The Philosophy of Jesus*, in 1983 (Adams and Lester, *Extracts*).

2. See Sanford, *Religious*, 104: "This material [the Jesus books] supplements and supports the beliefs about Jesus Christ that are revealed by Jefferson's Letters. Jefferson, "Writings" (1984). *Against the above approach the notion here is that the LMJN cannot be studied only by choosing representative passages from the LMJN or from familiar themes known from his letters; we need a holistic and immanent approach.*

3. Adams and Lester, *Extracts*, 30.

4. Mabee, "Jefferson's Anti-Clerical Bible."

related approaches, seeking to discover consistency in Jefferson's thought between his letters and published pieces and his Jesus books, undoubtedly have merit, but *they fail to consider the inner logic of his actual Jesus portraits before they compare Jefferson's Jesus-book Jesus with his expressed opinions about religion.* Scholars need to develop a more exacting method to move the analysis beyond an impressionistic or generalized effort to confirm already-known ideas from the Jefferson corpus with findings in his *Syllabus* and *LMJN*, his Jesus books.

Finding a more sophisticated method is not easy, since, first, we are dealing with an editing and a condensing of four canonical portraits; since, second, we have to interpret what is not in the picture; and since, third, we are never quite sure whether what is in the picture comes with Jefferson's enthusiasm or simply with his lukewarm acceptance, with insufficient reason to exclude an item *(the principle of insufficient reason). The difficulty rests in the fact that Jefferson's Jesus is the sum of what he leaves in, in light of what he could have left in, had he not changed those canonical pictures. His Jesus actually is a combination of what he does and what he does not do*; obviously, not removing something sustains some value in the canonical pictures, but how much? Even more complex, what Jefferson leaves in often is reconfigured in new contexts and by being clustered with other texts.

In this book we offer an immanent interpretation of Thomas Jefferson's *LMJN,* one that proposes to uncover by a critical method the inner procedures of Jefferson's work. By "immanent" I mean to identify steps that obtain in the construction of the *LMJN,* independent of themes supposedly part of Jefferson's views on religion or of speculations about Jefferson's intentions for the work. *Indeed, the analysis brackets what we know about Jefferson's thinking. Therefore, at least in our first wave of interpretation, the question why the author of the* LMJN *does what he does will not be answered by inferring his motive from what he has hitherto written.* Rather, explanation will be limited to analyzing what happens and does not happen to the gospel texts and to generalizing from patterns of the author's selections and deletions. Only after we have completed the immanent exegesis of the *LMJN* will the results be related to insights from the Jefferson corpus.

Identifying Method in Jefferson's Procedure

Jefferson's method, of course, is an *apophatic* one; he takes away sizeable portions of the four gospel texts to create a cut-down gospel of what he regards to be the essence of the message of Jesus of Nazareth. It involves taking away content and meaning and then recontextualizing the saved materials in a new framing.[5] Because the apophatic approach is so central to the meaning making of the *LMJN* as well as the content and the structure, we cannot simply attend to the cataphatic content, that is, to the positive list of things Jefferson thinks are essential for understanding the figure of Jesus. *Jefferson actually re-creates what he takes to be the real Jesus and disposes of the other material. Why he believes the four gospels need to be essentialized we do not know from the work itself, and we will not speculate on the matter at this point. We also do not know why he thinks the real, better Jesus comes encased in materials that must be rejected. Nor do we know from the text itself why he recasts the saved materials.* Jefferson simply cuts up his Bibles privately, and the only clue concerning the how of the project we get is by tracing the immanent patterns of the editing. *The first moment of method involves listening carefully to the signals immanent in the text itself.* In this effort we do not proceed with a heavy methodological apparatus but a simpler watch-and-see approach.

Harmonizing

The *LMJN* presupposes that its author understands that the texts of the four canonical gospels are different versions of the same story that can be unified into a single, woven account. *The assumption is that the four can be unified and harmonized in the style of older harmonies of the gospel.*[6] The author

---

5. See the attractive characterization of our author's methods in Manseau, *Jefferson Bible*, 6–8. Manseau's analysis speaks of his hermeneutic as an "archaeological excavation" in which the author digs into the gospels to correct the past mistakes in the transmission of Jesus' message and to unearth the genuine nuggets. Thereafter, he creates a "collage" that ignores the original contexts and "remixes" the preferred content, recognized intuitively as genuine by the author of the *LMJN*. The archaeological approach to texts, of course, is typical of the Enlightenment. Manseau himself continues that hermeneutic as he proceeds to excavate the *LMJN*'s excavation.

6. Sanford aptly notices two aspects of our author's method in gospel research: first, his approach has been inspired by Charles Thomson's and Joseph Priestley's prior works to harmonize the main moments of the four gospels, an approach that goes back to Tatian's *Diatessaron* from the second century CE. Second, our author does not opt to construct a parallel construction of gospel texts that would illumine the differences among the evangelists' accounts. This approach, constructing parallel columns of each gospel's version of an episode, was pioneered by German source and redaction criticism and became the most important direction for gospel criticism. Interestingly, however, Jefferson was on the right trail in the history of Jesus research in that he recognized he had to separate the genuine Jesus from the accrued Jesus. But Jefferson chose the "wrong" path, so to speak, since his harmonizing method did not allow him to recognize the differences among the gospel accounts. He flattened the four into a single account in his effort to find the genuine Jesus; he led with his criteria for what is genuine without knowing about the source and redaction work that would be done first, before

reads the four texts in a flat, even eternalizing, manner without distinctions among the four messages and their contexts, their eras or their provenance; the four are simply candidates for the one harmonized story of Jesus.[7]

In terms of modern gospel criticism, the author does not distinguish John from the synoptic tradition and, of course, knows nothing of Q, Thomas, and other noncanonical sources. He does not have the advantages of the redaction critic, who can see that the four evangelists have different provenance, different themes, and different emphases in the way they spin the Jesus saga. He has no form-critical sense for the layers of meaning and use in a particular passage or of the reception history of Jesus material woven into the top layer. Rather, *the author conducts his editing as if the four sources are coequal pictures to be unified*. Each gospel offers a flatness of meaning from which he makes his choices. He never articulates their difference or why he is attracted to Matthew chiefly and uses Luke as a supplement to Matthew, why he so often ignores Mark, and why he commonly uses John at major turning points of the story. The four are all the same fodder for his editing task. Remarkably, the author succeeds in creating a more seamless story than some of the famous harmonies of the past do, simply by removing anything that does not fit his conception of Jesus, by patching a rough spot with a quote from another gospel, or by bringing on a transition from another source.[8]

Recontextualizing

When the author excludes substantial segments of the gospels but saves other texts, he easily removes the saved material from the narrative and literary context of a particular gospel. While he may not understand the historical, literary, and narrative contexts as we do today, nonetheless he does *recontexualize* the materials he saves: he jumbles, if not destroys, the narrative shape of the gospels; he flattens the historical references in them; he ignores the literary features; he vaults over time and place markers. Then he relocates what he saves into his own woven narrative and ethical context.

---

the what-is-genuine discussion begins among critics. So, Jefferson is on the cusp of modern gospel criticism (Sanford, *Religious Life*, 109).

7. Soon we will be able to introduce corroborative evidence in the Jefferson correspondence that points to his theory that priests have corrupted the original gospel message and story. But for now, we will bracket that explanation. We note that Jefferson does recognize some of the plurality of gospel accounts, yet he does not have a way to appreciate the plural visions of Jesus but only has his corruption theory to explain the differences among the gospels.

8. As Holowchak notes (Holowchak, *Bible*, 105).

If we believe that contexts shape meaning, then *the author has recast gospel materials independently of the context of the texts and has created new meaning*. He does so even as he preserves, say, 30 or 40 percent of the four gospels in pericopes somewhat related to passages in their original setting. Thus, *when Jefferson claims to be simply reporting concisely the real Jesus' message, he is not owning up to his actual new creation, that of a dramatically new gospel*, however much there are thematic continuities between his gospel and aspects of the canonical gospels.

Roughly, the author follows the synoptic narrative sequence from the beginnings of Jesus' ministry to his death. Roughly, also, he reassembles sequences of materials within a particular gospel; consequently, his recontextualizing is not comprehensively radical, since it follows the pattern for a gospel established by Mark. When some think of the *LMJN* as a synopsis of moral wisdom, they miss *the extent to which the author reconfigures and emplots the moral wisdom*. Think of how often we have seen Jefferson rescue some moral nugget from its relationship to a wonder that he suppresses. Think of his confusion over the audience for the centerpiece of Jesus' wisdom, the Sermon on the Mount. Think of his jumbled attitude toward the apocalyptic. It is simply not the case that our author is little more than a craftsman-editor. *He delivers a content-rich transformation of the canonical gospels*. His gospel is not without narrative, progressing toward a basic plot: it roughly follows Mark's invention of the gospel genre, but it is hardly the disembodied voice of the eternal moralist. Rather, it is *a displacement of the biblical stories into the particularity of a time and a place: Jefferson's time and place*.

The new context starts and ends in Jerusalem over an undetermined amount of time, while the synoptic accounts begin in Galilee. Remarkably, the author launches the ministry of Jesus by the housecleaning of the temple and surprisingly brings the ministry to an end with a second temple fracas! The latter one brings his death. *The dislocation poses a temple-to-temple story, a construction only in Jefferson, who combines John's placement of the event with its placement in the synoptic accounts*. The frame gets filled with much of the moral wisdom that the gospels have to offer, but not quite in a "listy" way. The *LMJN* focuses primarily on Jesus' sayings in their many forms. It cleans up redundant items, items that offend the moral life, ones that are inscrutable. In the midst of the moral cleanup the author saves as much context, time, and place as possible according to his standards and intentions. For all the disruption of the gospel accounts, *the author is conservative in that he saves text until he runs into materials that he dislikes or finds redundant*. He is also surprisingly conservative in that he does not remake the Heilsgeschichte *of Mark's creation: the plot that moves from its beginnings through conflict and powerful revelation to the persecution and death of the hero.* The things excised are usually predictable and include inoffensive, additional blocks removed as repetitions of things already considered. Jefferson sticks with a gospel progression until the topic of the gospel changes, until he runs into something that offends him, or until he finds a thematic way to add to the episode from another gospel. We can tell from the smooth, even graceful, way he moves from one gospel to another that he is often reading all the accounts of a particular topic to make his selections.

Clustering

One of the principal ways in which the author recontextualizes the gospel tradition is by clustering tests according to similar themes and related materials.[9] If one forgets the material that the author excises, the material flows fairly well according to his gospel reading for the day. The clusters often have an internal coherence, paralleling the original gospel order. Again, Jefferson may refocus the order when the gospel shifts or when something offensive to him emerges in the gospel. The unified story unfolds without too much repetition until the last third of the whole work, where he seems to discover materials in Luke, Mark, and John that he has missed. Even then, he saves what he regards as the good stuff and puts the collection of leftovers in a cluster of chapters.

Narrative Faithfulness

Despite the author's comprehensive recontextualizing of the gospels, the ghost of the basic narrative (the synoptic account constructed by Mark) shapes the new gospel. The new gospel moves from the emergence of the precocious sage who can duel with the rabbis at age twelve to a life of remarkable teaching and acts that raise hostilities and controversies, on up to his moving, martyr's death. Thus, *the reconstruction retains the* heilsgeschichtlich *shape of the canonical gospels, if in a somewhat submerged form.* The new gospel, thus, promises salvation, but the recontextualizing is not quite a de-narrativizing of the gospel. It may be a softening of the synoptic narrative but does not obliterate the saving-historical portrait of the Jesus figure. What changes is the aim of the ministry and passion of Jesus.[10]

    9. See the next point: the reclustering happens within a relative honoring of the shape of the gospels' narrative story.

    10. The conservative tendency of this radical book has been recognized in Bryan, "Reauthorizing," 22. Jefferson's Jesus wants to save the real Jesus from corruption at the

Selection among Redundant Texts

This study pursues whether our author favors one or more gospels over the others and thus selects accounts of a familiar text from one or more gospels where redundancy is evident. Does he have a favorite gospel? We then face the more nuanced concern, whether our author chooses to include particular texts from a gospel for some reason. Is there a pattern to his inclusions, one that may reveal why the author prefers one evangelist's account or why he consistently uses one evangelist's version according to some recognizable theme? Possibly, under the conditions of redundancy, when the author includes one account and leaves behind two or three similar accounts, we have either a general preference or perhaps an ease in using one particular gospel, or we have an explicit decision of preference for the shape or values of one gospel's version. More simply, the author decides to trim redundancies.

We have already indicated that the author uses Matthew as his framing account. We do not know why he prefers Matthew; he may simply go with the gospel that leads the New Testament, as indeed the church has done in most of its history. Perhaps Matthew is his favorite as the gospel because of the Sermon on the Mount. Clearly, Matthew has a right of priority, because his material on a topic is more likely to be included than what is in the other gospels. Obviously, he does not know of the chronological primacy of Mark as the inventor of the gospel genre and of the narrative frame of the synoptic story. Matthew carries the story (without the Christmas story) through the Sermon on the Mount, arguably the showpiece of the *LMJN*'s account of Jesus. He hardly drops a word from his quoting of the complete Matt 5–7. But Matthew's gospel of the higher righteousness demanded by Jesus fascinates him throughout the sequences of Jesus' ministry in the synoptic tradition. He likes Matthew's injunctions of high demand and his long parables, and lets Matthew and John lead the passion story. The reader senses that Matthew's ethic of the higher righteousness inspires the *LMJN*. One thing more: we must mention that Matthew emphasizes the conflict with the Pharisees, and, it turns out, the *LMJN* author makes Jesus' conflict with Jewish authorities his major theme. So, there are good reasons why Matthew is the leader into our author's Jesus.

Mark gets comparatively little attention. One wonders why. It is the shortest and, perhaps, the least polished of the gospels. Why does the author land lightly on Mark? Perhaps it is that Mark emphasizes so powerfully that Jesus is an exorcist that scares him away. Interestingly, Jesus' acts and reputation as a first-class exorcist dominate the account of Mark. If anything, our

---

hands of his followers and the priests.

author dislikes the exorcisms more than the healings, for whatever reason. On a couple of occasions, the author of the *LMJN* speaks of Jesus as a healer (even if he banishes accounts of actual healing acts), *but he never mentions anything related to the exorcisms.* In addition, Mark's use of Jesus' exorcisms places them squarely in the apocalyptic scenario of the coming of the Kingdom of God. Presumably, sending the demons packing enacts an anticipation of the Kingdom. When we see exorcisms and apocalypticism woven together in Mark's account, we understand why our author holds his nose.

Perhaps the fact that Mark is the gospel most dominated by the messianic secret confirms that Mark is the least interesting gospel for the *LMJN*. We know that the secrecy motif aims at the disciples first and the ordinary people next. Oddly, it has little to do with the conflict with Jewish authorities; indeed, if Jesus were to keep his mission a secret, the *LMJN* author could not sustain his theory that the gospel is about Jesus' fight with Jewish authorities. Jewish leaders would not have known of Jesus' danger, were it covered in secrets. As a matter of fact, since the *LMJN* author follows the gospel of John in putting Jesus' last event (the temple fracas) first in the ministry, there is no secret for him to keep about Jesus, and the Jewish authorities would immediately know he is a danger and that he must be killed (as John's account has it). Thus, *the assumption here is that the author dislikes the messianic secret and finds it illogical in his retelling of Jesus' story. Additionally, we see no interest in Mark's theory that parables mean to hide Jesus' meaning as part of the whole construction of the messianic secret.* Thus, Mark seems to get little attention. We should note that the *LMJN* shows no sense that Mark is chronologically the first gospel, that Mark creates the narrative plot of Jesus' ministry, and that Matthew and Luke depend on it for framing the narrative.

The reader senses that Jefferson gets to Luke late in his editorial process. He uses a lot of Luke, especially after the Sermon on the Mount and certainly mines Luke's Sermon on the Plain for every drop of moral insight. Clearly, he looks for good materials that add to Matthew's account. He loves the Parable of the Good Samaritan, and he highlights what is missing in Matthew's Sermon, the woes on the rich. If we put the failed Jewish leaders of the "Good Samaritan" parable next to the woes on the greedy rich, we sense that Jefferson shares something of Luke's moral sense that Jesus' critique aims rightly against the rich and the powerful. *With Luke's help, Jefferson makes the rich and the powerful the main target of Jesus' anger.*

We have already mentioned that the *LMJN* begins Jesus public ministry with the temple event from John, the overturning of the money changers' tables. Here is our clue that connects moneymaking and money people with the religious establishment. *For our author, the temple event does not symbolize the eventual fall of the temple, or more outlandishly, hint about the coming of the Kingdom of God. No, the event is about filthy lucre, and it forecasts the failed moral vision of the Jewish leaders.* But modern gospel scholars note that the first synoptic account of the temple event (from Mark's gospel) happens only at the *end of Jesus' ministry*, after he makes his first visit to Jerusalem. Indeed, Jesus historians routinely see the temple event as the last event of his ministry and the one that brought him to his death by the Romans. Unknowingly, the author misses this construction and puts the event at the beginning where the event is entirely an insult to the right and powerful people of Judaism. And immediately the scribes and priests of the temple decide to execute him. *While the plot of conflict with Jewish authorities is a genuine theme of the gospels, Jefferson makes it the dominant theme of Jesus' ministry and frontloads it into leading the gospel.*

Since John is not a gospel with lots of moral wisdom but rather is full of seven dramatic wonders and attached transcendental meditations by Jesus, there is little in it that advances Jefferson's project, once he has raided and displaced the temple fracas to the beginning of the epic. However, Jefferson dives into the passion according to John, and on the way to the end, those episodes illustrate the major theme of conflict with Jewish authorities.

Meta-Rules Governing the Analysis

This immanent study of the *LMJN* proceeds by bracketing certain methodological issues. It is now time to return to these, since it is not possible to proceed with a *tabula rasa* mindset. Of course, as an author I knew things about Jefferson, and I knew quite a bit about his views of religion before I began this work. And early on, I came to learn about the provenance of "Jefferson's Bible," as it has come to be studied. I cannot pretend that this reading of the text is simply a blank-slate analysis of it. I knew much and started to work with hunches, not so much about its contents, but about an appropriate approach to the text. Indeed, my growing sense was that the *LMJN* needed an immanent analysis. I realized that a bracketed reading, setting aside what scholars know about Jefferson and about Jefferson on religion, say, could not be strictly and nakedly immanent; the reading would have to be an informed, dialectical exercise.

Up front, my analysis began with the observation that the *LMJN* is an inherently difficult text to interpret. Its difficulty rests in the strange character of Jefferson's writing of it; we recall that Jefferson keeps his views of religion quite private. In addition, we know that he likely viewed his project with Jesus and the gospels to be for private meditative purposes; we know for certain he did not publish the work publicly.[11] Then, with a modest amount of study, we face the odd, apophatic character of the project, since Jefferson takes away materials from four sources to construct his book. *The book requires an approach that identifies and appreciates what Jefferson is not saying.* Of course, if readers come to the text of the *LMJN* with no particular knowledge of the Jesus saga, of the gospel sources, the oddities of the book will not strike them so powerfully; the text appears like other books of favorite quotations of famous humans. It reads like a Jesus "commonplace," as educated people called the genre in the late 1700s, a gathering of fine quotes of a respected author.[12] But if one comes to the text with some knowledge of the gospel texts, of gospel history, and of the narrative aspects of the gospels, of how they work, then the texts have meaning in the negative, in the removing of things expected. Of course, we learn that the best hermeneutic aims to let the text speak for itself.[13] We readers ought to go with what is in the text itself and not produce an interpretation that worries about what is missing, what could have been there, what has been there once in the biblical texts. So, *an immanent reading is at cross-purposes with itself,* especially if one knows something about gospel criticism. Here the interpreter has to make a meta-methodological decision whether the things left out matter to one's interpretation: ironically, there is nothing immanent about that decision.

Meta-Rule No. 1: This study of the LMJN *proceeds with an approach that sets aside Jefferson's known ideas, particularly on religion, on the gospels, and on the figure of Jesus.* Such knowledge can be employed only upon the completion of the immanent analysis of the text.

---

11. Though at one point he would finally allow it to be printed in Europe without his name.

12. See Jefferson, *Literary Commonplace.*

13. And while the general hermeneutical principles shall be that we ought to let the text speak for itself without imposing meta-meanings on it, we know that this rule is a caution against manipulation of the text's meaning. Further, we know that good interpretation does not happen without an interpreter's presence within the hermeneutical circle. Jefferson aims his method to discover the real Jesus. We can hope he finds the real Jesus, and modern scholarship can help him in his dated efforts. But the interpretive problem he would have to face is what and how a genuine item can have meaning. *He seems to assume that once he has discovered the genuine, its meaning is self-evident. At this point Jefferson is quite naïve.* Consider obvious issues such as the ones he would have to answer in items of the genuine Sermon on the Mount. What are the parameters of the enemies in the love-your-enemy logion? How do we define "hunger" in the Beatitudes? Who is my neighbor? How do we live as eunuchs or as naked when others are without clothes? None of these is transparent; these and other issues would require a next step in the interpretive process.

Meta-Rule No. 2: This study of the LMJN proceeds as an immanent exegesis with attention to an author's deletions, inclusions, combinations, and reframing of the materials of the four gospels of the New Testament.

While the above rules do not flow from an immanent exegesis, they have warrants. Recall that the book is an odd one, composed using a cut-and-paste method. Recall that Jefferson hides his views. Then add the fact that Jefferson discloses his frank views on religion only to a few confidantes in a set of letters that are the primary texts for Jefferson's personal religious views. At this point the interpreter could follow the standard pattern by which scholars have found meaning in the *LMJN*, by applying the ideas of a few letters to its interpretation. But the themes of the letters can filter and even dominate what the researcher finds in the Jesus book. There are two difficulties in this approach.

(1) Such a hermeneutic can apply only to large-framed themes of the text. Perhaps it can determine that Jefferson's modern sensibilities allow him to discard the wonders of the gospel accounts; perhaps it can determine that Jefferson sees the God of Jesus within the family of deist God conceptions. But this approach, applying the themes of the letters to the text, is less helpful in determining the values involved in the *details* of Jefferson's method. For instance, why does he prefer one gospel account of a story over another one? Why does Jefferson allow more supernatualistic-seeming pericopes as the narrative moves toward the passion story, or why does he allow Jesus to be a prophet at the end of the story after eliminating virtually every hint of prophecy/fulfillment early in the story? Moreover, the hermeneutic cannot illumine all the microdecisions of the editor's cut, since the letters treat only large-stroke judgments. Of course, we can guess at Jefferson's values and decisions by applying this or that insight from the letters; we can guess what Jefferson really means about Jesus according to our knowledge of Jefferson and of Jefferson's views of religious topics as reconstructed from the public record. But guessing a writer's editorial moves from the reconstruction of the intentions articulated in letters, then applying inferred intentions to a judgment about his psyche, and finally extending the psyche and the intentions to particular episodes in the text, well, that is a whole load of speculation! What values apply? When is Jefferson being anti-miracle and when is he anti-Judaic? How would we guess why Jefferson warms up to apocalyptic? How would we unravel what titles he would settle on for the figure of Jesus? Therefore, *interpreting the LMJN through the letters is always speculative*, but more importantly, it cannot illumine the minute editorial decisions Jefferson makes. That is, it is rather clumsy and inexact in answering many of the most crucial issues posed by the text.

(2) The standard approach to the interpretation of the *LMJN* does not allow the text to present itself with any independence from the reconstructed speculations of the interpreter's Jefferson. The typical method restricts the voice of the text. For instance, filtering that voice through the applied ideas of the letters deemphasizes what in the *LMJN* does not quite fit those ideas. Or consider how we are to know whether the editor begins to think differently or more concretely about the message of Jesus in his exegesis than in his abstract and early letters to his coterie? Therefore, the method to interpret the *LMJN* through the public ideas, or even the semipublic letters, of Jefferson on religion has limits. Certainly it should not lead the interpretation of Jefferson's Jesus book.

In the above analysis we proceeded by bracketing knowledge of Jefferson. We do not even refer to Jefferson, nor do we solve exegetical difficulties by applying the known themes from the Jefferson corpus. Rather, we proceed with a studied blindness to Jefferson and his expressed themes. Of course, as we chip our way through the "author's" selections, we do find some confirmation of the themes we have bracketed: Jefferson does indeed drop virtually every sign and wonder in the four gospels. But he does so many other things for which we do not have a script from the Jefferson corpus. Why, for instance, does he allow a hubbub about the very exorcisms and healings which he bans from his account? We have to account for these tensions, and *the only way to uncover the values and emphases operative in the text is to discover the facts of his selections, then his de-selections, and then the patterns of his editorial moves*. The interpreter can build up analogies from similar selections to related clusters. The omitted becomes a negative confirmation of fact and pattern; all three become the clues to values central to Jefferson's Jesus.

(3) We have to consider the object of our analysis. Because of the peculiar character of the text, the object of our study is surprisingly complex. Of course, on a simple level the object of the portrait of Jesus is a gathering of what emerges on the pages of the *LMJN*. *"Jesus" is the gathering of episodes included in Jefferson's text; Jesus is what is pasted onto the folio sheets.* He is a talker and an ethicist; he gets into immediate trouble with Jewish authorities who object to his radical ideas and eventually dispose of him. Unfortunately, a Jesus gathered from the included episodes is a partially unsuccessful picture of Jefferson's Jesus. The point is not that Jefferson's Jesus does not match any biblical Jesus; rather, it is that *Jefferson's assembled Jesus presupposes the Jesuses of the New Testament gospels, and that Jefferson's constructive editorial work alters the Jesuses of the gospels and does not resemble any one of them.* That is, a good idea or a saved episode does not mean what it means in the gospels, when it is stripped out of the context of the gospel. What is it to love

one's enemies unless we know to whom the injunction is addressed? Consequently, Jefferson's Jesus is not simply the assembled images and values of chosen pericopes taken out of the New Testament. Indeed, *Jefferson's Jesus depends on the Jesuses on the floor of the cutting room*; the inner logic of the presentation presupposes elements of the gospels' Jesus. For instance, we note that Jefferson shapes his Jesus story according to the narrative pattern of Mark, the original gospel, but he primarily follows Matthew's version of Mark's narrative pattern. He makes the story move toward the passion story. We note that Jefferson changes the aim of picturing Jesus, according to the way that the gospel of John wanders away from the time and place of the synoptic accounts. In some sense, then, *Jefferson's Jesus is the sum of what he leaves in, in light of what he could have left in, had he not changed those canonical pictures. His Jesus actually is a combination of what he selects and what he lets fall to the editing floor.* Jesus the great Sage is not simply a sage but a sage so far as he is not a wonder-worker. A Jesus parable cannot have the same meaning when it is stripped of its location in the coming of the Kingdom of God.

Therefore, we must formulate *Meta-Rule No. 3 for research on Jefferson's Jesus: that what is in the LMJN's picture must be read in relationship to what is not there.* More specifically, we must enact the above meta-rule by paying attention to the locales where the difference between Jefferson's selected Jesus from that of the Bible shows up.

First, we must *track how Jefferson contextualizes what he saves from the biblical Jesuses in relation to the received contexts of the canonical gospels*. Do Jefferson's selections strip an episode from its context to recontextualize it in a new plot? For instance, we note that so often Jefferson takes episodes and sayings out of their apocalyptic settings; by purging the apocalyptic from the Jesus saga, Jefferson creates a new meaning for the episode. Second, we must trace how *Jefferson's selections are led by redactive tendencies in the particular gospels*. Undoubtedly, Jefferson is not aware of the important differences between the synoptic gospels and John. Nonetheless, his choices shape his meaning. For instance, his basic source is Matthew's account, and, in so favoring Matthew, he presupposes Mark's invention of the synoptic narrative. He norms Jesus' ethics from Matthew's Sermon, mostly absent from the other three gospels. And Jefferson takes the Sermon mostly stripped from its midrashic conversation with Torah and its apocalyptic frame. Also, Jefferson's use of John in significant moments transforms the message and ministry of Jesus, as we have seen. That is, Jefferson's use of John's account frontloads the temple event to the beginning of Jesus' ministry, thereby displaces the time and locale of it, and turns the main theme of his ministry into one of conflict with Jewish authorities. It is not a ministry devoted to the coming of the Kingdom of God, as most scholars think, or of the effort to reform Judaism.[14] Even though Jefferson basically follows the synoptic account from Matthew through Luke (and Mark, to a lesser degree), his use of John gives Jefferson the foundation for his construction of Jesus, the great crusader against Jewish authorities.

That we value the apophatic in the construction of a Jesus picture means that we have approached the immanent exegesis without heavy-duty application of method and analytical categories. On the one hand, we do not want to have a finished method and theory about the meaning of the text before we have examined it immanently. Yet we cannot pretend we know nothing about text but what we see in front of us. Admittedly, we work with a dialectic between a bracketed blinder and some experience in Jefferson studies. But in so doing, we do not apply a heavy interpretive grid on the actual text until after we see where it goes. *We know our bracketing works because we have been surprised by the way that Jefferson remakes the gospel account, and our surprise does not rest on the obvious ways his Jesus differs from Jesuses of the biblical gospels; rather our surprise stems from the way our author stretches elements of the canonical gospels so that insights from the Jefferson corpus become only relatively helpful in understanding the LMJN text.*

Immanent Rules of Jefferson's Jesus

Once we have sketched our meta-approach to the entire analysis, we turn to identifying the immanent patterns that govern as rules in Jefferson's detailed selections in their exclusions, inclusions, clustering, and rearranging of the gospel materials. *Our first rule: things missing from the four gospels often tell us much about the shape of Jefferson's Jesus.* When we see that Jefferson eliminates the wonders of Jesus or the prophecy/fulfillment frame, we learn much about Jefferson's conception of Jesus. When we notice that he consistently deletes elements of the supernatural, suddenly we have before us a major interpretive issue. The discovery of a consistent pattern evokes the criterion Jesus scholars have used for decades: the use of *multiple attestation* to secure likely genuine Jesus sayings and actions within the synoptic gospels. For instance, in gospel research, scholars notice that the theme of the coming of the Kingdom of God is pervasive in so many of the logia and episodes in the ministry of Jesus. Therefore, scholars are assured they are dealing with evidence closest to the historical Jesus. *In the instance of Jefferson's Jesus we can use multiple attestation as a modest help in discovering*

---

14. Of course, Jefferson's Jesus is a reformer, but of what? Of Judaism, but without the "religion" of Israel.

what Jefferson thinks Jesus was really like. It reveals, for instance, how Jefferson seeks out every hint of the moral instruction. He drags from Luke all the important pieces of moral wisdom not in Matthew's Sermon. Indeed, in another example, we notice that Jefferson finds a moral nugget in most of the actions and the parables he chooses, whether there is one there or not.

We should observe that *multiple attestation of a theme or saying is a strong indication of Jefferson's approval.* But it is not infallible, given the blocky way that Jefferson edits the texts and his effort to reduce redundancy from the four gospels. Since he cuts out materials in large chunks and rarely takes out individual words or phrases, Jefferson's commitment to a theme or passage means that he will likely use an entire block of material he likes. But the same whole pericope may drag with it elements he is not so keen on; nonetheless, he accepts the whole block. We interpreters wonder why he would allow Jesus to say such and such, when we have seen the element deleted in other instances. The most obvious example of multiple attestation is Jefferson's general inclination to hone in on every moral item in the Jesus saga or more narrowly his developed radar for instances in which ritual and morality seem to the author's mind to be in tension.

More important for Jefferson research, however, is the inversion of the multiple-attestation criterion to *multiple nonattestation*. To say it bluntly, we may be assured we are dealing with a major theme (albeit in the negative voice) when Jefferson repeatedly rejects certain materials from the gospels. The obvious example is when Jefferson consistently wants nothing to do with supernatural phenomena. Again and again, he vaults over such opportunities in the biblical texts. Simple nonattestation is not as revealing a criterion as it might be, however, since Jefferson attempts to shorten the four gospels into a single, trim account. The single account often leaves out repetitions of material[15] in particular from the synoptic gospels, and of course, categorically omits a large amount of the actions of Jesus (often identified with the supernatural). Meanwhile, *single nonattestation* is of limited but not no value. For instance, that he eliminates the Christmas stories and the genealogies in Matthew and Luke shows that he finds find no value in the mythic details of the story and in the contrived lineage of Jesus of Nazareth. Items that appear by single nonattestation must be secured by other criteria, such as *coherence*. That is, *if an item is left out of Jefferson's story of Jesus, its absence gains in importance if it resembles other rejected materials.* For instance, if interpreters were able to notice that Jefferson leaves out one of

---

15. See Holowchak for nifty criteria for determining when Jefferson leaves out and adds materials (Holowchak, *Bible*, 105–8).

Jesus' comments on divorce, they could not be assured that the omission was meaningful unless the author were to leave out other such comments.

Multiple nonattestation is more promising, but obviously we would not discern its importance, if we only read the cataphatic text of the *LMJN*, since what we learn from *the use of the criterion makes sense only in relation to what is not there!* The author's apophatic project depends upon the cataphatic claims of biblical text. Were it not parasitic, the *LMJN* would offer the sayings of a great moralist simply in an even flatter way than it does. *Jefferson's Jesus is not simply the great Sage, but he is the great sage who makes his wisdom work without the miracles.* And even if we know that the *LMJN* author claims that Jesus is the greatest moralist ever, he does not leave the Jesus ethic simply as a list of sayings; he tells an entire emplotted narrative of the moralist. It is not the narrative of the Synoptics or the one from John, but nonetheless he puts the moral plot of Jesus into a story that scoops up the Mark/Matthew frame and many gospel episodes and stuffs them with sayings, parables, and example stories. His moral use of a story is not identical to the use of the same story in a canonical gospel. More significantly, *he wants a drama, even a tragedy that builds through initial opposition all the way to the execution. Indeed, the author evidently replaces the saving-historical, transcendental account of the death of the Son of God with a conflict-plot of the noblest Sage who runs into enemies plotting to depose him.* The moralist lives within a successful Jewish crusade to remove him, but this conflict is different from the biblical conflict with the Pharisees in Galilee over Torah. When we recognize that our author replaces the passion of God's Son with the passion of the great Sage, we face the obvious questions: Is Jefferson's Jesus a new Socrates, the great moral leader taken down by evil and misunderstanding people? And has the passion of the great Sage become something different from the passion stories of the biblical gospels?

We can begin to identify certain qualifications for the application of nonattestation: *incidental nonattestations* may be simply a matter of eliminating repetitions. Or they may be the result of the *LMJN*'s boxy attempt to remove something really offensive. Consider all the content that goes down with the sinking of a miracle and recall that Jefferson's method usually removes whole episodes rather than individual bits of offensive material. We can speak of this incidental deleting as *collateral nonattestation*. The remarkable feature of the author's method of editing is that after he determines whether he likes a passage, his only next step is to decide *where to start and where to end the passage; and generally, he must cut a straight line across the page at the beginning and at the end of a chosen passage.* In other words, he has no technique that allows him to make fine, single-word or single-phrase, editing maneuvers and, thus, no way to eliminate or include a little piece of meaning.

Obviously, *double or multiple nonattestation* makes for a stronger case to the interpreter for something that Jefferson wants to avoid in a portrait of Jesus. We do not have positive content of his image, the inverse, as it were, but we do know with clarity what he rejects. For instance, the author is reluctant to show much of Judas as a betrayer of Jesus and Peter as his denier. If we did not include what is missing in the author's picture, we would never wonder why he softens the bad behavior of Jesus' disciples. We shall have to return to this point later.

Both the criteria of attestation and nonattestation have more power so far as the content of the materials included or omitted more examples from the four gospel sources, when the editorial choices move from sayings to actual deeds, and when they jump across genres within the gospel traditions. Thus, including or deleting becomes more persuasive when the editorial action is not isolated but follows a pronounced tendency in the editing. Consider how the author of the *LMJN* early on eliminates the apocalyptic from Matthew, Mark, and Luke, and corroborates his elimination with considerable use of the noneschatological John. Indeed, his reading of Jesus, as we have seen, is heavily shaped by John. Think of how he eliminates supernaturalist materials from every story and genre within the gospels, or think of the radicalized moral demands of Jesus that the author affirms without qualification, from the logia of the Sermon, from the parables, the aphorisms, the conflict stories, and the example stories. From all of these patterns we see that Jefferson thinks of Jesus as a nonapocalyptic and a very edgy moral sage.

Meta-Rule No. 4 suggests that an internal criterion of coherence can illumine Jefferson's selection process. The rule can be employed both with the attestation and the nonattestation criteria, and it looks for materials of similar themes such as securely excluded or included episodes. Material judged as coherent fills out our picture of the *LMJN*'s Jesus, even if it cannot provide a foundation for it. Take, for instance, the pattern that the author routinely omits all titles and honorific designations for Jesus; we start to see he is very consistent in the pattern, and we can move from one category to another without puzzlement. Clearly our author is allergic to honoring Jesus with the inherited ecclesiastical and biblical titles (and will struggle to find a proper way to name his greatest moralist). So, we have the pattern, and we know it sprawls out to virtually every title. *When the author violates his patterns of consistency, we realize something meaningful must be happening.* Thus, he surprises us by occasionally using "Son of Man" in and around Jesus. That fact is remarkable enough, especially since he does not have the advantage of the modern critics who see in the phrase several different meanings. We note that he does not remove all the "Son of Man" references, and his inconsistency presses us to figure out how later he can use a title he rejects at the beginning of his gospel. We note that his use of the category comes as Jesus is facing the end of his life. Perhaps the author is running out of ways of naming his sage when typical church titles prove to be unacceptable.

Why does he use the term at the end of Jesus' ministry and in the midst of Jesus' developing sense of persecution? Of course, the *LMJN* uses the term "Son of Man" without any hint of Daniel's apocalyptic use. But the term is all over the gospels and it is used with different senses. Perhaps our author has backed into a use that would have surprised him at the beginning of the *LMJN*: one traditional notion that the term is a self-reference or a developed generic/representative category for humankind. Conceivably, then, we have a modest designation useful in Jefferson's sophiological christology, namely, that the Jesus may identify with this Son of Man who represents all humans.[16] Tellingly, the term appears frequently as the Sage is heading to his death.

Finally, we need to identify smaller categories for interpretation. We have already noted that some attestations and some nonattestations seem to carry little weight for Jefferson. Some are *false positives* where things are included in Jefferson's account that he likely does not think are important. For instance, he includes place/time markers drawn from the four gospels even as he constructs a saga for Jesus that is quite atopic, even as he is displacing the synoptic chronology and geography. Both of these moves suggest that *Jefferson is relatively inattentive to the space/time markers in the gospels*, even as he is displacing the synoptic account to produce a new gospel. We note, then, that Jefferson seems inattentive to the time/space markers, while we interpreters of his work may see enormous significance in the way he reconstructs the space and time of Jesus.

One caution is in order. The fact *that the author of the LMJN includes an item in his Jesus book does not mean for sure that he is enthusiastic about the material.* Since his method of editing is, as we have called it, blocky, he has to commit to a block of gospel or decide to remove a block. Again, he does no excising of individual words or phrases. For a block to be included in his new book, he commits to the content of the entire block and has to do so even if there are elements in the block that he might regard as suspect. So, too, if the author commits to removing a block, he decides to eliminate all of

---

16. See the classic modern work on the meaning of the "Son of Man" category. Tödt identifies the Danielic use, the self-reference use, and the representative model (Tödt, *Son of Man*, 222–77).

the content of the block. The door is, therefore, open at times to suspected materials entering the *LMJN*, possibly against the mainstream of the author's values. Possible instances of this *incidental inclusion* may be the growing inclusion of apocalyptic material at the end of the Jesus account. After all, think how complex is the end of Jesus' story and how comprehensively apocalyptic themes and the figure of the Son are woven into the account. How could one remove these themes without exploding a valued passage? Are inclusions truly incidental, or do they represent a changing view in the author's mind? Again, perhaps he realizes he needs a way to speak of his Sage, and the best notion is that the Son-Sage represents all who stand with him in his wisdom. Surely, the end of the synoptic account of Jesus' life is so saturated with apocalyptic that our author may not avoid it all through his blocky method. Of course, we have already speculated on different explanations for his warming up to the apocalyptic.

Incidental negatives appear where the author throws out things without a serious statement. These items often disappear when he removes larger and offensive pericopes. The *LMJN*, for instance, seems to forget the "salt of the earth" theme even though the author quotes all the parallels in the complete Sermon on the Mount: leaven, city on hill, light of the world. Perhaps the omission means little.

The Use of External Coherence for the Interpretation of the *LMJN*

Scholars of the *LMJN* have assembled a relatively clear picture of our author's religiosity. We will attempt to summarize these insights presently. But first we need to note that scholars have a repository of ideas and values that can be applied to the interpretation of *LMJN*. We have been critical of the premature application of these insights to the text of the *LMJN* because such application leads and controls the interpretation of the text itself. We have argued for the necessity of a prior, immanental reading of the text, one that does its work before the external task of matching ideas in the research on the Jefferson corpus to the themes of the text. *If the external coherence stops or distracts from the results of an immanent reading, it is a misplaced interpretive danger.* In an extreme case, the meaning of the *LMJN* could be limited to the application of known items in the Jefferson corpus for the interpretation of the text itself, and the book itself then only reaffirms what Jefferson has already said in private letters. In that case the book has no autonomy of meaning on its own. But what if the immanent reading uncovers themes that do not match the main, known ideas on religion in Jefferson? What if the known ideas do not fit exactly? Or what if the text moves in ways that depart from the well-known?

In order to let the book speak without the cluttering of extratextual ideas of what Jefferson really meant, we propose that *an external-coherence criterion must be applied only upon completion of the internal analysis.* It may be that the immanent reading will uncover ideas from the *LMJN* that the scholars have not seen. It may be that the *LMJN* can confirm ideas in the public corpus. Or it may cause scholars to reconsider settled issues. Possibly the author develops ideas or even changes his mind. We do not know unless we start by bracketing the known to test whether and to what extent the already known helps with the interpretation of the book. *What is at stake is the question how the external-coherence criterion can be used.* Possibly, an immanent approach will illumine ideas not much recognized. Possibly, a theologian familiar with gospel research can recognize new ideas in the text. In any case, the point is that *we cannot offer theories about the meaning of the* LMJN *until we have first sorted out the insights of the text itself.* Then we open the door for other ideas from other sources, confirmation of ideas already known, and modifications of the known.

A final word is in order on the apophatic procedure in the author's editing. We can imagine good reasons (from his view) for eliminating many episodes of the gospel story. If we have good reasons to explain by internal and external coherence why he drops some material and why he drops the same sort of materials over and over (e.g., the miracles), we not only have a major characteristic of Jefferson's Jesus, but we may have a basis to explain why the texts of the gospels got the story wrong. We will see how the author comes up with a theory of the genesis of error in the gospels. In any case, we have to note that the criteria we employ aim to deliver what the author takes to be the real Jesus. How the real Jesus becomes unreal and corrupt remains for us to see. Obviously, the *LMJN* itself cannot by definition comment on a theory of corruption.

Apophatic Results

The negative naturally gets the first notice when we deal with the *LMJN*'s reduced Jesus. This reduction, not very original among critics of religion, looks like a shopping list of criticisms of religion from the Enlightenment. Jefferson eliminates what modern educated humans judge to be scientifically impossible (*the modern-science criterion*), what modern historians regard as historically improbable (*the Hume criterion*), and what enlightened persons judge to be illogical—inconsistent, contradictory, or flawed (the *enlightened-reason criterion*) and morally compromised (a *moral criterion of some kind*). From day one, Jefferson believes that reason tests all things regardless of the risks.[17] These are familiar standards. But Jefferson adds a moral criterion that extends the scope of the epistemological criteria somewhat: this one is a *moral-offense criterion* that eliminates things that are morally indecent or unacceptable, particularly to many modern people (e.g., the denial of free will). Actually, the moral-offense standard Jefferson seems to unpack in what we could call a *theo-propos criterion*, in which he rescues the Jesus story from unacceptable views of God, an *anthro-propos criterion*, where Jefferson norms what good humans can and should be like. These moral criteria, familiar from d'Holbach's Enlightenment Jesus,[18] can overlap with the epistemological appeals but often add judgments on the moral consequences of an idea or practice.

Again, we are working criteria negatively, often to explain what is not there. Without any explanation of an absence, the criteria have to be discerned in the sheer fact of an item's absence, and especially in the consistent patterns with which such items are missing, and eventually, from a check against ideas expressed in the author's other writings, for instance. The epistemological criteria always work to flush from the received text things we cannot know, while the moral criteria may be deployed positively to suggest, for instance, what kind of a (good) God Jesus really believes in.

To these criteria we add a couple of formal, methodological criteria: the author norms his Jesus story with a *protestant criterion* in which the earliest and the simplest he judges as the most authentic. Here, intelligent reading of the received texts requires cutting through the corruption of ideas, texts, and practices, regarded as unsavory developments and corruptions.[19] We see in the author, then, a form of the *protestant "myth of*

---

17. See his famous advice ("reason is the only oracle given by Heaven") to his nephew Peter Carr. Letter to Peter Carr, August 10, 1787 (Jefferson, *Writings* [Peterson, ed.], 901–2).

18. Conceivably, Jefferson could have learned of d'Holbach's criteria in *Ecce Homo!* from 1813, since he read d'Holbach and was aware of his views and those of d'Holbach's contemporaries on religion. See D'Holbach, *Ecce Homo!* It is intriguing that two of the earliest modern reductive readings of the biblical Jesus appeared within a few years, and that they were both from materialists with French connections. We know Jefferson has read d'Holbach's *Système de la Nature*: Letter to Adams, April 8, 1816 (Braden, "Ye Will Say I Am No Christian," 164).

19. Here we see the dependence of the author upon the writings of Priestley (Priestley, *History of the Corruptions*). See the discussion of Priestley's influence on Jefferson in Gaustad, "Religion," 283–84. Also, Conkin, "Religious Pilgrimage," 29–31, where Conkin suggests that Priestley's book had "the greatest influence on Thomas Jefferson in the world of religious ideas."

Christian origins,"[20] which assumes that an initially simple and untroubled moral vision in Jesus gets corrupted by predictable "catholic" developments. Actually, we will learn that the *LMJN*'s Jesus is doubly protestant, in that Jesus is a "protestant" style reformer of the Jewish "catholicism" of his day, and that the *LMJN*'s Jesus possibly could act as an agent to reform religion and Christianity of the author's day.

---

20. Wilken, *Christian Beginnings*, xi–xii. We know that the ancient idea of an original purity to the Christian movement comes to Jefferson via Priestley (Priestley, *History of the Corruptions*, ix). Priestley teaches Jefferson the logic of the corruption theory: the original purity of the man is corrupted by ignorant followers and nefarious clergy; the deception is uncovered, and what follows is reformation, apology (defense of the faith) to unbelievers, and the restoration of the honor of the Christian religion.

12

Immanent Theological Conversations

The New Framing

We have seen that our author shuffles the patterns that shape both the synoptic gospels and John, even if he roughly follows the movement from the inauguration of the ministry through conflict to execution. Yet *he has trouble with the do/say pattern of the biblical gospels*; both the Synoptics and John have Jesus complete an act and then offer some kind of explanation, lesson, or example story.[1] But the "do" part often involves the wonders and the exorcisms that our author must delete. The middle of the Jesus story is almost entirely a sequence of doings and sayings; *without such doing, the author has almost no frame on which to hang Jesus' sayings. The effect is to generalize the moral teaching from its context and to make each item more abstract and universalized.*[2] Notice that a saying, perhaps a parable, does not have the meaning it has in the canonical gospels when it has been extracted from a wonder or from a mythic frame like the coming of the Kingdom of God. In other words, a saying has no gospel meaning at all when it has been abstracted from its primal contents; indeed, it becomes a completely different speech act when its frame is gone. *What is the Sower without the*

---

1. Or vice versa: say/do.

2. Very possibly our author may not see the abstraction of the ethic to be a problem, given his interest in universalizing all things tribal, and given the way that a "commonplace" hermeneutic schools him into gathering moral nuggets and assembling them in a notebook.

Kingdom? It ceases to be the performance of the coming of the Kingdom and becomes a moralized reminder to be good soil. Notice that, whether by design or accident, the *LMJN* frontloads the Jesus story with the temple event and thereby re-encases the moral advice in an all-consuming account of conflict. Of course, much of Jesus' moral contributions have nothing to do with conflict with the Jewish authorities. Almost nothing in the Sermon pertains to that conflict. *Our author re-creates the Jesus story and reconceptualizes the moral advice of the Sage as an in-your-face affront to the way the Jewish authorities shape their world.*[3] In so doing, he displaces the moral advice of Jesus, just as he re-places the saving-historical mythos of the biblical accounts with a constructed conflict account. The result is that *the gospel of the LMJN appears as a conflict story with a tragic ending.*

We have seen that the movement to Jerusalem, though *confused, remains despite the fact that the* LMJN *begins the tale in Jerusalem. The author sets the instantaneous conflict with Jewish authorities as the leitmotif in the progress of the story.* Additional themes we observe are our author's formal reliance on Matthew, his use of Mark and Luke as supplements to Matthew's story (until he turns to the sermonic and parabolic materials of Luke in a block), and his rare and significant insertion of materials from John, particularly at the end of the story. Mark never gets more than a supplemental role, likely because Mark, dominated by exorcisms and wonders, lacks a distinctive teaching section. Roughly speaking, the *LMJN* has John pose the issue of conflict, then turns to Matthew and Luke to deliver the new teaching to counter the failed morality of the Jewish authorities. Luke especially brings strident critique and judgment of the Jewish failure, and finally the *LMJN* lets Matthew and John dominate the passion story of the Sage with some help from Luke.

The displaced frame of the *LMJN*'s gospel challenges theology to see if it can live without the old saving-history plot, as it has been classically defined. *What is the cost of the displacement?* While the old saving story goes back at least to Mark, if not to Jesus himself, how much loss is there to gospel and theology without Christmas and Easter, without Jesus as an exorcist and a healer, without Jesus as the great includer of the broken and marginalized, without the one who is prophesied and the one who fulfills prophecy, without the one who struggles to redefine Torah and Judaism, without the messianic claims and titles? The cost would be tremendous, of course, but would those losses create opportunities for a postclassical, sophiological theology? Perhaps.

---

3. And the conflict and affront must be shattering in order that the *LMJN*'s storyline can pass the execution criterion.

The Transformation of the Jewish Authorities

In our analysis of the text we noted over and over that the *LMJN* clumps all Jewish authorities into a group continually challenging Jesus. Of course, the author does not have modern knowledge of the differences among Jewish leaders and parties, and the fact that he leads with the temple event means that the Sadducees are immediately hostile to Jesus, when in the synoptic accounts the Sadducees really do not make an appearance in Jesus' ministry until the last week of his life. But in the author's reconstruction, dealings with the Sadducees begin as well as end the story. In the middle part of the story Galilean scribes and Pharisees take over as substitutes for the Sadducees and their anger with Jesus. Of course, the *LMJN* misses that the Pharisees are primarily tied to the synagogues away from the temple in Jerusalem, and that their thing is to interpret Torah, not offer sacrifices in the temple. The Sadducees do not take on a new role in the *LMJN*, though they do get involved much earlier and, early on, they protect their turf, the temple in the midst of a colonial Roman city, in the same way they do at the end of Jesus' ministry. They protect their privilege with the Romans by keeping the city free of disorder during holy days.

The Pharisees, however, come to be a different reality under Jefferson's knife. The most dramatic transformation of the Pharisees comes in the way that they are instantly drawn into the hostility caused in the temple event, as if they have a stake in keeping order at the temple. *They pick up the Jerusalem-based Sadducees' project of shoring up the sacrificial system and relations with the Roman colonists. They pick up the Sadducee anger also.* Obviously, the *LMJN* does not know or care that the Galilean Pharisees have a different focus from the Sadducees. Instead, *the author wants to indict them in the Sadducean-led plot to kill the great sage. From his viewpoint there is no serious difference between the two Jewish groups. Not surprisingly our author has no patience for points of interpretation of Torah; negatively put, his only concern is that the hypocrite Pharisees get distracted with legal or ritual details and miss the moral calling of the day. Most seriously of all, the Galilean conflict between the Pharisees and Jesus collapses into the challenge Jesus poses in Judea to the Sadducees and their temple.*

The LMJN *actually intensifies the conflict traditions in the gospels by collapsing the issue of the Pharisees into the order-keeping cause of the Sadducees.* For instance, by drawing on John 2 at the beginning of the story, *the* LMJN *author is more or less wedded to John's geography and chronology.* Consequently, Jesus' first act is to get to Jerusalem and clean out the temple. He launches reasons for conflict early in the story for the entire ministry of Jesus. Still early in the story Jesus has to leave Judea for Galilee because the (Judean) Jews plan to kill him (John 7:11). Once Jesus is in Galilee, "the Jews" do not believe him; the people are murmuring, and are afraid of the Jews who seek Jesus. As the story develops, *the generic struggle with "the Jews" turns into a pitched battle with the Pharisees,* who dominate "the Jews" category until the last week of Jesus' life when the priests, the elders, and the Sadducees appear and the Pharisees all but disappear. But from Jefferson's point of view, Jesus gets in trouble at the beginning of his ministry with the Jews, the Pharisees pick up the ball, attack him, and turn him over to the Judean priestly/aristocratic caste that puts him away. Of course, at times Jesus does bait the Pharisees in the middle of and at the end of the story, but *we know that the gospel conflict with the Pharisees pertains to rival Jewish readings of Law and holiness, not the fracas that horrified the Sadducees* (which, according to the Synoptics, has not yet happened at the time of Jesus' controversy with the Pharisees). Therefore, *our author collapses two different moments of conflict and thereby intensifies and broadens the conflict that started with the displaced temple event. In so doing he conflates the entire Galilean conflict on holiness with Jesus' final, Judean affront to the order kept by the Sadducees.*

We see, then, that *the Pharisees function for the* LMJN *author as his stand-in Jewish opposition to the moral greatness of Jesus.*[4] Such a view hardly surprises us until we notice what the *LMJN* excludes about the Pharisees and what it includes. Recall, for instance, that Jefferson omits references to suspicious Pharisees when they are questioning Jesus' exorcisms (Matt 9:34, 12:24) and healings (Matt 12:19) and feedings (Mark 8:15), or when they want a sign from Jesus (Matt 12:38). *Our author is not interested in the Pharisees who battle Jesus over ritual, tradition, defilement (Matt 15), table fellowship (Luke 5:30), Sabbath law (Mark 2:24), fasting (Mark 2:18), divorce (Mark 10:1), and messianism (Matt 22:41); or in the Pharisees who try to trick Jesus with points of Law (Caesar/God dispute [Matt 22:15–22; Mark 12:13–17; Luke 20:20–26]); or finally in those Pharisees who wrangle with him over forgiveness and adultery (Luke 5:21). The list of the deletions of Jesus' dealings with the Pharisees is astounding because it covers some of the juiciest topics of the Galilean ministry.* Consequently, we realize that the author is not much interested in the Pharisees of the gospels who debate over decidedly "religious" and Jewish topics, the very things the Pharisees are trained to interpret. He is not interested in conflicts that arise from issues of Israel's identity or from the interpretation of or the following of Torah. Oddly, as much as the Pharisees represent generic Jews in the *LMJN*'s drama, its author finds little interest in their specific Jewishness and their specific focus

---

4. Notice that Jefferson does not emphasize the rejection by the people of Nazareth.

on interpreting Torah. In other words, *the author's editing makes the Pharisees the clustered representations of all the Jews, if not of the generic humans who oppose Jesus' moral campaign.*

We have to qualify these claims a little. If the author were to throw out all the intra-Jewish conflicts of the gospels, after he has removed the supernatural elements of the story, he would fail the *criterion of opposition*: that is, he would not present sufficient reason to explain the opposition to and the eventual execution of Jesus. *Our author seems to sense that he must provide a full explanation why Jewish leaders oppose Jesus. Therefore, he re-aims the given intra-Jewish conflict over Torah and holiness and establishes it as the continuing Jewish opposition to Jesus started with the temple fracas.* For instance, in nearly the first act of the moral master he permits his students to pick corn on the Sabbath (Matt 12:2) and immediately the Pharisees and Jesus begin to debate whether this act is permitted by the Torah. Thereafter, the Pharisees try to catch Jesus on the issue of healing on the Sabbath (Matt 12:9).[5] Again, a debate ensues. Likely, we are not to think our author worries much about the integrity of Sabbath law and certainly not about healing (by the *criterion of coherence*). Rather the *LMJN* reveals what is on the author's mind in the way that he interrupts all the stories of Matt 12 about the Sabbath with the Mark 2:27 one-liner: "The Sabbath was made for man, and not man for the Sabbath." Here the author shows his hand by juxtaposing thematically related items and by escaping the world of Jewish ritual into the morally universal.

The *LMJN* vaults over the putative fact of healing to make a general point about Jesus as a moral leader. So, too, in the next encounter (Luke 7:37–39) we have Jesus dueling with the Pharisees about whether the "sinful" woman should anoint Jesus' feet. In this intriguing passage, our author establishes the Pharisaic point that Jesus is not a prophet, since he would have known she was in sin. Jesus should have refused to be touched by her. But the lesson our author derives, it seems, is not about ritual defilement but rather about the inclusive love of the Master. The parable he gives (the two debtors: Luke 7:41–43) secures the notion that love extends to (and may favor) the most sinful. The point is a moral one about the extension of love. If we have not gotten the point already, the author immediately adds from Mark 3 the encounter of Jesus with his family. Here he extends the notion of family to all who "do the will of God" (Mark 3:35). Therefore, we get a second insight into the moral reformation of the teacher; and, naturally, the Pharisees do not like it.

---

5. The use of this passage that refers to healing is quite daring, given Jefferson's allergy to supernatural phenomena. But again, he is establishing the plausibility of opposition.

The Pharisees are unwilling to take these moral steps and decide to destroy Jesus (Matt 12:14). The *LMJN*'s Jesus is unintimidated. He proclaims that his disciples must do better than the Pharisees (Matt 5:17–20). Again, our author uses a text that tends in directions different from what he typically favors, for it seems to read plainly that Jesus' disciples must outdo the Pharisees in their fussy legalism. But like many interpreters, the author hears the call of the reformer who wants to clean up practice according to high moral standards. Modern critics understand why our author makes his mistake: they have a better reading of the exact battle between Jesus and the Pharisees, namely, the status of the oral Torah.[6] The Pharisees support it and Jesus seems to take a stand on only the written Torah. But our author has no interest in the actual Matt 5 text as written and, of course, no knowledge of modern gospel criticism; his concern is to hear Jesus as a reformer of decadent and narrow Judaism, and since he does not distinguish Pharisees from Sadducees and sees all Jewish authorities mixed into the role of opposition to Jesus, he is blind to what "outdoing" the Pharisees might mean in Matt 7.

Just as Jesus' ethic becomes for the LMJN *a cipher to the universal moral law, so the Pharisees stand in for all who from ignorance or greed impede the moral life and oppose the moral giant.* Consequently, our text effects a transformation of the causes of Jesus' death. The Pharisees and Jewish authorities are to be blamed. The key text is a long section from John 7:10–44 where the author lets John show that the whole of Israel does not keep the Law even as the Jewish leaders seek to kill Jesus. Jesus the reformer ups Moses's ante on obedience, and for that, the Pharisees (in league with the priests) set out to destroy him (John 7:32). Recall that Judas is not to blame, and it never occurs to the author to blame the Romans. Even the Sadducees' involvement gets twice reduced (see Luke 19 and 20) and rolled into the Pharisaic campaign. Over and over, like a chorus at the end of each episode, the *LMJN* author repeats the words "Jews seeking Jesus' death." Indeed, he enhances the gospels' attempts to absolve Pilate and the Romans for Jesus' death by keeping the trial before Jewish authorities and by minimizing the Roman trial.

---

6. Modern scholars have long recognized that the role of the Pharisees in Matthew, especially, has been shaped by third-generation Christian polemics against Jewish communities. This line of thinking is familiar within Jefferson, *Bible* (Beacon ed.): the Jesus saga came to be transformed into the famous Galilean conflict traditions, in which the Pharisees conveniently pop up as Jesus' foils so that his message becomes distinct from that of Second Temple Judaism. The best of Jesus research today sees little to no actual conflict between Jesus and the Pharisees, with the exception of the issue of the status of the oral tradition of the Torah. So, Jesus is no longer viewed as one who breaks with Torah on any serious point; see Sanders, *Historical Figure*.

The Pharisees are to be blamed for Jesus' death, but in a specific way. The text from John 7 is crucial, since it gives voice to a rationale for opposing Jesus. The *LMJN* needs such a text to explain Jesus' death (the *execution criterion*), particularly since it omits the wonders and the holiness/kosher battles. *The author of the* LMJN *discovers that the real conflict with the Pharisees centers in Jesus' moral reformation.* And when Jesus accuses the Pharisees of not doing "the law," we wonder if our author hears this Law to be the moral law within every human. Certainly he is not thinking of Mosaic Law, neither of the oral Torah nor of the written Torah. No, Jesus brings a reformation some do not want. The *LMJN* has a favorite word for the Pharisaic failure: hypocrisy. Hypocrisy is the slippage between saying and doing (see Luke 12:1–3). Immediately after the author has established the Sabbath point and the extension of love, he turns to Luke's critique of the Pharisees' hypocrisy and eventually gets to the woes on them (Luke 11). They are unwilling to incorporate sinners into the community (that is, forgiving the debts of sinners: Luke 7:40), and if that were not bad enough, they spend their time on showy things (Luke 11:43–46).

In the treatment of the Pharisees, we see that our author takes materials, some of which must make him wince, and redirects them subtly to moral issues.[7] *The problem of the Pharisees is not their intra-Jewish concern for holiness and the interpretation of what Torah requires. Rather the author gives the problem of the Pharisees a moral reading.* Of course, he has the help of the gospel texts for this task. But the issue is how we define the extent of the moral universe. The Pharisees are finally not problematic in that they are wooden legalists and hypocrites in the common senses of those terms. *Their problem is that they are immoral.* They have missed the full requirement of moral law and have thus been unjust in excluding many. The *LMJN* calls them "covetous" (Luke's word: 16:14 KJV) and "wicked" (Matt 22:18 KJV). They oppose Jesus and his inclusive message, they take it as their task to tangle with him, and they begin to fear the crowds who now regard him as a "prophet" (Matt 21:45–46).

The *LMJN* repeats the inclusion theme. In the "follow me" call of the tax collector, Levi, we get to see Jesus hanging out with "publicans and sinners" (Mark 2:15–17; 5:27). We see that Jesus eats with the wrong people and that the Pharisees oppose such fellowship (Mark 2:16). And in a rare moment the text allows a departure from common references to Jesus: the author allows Jesus to be "Master," and lets Mark's Jesus suggest that it is the sinners who need the "Physician" (Mark 2:17). Such inclusion marks the new moral day, and in a rare moment the *LMJN* author allows these

---

7. See the Pharisees' discussion about divorce in Matt 19.

two christological categories. To accent the reformation, Jefferson turns immediately to Luke 5:36–38, the famous "new wine in old wineskins" image: it is time to be wise.

The Transformation of Nature and Supernature

We began our analysis of the portrayal of Jesus in the *LMJN* with the most obvious feature:[8] the author omits as many of the so-called supernaturalistic features as he can according to his method. His commitment to a naturalized picture of Jesus shows immediately in the beginning (including in the transfiguration stories) and the end of the Jesus story; more powerfully we see it in the way he purges the synoptic gospels of all healings (and references to healings, approximately fifty-eight opportunities in the gospel narratives), of all exorcisms (about thirty-two references), of all so-called nature miracles (about twenty references, including feeding wonders), and of virtually all references to angels and the devil (Mark 3:23).[9] The Jesus of the *LMJN* does not live in a supernaturalized world. So, too, its Jesus does not commission his disciples to heal or to cast out demons (Mark 3:14). The temptations Jesus undergoes do not involve wrestling with the devil (or God) but are introspective self-clarifications (Mark 6:32). And more generally, this account of the life of Jesus largely lacks the doing-and-saying pattern of the wonders in both the synoptic gospels and in John.

One of the remarkable consequences of the author's purging of the traces of supernaturalism is that the doing-and-saying pattern of the gospels is exploded. Frankly, *without the wonders and the exorcisms, Jesus does not have much to do. As Manseau notes, Jesus becomes all talk in the* LMJN. He does not do anything, and when he is involved in events, often they are done to him. His life is rather empty of action after he throws his temple fit. He moves about Palestine and meets people with whom he talks: one act and he is finished, so to speak. Thereafter, he talks and gets a following and cultivates enemies. As we have seen, the *LMJN* has to struggle to find sufficient cause for his execution.[10]

---

8. The hostility to supernatural phenomena lives in Jefferson's thought well before the issue of supernaturalism in the gospels: see the Letter to Adams, February 10, 1812 (Braden, "*Ye Will Say I Am No Christian*," 25, where Jefferson identifies supernaturalism with craziness. See the treatment of the supernatural theme in Frank, "Religious Journey").

9. Jefferson purges the supernatural from all four gospels, but since he uses John very little, his opinion of John must be that it is essentially supernaturalistic.

10. See the discussion of the inactive sage in Manseau, *Jefferson Bible*, 68–69.

A theological reflection on the *LMJN* would have to offer a de-supernaturalized theology, rather in the mode of Schleiermacher who worked out his theology at the very time of the writing of the *LMJN*. But be clear, the theology of our author would not be without God, as we will see.

The Transformation of God

Our author takes his Jesus beyond the older views of God, with their heavy emphasis on personal theistic language, on inward moments of revelation, and on weighty metaphysical frames.[11] The real Jesus rarely speaks of God as Father and only once as "my Father": see our author's omissions of Matt 5:48 and 10:32 and most of the book of John. Even the elevated moral insight "Be ye therefore perfect, even as your Father which is in heaven is perfect" (Matt 5:48) the author drops, presumably because he does not like the personal language for God.[12] Recall also that he substitutes the mercy of God for the perfection of God. *We have supposed that our author thinks that divine perfection is an unreasonable moral expectation for humans.* It smells of an idealistic (platonic) or apocalyptic extremism that violates the moderation of the real Jesus.

We can see, then, *the God-language in the* LMJN *seems to move from the implied theism of the Bible toward the deist family of terms. We should note, however, that, while the* LMJN *avoids personal language for God, it does not thereby turn God into a cold and distant divinity.* Recall the care theme as it is woven into the beatitudes and the lilies/birds images of the Sermon, not to mention the entire beatitude/woe patterning of the gospel in the *LMJN*.

The *Theo-Propos* God

Here we will not rehearse the author's epistemological criteria for theology, but will focus specifically on the moral implications of the life Jesus commends. Jefferson's use of the *theo-propos* criterion reveals a complex dialectic with nature. Since for the *LMJN* divinity is the author of nature, then the patterns and the laws of the universe are directly analogical to God. God works as the world works, in and with the regularity of nature. To attribute to God what is not in the way of the world leads not only to unintelligible claims about events but to theologically and morally defective

---

11. Boorstin, *Lost World*, 54–55 for a helpful orientation to a new model of God.

12. The omitted verse is remarkable because it is the only line the author leaves out of the Sermon from Matt 6 and 7. We have already suggested that the *LMJN* prefers the mercy of God to the perfection of God as the ideal for humans.

views about God. *A God who departs from the regularity of nature would not be a decent God.* Such a God probably could not be known also, since a tear in the regularity would prevent the Newtonian cosmological logic from supporting knowledge of God. When our author has to choose what things in the Jesus story are most revelatory of divinity, he does not turn to special revelations or to prodigies, as we know; but he turns to the deity who rains on the good and the evil both.

His model for thinking about God rests in the daily rhythm of natural cycles. But those lessons tell us about God, he thinks: God does not favor some over others; God does not play a Deuteronomic game of blessings and curses with humans. Therefore, *God cannot be tribal and exclusive,*[13] since the regularity and universality of the ways of nature would prohibit such views of divinity. It is reasonable to define the reasonable according to the mind's attention to the patterns of nature and not let it fly far from natural law. Quickly the ideas our author connects identify the reasonable with the life of God. God is a reasonable Deity. The real Jesus gets us to the reasonable God, who is not a tribal God playing favorites, not a God distant from the launched system of nature, and certainly not a grumpy and vindictive judge. *The LMJN thus shows how Jesus enlarges and enriches the view of God, and this enhancement of the qualities of the divinity presents itself as one of Jesus' most powerful christological activities. Jesus actually transforms the notion of God.*[14]

---

13. The critique of religious exclusivity is quite strong in the *LMJN*. Exclusive or tribal notions of religion or divinity undermine the justice of God. Reading Paine possibly prompts the author to these views.

14. If the new Jesus helps modify the notion of God for the author, beyond the critical notions with which he struggled early, we note the irony that the author's view of God is changing because of his critical rescue of Jesus from the impostor that the early church made of him: *a new God in and because of the new Jesus*. When the author discovers that Jesus is not an impostor, he begins his retrieval of Jesus and ultimately of Christianity. The author actually progressed on his God project before he sorted out the new Jesus. But *the values of the new Jesus seem to imply elements in the new divinity*. Take, for instance, that *via Jesus God is discovered to work with mercy not perfection, or that Jesus teaches that God anchors an other-regarding, nontribal morality*. Behind these theological developments we can see an author who, like many modern theologians, begins to remake both classical theism and the Omni-God and the demands of Chalcedonian christology. Sometimes one senses that Jefferson scholars know nothing of the history of modern theology, when often they take criticism of old theologies and old christologies as the death of the theological show. But Jefferson is neither very revolutionary nor very inventive in his theology, and when he embarks on his criticism of classic theologies and christologies, Jefferson scholars should not assume Jefferson and his sources have killed theology. The Germans were midcourse in their rebuilding both God and the Christ when Jefferson offered his *LMJN*. *Note that the young Jefferson speaks of the perfection of God quite freely; but it is only in his conversation with the Jesus*

With the real Jesus God shows up as preveniently fair to all, warmly involved, and willing to establish disinterested justice. We may suspect that Jefferson has not worked out how elements of a proper God hang together coherently, and we certainly see little more than formal hints of such in his Jesus book. For instance, how can one think of God in nontheistic ways without special divine acts and revelations and still pull off a compassionate and involved God?

Lessons on the Trinity

We have already noted our author's critique of anything that looks like trinitarian thinking. Here we add a small but important example the author makes via his Jesus studies. In his "Notes on Heresy," he takes his more general concern with the doctrine into the murky water of the immanent relationship within God.[15] His general orientation to the three-is-one problem leads him to be suspicious of the church's doctrine of the *homoousios* relationship of Father and Son. He formulates his suspicion by careful reading of Origen, Irenaeus, and Eusebius, who convince him that "belief in a consubstantial Trinity was contrary to early Christian thought."[16]

Intriguingly, the author of the *LMJN* combines his suspicion with remarkably skillful literary-critical insight into the gospels. The former literary work teaches him a familiar Enlightenment hermeneutic whereby he approaches the gospel texts as having layers of meaning.[17] The earliest and

---

figure that he comes to believe that God's mercy is more interesting and more characteristic of God than God's perfection. Here is another Jesus-founded transformation of Jefferson's God concept.

15. Our author has a complex relationship to the category of heresy. We know he himself is under accusation of heresy from his Federalist and New England Calvinist opponents; they would have good reason to use the category, were they to know what he really believes. The sheer idea of editing, much less literally cutting the Bible would be scandalous. But in his lifetime, our author's cut-and-paste method would not have been known, but his critics could smell his heretical status mostly from his public acts and pronouncements alone. Our author, of course, came to a construction that told him that much of the scriptural and creedal tradition had been seriously corrupted. Therefore within that construction the author's reform and rescue of the genuine Jesus materials from the corruption allow him to see that his opponents are the actual heretics, and that even the dreaded Christian pillar, Calvin, is the real atheist. See the Letter to Adams, August 22, 1813 (Cappon, *Adams-Jefferson Letters*, 367). Jefferson's hatred of Calvinism is deep and disturbing: see the Letter to Salma Hale, July 26, 1818 (Adams and Lester, *Extracts*, 385).

16. See Vicchio, *Jefferson's Religion*, 40.

17. The notion that texts and especially sacred texts have layers of meaning is an ancient hermeneutic, of course. We need to go back only to the history of allegorization

most genuine meaning can be found under layers of extension, development, and especially of corruption. The critical work on the gospels operates with a very modern theory that one can determine the core within the layered text by judging a particular item against a sense for the whole of the work. *The combination of the two brings Jefferson to a visionary, if ad hoc, recognition that the gospels do not support well the trinitarian views of the second and third centuries.* In fact, the author is so impressed with his negative discoveries, that the gospels and the earliest theologians do not match Nicene theologies, that he has little appreciation that certain early Christian materials do, in fact, anticipate Nicene doctrine.[18] Nevertheless, he presses a recognition needed in his day and ours, namely, that an Arian Christian theology might easily have won the day as orthodox against the Nicene-style options. More generally, our author comes to a keen notion that doctrine is developmental, that it has a history; but given his myth-of-Christian-beginnings orientation, that history usually weighs in as negative corruption from its pristine beginnings.

The Transformation of Christology

The editorial signals suggest our author purges all traces of high christologies. These we see in the titles and prologues to the gospels, the patterns of naming Jesus, the typologies of prophecy and fulfillment, and especially the Johannine passages in which Jesus shows a serene and lofty sense of his status in the divine plan and the life of God. Also, Jefferson does not include the elaborate, theological genre, the disquisitions of John. Indeed, Jefferson prefers a modest, laconic Jesus crafted under in the value of humility. In a sense he wants the shy and elusive values of Jesus of Mark's messianic secret without the secrecy, without the titles, without the big revelation of the secret at the end.

The matter is a tricky one, however. The *LMJN*'s broad strokes emphasize that Jesus is a revealer of the divine, moral wisdom and that our author opposes the secrecy surrounding the figure of Jesus, especially in Mark. Recall that a major theme of the middle of the heavy moral teaching

---

of the biblical texts to see the recognition of the layering of texts. In the modern period Hume's *Natural History of Religion* (1757) beats Jefferson's account by over sixty years. In the meanwhile, Jefferson gets inspiration from Priestley's theory of corruption to begin to unearth the "diamonds in the dunghill" (Manseau, *Jefferson Bible*, 32).

18. Jefferson does not work with a positive developmental notion of the history of doctrine, one that emphasizes that doctrinal developments unfold ideas and images implicit in the revealed tradition. His development, of course, is tied to the corruption theory, where historical change is read as a loss from pure origins.

has Jesus oppose secrecy about his message. We suppose that the *LMJN*'s Jesus wants to open the door on all secrets because the openness is central to Jesus' whole mission. Apparently, for the author, *hiding the wisdom of the great Sage would be incoherent with his mission and, by the way, would undermine the possibility of accounting for opposition to Jesus.*[19] His enemies, the Pharisees, keep secrets, but would need to have access to Jesus' words and actions before they could develop their campaign to take him out. The author must feel this need particularly, as he has decided that there could be no opposition to Jesus based on his wonders and his exorcisms.

So, the Sage, to be the great revealer, must make a big splash at the beginning of his ministry: hence the temple event at the beginning of the ministry. Then the author constructs the notion that Jesus' ministry is a fight with the Jewish authorities, and without the miracles every speech act of Jesus is an affront to them. They have, then, plenty of reasons to get rid of him. Secrets are bad because they delude people and work in favor of the clergy. Jesus cannot be the secret Messiah, as the logic of the conflict requires him to uncover every secret. While Jesus opposes secrecy and would not hide his words, he reveals the great Wisdom. Remember, the Wisdom opposes the prideful and oppressive ways of the clergy class, and indeed Jesus strikes first against them, in the first temple fit. Jesus starts it! No wonder the authorities are hostile! Jesus' obvious takeaway from his first temple attack is that *he will stand opposed to everything haughty about the clergy class.* He would be the humble Sage, one who would bring down the proud, efface himself, and live for others. Inherently, then, Jesus eschews christological appellation. He and his author would not be into high-flying claims for the status of the Sage.

Therefore, the *LMJN* crusades against traditional christological claims and titles. It does so by dropping christologically rich passages. An interpreter is easily tempted to think that the force of its rejection of traditional christologies means that there is no christology in the *LMJN*. A fairer claim suggests that the author's christology fits among the so-called low christologies. Here "high" and "low" categories usually depend on an attitude toward the several classic theories of atonement and, while there is little commonality among the theories, they all are supernaturalist, and all tend to locate the overcoming of alienation from God via the particular work and person of the Christ with a focus on the sacrificial death. The author of the *LMJN* shows no interest in the one-for-all atonements. *Therefore, he would have to join the "moral influence" ranks among atonement theorists where the One would not do all atoning with God for all the many but would provide*

---

19. Here we have an instance when the criteria of opposition and execution are under pressure to account sufficiently for the opposition to Jesus and his execution.

something like an example, a guidance, a leadership, a representation, and possibility more. Of course, we see what is at stake for the author: *the Sage cannot do for us what we must do in our free will.* Of course, *we can see the Sage as a moral exemplar in the* LMJN. But our analysis of the *LMJN* may have ideas that stretch his role further.[20]

The Transformation of the Son of Man

The "Son of Man" category is quite complex, of course, in biblical scholarship. The author of *LMJN* seems to intuit some of the variety of meanings and uses of the term, since he both allows it on occasion and suppresses it at other times. What he clearly rejects are passages that are apocalyptic in the Danielic sense (e.g., Matt 24:30) and that seem to suggest elevated reference for Jesus (see Matt 16, 17, 18, and 20). By extension, he does not accept the Son of Man who is the Lord of the Sabbath (Mark 2:24, 28), who forgives (Mark 2:7), who condemns the generation (Mark 8:38), who is to suffer (Mark 8:31), who predicts his suffering (Mark 10:33), who is to be crucified (Matt 26:1) and betrayed (Matt 16:21). The uses of the "Son of God" title that the *LMJN* embraces are the ones where "Son of Man" is an indirect, even modest self-reference, or where the term means an identification with human nature as if the Son is a representation of humanness. In this reading the "Son of Man" clearly opposes the rejected "Son of God" title, because it seems christologically safe to the author, since he takes the term as human and worldly.[21] He can use it in his theology.

---

20. Note that if one has in mind Chalcedonian christology with hypostatic union and two full natures, Jefferson and his modern Enlightenment colleagues look like modern pagans. But there were all kinds of new christologies emerging in the Enlightenment and after; Jefferson's modest one is not very distinctive or daring. So too with atonement theories: if one norms atonement by one of the classic models, Jefferson is without an atonement theory. And in both his christological and atonement thinking Jefferson is trapped by orthodoxies he naturally must flush. Nonetheless, we will see that he offers a medium-low idealist christology and a real atonement view centered in the message and the performance of the Sage who is executed for his wisdom. It is a kind of moral-influence atonement, one without guilts, ransoms, deals with the devil, cosmic battles, and the like, but one that is just begging for the help of Schleiermacher from a few years later in the 1800s. *When Jefferson scholars see his criticism of christologies to mean he has no christology, they are making a serious mistake.*

21. Even though the earliest use of the term in Daniel refers to a divine being who comes to bring in the Kingdom of God.

The Anti-Christology Christology

Not surprisingly, when the author of the *LMJN* completes his reduction, he is left with negative elements of an anti-christology christology. In its oppositional or prophetic mode, his christology seeks to criticize the Christs of Scripture and church. The real Jesus negates, first of all, the religion of Judaism, but then, of Christendom and the classic Christs of the Western tradition. Much of the power of the *LMJN*'s Jesus rests in negation, in being over against bad religion and narrow moral visions. *This Jesus is christic in so far as he becomes a prophetic agent to return religion to its purity.* Jefferson has internalized the Christs of the tradition to be over against them with an independent take on christology. We use the term "prophet" in a generalized way for any over-against critic of religious life. Of course, the author himself does not value the narrower sense of prophet, tied to biblical prophecy/fulfillment. The christic reformer of religion is a teacher, to be sure, and his teaching has personal importance for piety. Possibly, if the reformation of Judaism takes hold, the teaching may even have importance for the hopes of a nation. While there is a clear application for reformed disciples, true Christians and their piety, we do not get a clear signal for Christian life in the world from the text of the *LMJN*.

A Sage Christology

Once we have seen the prophetic, apophatic side of the new christology, the author can turn to fragments of a cataphatic orientation to christology. First, he constructs the moral wisdom of Jesus, bereft of much of the narrative contexts, and then clusters images of the new Christ by associating ideas and images and by constructing huge sermons drawn from various locations. The *LMJN* creates, somewhat unwittingly, the vision of the great Sage: *Jesus is "this first of human sages" and "the true sage."*[22] The *LMJN* uses the teaching word "master" to identify Jesus, but it also features the term "sage" or wise man. Eventually, the author will identify Jesus more and more with the category of "Son of Man."[23] Remember, the teaching in question is that of a moralist making recommendations about the moral life. One could call Jesus a philosopher, as Jefferson does in his first Jesus book. But "sage" works well as a descriptor when we think of Jesus in the company of Jefferson's beloved moral fragmentist, Epictetus.

---

22. Here we find one of the first and most secure christological terms the *LMJN* will use: Letter to Van der Kemp, April 25, 1816 (Jefferson, *Writings* [Peterson, ed.], 63).

23. See the section above for the complex use of the term in the *LMJN*.

Actually, the sapiential Jesus lines up nicely with the sages constructed in contemporary Jesus research, the Jesuses that emerge from contemporary historical reconstructions, freed of the narrative constraints of the gospels and informed by the gospel of Thomas and by Q. The *LMJN*'s Jesus would be a friend to the Jesuses of the new sapiential paradigm in Jesus research, for that Jesus is commonly an aphorist, a cynic philosopher, a fragmentist, an ethicist with a countercultural message, and, most of all, a naturalistic reformer of Israel: portraits of Jesus that the author of the *LMJN* could comfortably endorse. But Jefferson, shy of miracle and exorcism, turns to something more than a moral lesson: his Jesus performs the message.

The Shepherd-Sage

Reconstructing our author's cutting and pasting is hardly easy. Apart from his letters, all we have is what he does with a given text and what he cuts.[24] We can figure out, however, that he has major difficulties with the theologically advanced telling of Jesus' life in the gospel of John. After all, he omits most of John and, appropriately so, given his set of values. One can hardly imagine, for instance, the *LMJN* author tolerating the Jesus of the Farewell Discourses, with their portrait of Jesus' intimate relationship with his Father. In addition, as we have suggested, the author may simply have run out of time and energy to use the huge paragraphs of John. In any case, when he does draw material from John, we can safely bet he likes it. *Remarkably, then, Jefferson quotes much of John 10's sermonic allegory on the Good Shepherd. Even more remarkably, the passage is key in filling out the LMJN's constructive christology*. Indirectly, we hear much from our author that identifies what the real Jesus is not. And when he carves away all he does not like, he can be left with a noticeably bland, real Jesus, one who travels in bloodless, moral universals. But here, with John's help, he warms up to Jesus and gives him some concrete and substantive content. We have already seen that the *LMJN* loves the sheep images of the gospels; *here he shows Jesus as the Good Shepherd*.

Surprisingly, *in the author's use of John, we find most of his cataphatic moves*. If John's Jesus gives him shepherd-like leadership, it also gives him the theme of that leadership. From chapter 12 of John, our author omits the Lazarus story, naturally, and the entire "troubled soul" discourse that leads into Jesus' farewell, where he speaks of his commission "to save the world" (12:47). We expect these passages to be omitted and we expect Jefferson to use little from John. But out of the blue he surprises us by inserting 12:19–24

---

24. Plus, the *Syllabus* and *The Philosophy of Jesus*.

completely. The passage makes almost no sense in the King James Version our author has before him. But in the NRSV we know that Jesus has just gotten the donkey for his entrance to Jerusalem on Palm Sunday; his disciples do not understand the prophetic character of the act (until later). The crowd is still swarming about Jesus after the "sign" he performed with Lazarus, but, of course, we do not get to see the sign. At this point the Pharisees (v. 19) shake their heads at their inability to stop his fame among the people. Then Greek festival folks come to the disciples to see Jesus. When Jesus learns that these Greeks press to see him, he delivers his big line: "The hour has come for the Son of Man to be glorified." The passage sounds redemptive, anticipatory of suffering, fulfilling of prophecy, slightly apocalyptic,[25] and surprisingly resurrectional—in short, it sounds exactly like what the author of the *LMJN* would avoid. Yet he includes this passage, which ends in the punch line: "Verily, verily, I say unto you, except a corn of wheat fall into the ground and die, it abideth alone; but if it die, it bringeth forth much fruit" (John 12:24 KJV). There is no good reason that the author of the *LMJN* would save such a passage, were it not connected to the *bringing-forth-fruit meaning*, a favorite image in the *LMJN*. We can figure that our author finds that theme especially important because he omits the follow-up words of Jesus in the same speech: those about hating life to keep life unto life eternal, about following Jesus, and about serving Jesus as equivalent to honoring "my Father" (12:25–26). These ideas lead into John's Jesus' "troubled soul" discourse, which the *LMJN* does not include.

The author clearly wants us to focus on the fruit of the planting upon the "death" of the seed.[26] The theme coheres nicely with other items he emphasizes, and matches his expressed views on ethics. Showing good fruit represents active moral leadership when so many allow the typical slippage between what we say and what we do; it is also leadership that goes beyond intentions and good ideas into the world of actual action. We see traces of the *LMJN*'s antispeculation theme and his commitment to practice in his show-fruit principle. *What exactly should the shepherd do to bring forth fruit?*

The Inclusive Sage

As if he were in the midst of twenty-first-century Jesus research, our author constructs a Jesus who posits that humans must move beyond tribal

---

25. Though in the spirit of John's transformation of Danielic themes into the revelation of the glory of the revealer.

26. Paul's old image for the resurrection in 1 Cor 15.

understandings of moral concern. Undoubtedly, he has his mind on the universal nature of justice and equality, those wonderful qualities he inculcates into American ideals. But just as likely he has his eyes on a careful reading of the gospel texts; the inclusive theme holds up well in Jesus research. We have mentioned that the author comes to believe that the Jews lived with an unacceptably narrow understanding of the scope of human concern for the other.[27] Interestingly, he sees the same limit in the classical ethical traditions: too narrow a circle of benevolence. *The LMJN's construction suggests that Jesus' inclusive practice prompts the conflict he has with the Jewish authorities and eventuates his execution.* But it is a moral leadership Jefferson embraces.

A Sublime Christology[28]

Jesus is the Christ because he is "simple." Jesus is the Christ because his ethic is "sublime." Jesus actually outshines the great religious and philosophical moralists.[29] Jefferson has done some of the comparative study himself and leans heavily on the work of other comparativists. Recall his judgments: First, Jesus' moral intuitions are knifingly simple and understandable to any child, he thinks, and stand in self-evident distinction from the bundling of his handlers and from the perversity of the clerical caste that overtakes the church. In the light of day, reason, under a *perspicuity criterion*, can discern the gold from the "dross."[30] Second, Jesus' moral sense is sublime, indeed the most sublime of any human's.[31] The elusive notion of sublime aims at

27. Recall the theme in the Letter to Short, August 4, 1820 (Adams and Lester, *Extracts*, 396), where Jefferson contrasts the same tribal limitations of the classical narrow, ethic concern of the Jew with the capacious benevolence for all in Jesus' ethic.

28. In this section we have to show a little Jefferson in order to make the subtle points about the sublime.

29. Jefferson's discovery that the great and much-admired Greek ethicists cultivate the inner calm of the person but do not create a fellow-feeling with open doors to others is one of the great turning points in his intellectual career. It opens the door to a reconsideration of the figure of Jesus.

30. Letter to Short, October 15, 1819 (Adams and Lester, *Extracts*, 388).

31. Likely one of Jefferson's heroes, Shaftsbury (Anthony Ashley-Cooper) offers him the sense for and importance of the sublime. See Letter to Adams, October 12, 1813 (Braden, *"Ye Will Say I Am No Christian,"* 99). Note that "moral sense" is a technical term for Jefferson; it refers to the entire intuitive sense that humans are born with; the sense or feeling, as he calls it sometimes, is a major epistemological and ethical category for Jefferson. He comes to the idea early, and it becomes the sense by which humans have a *primal orientation to virtue.* It is not reason, to the surprise of many a Jeffersonian (who tend to make Jefferson a hyperrationalist). But it is not irrational or anti-reason either. Rather it is the primal sense for the point of moral concern. Koch

something that knocks one's socks off, and in the eighteenth century it was nature most of all that could give people a mountaintop experience. The author of the *LMJN* certainly shares with his contemporaries the aesthetic contemplation of nature, but his sense of wonder always leads him to observe the regularity and design of the whole world. Like others of his day, he connects with the aesthetic contemplation of nature, not with unruly and uncanny features of the romantic, but with the amazing order of the whole. Recall the author's incredulity that some could look at nature and not see the Divine at work. Consider the lilies.

The encounter with the simple and the sublime is revelatory, if we dare to use a word our author wanted to avoid. We know he spent his religious life avoiding categories and doctrines associated with Christian and positive religion. Nonetheless, if we loosen the category of revelation from special revelation and turn it back to a general doctrine that might appeal to deistic people, we have to account for *a discernment moment. When reasonable humans encounter a trigger that launches their wonder, when the wonder leads back to a Creator, when the wonder demands a moral pattern for human life, personal and social, we have an epiphanous moment.* We can and do call it a mountaintop experience. But mountains usually do not give clues to the moral life. Our author clearly has a *lifelong "aha!" moment in pondering the sublime and simple wisdom of Jesus. That wisdom is generally revelatory for him.*

Yet pondering the beauty of nature seems insufficient for the *LMJN*. It has value, of course, and our author's life is a record of his observational and technical work with and of his aesthetic wonder about nature. But he goes beyond these sentiments in *a lifelong search for a moral shepherd*. This search takes him beyond Epictetus to Jesus. It also encourages him to take on some daring themes from the gospel record of Jesus. Or to put it in the language of the *LMJN*, he discovers *the real and self-evident Jesus to be a moral marvel.*

We have considered the role of the important fruit-bearing principle and his use of John 12. His use of John 13 is similarly complex and daring. Recall that our author uses little from John. Apart from locators, he employs John 7 to establish the opposition to Jesus' moral reformation. Then *he turns to John 10 to establish Jesus as the Good Shepherd and to chapter 12 to set out the bearing-fruit principle*. In chapter 13, his last substantive use of John, Jefferson ignores, as we expect, the theme that the "hour has come" to turn the world over to the Father (13:1), and that Jesus, coming from God and going

---

notes that the moral sense is early in Jefferson, is central for ethics as an "intuitionalism" in his thinking, is independent from but informed by reason, and is unevenly thought out in his development (Koch, *Philosophy*, 15–22).

to God, receives all from the Father. No surprises there. Then he includes the foot washing ritual, an uncharacteristic reference to the betrayal (by an unmentioned Judas), and some very surprising passages (v. 13) where Jesus declares himself Master (or Teacher) and Lord!

Including such passages defies our expectation. Jefferson is not being himself, it seems. He finds himself choosing passages inconsistent with his signals so far. Until we go a step further. He embraces the humility of the Master in foot washing, against Peter's demurring. Jesus, suggesting that Peter will understand the meaning of the act only later, goes ahead and interprets it: the Master and Lord washes the feet of his followers, and they are to do likewise among themselves; for this act is an "example, that ye should do as I have done to you" (v. 15 KJV). We get, then, another piece in the *LMJN*'s christology: *the notion of the Master's example.*

We need to go one step further in exegeting John chapter 13. Jefferson omits the prophetic reference to eating bread together, and a dense Johannine bit of self-reference (vv. 18–20). Then he daringly includes Jesus' predictive naming of Judas as his betrayer (vv. 21–26) but omits how Satan enters Judas and that Judas then leaves the group (vv. 27–30). There may not be much significance in these choices, but surely our author would not want to suggest that God forces Judas's act, and surely, he needs a mechanism to get the Pharisees' intention to kill Jesus catching the attention of the priests in Jerusalem. The surprise rests in the *LMJN*'s second and third Johannine uses of "glory" in the next verse (v. 31 KJV; see also 12:23): Jesus says, "Now is the Son of Man glorified, and God is glorified in him." These words seem dangerous to include for a man with our author's critical views, yet he includes them. They employ an exalted notion of the Son of Man and an uncharacteristic intimacy between Jesus as God's Son and God. What our author does is to add the theme of "glory" to his unfolding constructive christology.

Glory is sublime, but not sublime in quite the manner in which John uses "glory," which is the communication of the very life of God by dying.[32] Our author trims back John's complex dialogue on glory, and eliminates the continuation of the glory theme in v. 32 ("If God has been glorified in him, God shall also glorify him in himself, and shall straightway glorify him"). We do not know why. Perhaps he gets scared by John's talk of glory, which simply looks too religious or too speculative. More likely, the little addition of glory, that "God will also glorify him in himself" (NRSV), sounds as if the theme of glory aims at the inner life of God, the Trinity. Again, the author

---

32. McGill, *Death and Life*, 66.

suppresses the notion that the disciples are children (John 12:33) and shies away from the going-off-to-heaven expressions of 12:33 and 37.

In the *LMJN* glory may be sublime, but it is not supernatural, and it certainly is not John's sense of participation in the communication of the inner life of God. By purging what comes before and after the double glory passage (12:31) and immediately turning to the "new commandment" of love, we get clear that the author thinks the *glory of the sublime morality of Jesus rests in the mutual love of Master and disciples*: "That ye love one another; as I have loved you, that ye also love one another. By this shall all men know that ye are my disciples, if ye have love one to another" (12:34–35 KJV). Here the author gathers most of his constructive ideas. We know the content of the moral life; we know how the disciples learn of it, by the instance of the Master's love for the disciples; and we know how we determine who are the true disciples: those who follow the Master's lead.

Such glory is sublime in the moral province. This glory is authoritative, if not in a supernaturalistic way, but in a normative way worked up from the Master's messages and performative acts. Jesus moves with singular compassion, the author of the *LMJN* thinks, but not in miracles or exorcisms (Matt 9). We sense that our author scrambles to identify Jesus' compassion, since he rules out the obvious candidates for compassion tied to the supernatural. He also gets no help from what we might call intra-Jewish struggling with the meaning of Torah. *In fact, he struggles to find a thick meaning in Jesus' death.* So, what is left? On what can the sublime rest? The options are few: (1) *Jesus can be the greatest epitomizer of the moral ought*; or, (2) on a related point, *Jesus can bring the moral ought to the people, to all the people in a simple, essentialized way*; (3) *Jesus can intensify the Law with clarion urgency*; and, most likely of all, (4) *Jesus can extend moral concern to love for those who are beyond our natural affections and commitments.* Recall the critique of a narrow vision of justice in the classical ethicists from the *Syllabus*; recall that the author is the one who thinks Jesus brings Jew and Greek to "embrace with benevolence the whole family of mankind."[33] And then he returns to the conclusion above, that Jesus represents a God who rains on good and evil, and suddenly, *we see the way that Jefferson, through Jesus, is redefining justice to include "benevolence" toward all.*[34] (5) These points live in *one who can model what he says in what he does. Jesus bears fruit, and the way that he bears fruit is authoritative, even christic, we can say, as the one who bears the fruit that bears fruit in others.* Not only does Jesus the moral

---

33. *Syllabus*; and Letter to Rush, April 21, 1803 (Jefferson, *Writings* [Peterson, ed.], 1122–24).

34. See the discussion in Foote, *Religion*, 54.

exemplar launch the community of the disciples; he launches the recognition that the outsider requires the highest moral concern, and Jesus thereby extends the moral law. Conceivably, *Jesus understands himself to be divinely inspired for his moral campaign.*[35] But the central thing for the LMJN *is not what Jesus thinks of himself but the perfect character of his sublime system of morals.*[36]

A Reformer Christology

The *LMJN* allows its theology to continue to *develop a reformer or prophetic christology.*[37] To be sure, this contribution defies some imaginations, since it presses christologically against the inherited christologies, but it does offer *a modest christology that stands permanently against various forms of moral and intellectual abuse, particularly in the area of religion.* Its great virtue lies in its willingness to deploy a proper Jesus, one that is *Christo-propos*, for the life of the nation, and to do so without making Jesus a function of a Christian theocracy. This Jesus is always suspicious of power grabs, of obfuscating doctrines, and of part-for-whole religious mistakes. In the most specific sense, the mistakes are that of the depraved religion, Judaism, and Jesus would be its reformer.[38]

---

35. As the Letter to William Short seems to suggest: Letter to Short, August 4, 1820 (see it on the *Founders Online* website from the US National Archives, listed in the bibliography; or see Jefferson, *Writings* (Peterson, ed.), 1430–35.

36. See the Letter to Rush, April 21, 1803, Jefferson, *Writings* [Peterson, ed.], 1125 for an example of the many-time repeated praise of the sublime character of Jesus' system.

37. Sanford argues that Jefferson is to be credited with the insight that Jesus was a reformer of society among deists who had, until Priestley, largely ignored the social program implied in Jesus' message. As Sanford suggests, it was Jefferson's concern for building a republic that got him to see social-ethical opportunity in Jesus (Sanford, *Religious Life*, 39; see also Waldman, *Founding*, 72).

38. The Letter to William Short with the *Syllabus*, October 31, 1819 (Jefferson, *Writings* [Peterson, ed.], 1431). There must be a hundred references in the Jefferson corpus to his hope for reformation of Christianity and to his sense that Jesus, properly cleaned up, could be a permanent beacon for reform of religion and morality. Nonetheless, scholars who de-emphasize Jefferson's religious intentions and concerns, or who make him essentially a secular, political figure, still reject the notion that he would reform church, Bible, and culture with his figure of Jesus (see Halowchak, *American Messiah*, 91–92). For a view where Jefferson's religious convictions can be seen to found many of his social and political values, see Sanford, *Religious Life*, 55. The Letter to Thomas Law, June 13, 1814, one of the most important documents on Jefferson's moral sense, reminds us that Jefferson values social reality over individual and claims that "self-love . . . is no part of morality" (Jefferson, *Writings* [Peterson, ed.], 1336).

A Naturalized Christology

We have to point out that *our author probably would not admit that he has a christology at all,* since the notion of a christology is defined for him by the *classic* atonement theories and high christologies, and tied to what he regards as arcane and irrational doctrines.[39] If we can set aside his abhorrence of doctrine and not be affected by the belief that there can be no christology without supernaturalism, we open the discussion of a *possible naturalized christology for a "demythologized" Christianity.* Our author has naturally been inside the very room from which he and others would flee. Of course, Jefferson will not budge in his hostility to the supernaturalism of traditional christological doctrine. Whether that position seals the deal or not for him depends on a particular kind of constructive theology. He lives in an era when both stinging criticisms of historic christologies (e.g., Reimarus's or d'Holbach's *Ecce Homo*) and promising new-style constructive christologies (as in the Germans, like Kant, Schleiermacher and Hegel) are out there.

Upon finding the real Jesus under the corruption, the author of the *LMJN* is able to call himself a Christian, albeit in his specific mode of honoring the moral doctrines of Jesus. Indeed, once the author has purified the corruptions, Jesus no longer is the deluded "impostor"[40] and can be retrieved from the excessive supernaturalism of the canonical picture of Jesus.[41] Of course, his naturalism and his liberation from supernaturalism has permanent value in faith and a theology, even among those who can put their minds around a supernatural savior. Namely, it calls back Christian theology to this world. Whether we make the point negatively (about the dangers of otherworldly thinking) or positively (about the importance of thinking incarnationally), good theology must embrace the worldly. It finds theological inspiration and a permanent correction of many religious ideas in the author's scientific marvel at nature and his sense that reason must conform to the observation of nature. The *LMJN*'s materialism is a good,

---

39. If he even has studied theology. His unnuanced understanding of Trinity does not make one confident that he knows much actual theology.

40. Letter to Short, August 4, 1820 (Jefferson, *Writings* [Peterson, ed.], 1435).

41. See the story of the rescue of the deluded impostor in Sanford, *Religious Life*, 114–16. The original text for the impostor category is from the Letter to Short, August 4, 1820 (Jefferson, *Writings* [Peterson, ed.], 1438). What is at stake in the cleaning of Jesus of the piled-on corruption is the revelation of his authentic character. Jefferson's famous words for his *LMJN* are that the book is to be a "vindication of the character of Jesus": also Letter to Short, August 4, 1820 (Jefferson, *Writings* [Peterson, ed.], 1436). Kilgo recognized in the early 1900s the transformation of the Christ figure and the project to vindicate Jesus (Kilgo, "Study").

even as it struggles to make sense of the world of "spirit." This position is so, especially since his materialism rests on low-level metaphysical claims.[42]

The critique of supernaturalism can function in all the ways the Enlightenment figures saw: broadly, it can cut people free from foolish claims about their world. Our author spends most of his efforts, not on that epistemological point, but on the moral point. The foolishness about what we can know leads to foolish and crass actions in the moral life. Those who are suspicious of supernatural phenomena frequently work with a sensitivity to figurative modes of interpretation, which they employ to get around, for instance, the zapping of a fig tree.

The Transformation of the Message of Jesus

The Transformation of Miracle

Of course, all of the healings and the exorcisms have been banished from Jefferson's account. Whatever a man educated in the eighteenth century would find as supernatural has no role in the story of the real Jesus. Over and over as editor, our author faces gospel accounts of healing or exorcism, but his cutting takes the reader right to a moral issue, often to some universal lesson. Commonly, it is an insight that distinguishes the merely ritual from the moral; or it may distinguish the superficial and showy from the truly moral. The *LMJN* always has a ready pericope in which Jesus' behavior can be challenged by his enemies. We who read the biblical gospels know that many of his offenses come from the very items that the author purges. But since he begins the story with the temple explosion, he must hang on to the issues that build on the conflict theme, issues that advance the opposition and make inevitable its tragic ending.

---

42. Locke persuades Jefferson of an English-style, moderate materialism (against the French model) that brings with it the notion of a Creator-sponsored origin of matter: see Letter to Adams, March 14, 1820 (Jefferson, *Writings* [Peterson, ed.], 1440–45). Thomas Cooper evidently convinces Jefferson that Jesus was a materialist like him; see Jefferson's Letter to Thomas Cooper, August 14, 1820 (Jefferson, *Writings* [Lipscomb and Bergh, eds.], 15:109). It seems likely that Jefferson is consistent in his materialism, that it is a softer materialism, and that it includes elements of what idealists call spirit: soul, agency, free will, feelings, and the moral sense. Koch calls him a "conservative materialist" because he internalizes Locke's notion that matter could be endowed with thinking by the Creator (Koch, *Philosophy*, 35–36, 97–101). Interestingly, Jefferson thinks God and Jesus are both materialists!

The LMJN's Jesus is not the Galilean wonder-worker and exorcist who gets little notice until he finally goes to Jerusalem in his last week. He is a troublemaker for the Jewish authorities right off the bat. The conflict keeps building and eventually Jesus begins to fight back. But the author runs out of conflict materials and especially ones generated by the temple event; he must turn to the Galilean-based clash with the Pharisees and incorporate the Galilean controversy, largely over the interpretation of Torah, into the one launched in Jerusalem with the Sadducees. Consequently, *we see how putting Jesus' temple fit in the front of his ministry displaces the entire story. Placing the conflict at the beginning means that the entire mission of Jesus has been swallowed up into the conflict plot and a morality play. So far as the author absorbs the Pharisaic conflict traditions, he transforms the content of those conflicts by yoking them to the Jerusalem-launched challenge to Sadducean authority and Jesus' new moral campaign.*

As Jefferson converts the Galilean conflict traditions into the Judean plot, he must draw in the materials that surround the wonders and exorcisms, both to claim them for moral value but also to find enough material to fill out his plot. He allows Jesus to be known as a healer and an exorcist, as we have seen. He mentions healings after the evangelists have described wonders and exorcisms in the Jesus saga. We have wondered why he allows so many hints of the very supernaturalism he rejects. *The only explanation can be that he sees in the wonders, properly demythologized, sermons on the moral life.* Think of the way the author's gospel brings up a blind man—was he just healed?—and Jesus turns the blindness into a lesson on sin and infirmity (John 9:1–3). Consider the way he mentions the fig tree without the painful miracle, or how Jesus turns the tree without figs into a parable of judgment on the unfaithful.[43] With a little imagination, we can surmise that in the author's mind, *a simple parable or lesson can become distorted in ignorance.* Thus, *the supernaturalizing of the Jesus saga is part of the corruption that has overtaken the simpler, moral story.*[44] There are hints in the *LMJN* and corroborations in Jefferson's letters that the pure moral vision of Jesus gets laced with supernatural prodigies under the influence of the uneducated disciples. *Here we have an explanation how the moralist's pristine message becomes corrupted and a clue how the author employs a theory of corruption.* To corroborate this point, we remind ourselves *how quickly our author turns a parable into a performative substitute for a miracle.* A good parable sets up the moral punch line as would a miracle. *It is as if Jefferson understands*

---

43. Jefferson, *Bible* (Beacon ed.), 63; folio 16.
44. Though, admittedly, an immanent reading of the *LMJN* cannot see directly a corruption theory, until it registers the impact of Priestley's work on Jefferson's project.

that the parables and the wonders are on the same level of generality: one is a distorted version for the masses, and the other is a genuine substitute, possibly as a symbol for the educated consciousnesses. The transformation of the miraculous, thus, is much more complicated than having an editor simply excise them.

Gnostic Wisdom

We have already analyzed the way in which the *LMJN* turns the Sermon on the Mount into a *gnostic assemblage of wisdom*, a turn dependent on the stripping away of the Mosaic foundation of the Sermon and the abstracting of its audience and the context for the Sermon. *Here we will add a second gnostizing element of our text.* When the author of the *LMJN* abandons so much of the narrative, when he clusters like sayings and parables, *he gives the teaching of Jesus a gnostic and disembodied form.* In part that impression arises from the fact that the author shies away from the actions of Jesus, since they are often embedded in the supernatural. Then, he typically assembles sermons of parables and aphorisms with a universal or moralizing byline that functions as the rationale for the cluster. Again, what he emphasizes in his selections is the moral-allegorical application of a parable. Actually, our author does not distinguish between an allegory and a parable, and, thus, he moves immediately to pick up the (later-added) allegorical interpretations of many of the parables without recognizing the two genres are quite different.[45] Of course, he does not have the benefit of modern parable research.[46] We cannot fault him for this issue. But importantly, as parable researchers have noticed for a hundred years now, *the allegorical interpretations probably do not go back to Jesus but are indeed the constructions of an early church that does not understand what Jesus means by many of his parables.* The key point is not the provenance of the allegorical interpretations but *that they are already moralized readings of the parables.* Thus, the LMJN *author doubly moralizes the parables of Jesus: not only does he look for the moral nugget in every parable, but he typically adds to the allegorical interpretation of a parable as the point of the parable.*

The irony, of course, is that in the case of the parables and a few other language forms, the corruption theory is on the right trail. It assumes the expression of the master is not the expression in its original form, and that

---

45. If anything in the gospels is a good representation of the theory of corruption, the allegorical interpretation of Jesus' parables is a perfect example.

46. Seeing the parables as productive and not reproductive forms of speech probably depends on Crossan's *In Parables* or Zimmermann, *Puzzling the Parable.*

interpreters must dig deeply according to some method. The modern scholar of the parables is likely to set aside the church's allegorical interpretations as primary for the message of Jesus, while our author simply eliminates what is judged as a crust over the real words of the Master. Both methods are informed by Enlightenment hermeneutics but they differ in their judgments on the crust. Generally, accepted parable scholarship sees that what encrusts the parable is usually the applications of the church in subsequent eras, while the corruption theory posits a deception and an evil cover-up.

Today we are apt to think of parables as productive of meaning; in Jesus' ministry they draw out people and give them a little entrance into the Kingdom of God, or into that life in which everyone gets a fair wage. Our author is looking for a moral lesson when he examines the parables, and then he often latches onto the allegorizing of the parables. *The surprise is that he first takes away the supernatural, before he takes the parables out of their narrative context from the gospels; then finally he ignores their performative character for a preferred, moralized meaning of the parable.* The *tendency of his exegesis leans toward the moral universal*, and whether he gets the moral right or not, the nuggets of wisdom tend to be abstract. *Under his theory that the parables teach a moral, the parables stand independently first from the wonders, then from their narrative frame, and finally from their genre in a constructed list of abstract insights. His abstracting of the parabolic discourse of Jesus is almost inevitable, once our author strips the parables out of their contexts and separates them from the ministry of healing and exorcism.*

At this point we have to identify a tension in the *LMJN*'s theory of parable. Against the notion of the gospel of Mark where the parables help hide Jesus' messianic message, Jefferson has Jesus open every secret. In so doing, his interpretation of the parables is closer to the pre-Mark meaning, in that the parables were meant to be understood by ordinary people. However, Jefferson strips the parable from the context offered by the healings and the exorcisms. When he drops most of the "Kingdom of God" language and certainly teaching about an apocalyptic Kingdom and isolates the parables from nearly the entire (religious) life of the first-century Jew, he leaves them as pale, moralized truisms. So abstracted is the message of the parables, so allegorized is their meaning that they read like the bland gnostic apothegms of the Gospel of Thomas. What Jefferson does with the parable is as acontextual a rendering of the message of Jesus as possible. But naturally so, since he will not permit the parables to live in the context of Jesus' actual Jewish life. The result is a gnosticizing of the Jesus story in which the parables become secreted in a bland, universalized interpretive frame. Recall that the *LMJN*'s Jesus' enemies, the Pharisees, trade in secrets, and Jesus is supposed to be against secrets, according to the theory of the *LMJN*. Therefore, the text's concrete practice of interpretation conflicts with its announced notion for the parables.

We may wonder why our author goes against the secrecy theme and associates the Pharisees with secrecy. The secrecy motif is very strong in Mark but there is little evidence that the Pharisees trade in secrets. Why then is secrecy such a big deal for the *LMJN*? We find no direct answer to the question in the text itself, until we recall that our author consistently stands against tribal moralities and has Jesus stand for a universal ethic. The Jews get pegged with the concern for the tribe while Jesus raises their moral vision to include regard for all humans and communities. At this point the logic is clear. Once the *LMJN* universalizes the Sermon ethic in Jesus for all people and times, it represents the natural law fully knowable and available to all humans. And once the *LMJN* determines that the Jews are angry with Jesus' ministry from the start, *the failure to appreciate his moral vision must arise from their secretive and narrow moral vision*. So, the one who can deliver an ethic coterminous with the natural law stands as an enemy to the secrets of the tribe.

As Holowchak notes, sectarian religion is always esoteric; we can understand why the two ethics are combatants.[47] Is the great ethic of Jesus a secret? No, it could not be, or it would be trivial and less than universal. A secret ethic would be far from the natural law, and the messianic secret must be part of the corruption of the gospel.[48]

An Abstracted Ethic

Not surprisingly, though our author wants to heighten Jesus as the great moralist, he often reads the moral wisdom of Jesus in a puzzlingly flat way. He frontloads the words of calm and comfort from the Sermon at the beginning of the message of Jesus, as if to emphasize them and not the biting sayings of the body of the sermon.[49] In so doing, *he is at cross-purposes with himself: he needs the most radicality from Jesus the moralist, or he cannot account for the powerful hostility to Jesus from Jewish authorities*. And yet, he

---

47. Holowchak, *Messiah*, 53.

48. Here Jefferson's intuitions are right about secrecy and sectarian ideas but for the wrong reasons. The messianic secret is indeed an interpretive application added to Jesus' parables in Mark's theology but to explain Christian dealings with Jews in the third generation after Jesus. The irony of Jefferson's rejection of the secrecy motif comes when we recall that Jefferson himself is the chief keeper of secrets about his religion. In this inconsistency he becomes a pharisee tribalist in his private life even as he advocates for something like a civil religion for the nation.

49. Jefferson, *Bible* (Beacon ed.), 56; folio 16;

often prefers the calmer, rational, and moral recommendations and thereby undermines his campaign to account for the deadly conflict out of Jesus' sayings, not actions. Recall that the *LMJN* incorporates some of Luke's and Matthew's most powerful sections on issues of wealth and gender without cuts, yet the text often suppresses the edgiest sayings or parts of sayings (e.g., "hating" one's mother . . . ; the "dead bury their dead" in Matt 8:20 and Luke 14:26-27; or the "bringing a sword on earth" in Matt 10:17). Perhaps our author simply omits what he does not understand or accept, such as Jesus' norming children as the citizens of the Kingdom of God (Mark 9:37) or the cryptic "render to Caesar" logion (Mark 12:14).⁵⁰ Sometimes he simply quotes a radical saying as if he does not see or hear its radicality (e.g., the celibacy theme, the critique of property [Luke 18], the critique of riches [Mark 10:21, 25], the antitheticals from the Sermon [Matt 5:21], the plucking-out-the-eye passage [Matt 5:29], the no-divorce theme [Matt 5:32], the no-hate requirement [Matt 5:38], the nonresistance-to-evil requirement [Matt 5:39], Jesus' aggressive egalitarianism, and so forth). Surely, that our author quotes these passages but does not tune in to their implications is stunning for someone who celebrates Jesus as a moralist. *How can the* LMJN *pay so little attention to such potent moral recommendations?* Inexplicably, in a celebrated step, the author simply drops from the text of Matt 19:11-12, the part which commends being a eunuch for the Kingdom of God.⁵¹

This tangle of groundings captures the fix that Jefferson has gotten himself into: *he begins his editing of the Jesus story with an unthematized assumption that basically the ethic of Jesus avoids the trouble he finds in the actions of Jesus.* We know, for instance, that our author recognizes that Jesus is rejected by his family and hometown, and that Jesus turns to an itinerant ministry. But our author does not pay much attention to the radical lifestyle issues involved in this ministry (Mark 6:9). Since he omits the losing-life/gaining-life logion (Luke 14:33) and the four images of the Jesus people (light of the world, leaven, city on the hill, and salt), he makes it clear *that his followers are no sect against the world* (Luke 14). Yes, he includes Jesus' recommendation for living and begging on the road but without any of the apocalyptic frenzy or asceticism apparent in Jesus (as in Luke 18).⁵² We can wonder why.

Evidently, *radical moral dissimilarity bothers our author*. Either he is tone-deaf to Jesus' moral radicality or, when he sees it, he chooses to

---

50. Admittedly, the texts he abandons frequently are inscrutable, but they are even more unintelligible without their contexts.

51. Scholars wonder if the omission was simply a mistake, or if Jefferson was flummoxed by the strange expectation.

52. Jefferson's letters show no interest in these themes.

downplay or suppress it altogether. One wonders how our author would respond to the common criticism that the Second Mile Ethic is humanly extreme and, at points, unlivable, unrealistic, even irrational. How can he rave about Jesus the moralist when Jesus says such things? How can he include such sayings and walk away with the notion of a calm, reasonable Jesus?[53] Of course we know that the ethic of Jesus has been domesticated for centuries and that the author hears the ethic through a muffling system. *The morally harsh things in the ethic seem to roll off the author as easily as they do the orthodox Christians he dislikes.* Yet he does meet some tough issues head-on. He reads the gospels carefully and intuits many historical-critical points. When he finds harsh or demanding Jesus sayings, he has only three options for handling them: He can decide (1) that the outlandish demands are part of the "eastern hyperbole" he recognizes in Jesus; (2) that the demands represent the intense enthusiasm of an early moral genius, one who stretches people to the high ideals of the moral life; or (3) that the truly irrational or immoral demands are part and parcel of the corruption of Jesus' record by the disciples and church officials.[54]

None of these views is completely convincing, since *the letters show little awareness that he must adapt Jesus' ethic as much as Jesus' actions.*[55] He is tone-deaf to the problematic character of the moral requirements of Jesus while he is hypersensitive to any hint of the supernatural in the actions of Jesus. It seems that our author takes on Jesus' ethic with something of a tin ear, whereby he easily finds the ethic he already believes in and believes all reasonable humans would honor. That is, hearing Jesus in an already-flattened way, he discovers a cypher to the universal moral law. Jesus is radical, yes, but because his ethic is exquisite and encompassing, not because it is unlivable and irrationally harsh. *The ethic of the real Jesus never strikes our author as problematic, as the healings of Jesus do.* He never problematizes the ethic of Jesus, and he shows little recognition of how Christians have struggled to handle Jesus' too-hot moral demands. When we say that our author flattens the moral vision of Jesus, we mean he seems to emphasize the calm, happy, and untroubled recommendations for the moral life and condense them into a range of formal moral principles, such as justice, equality, love, and

---

53. Is it possible that Jefferson can simply not remove some things he knows are corruptions of Jesus' simple and reasonable morality without editorial comment?

54. The legacy of Priestley's *History of the Corruptions*.

55. With the exception of his sense that the message of Jesus has been distorted. Nonetheless, the stuff in the moral record, properly cleaned, is unproblematic in a way that the wonders and exorcisms are not.

mercy.[56] In other words, Jefferson finds universal principles in the tough demands he sets out.

When the author moves toward an abstract ethic, he drags with him an unforeseen consequence. *A bland, acontextual reading of Jesus risks the danger of interpretive retrojection of the author's vision and values onto the Jesus figure. The reason for this retrojection is that the episodes reveal no contextual grit to offer as resistance to the values of the author.*[57] Thus, authors like Byron can recognize that the reconstructed Jesus of the *LMJN* looks like its author, a subversive skeptic.[58] The abstracting hermeneutic in the *LMJN*'s portrait of Jesus actually encourages the notion that Jesus looks like his author, since the hermeneutic removes so much of Jesus' historical particularity. The irony, of course, is that Jefferson protests that he is not writing about his views in his Jesus books but representing only the real Jesus.[59] The author can present his method as if he is writing a gospel commonplace, as if he is simply saving the good stuff of the gospels. And scholars sometimes are taken in by his simple procedure. In fact, the evidence of our analysis here shows our author to be offering an original interpretation of the figure of Jesus compared to any of the gospels.[60]

---

56. See the way that Jefferson suppresses the "hate your mother" logion and turns Mary's visit to Jesus into a general lesson on who does the will of God (Jefferson, *Bible* [Beacon ed.], 57; folio 16.

57. See my analysis of the structure of retrojection onto the figure of Jesus (Wilson, *Christic Jesuses*, 1:149–67).

58. Bryan, "Reauthorizing," 21. Note that Bryan recognizes that Jefferson strips away the cosmic or metahistorical elements in the gospels' picture of Jesus, and she sees the Jesus of Jefferson to be "enmeshed in first-century Jewish life." I would debate with her second point and refer to the extent that Jefferson ignores actual Jewish life. The result is a doubly abstracted picture of Jesus without the metahistorical frame and the concretion of Jewish religious life (Bryan, "Reauthorizing," 23). Consequently, I do not think Jefferson's Jesus is a man of his time.

59. If Jefferson's Jesus looks like Jefferson, then Jefferson's protestation about finding the real Jesus is wrong, or better, a false consciousness, since his gospel selections substantially match the values of those in a lifetime of letters. If so, scholars who emphasize that Jefferson is not like Jefferson's Jesus (i.e., Holowchak, *American Messiah*, 59) simply do not own up to retrojective construction of the figure of Jesus. For the original protestation from Jefferson, see the Letter to Short, April 13, 1820 (Adams and Lester, *Extracts*, 391). There is a second irony in Jefferson's hermeneutic: he advocates a plain, nonallegorical reading of the gospels and ascribes much of the corruption to the Jews and their allegories. Yet, as we see throughout the course of the cleaning of the Jesus saga, he finds a Jesus who increasingly looks like a mirror image of himself: see the Letter to Adams, April 8, 1816 (Cappon, *Adams-Jefferson Letters*, 2:468–69).

60. Thus, Burstein is mistaken when he affirms our author's claim not to interpret the Jesus story. The issue rests in a contemporary hermeneutic that suggests that the procedure of the commonplace does a major disruption of the materials of a chosen passage when it strips the passage out of its original contexts (Burstein, *Inner Jefferson*, 260).

A Reputable Moral Life

The *LMJN*, then, flattens the pointedness of the Jesus ethic. There is another current: the text consistently purges the bad rumors about Jesus' conduct and suppresses instances when he inexplicably looks bad. Those of us who listen to the canonical accounts of Jesus hear a complex, unpasteurized Jesus. He demands outrageously; he separates his people from the rest; he zaps the demons; he fights the scribes and Pharisees about points of Torah and on holiness requirements (Matt 12). He criticizes his hometown and rejects his mother. There is much in the unpasteurized Jesus that makes the morally fastidious wince. But under the *LMJN*'s surgery *the real Jesus emerges mostly as a model citizen*. His ethic is sublime. He teaches moderation: the moral demands are serious but not extreme. His actions do not offend family or community; he does not campaign to offend his people, the Jews. There is nothing "countercultural," as we say, about Jesus' ethic. It affirms the best of human values and is inherently rational. In fact, only really rotten people would object to this ethic.

The people in the Jesus story are also well-behaved, for the most part. The *LMJN* does not show a Jesus having great trouble with his family and his hometown. The people of Samaria do not reject him wholesale (Luke 9:53). He does not denounce whole sections of the country (Luke 10), nor does he condemn the whole generation for its failures (Luke 13). Jefferson typically leaves out the apocalyptic sense of strife within families (Mark 10:29). Only the Jewish authorities act irrationally and immorally against the sublime teacher. Only they get Jesus' woes. And it is irrationality that we see, since we can hardly imagine what would motivate them so to oppose Jesus. We have to rely on our author's own words to explain their inexplicable behavior, since so little that Jesus does seems to evoke opposition: it must be a kind of jealousy that lies behind their wickedness, jealousy of Jesus' popularity, jealousy of his moral vision, perhaps. We do know that the *LMJN* omits Jesus' reputation as a glutton who parties with disreputable followers (Matt 11:19; Luke 7:34); *our author clearly wants to clean up the image of Jesus, by eliminating troublesome images in the biblical record.*

Central to the *LMJN*'s cutting is the sense that the real Jesus does not deserve his own death, and that the gossip in the gospel record is mistaken. It is unreal, but in a different kind of unreality than the unreality of the wonders and exorcisms. Wonders are simply mistaken impressions, not unlike the notion that Socrates corrupts the youth of Athens, while exorcisms are fantastic for the author, who notices that even the "neutral" Pilate recognizes Jesus' noble qualities. The author endorses the gospels' attempts to absolve Pilate and the Romans for real guilt in Jesus' death. He goes out of his way to let Pilate wash his hands of the whole deal and affirms the Roman view of truth against that of the Jewish authorities. Jefferson even allows Pilate to confirm Jesus as "King of the Jews" at the death scene, a seeming insult to the Jewish authorities, when Pilate places the sign above the cross (Matt 27:37). *Nothing in the* LMJN's *entire gospel indicts the Romans.* Pilate's role proves that Jesus is a model citizen. Even the much-blamed disciples our author rehabilitates at the end of Jesus' story. He suppresses their jockeying for power and position (Mark 10:37; Luke 9:46). He does not emphasize either Judas's betrayal (Mark 14:9; Luke 22:47–53) or Peter's denial (Matt 26:69–75; Mark 14:66–72; Luke 22:54–62). He does not even want a disciple to cut off the ear of a servant in the garden (Mark 14:47). In all of these subtle moves, *the* LMJN *shows that the people influenced by Jesus do their best to be good citizens, too.* Meanwhile, the Jewish authorities look very wicked indeed.

The Transformation of Authority

It is no surprise that the *LMJN* moves the discussion of the authority of Jesus away from a supernatural basis, away from a special intimacy with God, and away from the power of prophetic realization. Jesus does not gain status by discerning signs of the times or by playing prophet (Luke 11). Jesus' authority is not predated to his conception, his birth, his baptism, or any flashy things he does.[61] His is not the authority of healings and exorcisms (Luke 11). Jesus is not a prophet, and his meaning does not flourish within a prophetic mode of interpretation. Still, he is authoritative. Jesus' authority is not immediate but must be built up, though it is recognized already at age twelve. The *LMJN* has the gospels speak of the surprise when people discover his authority. They are "astonished" (Mark 1:22; Matt 7:28; Matt 13:54); "the Jews" marvel at his learning (John 7:15, 21), at his "speaking" (John 7:45); and, once the text cuts away corrupted notions of authority, it reveals that Jesus possesses a specific kind of authority: a teaching authority. We notice how often Jefferson reminds us of Jesus' authority: from his first, youthful sermon (Mark 1:22) to the end of the Sermon on the Mount (Matt 7:28). We notice how often the *LMJN* allows the people to recognize this kind of authority and permits even the enemy, the Jews, the Pharisees, the officers of the priests (John 7:45), to be amazed at and to debate over what this authority means (e.g., Mark 11:29; Luke 20). And we notice that Jefferson designates the authority of Jesus with the teaching word, "Master" (Luke

---

61. Of course, only his youthful encounter of Jesus with the rabbis in the synagogue anticipates his true authority as a sage.

10:25; 12:13; 11:45; John 8:1; Matt 19:16). Recall that we have seen that the *LMJN* purges virtually all of the titles for Jesus, but saves the "Master" title. We may say that the category is *a foundational choice for Jefferson's christology: Jesus is the master of wisdom.*[62]

The people's astonishment comes out of the blue, when they find authority where they do not expect it. *The authority rests in wisdom, not wonder.* It astonishes that such an uneducated person teaches with authority. They marvel that such teaching can come from Nazareth, of all places. Even the Pharisees are amazed at "these words" (Matt 22). Naturally the astonishment grows into debate. People argue about the status and the genesis of such authority. Where does he get such "doctrine" (John 18:19)? Soon debate turns to suspicion ("murmuring": John 7:12) and opposition comes out.

We can summarize the main ideas of Jesus' doctrine here by simply naming the elements: the doctrine centers on the moral life; it has to do with Jesus' trenchant insight and new moral expectations; these new demands go against older and narrower moral visions in a reformatory way. Jesus is the moral Master, but surprisingly he is a modest one who sets in place a new way without an inflated self-importance.[63] Notably, the real Jesus defers claims for himself; he does not make bombastic predictions about events, and certainly, he does not do attention-getting wonders. He remains silent in the face of the trials at the end of his life; he lets others brag about him. Tellingly, the one designation Jefferson showcases comes from the Roman, from Pilate, who, in the face of Jewish authorities, insists on designating Jesus on the cross as the "King of the Jews." Of course, we need the story of Pharisaic opposition here, but it is Pilate (along with the Centurion) who recognizes the teaching authority of Jesus and declares it "Truth." At that point the reformer's doctrine among Jews opens up to the Roman world and becomes normative as the universal moral law.

We note one final point on the *LMJN*'s transformation of authority. With the exception, say, of the last point about the moral law, the author says nothing that is not in the gospels. But by exclusion and reconfiguration of materials he lets a christology grow in a distinctive way. Remarkably, because of what he excludes as authoritative, *Jefferson must eke out all fascination with and hostility to Jesus from his teaching authority alone.* He cannot find authority in a divine provenance, in his lineage, in the worlds of prophets, in the signs and wonders or the exorcisms, in religious insights

62. Until the end of the saga, where Jefferson will allow "Shepherd" and "Son of Man."

63. Interestingly, on Jesus' modesty Jefferson in the early 1800s matches present-day Jesus research.

about Torah or holiness codes. The logic of the *LMJN*'s project requires that Jesus' authority rests on the explosive charisma of his moral message. For good or bad, that is a lot of work for a teacher. The pressure is on Jefferson, if not Jesus, to achieve this authority. Actually, *the author makes his task even more difficult in that he sometimes moderates the intense demand of the Jesus Sermonic ethic.* As we have seen, the *LMJN* consistently moves toward the universal and the "reasonable," as a man of the Enlightenment would want it. While the method heads toward a bland moral vision, the *LMJN* saves the project by enlarging it to the maximum as a life-or-death struggle with the Jewish authorities and by simultaneously shrinking Jesus' attention to the interpretation of Torah and holiness.

The *LMJN*'s transformation of Jesus' authority actually presupposes the author's own move beyond the inherited notion of the authority of sacred Scripture. *He conducts himself with authority to judge the authority of Scripture,* the sacred cow of revelation. We know why and how he does it, but we should also appreciate how daring he is to set aside the authoritative and traditional to replace it with a cleaned version of the gospels offered as authoritative. The truly authoritative must be achieved; it must be liberated by our author's own intuitions that allow him to distinguish the "diamonds in the dunghill," as he puts it over and over in *his repeatedly used symbol.*[64] And while he presents his hermeneutic as the judgments of a gut intuition, he would defend the decisions he makes according to the standards of intelligent and informed reason. Playing off Descartes, he declares, "I feel; therefore I exist."[65] Oddly, he does not make such justification in the conduct of selecting passages from the gospels; he simply cuts out what pleases him intuitively and leaves the rest on the cutting room floor. His action is intuitive—he knows what is possible in the world, probable in history, and morally appropriate for a human or a god, while his justification appears elsewhere in his letters. Susan Bryan argues that Jefferson's procedure actually is not as spiritually and intellectually arrogant as it may seem, since *he refuses to be the author of his Jesus book.*[66] That is, he views himself as a craftsperson, not a creative author. His Jesus book assembles the real Jesus, and he and his Jesus are reformers. The question remains whether the

---

64. For instance, the Letter to Adams, October 12, 1803 (Jefferson, *Writings* [Peterson, ed.], 1301); or the Letter to Short, October 31, 1819 (Jefferson, *Writings* [Peterson, ed.], 1431).

65. Letter to Adams, August 1, 1820 (Jefferson, *Writings* [Peterson, ed.], 1443). Jefferson means his parody of Descartes to illumine his own materialism, but it also serves to remind Jefferson scholars not to treat him as a simple Enlightenment figure who is only interested in reason.

66. Bryan, "Reauthorizing," 23.

author is dissembling, or whether the private and secretive side of his religious views keeps him modest. In any case, the hermeneutic moves beyond the givenness of the authority of Scripture to an authority ascertained by the implied criteria of the *LMJN*'s selection-making.[67]

The Transformation of Judgment

Even though one can imagine an Enlightenment figure would draw away from judgment, that theme actually plays heavily in Jefferson's Jesus. The surprise here is that the author's actual Jesus seems to value judgment in a way that we would not expect, and he even warms up to some sort of apocalyptic as we near the end of the story. We will have to interpret this fact later. First, we must note the kinds of judgment the *LMJN* leaves out of the account: first, judgment connected to prophecy (Matt 21), as we expect from his repudiation of the prophecy/fulfillment pattern; second, judgment connected to a very vivid/literal apocalyptic scenario (Matt 23-24); and third, judgment tied to anything that looks like an atonement doctrine. We have to say that the *LMJN* omits the whole of apocalyptic if by "apocalyptic" one means a catastrophic end to history (Mark 13), but the *LMJN* does allow some of the language of apocalyptic in certain passages, especially at the end of the story, and it does so without an apparent sense that such language lives properly within a cataclysmic worldview and may compromise its author's values. Moreover, fourth, the author omits the judgment theme when it pertains to forgiveness (for instance in Luke 6:37); this omission surprises, especially since our author uses the material before and after that single verse. Why would he reject "Judge not, and ye shall not be judged"? Possibly, the verse seems too apocalyptic for him. We know the author consistently reduces stories of conflict (e.g., in families: Matt 10:34-36 or the "peace on earth" episode; Mark 10:29-30; Luke 12:51-53). Possibly, he sees partisan judgments or retaliation in the saying. Possibly, our author hears too much of the prophetic frame to take seriously common talk of judging (compare his omission of the Parable of the Wicked Vineyard Tenants in Matt 21:33-44). In any case, the judgment he is rejecting is not that of the legal system, but of *the quick opinions we make of people whom we fear or dislike*. We suspect we are dealing with the obverse of the forgiveness theme, one the author also purges. *If he suspects talk of forgiveness often to be corrupt cheap grace, he may judge judging others as quick and vengeful.*[68]

---

67. Bryan, "Reauthorizing," 23.

68. David Brown confirms that our author cannot imagine God as judgmental in our common sense of the term (Brown, *Biographical Companion,* 44).

But once cleaned of distortion, *the idea of judgment can serve the moral life*. And Jefferson steps through the minefield of a dangerous idea. He seems to seek some positive content from which he can endorse the notion of judgment. First, *Jesus begins to accept apocalyptic where it underlines the conflict theme with its dire urgency*. Jefferson is not thinking of cosmic battles at the end of history but of the conflict with the Pharisees and the Jerusalem authorities, who bring Jesus to his death (see, e.g., his use of Matt 24:1–2 and 24:16). Arguably, the moral retrieval of apocalyptic supports the *LMJN*'s uneven use of "Son of Man" language.

When apocalyptic language looks too cosmic and Danielic (or too self-referential to the Christ), the author cuts it; but when a "Son of Man" passage supports a moral reading, he may save it. In this sense, *our author seems to demythologize the main serving of apocalyptic and to affirm in it a moral use of judgment*. Second, our author has Jesus say over and over, *the tree will be known by its fruit*. We may assume he likes this idea. *True judgment is judging the fruit of a life*. It is not cheap grace, not simply talk, but a verdict calculated on a model of active righteousness. Significantly, the *LMJN* omits the long Parable of the Wicked Vineyard Tenants (Luke 20:9–19), undoubtedly because of its allegorical tone and reference to "my beloved son." But in the parable, the owner of the vineyard looks for "the fruit of the vineyard," while the husbandmen kill the son and use violence to steal the inheritance. Here we have two typical themes yoked: judging reduced to tribal or retaliatory acts, and the genuine standard of judgment looking to the fruit of a life.[69]

The Transformation of Love

Our analysis has been building a corollary to the above points, namely, that Jefferson uses the words of the gospels to suggest an extension of love to dramatic new territories. Above, we have used the language of "extension" of moral concern and "inclusion" to name elements of the transformation of love in the Sermon. These are contemporary words, but they capture the *Jesus who expects us to care about people and situations that are beyond our natural affections*. That is, such care is outside the comfort zone of our tribes and affiliations. We are to care for outsiders, children, and known sinners,

---

69. The tree that bears good fruit is Jefferson's favorite image for a genuine religion; bearing good fruit is the test of a noble religion. See the discussion in the Letter to Miles King, September 26, 1814. https://founders.archives.gov/documents/Jefferson/03-07-02-0495/.

and to share our space and table with them.⁷⁰ The author of the *LMJN* uses the stories and parables of Jesus to extend our vision of the territory of love. Recall that Jesus redefines the family, accepts the shady woman who anoints him, and embraces Levi the publican and other sinners, like Zacchaeus (Luke 19:1).

In one revelatory juxtaposition, the author secures the general theme that love must go beyond tribal commitments: namely, in the midst of his quoting of the entire Sermon on the Mount from Matthew he inserts a chunk of Luke (6:35–36). Matthew has been establishing the higher righteousness required to be truly moral: turn the other cheek, resist not evil, and the like from Matt 5. Then Matthew's Jesus begins to stretch the notion of love beyond loving one's neighbor: that love is commonly insufficient. One must love one's enemy and "bless them that curse you, do good to them that hate you, and pray for them which despitefully use you, and persecute you" (Matt 5:44). In this amazing extension of the moral turf, Matthew also revises how we commonly think of God: the real God does not favor the good, but shines and rains on all equally. We know by coherence that the *LMJN* endorses this revision. Matthew continues: if we are good only to the ones we like, we are no better than the ones we hold in contempt (e.g., the tax collector, Matt 5:46–47). Clearly Matthew's Jesus is extending the scope of love, and we can be confident the *LMJN* endorses this extension.

To secure his point, Jefferson interrupts the whole Sermon from Matthew by quoting Luke 6:34–36. The theme is exactly the same: If one gives only to get back the same, one has not stretched beyond what the sinners do. Rather, *give without calculating who is a sinner, and give without expectation of return.* Again, the author permits the connection of the moral extension to the nature of God. God is "kind unto the unthankful and to the evil" (Luke 6:35). We are to follow the model of the mercy of "your Father" (Luke 6:36).⁷¹ Thus far, the author continues to transform God and to secure the moral life by imitation of the divine mercy, not divine perfection.⁷² Remark-

---

70. The *LMJN*, of course, does not have a developed sense for the woman in a list of those specially noted for inclusion, nor does he dare to speak much about the sick and infirm and demon-possessed, since to deal with them might suggest Jesus traffics in the supernatural.

71. On occasion, the *LMJN* will permit "your Father" language for God without sufficient reason to suppress it; except for one instance (Matt 18:35), Jefferson will never allow Jesus to say "my Father," presumably to avoid anything that smells like trinitarian thinking.

72. Recall that the *LMJN* replaces the perfection of God with the mercy of God as the model for the moral life. Holowchak notices the theme and connects it to the primacy of the theme in the central parable, the Good Samaritan (Holowchak, *Bible*, 36, 57).

ably, even though the author of the *LMJN* retreats from the heavy personal language of the Bible possibly in a deistic direction, he refuses to imagine a God who is still unresponsive and uninvolved. We have no clockmaker God here, but a God whose daily compassion is evident.[73] Our author completes his remarkable juxtaposition of ideas by returning to two of his favorite ideas, found in Matt 6. Here Jesus criticizes people who look for rewards for their good actions and who are only interested in showy displays of their virtue. With this connection he emphasizes the humility of the really virtuous and the hypocrisy of the Pharisaic types.

Both positions actually break the healthy and moral connection between what we say and what we do in the moral life. We have seen the saying-and-doing connection in our consideration of *the first principle of the moral life: The tree bears fruit according to its inner value.* The *LMJN*'s Jesus affirms that what goes on inside of the person matters; indeed, it shows up in the fruit born. At once, *he affirms the internalization of the moral expectation—the pure heart—even as he insists that what is in the heart must and will be expressed.*[74] Reward-seeking tells us that the heart is not pure and is looking for things other than virtue. One thinks of the *LMJN*'s extensive use of Luke's criticism of wealth here (Luke 12:13–34) and his repeated employment of the "no-concern" theme of the gospels (compare Matt 10:30–31; Luke 12:4–7). Showiness represents the need to be approved of by others or to be impressed with oneself (compare Matt 11:29): motives inappropriate for moral considerations. And to come back to the main point, the fruit will show what is in the tree. Interestingly, in the midst of Matthew's Sermon sections on bearing good fruit, on expecting no reward, on not being stressed out by the world, the *LMJN* pads its points by adding a whole section of Matt 12. Thus, after four verses that assert the connection between the good tree and good fruit (Matt 7:17–20), the author repeats the lesson of the saying-and-doing principle (from Matt 12:35–37) with two twists: one, he lets Matthew remind us that *we can read backward from the good act*

---

73. Even if the author of the *LMJN* has not thought through how such compassion is metaphysically possible, given other value commitments in his theology.

74. Indeed, the author often scoops up the "defilement" language of concerns for holiness in order to express the connection between the inner and the outer in the moral life. His point is not the dangers of impure foods and customs and the defilement of ritual purity (Mark 7:3, 18–23), of course, since *he ethicizes the defilement theme to accent the importance of the pure heart.* In other words, part of Jefferson's misunderstanding of the message of Jesus rests in his inability to recognize the legal and the ritual as part of the holiness codes and his inability to understand how holiness partners with the moral. Notably, the author seems to have a tin ear for holiness, and if he faces an issue of holiness, he converts it immediately into an issue of the moral life.

to the heart behind it; and two, *we will be judged according to the manner in which we make the connection.*

Here we circle back to the transformation of the theme of judgment. True judgment lives independently of what we see: a version of the blindness of justice. Luke is carrying the day for the *LMJN*: he is accounting for the growing conflict with the Pharisees and for a growing sense that things are going badly with Jesus' ministry. Then, in a rare use of the gospel of John, the *LMJN* lets John's Jesus introduce *an analysis of why we have the conflict with the Jews.* They have been given the Law by Moses, but they do not keep the law (John 7:19). That is, there is a *slippage between what they believe/say and what they do.* Then John announces the blindness of real justice: "Judge not according to the appearance, but judge righteous judgment" (John 7:24). We know what we are not supposed to do: we are not to be hypocrites like the Pharisees, who want to appear just. What is righteous in judgment is to do what the *LMJN*'s God does: to be fair toward good and evil both. As we have seen, *the Pharisee is the type for the ones who do not do justice righteously.* When Jefferson ties the saying-and-doing connection to the theme of judgment and emphasizes the importance of fair judgments, we see that he has accounted for the Pharisaic opposition to Jesus and for the woe-filled judgments on the Pharisees' conduct. They will be judged: the bad tree (a fig tree) will be cut down (Luke 13:6-9). On the other side, where good trees bring forth good fruit, there will be, first, repentance and forgiveness (Matt 18:35; Mark 6:12; Luke 13:3-5), arduous discipleship (Luke 9:57-62), dangers and persecution ("like sheep among wolves": Matt 10:6, 23; Luke 10:3), an itinerant mission of repentance, but then a great harvest (see, e.g., the use of the parables such as the Sower, mostly in Matt 13), Great Treasure (Matt 13:52), and perhaps even a hint of some comprehensive, final judgment (Matt 13:49-52; Luke 12:40; 17-18).

The disciples are to mimic the shepherd, even as the shepherd mimics the compassion of God (Matt 9:36). *The mimicking of God, first by the shepherd and then by the lambs, seems to be at the heart of the author's christology.* Only once does the *LMJN* author permit Jesus to speak of "my Father": *when humans mimic God's forgiveness* (Matt 18:35). Only once does he let the gospel texts use the term "Lord" for Jesus. Of course, we are not to get excited about trinitarian possibilities here; rather it is a passage where the shepherd sends out the lambs on the treacherous mission of compassion (Luke 10:1, immediately following the extraordinary "my Father" passage above). In a revealing juxtaposition the author sets the Jesus who refuses to judge the adulterous women from John 8:3-11 next to Luke's talk of the Shepherd in chapter 10. *Jesus includes this woman in the sphere of care, and he does so as the shepherd.* Then the text turns immediately to the Parable of the Good Samaritan, with its "Who is the true neighbor?" question and its advice to follow the example of the one who shows mercy.

The "following Jesus" theme brings Lukan messages of comfort, of courage for difficult times, and messages about some surprising reversals (the lost will be found, the prudent will be rewarded: Luke 15–16), and about the need to decide for and follow the real master. And with these, the master is turned over to the Sadducees and to the scribes (who call him, perhaps with irony, "Master"). The last week is ready to begin. If we have not thus far gotten the plot of Jesus' life, the *LMJN* repeats that the scribes and Pharisees are the representatives of Moses but do not do what Moses says (Matt 23:3). Their behavior is hypocrisy (Matt 23:5); woe to the Jewish authorities (Matt 23).

13

Jefferson and Religion

Scholars and others have been puzzled by Jefferson's secretive views on religion and on Christianity. In the past and to this very day, people pick up multifarious and elusive signals from Jefferson's writings and complete them just like the duck-rabbit of psychology.[1] His views have been subject to mythicizing, to debunking critiques, and to religious and political attempts to co-opt him.[2] In popular discussions and amateurish research, Jefferson's views on religion have become fodder for defining an evolving national identity. To some extent, Jefferson brought on his own bendable and spinnable legacy because of the complexity of his thinking and because of the secrecy with which he surrounded his views of religion.[3] In addition, scholars differ on how important religion was for Jefferson's entire thinking: some minimize its importance to this intellectual giant, and some recognize that concerns about religion pervade his entire corpus.[4]

    1. See Vicchio, *Jefferson's Religion*, 2. Recently, Manseau speaks of interpreting Jefferson on religion as something of a "spiritual Rorschach test" (Manseau, "Why Thomas Jefferson," 10). See the Letter to Clay, January 27, 1815 (Jefferson, *Writings* [Lipscomb and Bergh, eds.], 19:233).

    2. See Foote, *Religion*, 28.

    3. Thus, scholars often make the move typical of virtually all imaging of Jesus: the notion that the artist or author constructs the duck/rabbit as an unambiguous self-portrait retrojected onto Palestine in the first century. As a longtime student of images of Jesus, I have to say that the imaging of Jesus in the *LMJN* looks quite a bit like a self-portrait of Jefferson.

    4. We will see in time something of the naysayers; here note the judgment of Mark A. Noll and Nathan O. Hatch in their foreword to Gaustad's *Sworn*: The great achievement of Edwin S. Gaustad's biographical study of Jefferson is its "demonstration of how religious concerns were central to many of Jefferson's main preoccupations" (Noll and Hatch, Foreword, x). Soon we will note the malleable character of Jefferson, subject to

Among informed critical scholars today, however, there is some agreement on many issues of interpreting Jefferson's view of religion, and where there is a lack of agreement, predictable lines of difference exist. Indeed, scholars have developed some assured results of scholarship, and, at the same time, have developed sensitive antennae for agendas and biases of all kinds. When recent figures have attempted to show Jefferson as an orthodox Christian for the Christian-nation ideology, or when others have uncovered Jefferson as a secular infidel,[5] their views have been efficiently relativized by persuasive research. In this report I will not take an independent reading of the large theme of religion in Jefferson, nor will I become a combatant in the unresolved controversies in the research. But in order to determine how the *LMJN* can contribute to issues in Jefferson research, I plan to identify the main points among critical readings of Jefferson's views on religion. I will simply summarize a reading of the several points:

Jefferson's Early Critique of Christianity

Every interpretation of Jefferson's view of religion notes that he moves away from the cultural and pious Anglicanism into which he is born, in which he is presumably baptized and dies.[6] Scholars disagree on how lackluster or how pious he is as a young man and how involved in actual church life. In addition, we do not know for sure how the moving away occurred, whether as a religious crisis or as an extension of his uneven attachment to his Anglicanism, and indeed, to Christianity.[7] But by his mature years he had repudiated virtually the entire doctrinal house.[8] He comes up with

---

the construals of particular scholars and their values. Here we note Gaustad's own assessment: "Thomas Jefferson was the most self-consciously theological of all America's presidents" (Gaustad, *Sworn*, xiii).

5. For instance, Hitchens's effort to make Jefferson into an atheist (Hitchens, *Thomas Jefferson*), or the attempt of Barton and Beck to dethrone Jefferson from the Christian-nation pantheon (*Jefferson Lies*). See Vicchio, *Jefferson's Religion*, 2, 12, 14 for a critique of Hitchens's view. For a discussion of the issue see Foote, *Religion*, 23. The category of "infidel" comes from the New England clergy in the 1800 election battle and hangs over Jefferson for years: see the Letter to Charles Thomson, January 9, 1816 (Jefferson, *Writings* [Peterson, ed.], 1373).

6. This idea is a supposition, as there is no evidence of his baptism.

7. Many scholars have argued for a faith crisis early in his life (Sheridan, *Jefferson and Religion*, 15), but the evidence is inconclusive. More likely, Jefferson started to drift into new ideas under the influence of the four remarkable freethinker professors he had at William and Mary.

8. In a Letter to William Short, a letter full of praise of Epictetus, Jefferson names the virgin birth, deification, creation via the Logos, the corporal presence in the Eucharist,

a pattern of evaluating the gospel materials: there is a core of real Jesus on which the corrupting layers of ignorance and greed accrue. The only other thing between the diamonds at the core and corruption is what Jefferson calls "eastern hyperbolism," namely, the charming, "oriental" mannerisms of Jesus' style as a moralist.[9] Note that Jefferson fixes on the first Christians who corrupt Jesus' message in the *LMJN*, but simultaneously he has been stewing over the threats from New England, Calvinist preachers for many decades. Indeed, in Jefferson's allegorical imagination, the Calvinists seem to play the role of the Jewish authorities in the modern production of the passion of Jesus/Jefferson. The battle line rests on the defense of freedom against the predestinarians.[10]

We should add an excursus here about Jefferson's own religion. While we walk our way through the many phases of Jefferson's life and career and think about what the *LMJN* may contribute to Jefferson research, we have to note a couple trends in the research. Earlier studies of Jefferson, it seems, did not pay much attention to Jefferson's religion and were rightly busy with Jefferson's history and politics. Some ignored the issue of religion; some suggested that Jefferson's criticism of religion meant that he was virtually done with religion; others saw his occasional interest in religious topics to be a cypher for his political maneuvering. More recent scholarship, founded on the earlier work of Foote, Sheridan, Brent, Sanford, and others, has established a sense that the topic of religion must be mainlined in Jefferson research. As Willard Frank Jr. says, Jefferson was an "intensely religious man,"[11] one who

---

the Trinity, original sin, the atonement, regeneration, election and order of hierarchy, as Christian doctrines he cannot tolerate: October 31, 1819. https://www.csun.edu/~hcfllo04/jefflet.html; also Jefferson, *Writings* (Peterson, ed.), 130–33. Note that the scholars debate whether the young Jefferson undergoes a religious crisis. The one position finds him a conventional and sincere Anglican young man, a participant in his local church life, who undergoes a rationally stimulated crisis of faith. This Jefferson is susceptible to the freethinking of his enlightened teachers at William and Mary. He then must spend the next decades crafting a postcritical religious consciousness. The other view tends to see the young Jefferson as a diffident and vacant attender of services without much of a piety; his encounters with freethinking in his college years and after aims him toward a critique of religion. His development in his maturity consists in a particular warming toward religion. Scholars fill in the blanks on the nature of the warmup: the discovery of a personal piety, a concern for the country, the strength of republican values, and so on.

9. Letter to Short, April 13, 1820 (Adams and Lester, *Extracts*, 391, 396). Concerning these hyperbolisms, Jefferson asks for "indulgence from the circumstance under which he acted."

10. Waldman, *Founding*, 75.

11. Frank, "Religious Journey," 8. Frank suggests that Jefferson underwent four phases of his religious life, not a single one of which was nonreligion.

is haunted by and taken by his religious agenda all his life. And as the recent studies of topics in Jefferson are starting to show, current researchers now must respond to Jefferson's religion, no matter what topic they study. Thus, *Jefferson's religious life is not reducible to a thing he outgrew, to an ideology for his politics, or to an obsession of a youthful Anglican or of an old man facing death.* So also, Jefferson's phases of criticism of Christianity, his alienation from it, and his warming up to a kind of Christianity should not be taken as an end to his religious consciousness. Thus, *a nonreligious interpretation of Jefferson's religion is either false or only a partial or reductive account.*

The Materialist Commitment

Early on Jefferson comes to think of himself as a materialist.[12] Sidney Ahlstrom claims that he was among the most doctrinaire materialists of the deists of his time.[13] The real is matter and motion.[14] For Jefferson, what is not matter is nothing at all.[15] While we may not be able to unravel some of his interpretive steps, we know his claim is based on empirical science and observation. Jefferson is a capable and curious scientist, as modern science defines science. We know he knows that the way to knowledge about anything matches the empirical way of Locke and others.[16] For instance, he articulates empirical standards for history-writing familiar to all modern historians.[17] While he does not spend time crafting an epistemology, we know he understands that being a materialist distinguishes him from spiritualists of all kinds, whether of the Christian or platonic sort. In the world of philosophy, Jefferson blames Platonists for the metaphysical, transcendental hypnosis of Western philosophy, and he notes that Platonists have hijacked Christian religion.[18] The Christians also tend to get into speculative things

---

12. Jefferson's fullest explanation of his materialism is in the Letter to Adams, August 15, 1820 (Jefferson, *Writings* [Peterson, ed.], 1443–45). See the discussion of his materialism in Sanford, *Religious Life*, 147–52.

13. Ahlstrom, *Religious History*, 36; Letter to John Adams, April 11, 1823 (Braden, "Ye Will Say I Am No Christian," 220).

14. Letter to Adams, August 15, 1820 (Jefferson, *Writings* [Peterson, ed.], 1444).

15. Letter to Adams, August 15, 1820 (Jefferson, *Writings* [Peterson, ed.], 1444).

16. See Foote, *Religion*, 13.

17. Letter to Short, August 4, 1820 (Jefferson, *Writings* [Peterson, ed.], 1430–35).

18. The Letter to Adams, July 5, 1814, provides a fine summary of the criticism of Plato from our author (Jefferson, *Writings* [Lipscomb and Bergh, eds.], 13:390). See also Letter to Short, August 4, 1820 (Jefferson, *Writings* [Peterson, ed.], 1435–36). There are two issues in the critique of Plato and the platonic tradition: the ideas of Plato themselves, which Jefferson regarded as mystifications, and the way the platonic

because of their fascination with mystery and magic. The speculative and mythical urge within the religion is overtaken and misused by Christians interested in power and profit.

Jefferson's materialism never lets him warm up to what he calls Platonism, even as he comes to see a despiritualized Christianity as morally powerful and useful. Once he has walked the path of a comprehensive materialism, he has no choice but to argue that Jesus was a materialist of some kind. Thereafter, he starts to warm up to the figure. Under his rationalist version of Christianity Jefferson understands that the Creator creates matter and endows matter with thinking and action.[19] Jesus, therefore, is a critic of immaterialism, and even the language of "spirit" in the New Testament refers to a special kind of matter.[20]

Before we leave the topic of materialism, we need to make a qualification. Yes, Jefferson is an ardent materialist; and yes, he values empirical evidence and is a rationalist. But his epistemology includes an *appeal to moral intuition*, some kind of an *immediate feeling for what is right*. This feeling does not quite fit classic materialism or empiricism. *He uses "intuition," "sense," and "feeling" for this immediacy, and it is not exactly reason and not perception in the world of sensation, though it is not and cannot be anti-reason either.*[21] It must be an immediate apprehension of what is right, what is just,

---

tradition enveloped and transformed the Jesus saga, which he regarded as one of the prime causes of the corruption of Jesus' message (see Malone, *Jefferson*, 4:202).

19. Letter to Adams, August 18, 1820 (Braden, "Ye Will Say I Am No Christian," 211).

20. Letter to Adams, August 18, 1820 (Braden, "Ye Will Say I Am No Christian," 211). Jefferson explicitly connects his view that spirit is a kind of matter to a study of the church fathers and their identifying "spiritual matter" as matter without a heavy corporal character (212). Interestingly, if Jesus is a materialist and God is matter, those who deny the materiality of God are the real atheists (212).

21. See one of the many evocations of the intuitive sense in Letter to Adams, April 11, 1823 (Jefferson, *Writings* [Peterson, ed.], 1466–69). The feeling does not belong to the brain in its cognitive faculty; it gives rise to a moral sense that is primal and intuitive and as it pertains to the life of a community, it gives the individual a sense of justice. See the Letter to Francis W. Gilmer, June 7, 1816 (Jefferson, *Writings* [Lipscomb and Bergh, eds.], 12:315); and Letter to Thomas Law, June 13, 1814 (Jefferson, *Writings* [Peterson, ed.], 1335, 1336–39). The moral sense is from the Creator of all the faculties, and it focuses the person on an intuition of duty, aiming it at well-being and happiness: Letter to Peter Carr, August 10, 1787 (Jefferson, *Writings* [Peterson, ed.], 814–18). A reading of a lot of Jefferson criticism suggests that many researchers ignore or downplay the intuitive moral sense and think that Jefferson is exclusively a cognitivist on all matters. *Such an orientation makes it almost impossible to understand his ethic and his understanding of religion.* Koch reminds us how important is the moral sense, how much it challenges interpreters who see Jefferson as a scientized rationalist, and how much he starts to historize the moral sense. It is indeed an aptitude born with us but it develops with

and, since the moral element is constitutive of religion, religion is rooted in this sense.[22] Therefore, we face an issue that the philosophers continue to debate: While Jefferson is undoubtedly a materialist, what kind of materialist is he? Does he take his materialism in a hard or soft direction?[23]

The Critique of Supernaturalism

Naturally, a criticism of supernaturalism flows directly out of Jefferson's materialism. His views on this point match the epistemological commitments of English/Scottish thinkers of the Enlightenment. He believes there is nothing real about various prodigies, period. All such things are mistakes, confusions, misunderstandings, or the ignorance of people who do not live in the maturity of science. Eventually all thoughtful people will view the

---

our lives as we face new circumstances and challenges. One thinks of Jefferson's early enthusiasm for classic moralities and his subsequent discovery that Jesus extends the moral scope to include other-regard: he cools with Epicurus and sees the power in the Sermon on the Mount. Koch claims that the moral sense and its development depends on Lord Kames's *Essay on the Principles of Morality and Religion* (Koch, *Philosophy*, 23–26). We notice that the scope of the moral life in a human suggests that Jefferson is no longer a classic American Enlightenment rationalist, even as he allows the moral sense to be informed by reason. Indeed, the application of some utilitarian concern to the notion of reason further moves Jefferson from the classic rationalist (see Yarbrough, *American Virtues*, 36–38).

22. Note that scholars debate whether religion is completely reducible to morality or if it has a suppositum not claimed by morality. Those who regard Jefferson as a religious person tend to see that religion has some independence in his view, while advocates of a more secular reading of Jefferson think there is no residue when religion gives way to its essential morality.

23. Years ago, Koch argued for a *soft materialism* in Jefferson, one that could be distinguished from that of d'Holbach's. But Koch's Jefferson is unwilling to be consistent about his materialism when it comes to the intuitive dimension of his ethics and his care for religion (Koch, *Philosophy*, 34). More recently, John Colman argues for a hard version, and that Jefferson's other commitments, say, to be serious about religion, reveal that his philosophical views do not fit his values. Jefferson must scramble to find a consistent materialism that still allows his values. See Colman, "Diamonds" for Colman's reading of Bolingbroke, Pierre Flourens, and Thomas Cooper. He reacts eventually by asserting the notion that matter can be ert, moving, and thus capable of what we used to call spiritual things (Colman, "Diamonds," 346). Colman appeals to the study of Douglass Wilson on the early Bolingbroke *Commonplace* as evidence for a hard materialism in Jefferson (Wilson, "Jefferson and Bolingbroke"). Without intruding on the debate, we want to note that the appeal to Bolingbroke argues from very early materials of Jefferson and does not consider developments in his thought toward the end of his life. The brain studies of Marie Jean Pierre Flourens electrifies the old Jefferson because they appear to show that brain function and locations account for things hitherto ascribed to spiritual mentality and thereby to confirm Jefferson's materialism: see the Letter to Adams, January 8, 1825 (Braden, "*Ye Will Say I Am No Christian*," 227–28).

Virgin Birth of Jesus like the generation of Minerva from the brain of Zeus.[24] So when Jefferson literally cuts out the supernatural from the gospels' Jesus story, he enacts his judgment that there is nothing to retrieve in accounts of the supernatural. The reduction is complete. So far as Jefferson defines belief as "the assent of the mind to an intelligible proposition," we can be certain that the supernatural can have no role in real religion.[25]

The Critique of "Platonic Mysticism"[26]

The materialist in Jefferson wages a lifelong battle against speculative thought, what he calls "mystical theology."[27] From college on, Jefferson's fine mind would be directed to practical things and to ethics. In terms of our consideration here, *Jefferson blames the platonic tradition for the corruption of the simple gospel of Jesus.*[28] In this theory church leaders and priests ally their interests to use religion for power and profit with the mystifying hypnosis of platonic thinking. Platonists can be blamed for the doctrine of the Trinity[29] and for systematizing the plain teaching of Jesus.[30] In Jefferson's

---

24. Letter to Adams, April 11, 1823 (Braden, *"Ye Will Say I Am No Christian,"* 225).

25. Letter to Adams, August 22, 1813 (Braden, *"Ye Will Say I Am No Christian,"* 88). Obviously, we have the motivation for eliminating the supernatural from the Jesus saga, an elimination that leaves the gospel story in the *LMJN* without a clear basis for the persecution and execution of Jesus. See the discussion in Manseau, *Jefferson Bible,* 71–72. Notice that this definition is of belief, not faith, and not the more ephemeral moral sense we have just discussed. Belief is cognitive assent for Jefferson, and it properly fits where reason does its work to persuade one. We note that Jefferson's rationalism, especially in his early years, directs his thinking away from the Protestant tradition that belief is an existential faith, not a cognitive truth. As he begins to unfold his notion of a moral, intuitive sense that prompts and informs the moral life, he moves away from the classic Catholic Christian model of faith as cognitive assent.

26. Concerning blaming Plato for the corruption of the simplicity of the real Christianity, see the Letter of Adams, July 5, 1814 (Braden, *"Ye Will Say I Am No Christian,"* 138–39; see also Vicchio, *Jefferson's Religion,* 8).

27. See the ridicule of platonic thinking Jefferson shared with John Adams in the Letter of Adams, June 28, 1812 (Braden, *"Ye Will Say I Am No Christian,"* 32–34). Platonists and Philo of Alexandria bring "oriental ideas" from Egypt into the Christian religion; see also the Letter to Short, August 4, 1820 (Jefferson, *Writings* [Peterson, ed.], 1435).

28. Letter to Adams, October 12, 1813 (Braden, *"Ye Will Say I Am No Christian,"* 99); Letter to Short, August 4, 1820 (Jefferson, *Writings* [Peterson, ed.], 1435), where Jefferson suggests Plato corrupted Socrates himself and thus the pattern of followers doing harm to the charismatic moral voice is established long before we get to Jesus.

29. Letter to Adams, August 22, 1813 (Braden, *"Ye Will Say I Am No Christian,"* 87).

30. Letter to Adams, January 24, 1814 (Braden, *"Ye Will Say I Am No Christian,"* 139).

analysis, he and his critical allies should prepare for the "euthanasia for Platonic Christianity."[31]

The Incoherence of Doctrine

Jefferson's resistance to speculative thought of any kind leads to an early and lifelong criticism of the doctrinal tradition.[32] Doctrine is complex when religion is simple; *doctrine is corrupt because it is obfuscating*, when true religion offers an other-regarding morality. When he blames Platonism for overtaking Christian religion, he makes doctrine the enemy, for here the speculative urge combines with the mystical urge of religion to produce the reified incoherences of Christian theology. For Jefferson, the symbol of this unfortunate marriage is the Christian doctrine of Trinity, which he ridicules over and over.[33] In particular, he repeatedly blames Athanasius as the culprit who invents inappropriate, dangerous, and obfuscating doctrine.[34] Three is not one; one is not three, such is Jefferson's unsophisticated suspicion of trinitarian affairs. Actually, Jefferson seems completely unlettered in the history of the doctrine and likely unwilling to be tutored on the point. Instead, he leaves the matter of the Trinity with a recognition that the Christians have become polytheists. Here Joseph Priestley's Unitarianism influences Jefferson's insistence on the oneness of God. We note that he finds other Christian doctrines, such as the Virgin Birth, the two-natures doctrine of christology, and the resurrection of Jesus, as unintelligible as is trinitarian thinking.

---

31. Letter to Adams, October 12, 1813 (Braden, "*Ye Will Say I Am No Christian*," 101).

32. Consider Jefferson's repetitious catalog of complaints with doctrine in the Letter to Rush, April 21, 1803 (Jefferson, *Writings* [Peterson, ed.], 1125).

33. See Sanford, *Religious Life*, 88–90.

34. For the blaming of Athanasius, see the Letter to Sparks, November 4, 1820 (Adams and Lester, *Extracts*, 401); the Letters to Waterhouse, June 26, 1822, and July 19, 1822 (Adams and Lester, *Extracts*, 405, 407). See the discussion in Vicchio, *Jefferson's Religion*, 32, 38. Sheridan notes that Jefferson complains about the doctrine of the Trinity "with greatest feeling and frequency" and suggests that the doctrine is the heart of Jefferson's difficulty with Christianity (Sheridan, *Jefferson and Religion*, 65–66).

The Theory of Corruption and Priestcraft[35]

Jefferson's foundational philosophical point comes yoked with a typical Enlightenment critique of priestcraft.[36] He works up a theory of what goes wrong with Christian religion, namely, that it departs from the natural priestless foundation of all religion.[37] We need to note, however, his early views that religion itself exhibits, and too often all religions contain, weaknesses and limitations even before they are corrupted. Specifically, Christian religion is a religion conceived in the infancy of human life, before the age of reason, before the start of observational science. Consequently, it is subject to an "eastern hyperbolism."[38] In addition, Jesus' doctrines are incomplete and "defective."[39]

Jefferson's early suspicion of religion, and especially Christian religion,[40] gets some teeth when he discovers Priestley's doctrine of corruption.[41] Priestley's importance for Jefferson's religious development cannot be overestimated. It is especially his work *The Corruptions of Christianity* that equips Jefferson with a way to account for the unpleasant, unacceptable features of orthodox Christianity that he detests: the decent religion of Jesus has been corrupted.[42] In this corruption theory Jefferson learns of

35. See Vicchio, *Jefferson's Religion*, 8.

36. Jefferson calls priests "cannibals" (Vicchio, *Jefferson's Religion*, 9). If Jefferson is more influenced by English deism, the cause may be in his view that the clericalism of France dominates both French freethinking and the character of France's revolution. He really dislikes the Catholic Church's domination of French life and government. His enemies, however, linked Jefferson more to the French tradition of freethinking.

37. As he finds in the Indians of America and the Quakers, whom he admires: Letter to Adams, August 22, 1813 (Braden, "*Ye Will Say I Am No Christian*," 87).

38. Letter to Short, April 13, 1820 (Adams and Lester, *Extracts*, 392). Note that what is a defect in Jesus for the young Jefferson becomes a charming orientalism, as they call it, for the mature Jefferson.

39. *Syllabus* (Jefferson, *Writings* [Peterson, ed.], 1123–26; see Foote, *Religion*, 55.

40. Probably informed by Viscount Bolingbroke, whose ideas on Christianity Jefferson saves completely, word for word, in his notebooks (Sheridan, Introduction, 16). We may assume that via Bolingbroke Jefferson questions revelation; the quality of scriptural revelation; the ethnocentrism of biblical views of God; and the patterns of creation, the fall, redemption, and the like. Manseau reminds us that Bolingbroke is the influence who schooled Jefferson in serious hostility to Hebrew Scripture (Manseau, *Jefferson Bible*, 21).

41. From Priestley, *A History of the Corruptions of Christianity* of 1782, a work that Vicchio describes as "a kind of metaphysical Bible for Jefferson." Sheridan reminds us that Jefferson had been pondering the notion of the corruption in the Jesus record before he devoured Priestley's work (Sheridan, Introduction, 16). See the discussion of the importance of Priestley for Jefferson in Vicchio, *Jefferson's Religion*, 41–44.

42. Vicchio, *Jefferson's Religion*, 41. Jefferson tells Priestley, who had inspired his

two conditions for the distortion of the religion, namely, that the origins of Christianity are obscure, and that the message of Jesus has been obfuscated. Part and parcel with these new discoveries is *the rudimentary notion that biblical scriptures come in layers of meaning.*[43] The first condition that leads Christianity to become distorted, that its origins are obscure, points to the ignorance of Jesus' disciples and to the distance between the gospel writers and the events of Jesus' life: the writers either do not know the details, do not understand them, or both.[44] Jefferson regrets that Jesus does not have a smart and faithful Xenophon to write for him.[45] The second condition that leads to Christianity becoming distorted has to do with early Christian leaders taking over the "disfiguring" of the disciples so that eventually priests see in it an opportunity to manipulate the religion for power and profit.[46]

Clearly, Priestley's theory of corruption inspires Jefferson to look again at the accounts of Jesus in the gospels.[47] He now finds them as "paradoxical" with a schizophrenic view of Jesus, at once admiring and yet being irritated. At this point Jefferson launches his lifelong constructive crusade to save religion and the figure of Jesus from corruption[48] by purging the gospel of "amphibologisms."[49] *In Jefferson's hermeneutic, the interpreter,*

---

cleaning of the Jesus tradition, that the received story of Jesus represents a "perverted system" (Letter to Priestley, March 21, 1801, in *Writings* [Peterson, ed.], 1085). See Church, "Politics" for an account of the rise of the troublesome clergy, in Jesus' day and Jefferson's.

43. Priestley, *History of the Corruptions*. See the discussion in Manseau, *Jefferson Bible*, 31–32; and Burstein for an argument that the theme of corruption predates in Jefferson the impact of Priestley's notion of corruption (Burstein, *Inner Jefferson*, 53).

44. Since Jesus does not write and his followers are unlettered, they misunderstand much, they forget much, and they remember things at a distance. See the Letter to Adams, October 12, 1813 (Braden, *"Ye Will Say I Am No Christian,"* 99).

45. As Jefferson writes in his *Syllabus* (Jefferson, *Writings* [Peterson, ed.], 1124).

46. It is a likely allegorical feature of Jefferson's thought that he is thinking of the preachers with whom he fights, especially in the 1800 election, when he speaks of the Pharisee and the priests who oppose Jesus and of the early Christian leaders who distort Jesus' message. Possibly, Jefferson's obsession with the corruption of the clergy arises from his experience in France. In any case, the issue of corruption of the clergy in the *LMJN* resonates with the Jefferson, who has feared the intrusion of religion into the political province for decades; see Waldman, *Founding*, 75. Note that Jefferson understands himself as persecuted by the New England clergy: see the discussion in Waldman, *Founding*, 76.

47. See the Letter to Adams, August 22, 1813 (Braden, *"Ye Will Say I Am No Christian,"* 88).

48. Waldman, *Founding*, 77.

49. Jefferson uses this charming word, familiar to readers of Kant, to identify the way that the disciples attribute their misunderstandings of Jesus' message to Jesus: Letter to John Adams, October 12, 1813 (Braden, *"Ye Will Say I Am No Christian,"* 99); see

once enlightened, can discern the genuine Jesus voice in the texts by its moral clarity, eloquence, and imagination. Jesus' words will be self-evident, like "a diamond in a dung-hill."⁵⁰ Oddly, then, the "most perverted system" will emerge as the "most sublime & benevolent."⁵¹ When we bring together the theme of corruption and the image of the diamond, we have before us Jefferson's entire Jesus project. Note that part of Jefferson's corruption theory assumes that "all the learned of his [Jesus'] country, entrenched in its power and riches, were opposed to him, lest his labors should undermine their advantages"⁵²

Religion as Private

Jefferson views religion as essentially a private thing between the person and the deity.⁵³ This notion is the "God and a man" theme he repeats so often. The private character of an individual's religion is so sacred to Jefferson that he as a president and a statesman does not feel he should influence policy unduly with his own private view. He does not preach his views; he endures quiet, major misunderstandings of his views; and, painfully, he even tolerates people who do not tolerate his views of religion. He does not believe his religion is anyone's business, and he advises each not to meddle in others' religions; he tries to avoid religious controversy and wants to keep his *Syllabus* from public criticism.⁵⁴ While he does reveal his views to a few confidantes, largely through some famous letters, he works extremely hard to ensure that they do not share his views with the wider public.⁵⁵ Jefferson's sense of religion's private character unfolds into his doctrine of toleration of all religion and nonreligion and into the political doctrine that the state

---

the discussion in Church, Introduction, 17. See also the colorful language Jefferson uses to describe his method of separating "gold from dross" in the Letter to William Short, October 31, 1819 (Jefferson, *Writings* [Peterson, ed.], 1431.

    50. Church, Introduction, 18, 19. The Cartesian project of methodic doubt should be noted in his hermeneutic. See Letter to Adams, October 12, 1813 (Jefferson, *Writings* [Peterson, ed.], 1301).

    51. Letter to Priestley, March 21, 1801 (Jefferson, *Writings* [Peterson, ed.], 1085).

    52. *Syllabus*, Jefferson (*Writings* [Peterson, ed.], 1124).

    53. As seen, for instance, in the Letter to Rush, April 21, 1803 (Jefferson, *Writings* [Peterson, ed.], 1123).

    54. Letter to Adams, August 22, 1813 (Braden, "Ye Will Say I Am No Christian," 88); see the discussion of Jefferson's privacy about religion in Sanford, *Religious Life*, 13–14).

    55. In the Letters to Rush, April 21, 1803, and especially the one of January 16, 1811 (Jefferson, *Writings* [Peterson, ed.], 1122–23 and 1234–39, we see how obsessed Jefferson is about the privacy of his views on religion. He feared Rush's son would make his *Syllabus* known. See the discussion in Church, Introduction, 21–22.

and civil society can never be allowed to coerce in religious matters.[56] Indeed, the minute religion loses its "God and a man" character, it becomes tyrannous. Actually, Jefferson suspects that the opposition of the powerful consorts with the ignorance of the disciples to distort Jesus' teachings. The ignorance of the followers may be sad for the moral tradition but the powerful bring Jesus to his execution: "an early victim to the jealousy & combination of the altar and the throne."[57]

Undoubtedly, his sense of the private character of religion prompts his Jesus books, since they function to clarify his views on religion to himself and to a handful of close colleagues in times of challenge and critique. To them he reveals what he really thinks, and often his Jesus construction is his mode of articulating his wider views, both religious and political.[58] Undoubtedly, too, his view of religion contributes to his ambiguous and complex relationships to several kinds of ecclesiastical institutions. In one frank confession, Jefferson seems to have recognized himself as one who is not a "belonging kind" when it comes to religion: "I am a sect by myself, as far as I know," he says.[59]

The Subjectification of Religion

So far as Jefferson decides that his and each other person's religious life is a personal matter, he brings along both a theory of religion and one of the pillars of his political thought. The heart of religion is in the human heart.[60] It lives within the human subject and does not spill out into the public area.

---

56. Locke undoubtedly stands behind the value of religious toleration and freedom. See the discussion of the issue of religious freedom in Sanford, *Religious Life*, 24.

57. *Syllabus* (Jefferson, *Writings* [Peterson, ed.], 1124–25). Note that Wildman and others recognize the allegorical condition between those who persecute Jesus and those who criticize Jefferson aggressively: "The office of the reformer of the superstitions of a nation is very dangerous" (Letter to Short, August 4, 1820, Jefferson, *Writings* [Peterson, ed.], 1438). See Waldman, *Founding*, 80.

58. Michael Zuckert proposed a new view to consider: Jefferson's secrecy about his religion arises less from a complex desire to be private than from a genuine confusion about religion: a confusion about religion's problematic character, its immorality, the offense to reason, how to handle its corruption, and also how to deal with the attractive elements of Jesus, and so forth (Zuckert, *Natural Rights*, 87–89).

59. Letter to Ezra Stiles Ely, June 25, 1819 (see it on the *Founders Online* website from the US National Archives, listed in the bibliography; or see Adams and Lester, *Extracts*, 386–87).

60. One of the best introductions to the private side of Jefferson's religion can be found in Sheridan, Introduction.

Consequently, Jefferson is an enemy of theocratic nations.[61] We are not to worry about the views of the other persons who do not harm. Jefferson even does not want to know the other guy's religious views, nor does he want to reveal his own.[62] "Say nothing of my religion," Jefferson writes. "It is known to my god and myself alone. Its evidence before the world is to be sought in my life; if that has been honest and dutiful to society, the religion which has regulated it cannot be a bad one."[63] Here Jefferson finds a lifelong political principle in his belief in the private character of religion: namely, the government has no business intruding on religion where there is no public harm.[64] This principle is Jefferson's noncoercion doctrine, in which he argues that coercion violates God's plan for each human mind to be free.[65] To force belief while advancing one person's religion actually violates the divine purpose. Such religion is false. Therefore in the view of religion Jefferson is crafting, true belief does not impose belief in the public square. That is, the doctrine of noncoercion has a positive side: the principle of toleration.[66] Each of us must be publicly tolerant, even to ignore what is private to a person, while the government acts only to stop injury. The negative entailment of this principle is that there cannot be an established religion for the nation, not public support of a particular one.[67] And positively, it becomes the famous "wall of separation between church and state."[68]

61. Arguably, this is the reason he does not get along with the puritanical and Calvinistic religion and preachers of New England.

62. See Jefferson's fear that his frank Letters might be revealed in Lindsay's published *Memoirs*: Letter to Adams, June 15, 1813 (Braden, "*Ye Will Say That I Am No Christian*," 56).

63. Letter to Adams, January 11, 1817 (Braden, "*Ye Will Say That I Am No Christian*," 190).

64. In the important *Virginia Statute for Religion Freedom* (Virginia Museum of History and Culture, "Thomas Jefferson and the Virginia Statute").

65. See Virginia Museum of History and Culture, "Thomas Jefferson and the Virginia Statute."

66. It is interesting that the entire article about "religion" in his *Notes on the State of Virginia* from 1781 focuses on a critique of intolerance on the part of the Anglicans in Virginia. Jefferson notes that the Anglican establishment has controlled the thinking, the money, and the legal opportunities of the colony (Jefferson, *Writings* [Peterson, ed.], 283–87). The analysis of the domination of Virginia by the established religion seems to be the negative for which the "A Bill for Establishing Religious Freedom" is the positive (Jefferson, *Writings* [Peterson, ed.], 346–48).

67. See Jefferson's criticism of establishing religion in New England: Letter to Adams, May 5, 1817 (Braden, "*Ye Will Say That I Am No Christian*," 194). He speaks of the "disgrace" of establishing religion in America as a "Protestant Popedom" (Sanford, *Religious Life*, 22).

68. The same separatist principle underlies Jefferson's struggle to free his university

Identifying a theory of the private character of religion does not mean that Jefferson thinks religion is essentially or primarily emotive, nor does it mean that religion is unimportant for the world. Rather, religion is essentially subjective, in that it lives in the subjectivity of the individual.[69] But it certainly shows up in the public square when people act morally. It is possible that there is a tension between the private and the public in Jefferson's view of religion, and the scholarship on Jefferson's views on religion swings back and forth between scholars who emphasize the private and those who emphasize Jefferson's public concerns that proper religion strengthens the republic. The study of the *LMJN* becomes a perfect instance in the divide in the research: some scholars emphasize the evidence that Jefferson wanted the text to be his private devotional manual while others find evidence from the letters that the *LMJN* was settling scores with his critics and advancing a vision of the moral life for the republic.[70] In any case Jefferson himself would probably insist that privately moral, transformed persons act morally in the public square.[71] Once we have pointed out Jefferson's complex view of the religion of public and private, we understand how Jefferson got into trouble with Americans who are more of a theocratic mindset.[72]

The Moral Construal of Religion

Humans have a natural sense for right and wrong.[73] This natural sense is intuitive and does not come through reason; it is not irrational, but it arises

---

from ecclesiastical control. Foote calls Jefferson's struggle for religious freedom the "main challenge of his life" (Foote, *Religion*, 23).

69. One famous location for this theme in Jefferson can be found in his Letter to Margaret Bayard Smith, August 6, 1816 (Adams and Lester, *Extracts*, 376).

70. These two emphases between which interpretation swings are both grounded in textual evidence, and scholars repeat the battle concerning which emphasis is more Jeffersonian. From my point of view, the difference between the two emphases of the theme in Jefferson and in interpretation of the *LMJN* depends on *a particular scholar's comprehensive construal of Jefferson as a thinker*. In some sense, the difference depends on a scholar's values in relation to the evidence, particularly on the question whether Jefferson had a genuine and cultivated piety. The more religious interpretations of Jefferson tend to emphasize the private, devotional theme for the *LMJN* while the more political-historical interpretations see the book as contributing to building a republic.

71. The closeness of his approach to the moral life to Luther's here is striking; the approach is noticeably far from that of Calvin, whom he hated.

72. His work on religious freedom in the *Act of Virginia*, for instance, would be read by theocrats as proof of Jefferson's infidelity. Waldman uses the charming phrase "The Pious Infidel" to name how complex is Jefferson's alleged infidelity (Waldman, *Founding*, 72).

73. Sheridan thinks Henry Home persuaded Jefferson that God gives humans an

from a sentiment, almost an a priori triggered experientially.[74] Since for Jefferson religion is essentially about morality and an aid to the moral life, religion arises from the natural sentiment to believe in God. Though essentially a private thing, religion occupies the moral sphere of the human and aims to make the individual moral.[75] Then, as he recognizes that the heart of religion is the moral individual, his sources and influences insist that the moral sense must include a duty to the other.[76] Jefferson writes to Miles King, "I must ever believe that religion is substantially good which produces an honest life, and we have been authorized by One whom you and I equally respect, to judge the tree by its fruit."[77] That is, it is the voluntary capacity of humans to discern and live by the moral law; the moral law does not move in the affections or cognitive faculties but in direct intuitions.

Jefferson's Doctrine of God

Packed into Jefferson's sense that religion is a private affair is a firm affirmation of the need for a God. His view of God starts logically, if not chronologically, in his rejection of trinitarian thinking.[78] At an early age, he set in place the notion that God is one, and the only God he could believe in is a unity. Indeed, his mature interest in Unitarianism seems to center almost

---

innate faculty for right and wrong (Sheridan, *Religion*, 19).

74. The parallel to Kant's synthetic a priori is uncanny. See Holowchak, *Uncovering*, 147, 169–70 for an orientation to the sentiment that founds the moral sense and its essential separation from reason. Jefferson sets heart as different from head.

75. See the discussion in Sanford, *Religious Life*, 49–55. Note that there are probably several reasons that Jefferson hides his views on religion and Jesus: he may be puzzled by religion, he may sense he is out of step with many people's religion, he may worry about making changes in his views, he may worry about the political consequence of his views, or he may be afraid of confirming the already negative views.

76. Andrew Burstein notes that Jefferson's favorite early sources among the philosophers and the early, significant theological theme of Laurence Sterne, unified in their emphasis on developing sympathy for others. (Burstein, *Inner Jefferson*, 28).

77. Letter to Miles King, September 26, 1814 (see it on the *Founders Online* website from the US National Archives, listed in the bibliography). Note the tree/fruit images so important for our exegesis of the *LMJN*. The tree that bears fruit is the word that is acted upon. It is the image for Jesus' insistence that the moral life requires action and not simply fine ideas. It becomes the image that supports Jefferson's insistence that morality is centrally benevolence (Yarbrough, *American Virtues*, 49–50).

78. Sanford rightly sorts out Jefferson's typical language: an "atheist" means belief in no God, a "theist" means belief in a Trinitarian God and is associated with the old orthodox Christianity (see Sanford, *Religious Life*, 91), while a "deist" refers to one who believes in a simpler, single monotheism such as Jesus and the Jews. Jefferson gives a positive meaning only for the last term (Sanford, *Religious Life*, 130).

exclusively in the Unitarian criticism of the Trinity and the turn to a strict monotheism.[79] Jefferson speaks warmly of Unitarianism, seems to identify himself with the movement, and, in a famous prophecy, expects it will win the religious turn of the United States with its belief in the oneness of God. Yet for the most part, his attraction to the Unitarians takes the form of appreciating their rejection of the Trinity and of the two-natures doctrine in christology.[80]

Jefferson gives warrants for his divinity through classic cosmological reasoning: "It is impossible, I say, for the human mind not to believe that there is in all this design, cause and effect up to an ultimate cause, a Fabricator of all things from matter and motion, their Preserver and Regulator."[81] Jefferson looks at the design, the skill, the power, and even the compassion of the universe and works, effect-to-cause, up to an ultimate cause of the universe: Nature's God.[82] In this sense it is a view that matches the deism of many French intellectuals, but possibly with one qualification: *Jefferson happily thinks of the divinity as involved, compassionate, and present where humans use their God-given reason.*[83]

Once we follow the overlap between Jefferson's cosmological argument and his right opinion of nature, we face a tension in his understanding of God. The chain from the cosmological argument spans nicely to the revelatory power of nature.[84] On other days, in other letters, Jefferson plays the

79. Vicchio suggests that being a "Unitarian" in Jefferson's day meant simply rejecting the Trinity—and probably also the two natures of the Christ (Vicchio, *Jefferson's Religion*, 33). Jefferson speaks favorably of the Unitarians, grows in his affection for their positions, and at one point seems to identify himself with the somewhat amorphous movement. At one point he identifies the Unitarian option to be the "religion of all," as if it is basic, natural religion itself: Letter to Adam, August 22, 1813 (Braden, "Ye Will Say I Am No Christian," 87).

80. Vicchio sees considerable influence by Unitarian ideas, especially via Priestley's importance, but that Jefferson never joins the ranks of the church, nor uses the title for himself (Vicchio, *Jefferson's Religion*, 50).

81. Letter to Adams, April 11, 1823 (Braden, "Ye Will Say I Am No Christian," 222–23).

82. Daniel J. Boorstin picks up Jefferson's language for God and turns it into his major epithet for God: Jefferson's God is the "Supreme Workman" who caringly creates and sustains the world (Boorstin, *Lost World*, 41–47).

83. Even if he does not propose a theory how such involvement is possible in a deistic model. See Foote, *Religion*, 15. Clearly Jefferson wants some of the caring and personal values of theism even as he is blinded by trinitarian and christological difficulties when he regards classical (Christian) theism. Sanford's list of qualities that go beyond typical deism in a theology consists of love, concern, guidance, providence, protection, and wisdom (Sanford, *Religious Life*, 96).

84. Jefferson is so allergic to revelation, as in the biblical tradition and as opposed to reason, that he avoids talk of revelation. However, his expectations for the insights

agnostic sage who turns up his own apophaticism and claims we humans, even smart ones, are unable to speak meaningfully of God, who is so high and mighty that we are left with no words to express the divine reality. Often, he employs his apophatic moment against people that are too confident in using their finite words for God. In the Letter to Ezra Stiles of June 25, 1819, Jefferson assures the Calvinist Stiles that the two of them do not differ on the main moral business of religion, and famously declares himself a "sect by myself." Jefferson does not belong to any sect, but he has learned from the "benevolent and sublime Reformer" of the judgmental Judaism that God is good and perfect. But even Jesus does not define God, and Jefferson will follow his theology that words and ideas do not work to define God. In fact, we all should not define theology so to create divisions and schisms between rival dogmas.[85] When we add Jefferson's apophatic side to his secrecy about his own religious views and his argument for the privacy of each human's religion, we wonder how to integrate this negative-theological side with his bold claims for the innate cosmological access to God. Further, we wonder how the moral sense, and particularly a cultivated moral sense such as that in Jesus, fits with Jefferson's unwillingness to define God. If Jesus can offer a modest clarification of God, possibly he has still more insight.[86]

Sin and Evil

The *LMJN* gives only a limited view of sin and evil. We know that God creates everything and that everything is metaphysically good. We also know that people are perfectly able to be evil, in their free will. Thus, Jefferson accounts for the bad behavior of his enemies. We also suspect that he is making an allegorical application of Jesus' opponents to his own political opponents. We acknowledge their free will, and we see layers of motives prompting their acts of free will: acts that display hypocrisy, jealousy, envy, insults, and the like. Below exposing their enemies and exercising their political ambitions is their fundamental greed for money and power. Clearly such greedy people turn off the natural law and deflect from the fundamental good, though Jefferson does not give a metaphysical account of moral

---

drawn from nature seem revelatory, nonetheless. He rejects revelation handed to people by God that consists of information removed from, if not hostile to, the work of reason. Yet the divine presentation through nature comes to the imagination in the working of reasoning, and it resembles a mediated revelation.

85. Letter to Ezra Stiles Ely, June 25, 1819 (see it on the *Founders Online* website from the US National Archives, listed in the bibliography; or see Adams and Lester, *Extracts*, 386–87).

86. Here we anticipate Jefferson's struggle with the attribute of perfection for God.

evil. There seems to be an Augustinian assumption in Jefferson that one does not need much of a theodicy if the metaphysically good free will is involved in moral evil.[87]

The curious thing is that Jefferson does not speak much of sin even in an account in which Jesus is being bludgeoned by the Jewish officials. They are finally wicked, he will say, but he rarely speaks of sinners. One wonders why. He certainly experiences much sin, but he does not choose to use the category. Negatively we can guess why he avoids it: perhaps he does not want Jesus' ethic to be shaped by following the law, specifically Mosaic Law. *He thinks the inner duty now rules in the era of Jesus*; he is sure that *the moral is not really a relationship to a command but an interior signal to the self to progress on a eudaemonist life.* Perhaps, had Jefferson tied the issue of sin to the violation of the law of Torah, he might have developed a fuller sin-consciousness. It is not that Jefferson does not experience evil—he does and he is aware that he does—but he shies away from sin talk. We have seen his trouble with forgiveness and his concern that it can be misused as a category; he relativizes the counting of times for forgiveness as if he wants to avoid bean counting. Possibly he does not want to subscribe to a legalized notion of moral evil. Moral evil is more of a weakness, an ignorance, a confusion, and here he sides with the Greek tradition against that of Paul and Augustine.

Beyond these reflections, we can add little from the vantage of the *LMJN*. If we go outside the text to the letters, we can add one thing more to the problem of evil. Jefferson's sense of the goodness of creation will not let him think of humans being defective in their natural state. And surely, he cannot abide with anything like original sin, the hated "Calvinistic" doctrine. At every possible turn, his rather Pelagian defense of free will keeps him from a sense that the early human is damaged by primal sin, or that humans pass on their sinfulness. The doctrine of original sin and, with it, predestination are his least favorite of Christian ideas after the Trinity and the two-natures christology, since he holds that humans are not damaged creatures so that their freedom is not damaged. The only metaphysical place he can go, given the pieces on his board, is toward a Leibnizian sense that the Creator has created the best of all possible worlds. And when we cannot see all the goodness, this sense must rest in our perspective on the world and on God's continuing restorative wisdom. God could not have created an inferior world.[88]

---

87. See Burstein, *Jefferson's Secrets*, 148 for a picture of Jefferson's notion of evil as a moral disease for which we need no immense theodicy.

88. See the discussion in Sanford, *Religious Life*, 96.

The Rejection of Atheism

When Jefferson looks at life in the world, he reacts in amazement that anyone could deny the Creator. His point is as much a sense of wonder that requires an explanation as it is a mechanical appreciation of the where-from character of the universe. Recall that Jefferson is a materialist, though one who sees the necessity of a benevolent divinity behind the materiality of reality. He will not be an atheist. Indeed, he believes that the speculators, the spiritualists of a platonic sort, are the real, "masked" atheists.[89] God creates matter because God is material, corporal, not spiritual.[90]

It is, then, a great irony that Jefferson is branded as a "howling atheist" or "infidel" by his Federalist opponents and the New England clergy who support them.[91] They condense his apparent freethinking views into a single category in order to motivate the political opposition to Jefferson in the 1800 election.[92] However, competent historians judge the charges of atheism against Jefferson to be unfair.[93] His belief in a Creator who cares about the universe is quite genuine. But, to be truthful, we have to note that Jefferson's views are complex and at times hazy, and scholars (certainly not politicians) have not worked out nuanced ways to speak of the various religious views that do not match orthodox Christianity. Jefferson's reticence to speak about religion, of course, contributes to the misunderstanding and politicizing of his views.

---

89. Letter to Adams, August 18, 1820 (Braden, *"Ye Will Say I Am No Christian,"* 211).

90. In a tricky Letter to Adams, August 15, 1820 (Braden, *"You Will Say I Am No Christian,"* 212–13), Jefferson suggests there are really only three positions on God: the spiritualist position, which he regards as a disguised atheism; the materialist position that denies God; and the deist materialist position. It is the third position with which he identifies. Jefferson repeats his view that God is of a lighter matter or nature, in a Letter to Adams, April 11, 1823 (Braden, *"You Will Say I Am No Christian,"* 222–23).

91. Foote, *Religion*, 23, 47: Alexander Hamilton famously calls Jefferson "an atheist in religion and a fanatic in politics." Vicchio discusses the alliance between the New England clergy and the popular press, both of which are tied to the Federalist effort to block Jefferson's election as president (Vicchio, *Jefferson's Religion*, 23).

92. Vicchio, *Jefferson's Religion*, 6–7.

93. See Jefferson's rejection of the term "atheism" and his criticism of atheism as a defensible position (Vicchio, *Jefferson's Religion*, 14). See Vicchio, *Jefferson's Religion*, 20, for a summary of the evidence in Jefferson's correspondence that rejects the term "atheism."

The Issue of Deism

Jefferson is not an orthodox Christian, nor is he an atheist. Is he a deist? Scholars often debate the matter. Much depends on what they put into the category and which elements are definitive. We need to remember that there never has been a single thing called deism. It is not an ism at all, but more of an association of ideas on a spectrum of relations to other religious and philosophical ideas. Jefferson does not belong to any ism and he is quite proud of this fact. Remember that deism for Jefferson means belief in one God and a style of religious views that has not yet been packed into an ism that we identify with the eighteenth century. Jefferson thinks the Jews are deists, for all he dislikes the religion, and would correct the expression of its understanding of God. He thinks Jesus is a deist and that, in fact, wherever religion can live in its natural purity we have deism.

We know Jefferson drifts away from his Anglicanism; he hardly ever claims to be a Unitarian, nor does he use the "deist" word for himself. And anyway, the idea of belonging to deism is an oxymoron, both generally and for Jefferson, who likes to be a "sect" in himself.[94] If we were to judge Jefferson's religion by type, however, he would be within the deist family, primarily because he does not allow a divinity who intervenes and breaks apart the rules of the cosmos. He fits in the type of deism because he rarely uses personal language for God.[95] Here we can report two characteristics of Jefferson's entrance into the larger intellectual world of deism: First, his deism fits within the world of Virginia, where thoughtful deists commonly continue to be more or less affiliated with Anglicanism. The religious spirit of the Anglicans in Virginia is substantially different from that of the New England Anglicanism.[96] Jefferson attends Anglican services, supports several churches, and seems to enjoy the public, ceremonial side to that tradition, even as he is in some sense alienated from it. Second, Jefferson's religion feels the impact of English/Scottish thought, more so than other deistic

---

94. From the Letter to Margaret Bayard Smith, August 6, 1816 (Jefferson, *Writings* [Peterson, ed.], 1404).

95. See Sanford, *Religious Life*, 85–86. We note how rarely Jefferson uses personal language of God in the *LMJN*, and that he rarely quotes Jesus' personal language for God.

96. Significantly, Jefferson hated the New England style of religion and viewed it as heavily Calvinist. He ridiculed and demonized Calvin and found Calvin's view of God to be similar to the Jewish view: Letter to Adams, April 11, 1823 (Braden, "*Ye Will Say I Am No Christian*," 223). And naturally it was the New England clergy, allied with the Federalists, who found Jefferson to be a "howling atheist." Thus, for Jefferson, Calvin is the real "atheist": Letter to Adams, April 11, 1823 (Braden, "*Ye Will Say I Am No Christian*," 220).

American figures under the influence of French Enlightenment deism.[97] Indeed, Jefferson developed a nuanced sense for the differences among European Catholic deisms, English/Scottish Protestant deism, and the more radical French atheism of d'Holbach. He actually seems to combine the materialism of a d'Holbach with an English/Scottish style of deism.[98]

What characterizes Jefferson's religion as a type of deism? The most important points are these: Jefferson believes there is a simple, pure, natural faith in one God under the doctrines and the mysteries and obfuscations of positive religion.[99] Also, he opposes the idea that religion focuses on the revelation of secret truths of the faith and rather sees reason as the Creator's grace toward humankind. Finally, he thinks the true religion prospers without the trappings of positive religion (such as sacraments, rituals, clergy, creeds, or organizations). Jefferson's distinctive kind of deism is willing eventually to make peace with Christian religion, once the morality of Jesus has been purged of its corruption. In the spirit of their peace, Jefferson can announce: "To the corruptions of Christianity I am indeed opposed; but not to the genuine precepts of Jesus himself. I am a Christian in the only sense he wished any one to be; sincerely attached to his doctrines, in preference to all others; ascribing to himself every *human* excellence; & believing he never claimed any other."[100] Thus, he is able to move beyond a notion that being Christian is problematic and toward a notion that being Christian presents an opportunity to retrieve the essential moral truths of humankind.[101] In this transition, being a Christian means agreeing with the moral vision of Jesus, properly cleaned up.

Once we have traveled this far in the discussion of Jefferson's sort of divinity, we have to make one qualification. While Jefferson clearly works within a deist type, his understanding of God displays theistic qualities at

---

97. Holmes suggests the English trio of Bacon, Newton, and Locke did the most to shape the philosophical and scientific mindset of Jefferson (Holmes, *Faiths*, 40).

98. Letter to Adams, April 8, 1816 (Braden, "*Ye Will Say I Am No Christian*," 164–65).

99. Jefferson believes that the Jews were deists, and that Jesus was also. See Sanford, *Religious Life*, 130.

100. The Letter to Benjamin Rush of April 21, 1803 (Braden, "*Ye Will Say I Am No Christian*," 241) expresses his enthusiasm for "the genuine precepts of Jesus himself" against the corruptions of Jesus. In a Letter to Charles Thomson, Jefferson says his *The Philosophy of Jesus* is proof that he is a "Christian," which means to him that he is a disciple of the doctrines of Jesus: January 9, 1816 (Braden, "*Ye Will Say I Am No Christian*," 241).

101. Brent argues that the Rush letter suggests that *The Philosophy of Jesus* and the *LMJN* prove that Jefferson is really a Christian in his specifically defined mode (Brent, "Jeffersonian Outlook," 427).

one point: he holds to a God who while material[102] is caringly involved in the course of life in the world. Presumably, the involvement of God must be distinguished from the barging-in interventionism that he finds unacceptable. Jefferson wants none of the traditional delivery systems for such care, such as miracles, special revelations, and efficacious rituals. Yet he wants what they mean to deliver. *Jefferson's God is providential in a way atypical of that of most deists.*[103] However, he does not develop well how a deistic divinity can tend the details of life with care and avoid being a bull in the china shop of the world. Perhaps, since his favorite word for God's involvement is "superintending," he has in mind a caring overseeing.[104] He certainly thinks that the divinity's hand can be felt in the well-oiled order, beauty, and justice of the whole world, and that we need to adapt our expectations to that order. We do that in an intuitive feeling for the way of the cosmos. But sometimes he goes further and is willing to name actual events (e.g., the destiny of America and the defeat of Napoleon) as acts of God.[105] And sometimes *he suggests that the normal superintendence of the cosmos is insufficient and that God must somehow restore the cosmos.*[106] Unfortunately, he does not offer, or seem interested in constructing, a theory of how God can act, especially since he rules out supernatural models of action. One wonders why Jefferson would so name the destiny of America and Napoleon as examples of God's acts. His opposition to Napoleon may be a clue, however. Napoleon gets what he deserves, just as America will prosper if it lives up to its promise. The implied act of God can be confirmed as an act of *get-what-you-give justice*, and justice is woven into the created order.

When Jefferson opens the door to some sort of active management on God's part, the basic deist starts sounding more like a theist.[107] The question for Jefferson scholars is to figure out whether the more active model of divine action has been implicit in the deism of his early days, whether it is simply the unfolding of his original notion of the superintendancy of

102. Letter to Adams, April 11, 1823 (Braden, "*Ye Will Say I Am No Christian*," 222).

103. Sanford calls Jefferson's belief in God as "beyond deism" (Sanford, *Religious Life*, 96). Note, again, that Jefferson never actually calls himself a deist (Vicchio, *Jefferson's Religion*, 73). Even about deism he is not a "belonger" in religion.

104. See the discussion in Holowchak, *American Messiah*, 35–36.

105. See Waldman, *Founding*, 82.

106. As Holowchak notices (*American Messiah*, 36). Holowchak actually sees Jefferson as changing from a plain notion of superintendency toward a later notion that involves, somehow, more active divine action to set back chaos. Holowchak shows how important for Jefferson's deism and his view of God is the image of God's superintendency. Holowchak, *Messiah*, 35–38.

107. Thus, Waldman says that Jefferson is not a full-fledged deist (Waldman, *Founding*, 81).

the Creator, whether it has developed as Jefferson faces the challenges of his mature life, or whether it is a departure from the earlier position.[108] Two values remain, however: (1) Jefferson's sense that God cares for the world is constant, and (2) Jefferson cannot abide with a supernaturalistic model of God's act.[109] The former value suggests that Jefferson discovers new qualities in the divinity, a richer sense of what is *theo-propos*; while we see the effect of this discovery in the *LMJN*, we know from the letters that this discovery is mediated through his Jesus project.[110] That is, we have *a christologically mediated enlargement of Jefferson's divinity, undoubtedly a consequence of his studies of Jesus*. God is caring and actually works to restore creation from the chaos of human life in the world.[111]

The Problem of the Afterlife

Like any decent Enlightenment figure, Jefferson early on has trouble with elements of the traditional eschatologies of the philosophical tradition and the church. He is critical of the doctrine of the immortality of the soul in the platonic tradition. By extension, he is unhappy with notions of heaven and hell, with talk of resurrection and immortality and of apocalyptic struggles with the devil. Quite insightfully he identifies cultural Platonism

---

108. Holowchak can work the reader through the pros and cons of the issue; he opts for a nonimpositional deist theory with a notion that the so-called special actions of God are woven into the eternal cosmic plan of the Creator. Here things like correction for justice or retribution are simply anticipated in the comprehensive creation of the universe (Holowchak, *American Messiah*, 39–46). While I am not persuaded by Holowchak's reading of Jefferson's religion and find more sympathy with interpreters like Sanford, I am amazed that Holowchak suggests that Jefferson's God is not one to whom he can pray and that Jefferson does not believe in the efficacy of prayer, when there is so much evidence of Jefferson's nightly devotion before he retires (Holowchak, *American Messiah*, 45–46). See in support of the case for a serious life of prayer Sanford, *Religious Life*, 137. But then, perhaps, we need to have a discussion about models of prayer and various theories of prayer. In another recent opinion, see Manseau for an analysis of Jefferson's pious nightly practice and his use of the *LMJN* for devotional purposes (Manseau, *Jefferson Bible*, 74, 83).

109. The end of the Second Inaugural speaks of this capacious view of divine providence, that goes back to Israel, that covers the Americans in their youth with providence, wisdom, and power in their mature years. Jefferson asks the Americans to join him in supplications for enlightenment, for guidance in councils, and proper measures for good. The earnest language seems to suggest a very involved divinity. Jefferson, *Writings*, 523.

110. An insight from Sanford, *Religious*, 104.

111. See the Letter to Adams, April 8, 1816, Adams, *Extracts*, 1383–84 and Sanford, *Religious*, 91–92.

with wrecking the essential anthropology and eschatology of the Bible.[112] We expect, therefore, that he will reshuffle the elements of the inherited eschatologies. In these moves, he draws out the consequences of his firm materialism. But surprisingly, Jefferson does not simply dispose of the entire eschatological package. For instance, by 1803 *he affirms the doctrine of a future state* against the Jewish rejection of the afterlife,[113] even as he clearly throws out the resurrection and the dualistic, anthropological foundations of the doctrine of the immortality of the soul.

Recall that Jefferson's materialist commitments found his criticism of the world of spirit since spirit classically has a different reality from matter. Soon he works out a consistent materialism that views things hitherto of spirit to be particularly active matter: mind, soul, and even God. Nothing is disembodied, but *the notion of quickened matter makes room for some fragments of an eschatology.* As Jefferson becomes increasingly concerned with the problem of justice in the moral life, he insists that justice requires judgment in life and especially in a final reckoning with rewards and punishments. Here he no longer campaigns against the notion of a soul finding immortality, though he does not substitute the old platonic vision with a crisp new doctrine. Jefferson notes in the 1803 *Syllabus* that Jesus believes in a "future state."[114] He does pick up the providential thinking about God and emphasizes that according to Jesus, God will judge humans, and that judgment would require a future state of rewards and punishments.[115] But

---

112. See the discussion in Sheridan, *Jefferson and Religion*, 66–67. Jefferson actually recognized early that the Israelites had an undeveloped notion of an afterlife, but that Jesus in his campaign to reform Judaism sharpened it with a clear doctrine of a future state: Letter to Rush, April 21, 1803 (Jefferson, *Writings* [Peterson, ed.], 1126. Probably Jefferson is not distinguishing resurrection from immortality as sharply as we might today.

113. Letter to Rush, April 21, 1803 (Jefferson, *Writings* [Peterson, ed.], 1126. Concerning Jefferson's inability to distinguish clearly between immortality and resurrection, it is F. A. Van der Kemp who nails Jefferson with the tensions, if not the inconsistencies, in his eschatology: how can he reject the basic belief in the immortality of the soul and/or in the resurrection, and still dabble in a "future state" and a cosmic righting of justice? See the Letter to Kemp, July 14, 1813 (Adams and Lester, *Extracts*, 373).

114. See the *Syllabus* in Jefferson's Letter to Rush, April 21, 1803 (Jefferson, *Writings* [Peterson, ed.], 1123–26. So, also the Letter to Short, August 1, 1820, a late-in-life reference that criticizes Moses and the Jews for having no doctrine of a future life (Adams and Lester, *Extracts*, 396).

115. See Jefferson's Letter to George Thacher, January 26, 1824 (Adams and Lester, *Extracts*, 414). We note that this clarity about the afterlife comes two years before Jefferson's death. But notice that he is already pondering the matter in his Letter to Priestley, April 4, 1803 (Jefferson, *Writings* [Peterson, ed.], 374).

he is not prepared to buy a Judgment Day associated with apocalyptic world constructions.

Jefferson does not offer a triumphant doctrine of salvation, but he does insist that God's active care for the world continues in benevolence throughout the whole of life and world.[116] God is clearly an active deity who makes good out of evil in the world and holds people morally accountable. In language that seems to mimic Kant's position, Jefferson argues that such divine care for the world may require immortality as if it is a transcendental condition of moral seriousness and of the overcoming of evil. Do these ideas mean an actual future state of reward and punishment for souls? This is hard to know.[117] Whether or not Jefferson imagines such a state, he certainly envisions the moral cash value of the idea of that state, and the envisionment of such a state works transcendentally in Jefferson's undeveloped eschatology.

Jefferson's Freedom in Relation to Sacred Scripture

We have seen that Jefferson wanted to compare Jesus to other ancient moral sources, and that he learned that Jesus also was a fragmentist like Epictetus.[118] His hermeneutic develops with an interpretive freedom that liberates him from any lingering sense that the Bible is a sacred cow.[119] He boldly embraces the need to see it as a human document, on the one hand, and without special inspiration (except where its contents pass the test of

---

116. The Letter to Adams, January 24, 1814 (Braden, *"Ye Will Say I Am No Christian,"* 139) seems to show a departure from his early hostility to the immortality of the soul. Conceivably, his doctrine of salvation hints that all humans will be reconciled to God eventually, perhaps in the Universalist style: see the suggestion in Sheridan, *Jefferson and Religion*, 67.

117. Consider the Letter to Priestley, April 9, 1803 (Jefferson, *Writings* [Peterson, ed.], 1121), and that to Short of August 4, 1820 (Jefferson, *Writings* [Peterson, ed.], 1437). See Sanford, *Religious Life* for the notion that the questions of the afterlife are the most difficult to solve in Jefferson (141) and for a discussion of Jefferson's complex view of immortality in Jefferson's immaturity (144). Holowchak captures the uncertainty about Jefferson's view of the afterlife: there is no scholarly consensus on Jefferson and the theme of the afterlife (Holowchak, *American Messiah*, 13).

118. There is an interesting connection between the material point that Jesus is a fragmentist and Jefferson's formal re-creation of Jesus' fragments in a deepened fragmentary way. Bryan takes this theme to represent an assault on biblical authority and the objective power of the authoritative text ("Reauthorizing," 19).

119. The famous Letter to Peter Carr, August 10, 1787 tells the young Carr to judge everything religious by the authority of reason (Jefferson, *Writings* [Peterson, ed.], 902).

reason), on the other.[120] He would read the Bible as with Livy or Tacitus;[121] use your ability to reason, he says. He recommends interpreting the Bible under the methods of what we today call historical criticism.[122] Jefferson is free of the orthodox need to find special revelation in the text, and consequently, the plotline of his hermeneutic becomes evident when he decides to dig for the eternal and pure nuggets amid all the impurities. In his theory of the perspicuity of the genuine Jesus' moral wisdom, he is certain he can spot the "diamond in a dunghill."[123]

We should note that Jefferson's actual hermeneutic and practice of exegesis fits well into the founding of the biblical-critical movement, though his importance is often overlooked by historical critics within the world of biblical studies. Undoubtedly, Jefferson's contributions have been lost to the biblical-critical world because of his secrecy about his Jesus project and, probably, because he did not participate in German-based criticism. Yet, Jefferson shares much with Reimarus, the so-called founder of Jesus research, particularly in their common sense that the thing called Christianity emerges out of the mistaken ideas of Jesus' disciples. Thus, they share the notion that Christianity as developed is far from the concerns of Jesus.[124]

120. There is a good likelihood that Bolingbroke influenced the young Jefferson on the theme. Jefferson writes to Carr: "Your own reason is the only oracle given you by heaven" (Letter to Carr, August 10, 1787, in Jefferson, *Writings* [Peterson, ed.], 902).

121. Letter to Peter Carr, his nephew, August 10, 1787, Jefferson, *Writings*, 900–906. This is the famous letter in which Jefferson gives Carr permission to doubt God's existence, if he follows the lead of reason.

122. He mentions the need to reconstruct the context of a scriptural passage for good interpretation; he wants to guard against arbitrary applications, and against taking Scripture "figuratively, typically, analogically, hyperbolically," and with all the "figures of rhetoric" to make Scripture say what we wish: see the Letter to Adams, April 8, 1816, Braden, "*Ye will say*," 165–66, where Jefferson criticizes David Levi, a Jewish critic of Priestley. Jefferson rejects the allegorical tradition of interpretation particularly because it does not guard against fanciful readings of texts. Letter to Adams, October 4, 1816, Braden, "*Ye will say*," 183), even though he routinely embraces the Bible's allegorically moralized meanings added to the parables of Jesus. Sanford suggests that, while he did not know German biblical criticism, Jefferson had learned much from early English-language biblical methods of biblical criticism. Sanford, *Religious*, 106, 108.

123. Letter to Adams, January 24, 1813, Braden, "*Ye will say*," 130.

124. While Jefferson posits the protestant purity of Jesus and his moral vision and the bungling and ignorance of the disciples, Reimarus notes both the apocalyptic craziness of Jesus and the malevolence of the disciples to keep alive the movement of the cult. Both work with an Enlightenment hermeneutic that digs below the surface. Jefferson emphasizes the first disciples were mostly stupid while Reimarus' point reveals their deviousness to create a movement out of the prophet's ideas. In the Letter to Adam, October 13, 1813 Jefferson sets out a catalog of the mistakes of the disciples as they handled Jesus' message: forgetting, not understanding, giving their own misconceptions, and offering unintelligible expressions. Braden, "Ye will say," 99.

Jefferson boldly cuts and pastes according to his critical freedom in relation to the gospel texts. He exhibits no pious concern that would step delicately into his editing task. Indeed, he thinks it is obvious what belongs to Jesus and what is the corruption of bungling followers and crafty priests. He also has been emboldened by Joseph Priestley's theory that the good stuff is encased in corruption and could be extracted with ease. The hermeneutic simply removes the corruption. Of course, Jefferson knows nothing of the history of interpretation and of the history of interpretive ways to address difficult texts, the very ones that Jefferson throws out quickly. Of course, here we face both Jefferson's lack of learning in the area of religion and the power of the Enlightenment values he has internalized. In any case, Priestley's theory of corruption and Jefferson's abrupt cutting practice in interpretation consort to bring him to a surprising enthusiasm for Jesus that follows with him the rest of his life.

The Critique of Greek Ethical Resources

Jefferson's time at William and Mary College gets him excited about classical thought. He quickly develops an affection for ethical inquiry. His favorite ethicists come from the Epicureans and the Stoics; Epictetus is his top choice, and at one point Jefferson calls himself "an Epicurean."[125] Jefferson's *Syllabus* for a Jesus book takes him into a new area of inquiry, namely, comparative ethics. In a plan for a Jesus book, he would chart the differences among the moral wisdom of the Jews, of Epictetus, and of Jesus. We know from the *Syllabus* that his early admiration of the Greek ethical traditions continues but now in a more subdued manner. To be sure, he notes the Greeks' control of the passions and their commitment to duty to their kindred. But here we get a new position: that the Greeks practice justice among "neighbors & countrymen" but never bring the "circle of benevolence" to "the whole family of mankind."[126] Jefferson consistently pictures Jesus articulating the universal law of love, and, in that view, his is a superior ethic.[127]

---

125. For a discussion of the relationship of Epicureanism and Stoicism in Jefferson, see: Sanford, *Religious Life,* 37–40 and the Letter to William Short, October 31, 1819 (Jefferson, *Writings* [Peterson, ed.], 1430).

126. *Syllabus,* in Jefferson, *Writings* (Peterson, ed.), 1124. See also the Letter to Edward Dowse, April 4, 1820 (Jefferson, *Writings* [Lipscomb and Bergh, eds.], 15:114.

127. See the strong summary of the inclusive point in Sheridan, *Jefferson and Religion,* 66.

The Critique of the Jews

In some letters and in the *Syllabus*, we know the plot of Jefferson's reading of the Jewish moral tradition. The Jewish system is a "Deism" but one with "degrading & injurious" ideas of God: thus, the God of the Jews is cruel, vindictive, capricious, and unjust.[128] His brief study of Hebrew Scripture tells him that Israelite religion brings only limited moral advance.[129] He worries most about the brutal character of the Israelites: in their warring, in God's complicity in the violence, and in their narrow moral concern for one people only.[130] We also know that Jefferson is horrified by the Israelite notion that the sins of the parent fall on the children for generations;[131] undoubtedly Jefferson's prized sense for freedom as autonomy is offended by a notion of collective or inherited guilt. The Jews are despised and rightly so.[132] Certainly, he participates in cultural and Christian antinomian and anti-Judaic values.[133] But, significantly, his colleague Francis Adrian Van der Kemp criticizes Jefferson for going too far in his rough reading of the Jewish notion of God and of Mosaic law.[134] Likely, Jefferson's mind has been set

---

128. *Syllabus*, in Jefferson, *Writings* (Peterson, ed.), 1124. In the letter to Adams, October 1, 1813, Jefferson speaks of Judaism as a "wretched depravity of sentiment and manners" (Jefferson, *Writings* [Peterson, ed.], 1301). See the harsh language of criticism in the Letter to Short, August 4, 1820 (Jefferson, *Writings* [Peterson, ed.], 1438).

129. Compare his summary evaluation in the *Syllabus*: "Their Ethics were not only imperfect, but often irreconcilable with the sound dictates of reason & morality, as they respect intercourse with those around us, & repulsive & anti-social, as respecting other nations" (Jefferson, *Writings* [Peterson, ed.], 1124). See a full treatment of Jefferson's view of the Jew in Jesus' life in Sanford, *Religious Life*, 125–27.

130. In the Letter to Adams, October 12, 1813, Jefferson speaks of the ethics of Judaism as "wretched depravity" (Braden, "Ye Will Say I Am No Christian," 98–99). Note that Jefferson routinely connects the Jews to American people he dislikes or fights with, such as the Calvinists and New England Federalists: see Waldman, *Founding*, 75 for evidence of Jefferson's hatred of the Jews. Of course, the uncertain issues that remain are how much his dislike refers to modern Judaism in addition to the ancient and whether his anti-Judaic judgments sprawl into the moral issue of anti-Semitism.

131. Letter to Ezra Stiles Ely, June 25, 1819 (see it on the *Founders Online* website from the US National Archives, listed in the bibliography; or see Adams and Lester, *Extracts*, 386–87).

132. Letter to Charles Thomson, January 9, 1815, Adams, *Extracts*, 364.

133. Letter from Van der Kemp, July 14, 1816 (Adams and Lester, *Extracts*, 373). Sanford suggests that Jefferson's anti-Judaic bias appears already in his writings from Europe (Sanford, *Religious Life*, 126).

134. Letter from Van der Kemp, July 14, 1816 (Adams and Lester, *Extracts*, 373). Robert Brent declares, "Jefferson showed no respect for the Judaic heritage of Christians" (Brent, "Jefferson Outlook," 426). In theological circles, we would call Jefferson a Marcionist when we digest his claim that there can be no things more unlike than that of the Old Testament and that of the New (Letter to John Adams, August 22, 1813

about the Jewish moral tradition before he studies it for the Jesus book. To Adams Jefferson writes that the ethic of the New Testament and that of Hebrew Scriptures are so different that "no two things were ever more unlike."[135] Therefore, he does not hear the moral advance of the Bible. Rather he tends to see the moral value of Israel as defective. He calls the religion of Israel a religion of fear.[136] In fact, Judaism comes to epitomize nearly all the qualities of religion he dislikes: it embodies religion under corruption. Speaking of the Jews acts like coded language for all the religious types who oppose Jefferson politically.[137] What bothers Jefferson the most is *the tribal narrowness of respect in Judaism*.[138] We should note that while Jefferson is critical of what he takes to be the morality of Judaism, he sometimes suggests that Judaism, especially on its good days, is equivalent to deistic or natural religion.[139] When he wants to contrast the good old monotheism of Israel with the irrational trinitarian impulses of the Christians, then the Jewish way can be an early deism without the benefit of developed reason.

One painful consequence of Jefferson's lifelong criticism of the Jews is *his inability to locate Jesus within Second Temple Judaism*. His Jesus, as we have seen, has been stripped of the religious aspect of Judaism, of nearly all the things that make a Jew a Jew. And *the most problematic feature of that stripping away is that Jefferson cannot understand that the moral wisdom of Jesus is founded in the Mosaic covenant*. Of course, we do not know what causes what, but we do know that Jefferson's ethic heads toward a universal, natural ethic. The effort to abstract the gospel ethic from its concrete Jewish context overlaps with Jefferson's lifelong judgment of Judaism's depravity.[140]

(Adams and Lester, *Extracts*, 348). Sanford reminds us that Jefferson knew virtually nothing about Hebrew Scriptures, except for his favorite psalms (Sanford, *Religious Life*, 129). Malone notes that the young scholar Jefferson was always more critical of Israelite and Jewish ideas than of those of the classical traditions (Malone, *Jefferson*, 6:202).

135. Letter to Adams, August 22, 1813 (Adams and Lester, *Extracts*, 348). Actually, Jefferson's hostility to the religion of Israel is essentially a Marcionist position.

136. Letter to Adams, October 12, 1813 (Braden, *"Ye Will Say I Am No Christian,"* 101).

137. See Sanford, *Religious Life*, 118.

138. Note that the values here match Jefferson's criticism of the classical ethical tradition he admires so much.

139. *Syllabus*, in Jefferson, *Writings* [Peterson, ed.], 1124.

140. Here I would depart from Bryan's judgment that Jefferson is able to place Jesus into first-century Jewish life ("Reauthorizing," 23–24). See Conkin, "Religious Pilgrimage," 39 for an upbeat analysis from Jefferson about the Jews: in his hostility toward the Greek anthropological dualism, he happens onto the sturdy holistic anthropology of the Israelites long before Bible scholars discovered it. Oddly, Jefferson's exposure to Israelite materials permits him to find what he regarded as the materialism of the Hebrew scripture and develop an anthropology that allowed him to move away from Greek

Jesus the Reformer

For Jefferson, Judaism is a religion of fear; Jesus comes to reform it. In Jefferson's evolving view Jesus becomes a reformer of Judaism with a new, expansive moral vision.[141] He has the vision and courage to uncover and correct the religious errors of Judaism, like the "anamorphosis" of God and the defective doctrine of the future state.[142] In the *Syllabus*, he speaks of the "degrading and injurious" ideas of God among the Jews.[143] Jefferson writes in 1803: "I should proceed to a view of the life, character & doctrines of Jesus, who sensible of the incorrectness of their ideas of the Deity, and of morality, endeavored to bring them to the principle of a pure deism, and juster notions of the attributes of God, to reform their moral doctrines to the standard of reason, justice & philanthropy, and to inculcate the belief of a future state."[144] While Judaism may be the protodeism of the ancient world, it falls into typical errors of religion. Specifically, *its Mosaic insight collapses into a tribal view of duty toward others and of God's relationship to the world*. These are corruptions. Jewish religion, Jefferson thinks, is ethnocentric, and consequently it thinks of God's justice and governance of the world in narrow terms. And so far as Judaism departs from the true natural law, for Jefferson *the Jews are no longer the "chosen people."*[145] But Jesus brings Judaism to a more perfect doctrine, that of God's universal philanthropy to all.[146] If the Jew is narrow in moral scope and Jesus wants to broaden that view, the Jew also frames the moral life in terms of action and often superficial action,

---

dualism and the Greek notion of the immortality of the soul and, perhaps, eventually add some kind of hazy doctrine of the resurrection of materiality of the whole human. The later position is "iffy" in Jefferson but may signal the influence of Priestley on him.

141. The Letter to Van der Kemp suggests the *Syllabus* means to show Jesus as a "great reformer of the Hebrew code of religion": April 25, 1816, Jefferson, *Writings*, 369; compare the Letter to Rush, April 21, 1803, Jefferson, *Writings*, 1124 and the Letter to Short, August 4, 1820, Jefferson, *Writings*, 1438. Note also that in the Short letter, Jefferson not only riles against the moral depravity of the Jews but also against the useless distractions of the ceremonies, the rituals, and of holiness codes. Thus, *Jefferson has no serious appreciation of the moral heritage and of the holiness tradition of Israel*. The former is morally bankrupt and the latter is useless.

142. Letter to Adams, April 8, 1816 (Braden, "Ye Will Say I Am No Christian," 165). At the mature stage of his life, Jefferson affirms that Jesus has to correct the lack of an afterlife in Judaism: Letter to Short, August 4, 1820 (Jefferson, *Writings* [Peterson, ed.], 1438).

143. *Syllabus* (Jefferson, *Writings* [Peterson, ed.], 1124).

144. Letter to Priestley, April 9, 1803 (Jefferson, *Writings* [Peterson, ed.], 1121).

145. *Notes on Virginia* (Jefferson, *Writings* [Peterson, ed.], 123).

146. "Inculcating universal philanthropy" in *Syllabus* (Jefferson, *Writings* [Peterson, ed.], 1125).

while Jesus would turn it inward toward the essential and the pure heart. Jesus "pushed his scrutinies into the heart of man; erected his tribunal in the region of his thoughts, and purified his waters at the fountain head."[147] He would be a reformer of Judaism.[148]

We underline three points here: First, the religion of Israel can be corrupted as easily as the Christian religion. Religions get corrupted, after all. The difference between the two religions Jefferson finds in the moral progress Jesus brings. Jesus actually brings the recognition that all (who live morally) are God's chosen people. Note the corollary that follows: the corruption of Christianity returns religion to the very themes that characterize decadent Judaism. *We must suggest that the corruption Jefferson finds in Judaism first and in corrupt Christianity after Jesus reverses his notion of the pattern of decay in all religion.* Second, therefore, the theme to see natural religion hidden in all positive religion may be in some tension with the notion of moral progress. Natural religion does, however, provide Jefferson with the pedal point against which corruption and reformation can be judged.

And third, Jesus as reformer of religion, not surprisingly, matches Jefferson's own vocation, except that Jesus must correct the errors in Judaism while Jefferson's Jesus would clean Christian religion.[149] Ominously, in 1820, Jefferson sees the identification with the Reformer Jesus to be fraught with danger.[150] He knows what happens to Jesus; does he identify with the vilification of Jesus at the end of his life? However scholars secure

---

147. Here Jefferson mimics what Christian thinkers have said about Judaism since Paul: Jesus internalizes the expectation for the moral life. On the broadening of moral concern, see the Letters to Short, October 31, 1819, and August 4, 1820 (Adams and Lester, *Extracts*, 388, 396). See the discussion in Foote, *Religion*, 55.

148. Letter to Adams, October 12, 1813 (Jefferson, *Writings* [Peterson, ed.], 1301). See the discussions in Sanford, *Religious Life*, 111 and Manseau, *Jefferson Bible*, 48—and for a rejection of the reformer mode of interpretation, see Holowchak, *Bible*, 121.

149. I prefer the "reformer" category for Jefferson's Jesus, as it fits with his method in the *LMJN* to uncover the real Jesus under the corruption. Susan Bryan goes with "religious radical," one who wants a revolution. These two orientations to the same Jefferson's Jesus represent the duck-rabbit character of Jesus research generally and the way people find in Jefferson's Jesus a self-reflection of Jefferson, first, and then of themselves. The power of the retrojective imagination is unstoppable. Bryan's reading makes Jefferson's Jesus a subversive figure, and while there may be some basis for the radical judgment, it ignores how often Jefferson uses reform language and how often he appeals to cleaning the corruption. In his *Syllabus* of 1803 Jefferson speaks of the serious need for a reformation of Judaism, and that Jesus "corrects" the deism of the Jews (*Syllabus* in Adams and Lester, *Extracts*, 333–34). Of course, there is subversion and destruction, but the aim is to get back to the pure. So, I prefer the language of reformer. The real radicality of Jefferson's Jesus is that he drops nearly the entire orientation to the religion of Second Temple Judaism (Bryan, 'Reauthorizing," 24, 28).

150. Letter to Short, August 4, 1820 (Jefferson, *Writings* [Peterson, ed.], 1438).

his self-identification with Jesus, the larger questions remain: how radical is Jefferson about religion? Some scholars, more impressed with his radical departure from traditional Christianity or with his fundamental indifference to religious issues, present a more secular version of Jefferson and religion, while others, convinced of his lifelong piety and his efforts to save Jesus and his message from corruption, recognize that his hermeneutical radicality actually serves a conservative purpose.[151]

Warming Up to Christian Religion

Jefferson's early criticism of Christianity (as seen in his *Syllabus*) is harsh. Jesus has impossibly dull and dangerous followers who disfigure his message; he suffers jealousy from those with power and money. While he is a primitive moralist of insight, he is cut short before he develops a complete ethical system.[152] Conceivably, in his era and with his background, before the age of reason, he may be incapable of such a system. In any case, his followers mutilate and mistake his message. Were it properly recovered, however, it could be animated with style and spirit. To be sure, Jefferson never warms to what we call the "organized religion" of Christianity, to its apostles/disciples, or to its priests and institutions, doctrine and rituals, but only to its founding figure. In fact, Jefferson becomes increasingly charmed by the founding figure and repeatedly regrets that too often good-hearted people only see the corrupted form of the person and work of Jesus.[153] If there is no rescue of Jesus from Christian religion, we may never get a chance to see the power of his moral vision, "the most perfect and sublime that has ever been taught by man."[154]

Jefferson begins to make peace with Christianity once Priestley teaches him how to clean its truths of impurities.[155] Criticism is necessary but recovery is also. The recovery consists in going back to the origins of the religion and reconstructing the simple and pure truth and practice, and Jefferson

---

151. Actually, Jefferson's grandson Thomas Jefferson Coolidge calls him a "conservative Unitarian" (Sanford, *Religious*, 100).

152. Sheridan identifies the hand of Bolingbroke in the early view of Jesus (Sheridan, *Jefferson and Religion*, 105).

153. Sheridan notes this shift (*Jefferson and Religion*, 26). See also Sanford, *Religious Life*, 105.

154. *Syllabus*, Jefferson, *Writings*, 1125.

155. "It [Priestley's influence] increased his appreciation of Christian morality by demonstrating to his satisfaction that dogmas that had led him to reject the validity of Christianity in his youth were in fact perversions of the primitive Christian message rather than integral parts of it" (Sheridan, *Jefferson and Religion*, 27).

finally decides, after Priestley's death, to do the recovery himself. Consequently, the style of retrieval puts Jefferson's Christianity into the protestant type of Christianity. Once he has recovered the real Jesus, Jefferson glows with admiration at Jesus' moral insight: he is a "master workman" who produces a system of morality that is "the most benevolent and sublime" ever taught.[156]

The Simplicity of Christianity

Underneath the corruption of Christianity, Jefferson finds its simplicity. He is fond of saying that a child can comprehend the real teachings of Jesus.[157] They are "the sublime doctrines of philanthropism and deism" that are the stuff of "true religion."[158] Ironically, he asserts this simplicity as if it were a doctrine. We know how he finds the simple, by boiling off the complexities of the magic, the mystery, "the charlatanerie," the esoteric doctrines, the supernaturalism and the irrationalities that ignorant and power-hungry people have added to Christianity.[159] The hermeneutic itself orients the discovery to the simple and the pure. Once reduced by a critical recovery, the simplicity of the Christian founder reveals a passageway to natural religion, on which all reasonable humans can agree. These ideas are standard Enlightenment fare. Naturally, Christianity must be simple, since natural religion lives without the complexity of positive religion.[160] Indeed, the simple and natural religion of Jesus suggests that Jefferson puts him "within his own spiritual world."[161]

---

156. Letter to Adams, October 12, 1813 (Braden, *"Ye Will Say I Am No Christian,"* 99); see Church, Introduction, 10.

157. Letter to Adams, January 24, 1814 (Braden, *"Ye Will Say I Am No Christian,"* 139).

158. Letter to Adams, May 5, 1817 (Braden, *"Ye Will Say I Am No Christian,"* 195).

159. Letter to Priestley, March 21, 1801 (Jefferson, *Writings* [Peterson, ed.], 1085).

160. See Jefferson's vision that the Indians of America were close to the simplicity he imagines in natural religion and also in Christianity before it became corrupted: Letter to Adams, June 11, 1812 (Braden, *"Ye Will Say I Am No Christian,"* 28–31). Jefferson is especially delighted that the Indians, he thinks, live without a clerical caste, and he consistently thinks what he calls "Rational Christianity" will flourish on the frontier where life is not under decadence and prejudice: Letter to Adams, May 17, 1818 (Braden, *"Ye Will Say I Am No Christian,"* 201). One suspects that Jefferson's attraction to Unitarianism arises from the same motive: the Unitarians offer a simple doctrine of God and reject the complex doctrine of Trinity. All natural religionists are essentially Unitarians: Letter to Adams, August 22, 1813 (Braden, *"Ye Will Say I Am No Christian,"* 87).

161. In the words of Brown, *Biographical Companion*, 166. Brown's words prompt one to remember Jefferson's famous religious vocation (that he is a sect unto himself)

Christianity for the Republic

Once we have followed the trajectories of meaning in Jefferson's struggle with religion, we can understand why Edwin Gaustad calls him "the most self-consciously theological of all American presidents."[162] While we do not wish to undermine Jefferson's sincere personal involvement in religion, we do note how highly he values the importance of religion in its public functioning for civil society. Indeed, he warms up to Jesus at the point where he has a way to see something useful for his political and national aspirations.[163] After the controversial 1800 election, in which Jefferson was vilified by Federalists and their allies, he comes to see in a cleaned-up Jesus an ally in the survival of a republican kind of government.[164] Indeed, *Jesus was more than an ally: he was a virtual alter ego of Jefferson.*

The Public Function of Religion

Despite his privateness about religion, his toleration of others, and his subjectifying of the turf of religion, Jefferson nonetheless norms good religion by a civil-use criterion. We note that the more privatized view of religion seems to dominate early in his life and in later times of the attacks on him, the concern for the civil usefulness of religion develops. And we may judge that it develops as he finds a way to handle some of his Enlightenment doubts about positive, especially Christian, religion. In any case, he comes to believe that good religion ought to advance social harmony. The proposal leaps over, indeed leaps behind the particularity of the religions under the assumption that there is a natural religion within each that is unifying. Reasonable people have access to and can promote the social good with the moral inspiration of natural religion.

The two themes in Jefferson, the public and the private, seem to be in tension.[165] In the Americas generally, Jefferson's views have been important in the modern privatizing of religion. Yet Jefferson himself brings real religion back into the public square. We know his Jesus helps him with his piety, on the one hand, and with nation building, on the other hand. How

and confirms the way that Jefferson has found himself in the Jesus he has assembled.

162. Gaustad, *Sworn* (preface), xiii–xiv.

163. In addition to his discovery of the corruption of the pure message of Jesus from Priestley in the first years of the 1800s.

164. Sheridan, *Jefferson and Religion*, 24, 27. Benjamin Rush contributes to the Christianity-for-the-republic theme.

165. See how complex is the relationship of public and private religion in Jefferson and how they can be integrated (Buckley, "Placing," 145–46).

are we to imagine that a "God and a man" and "a sect onto myself" religion can find the public square? Jefferson can argue that the moral inspiration of the figure of Jesus, in another key and devoid of the melodies of positive religion, can actually change humans who then participate in public life. Certainly he has to make the real Jesus a public moralist among history's good moralists in order to bring him out of the bonds of Christian religion, its institutions, and its priests.[166] Those two steps seem fragile and insufficient, were he not presupposing the notion that the true, natural-religion underbelly of all religion unifies, so far as we have access to it. Education in reason then is central to what Jefferson offers in order to soften the tension in his ideas as an inconsistency between an individual moral focus and a social moral focus.

Jefferson's Self-Identification with Jesus

Without saying it in so many words, Jefferson self-identifies with the figure of Jesus he has rescued from corruption.[167] Once he sees the figure under the corruption, his thinking about religion becomes *a constant allegorical dance with Jesus*.[168] He finds himself within the real Jesus story as he publicly struggles with the Federalists and the New England clergy, his Pharisees in the drama of the 1800 election. Waldman reminds us just how awful was the 1800 conflict between Jefferson and the New England clergy, who showed him "no mercy," and who "crucified their Savior."[169] Just as his political opponents reveal the faces of Pharisees in America, so he must see himself in the figure of Jesus. The allegorical posturing is undeniable, since he likens the Pharisees to the Calvinist/puritanical preachers, and since he eventually

---

166. Buckley takes the public side of Jefferson's religious sensibilities to Robert Bellah's claim that Jefferson is the architect of America civil religion (Buckley, "Placing," 137).

167. One of the most striking moments of self-identification with Jesus comes from the August 26th Letter of Jefferson to Levi Lincoln in 1801. There he is complaining about the awful behavior of the republican federalists with their monarchical views and East Coast newspapers. He singles out the clergy as the worst: they showed no mercy, and "they crucified their Saviour." They now can expect no mercy for their "abuse on me personally." The allegorical format is undeniable. See it on the *Founders Online* website from the US National Archives, listed in the bibliography; and see also the discussion of the self-identification theme in Sanford, *Religious Life*, 118–19.

168. Boorstin provides a powerful argument that the entire coterie around Jefferson turned the cleaning of Jesus into an allegory of the Jeffersonian mind (Boorstin, *Lost World*, 155–59).

169. Waldman, *Founding*, 23, referring to the Letter to Rush, September 23, 1800 (Adams and Lester, *Extracts*, 319–20).

constructs a Jesus who shares most of his main values. His self-identification with Jesus consists of an "ever dangerous" office of reformation; his enemies are well positioned to take him down.[170] In any case, *the construction of a Jesus, then, steps dialectically along as Jefferson formulates who he will be religiously. In other words, his Jesus is an externalization of Jefferson,*[171] and, doubly so, since *he develops his own religious identity as he constructs Jesus' ethic. Therefore, his Jesus acts as a self-definer as he works to discover the moral insight of Jesus.*[172] The externalized Jefferson mediates for him a mode to bring some *harmony between the public and the private Jefferson. The crafted Jesus actually produces a sharpened, privately religious man who will be a new Jefferson as he faces the public life of a politician and statesman.* After all, he produces his Jesus mostly for his private meditative purposes. And yet, *it is that Jefferson-like Jesus who inspires Jesus-Jefferson to be a Republican statesman. Thus, a typical self-production through the objectification of Jesus takes on, in the case of Thomas Jefferson, a special function to mediate the public and the private in the vicissitudes of his career.* And remember that he is meditating on the Jesus words he has selected, as he faces the nasty political world of the first years of the nineteenth century.

Conclusion: The Constructed Jesus

Jefferson's Jesus, it seems, develops in the course of his career and, conceivably, reveals some tensions. For instance, the early Jesus of the *Syllabus*, who is an ancient, prescientific spiritualist, given to "eastern hyperbolisms," starts to give way to a figure who stands for the clear, simple, and grounded against the way of speculation. *The figure who is a private moral guide of*

---

170. Letter to Short, August 4, 1800 (Jefferson, *Writings* [Peterson, ed.], 1438).

171. Conkin sees the tendency as early as the *Syllabus*: "Jefferson's syllabus revealed more about himself than about Jesus" (Conkin, "Religious Pilgrimage," 37).

172. The power of Jefferson's self-identification is undeniable, but it only pertains to his identifying with Jesus' moral project. There is self-mirroring of Jesus, to be sure, but at different phases of his life, Jefferson notices things about Jesus that he does not like. Some of these complaints about Jesus arise in the early years before Jefferson has confidence about what he can throw out about the pictures of Jesus. He surely is self-identifying with the benevolent moralist, but he may be uncertain how to clean certain points in the Jesus saga, such as his eschatology, the theme of judgment, and the extent of forgiveness. At these points we get expressions of distance from Jesus: Jefferson rejects Jesus' spiritualism about God; he will not go as far as Jesus concerning the extent of forgiveness; he struggles with apocalyptic and the terms of a future state, and so on. He does recognize that Jesus has to pull some punches just to make his moral project work. See, for instance, the Letter to Short, April 13. 1820 (Adams and Lester, *Extracts*, 391–93).

a subjectivized religion comes to have public, corporate significance for the burgeoning republicanism of the new nation. In our reading of these developments Jefferson changes in his view of Jesus and finds use in Jesus in so far as he is able to recognize himself in the figure of Jesus. The middle moment of this shift seems to be a hermeneutical change, made possible by Priestley's theory of corruption. Through this new interpretive format Jefferson could see Jesus in a different light and see through the problems Jesus presents to focus on a new construction behind them. The newly imagined Jesus is more of a solution, more of an aid, than in the beginning of Jefferson's career when the specter of corruption dims Jesus' reputation. In other words, *Jefferson constructs Jesus as an ideated image of his own moral and republican consciousness.*[173]

In the end Jefferson's Jesus is a moral beacon who goes against the grain and is eventually slaughtered by jealousy and fear. His moral vision is without peer, Jefferson decides, and even his favorite, Epictetus, comes up short in comparison as a moral power for humanity. Jefferson attempts to reform the limited moral vision of Judaism and to expand the moral arena beyond that of the best classical ethicists run into conflict with the rich and the powerful. The blame can be shared, starting in the stupidity of Jesus' own followers and flowing out to the entire Roman world that is threatened by his expansive view of justice for all. He is executed, as wise people often are: a victim of wicked people, one who has become an example for individuals and nations, freed of the weight of a heavy atonement theory. Both the conflict traditions and the execution reveal a world willing to destroy a moral genius.

Epilogue

Though there is a constancy of mature views about Jesus in Jefferson, not everything he thinks about Jesus emerges in and out of his cut-and-paste treatment of Jesus. In a famous final letter to William Short (August 4, 1820), Jefferson undertakes to justify the *LMJN*: "My aim in that was, to justify the character of Jesus against the fictions of his pseudo-followers, which have exposed him to the inference of being an impostor."[174] We have

---

173. See the insight of Daniel J. Boorstin, the Librarian of Congress: "The Jeffersonian hand projected his own qualities and limitations into Jesus, whose career became his vivid symbol of the superfluity and perils of speculative philosophy" (quoted in Church, Introduction, 31).

174. Jefferson, *Writings* (Peterson, ed.), 1435. Note that the recognition of the character of Jesus as the "benevolent Moralist" is a condition of the possibility of recognizing the corruption that has been piled upon him. Indeed, the character issue and

seen the "vindication of the character of Jesus" theme[175] and the corruption theme before it, of course. But Jefferson adds a couple new wrinkles. "There are, I acknowledge, passages not free from objection, which we may, with probability, ascribe to Jesus himself; but claiming indulgence from the circumstances under which he acted."[176] The claim suggests, first, that Jesus has to go along with ideas and formulations that may rub against his better moral sense: we have come to this suspicion also from our exegesis of his actual text. Or alternately, there may be images of Jesus that Jefferson dislikes somewhat, but he relents to for a number of reasons. Then, by implication, the claim seems to suggest that Jefferson himself puts away his knife and leaves those passages in, even if they offend his moral conscience.

Here we have a little cipher that helps us understand the troubling feature of Jefferson's Jesus book: why does he let Jesus say and do things that seem un-Jeffersonian? In the Short letter, Jefferson tells us that *Jesus' accommodation to circumstances was a feature of his effort to reform Judaism and to correct the "cruel, vindictive, capricious and unjust" Jewish divinity.*[177] Under the hostile conditions of a reformation, where "priests of superstition" are setting traps for him, Jesus "was justifiable, therefore in avoiding these by evasions, by sophisms, by misconstructions and misapplications of scraps of the prophets, and in defending himself with these their own weapons, as sufficient, *ad homines*, at least."[178] *Jesus accommodates his ministry to the circumstances and has to say and do things that stretch his sense of what is appropriate; so also Jefferson puts up with passages that challenge what he regards as proper.* But Jesus, Jefferson says, manages to take "the best qualities of the human head and heart, wisdom, justice, goodness," to craft his view of God.[179] In a remarkable addition, Jefferson says that Jesus adds "to them

the corruption theme go hand in hand: Letter to Short, October 13, 1819 (Adams and Lester, *Extracts*, 388–89). Once Jefferson meets the corruption theory, he knows immediately, almost a priori, what belongs to the real Jesus and what is an accruement to his ethic.

175. Jefferson, *Writings* (Peterson, ed.), 1436.
176. Jefferson, *Writings* (Peterson, ed.), 1437.
177. Letter to Short (Jefferson, *Writings* [Peterson, ed.], 1437).
178. Letter to Short (Jefferson, *Writings* [Peterson, ed.], 1437). Jefferson speaks of "excusing" the passages in the gospels "which seem to bear marks of weakness in Jesus" (1438).
179. Jefferson uses the images of head and heart to identify the relationship of the cognitive/rational and the intuitive/sentimental, both of which he values. He does not want either to dominate or to be distinct one from the other. Consider how Jefferson turns the images into a leitmotif to navigate between two powerful orientations in his life and among humans, and how he understands the two can cooperate. The images appear most bluntly in Jefferson's letter "My Head and My Heart," to his English crush.

power, ascribed all of these, but in infinite perfection, to the Supreme Being, and formed him really worthy of their adoration." *Jesus then helps produce a worthy God.* Here Jefferson poses two snips of a careful and controlled christology: the first is the notion that Jesus intensifies the best of human qualities so to stretch humans to be *anthro-propos* and, second, that Jesus helps to produce a God who is worthy of worship (*theo-propos*). While the inspiration here is not that of a physical Son of God, it is of the wise Son of Man who believes in the reality of his inspiration.

If Jesus accommodates his hearers, if he persuades by using their language, if he sometimes says things that Jefferson doubts he believes, we have a sage who wisely adapts to his audience and works with their mental furniture. Jefferson himself accommodates his views to his audience, their capacities, his intention for them and the moral crisis they face. Because Jefferson is so accommodating (and perhaps he likes to avoid conflict and to please his audience), he too is something of a chameleon.[180] He is hard to interpret, and the interpreter wants to ask whether he really believes some things he writes, whether he does not see the tensions within his religious thinking, whether he is developing his views without fully recognizing it. William Gould writes about Jefferson: "His correspondence on the subject of religion varied according to the attitude taken by the individual he was addressing."[181] The insight is instructive for researchers who struggle with tensions, if not inconsistencies, in Jefferson's dealing with religion. We can make some sense out of his public/private values. We can see some development and changes in his thinking on religion. We understand his struggle to name and to clarify his views on religion, because of his uneven and untrained theological mind. We get used to his secrecy, his metaphysical weaknesses, his tendency to define his way out of conceptual issues. We get used to his concerns to avoid controversy. We step over his violent rhetoric toward the Jews and his hostility to Hebrew Scripture. But what is difficult

---

See the Letter to Maria Cosway of October 12, 1786, on the *Founders Online* website from the US National Archives, listed in the bibliography; or see Jefferson, *Writings* (Peterson, ed.), 866–76.

180. Zuckert summarizes Jefferson's reticence, shall we say: he adapts his speech to different audiences; he hides his own religion; he often says what his addressee might want to hear; he moves to peace, harmony, and easy social relations in most situations; he works to mediate and heal splits among people; he likes to avoid arguments; he is tactful and agreeable in his letters, and he finds points of agreement; and he seeks to convince, not coerce on points of difference (Zuckert, *Natural Rights*, 87–89). Holowchak too sees the chameleon-like character of Jefferson's views, especially about God (Holowchak, *Moralist*, 175). But as usual Holowchak is certain he can resolve the ambiguity by rereading all the evidence and all the interpreters.

181. Gould, "Religious Opinions."

is that once we get to his final contribution to the study of religion, *we do not know whether he really means what he says about Jesus, the Jesus reformation, and its consequence for religion.* Is he just riding with the values of the texts he snips out? Does he find himself saying things he knows better than? When he dabbles in some kind of apocalyptic language, when he flirts with the Son of Man, with the Shepherd-Sage, when his Jesus prophesies his own suffering, when he sets out the suffering and execution of the one who dies to share his wisdom, when this passion sounds like a very familiar atoning image, are we to take Jefferson seriously? Perhaps he simply goes with the flow of narrative. Perhaps he is so relieved to be done with the supernatural in the Jesus story, or he is relieved to sound vaguely Christian with his low-to-moderate christology. Nonetheless, he sets out more theology than old man Kant or young man Schleiermacher and we wonder why.

Does he mean it? And if so, do we have to rewrite at least the end of Jefferson's thinking? Perhaps he does not mean what he says about Jesus in his pared-down account. We might think that the *LMJN* is simply an exercise, a first draft, and that we should not fuss much over places where Jefferson seems to be saying things un-Jeffersonian. But then we remember that his Jesus project is at least a twenty-year private obsession for him. And if we think he is experimenting with ideas, led by the narrative itself, why would he not excise ideas novel to him, ones which he has already shown distaste for? He has his knife ready at all times, and no one is dominating what he can think. He does not have an audience to please.

We have to go with the most plausible thesis here: *he likes the theological vision of the suffering Sage.* He could have purged it otherwise. We know Jefferson is a professional at rejecting things he dislikes. By the end of the *LMJN* he is a pro with the knife; indeed, his cuts are more nuanced, smaller, and he seems confident that he no longer needs to take a whole block into his gospel but can reject material selectively. Consequently, we cannot imagine there is much in the final episodes that Jefferson would not embrace. Not only is he accomplished in his purgation, not only is he selective in his purges, but he emphatically rejects many predictable aspects of the passion story. When he saves the "Son of Man" theme, the Shepherd-Sage who dies for his wisdom, he saves many powerful episodes he could easily have deleted. We have to conclude that he likes his rather demythologized christology, and that interpreters of Jefferson and of Jefferson on religion may have to revise their estimates of his views. Instead of taking his privately held view from the earlier letters to norm the interpretation of the *LMJN*, they should reverse the direction of the study, from the *LMJN* back to the letters.

At his point we have only to suggest the factors why he lets his Jesus say and do un-Jeffersonian things. We can speak of factors conditioning his development: his aging and his growing frailty, the alienation of his Monticello final years, his years of grief. Maybe, it is his discovery that his twenty-plus Jesus project is stretching his ideas on religion and other matters; possibly the novelty in his ideas is informed by Jefferson's discovery of the tragic in Jesus and in himself.[182] Maybe he recognizes that a life lived for others is costly. Perhaps he has been building this recognition for a very long time and Jefferson scholars have not paid much attention to his private religion.[183]

Permit us to gather some of the radical things that happen at the end of the *LMJN*. We see the retrieval of the category of the "Son of Man." To be sure, the image is not Daniel's anymore, but it is of one who leads the world toward some categorical reckoning. Is it final reckoning? We do not know but we have hints that whole scheme of things weeps for justice. We know that the Son is the "good seed" image, associated with the Kingdom of God. But here is a human who will suffer and die as the Shepherd-Sage. What is at stake is the integrity of his wisdom against the wickedness of the fools; he must so identify with his cause that he dies for it. There is no apocalypse happening according to some scheme of cosmic battles, a gathering of the righteous elect, or a cataclysmic end of history. The Son knows what is happening, and he even can be a prophet of his own death! He calls for the angels. There is no question that his passion has a "for," a "for" for those who pick up on his wisdom. He serves the people by enacting a performance of danger that comes to the radical Sage giving his life for his wisdom.

---

182. An idea that is informed by a comment of Gordon Wood, as quoted in Yarbrough, *American Virtues*, xx. Yarbrough regrets that Jefferson did not put his private life of virtue into the public where it could inform the public good directly. In terms of our argument here, had Jefferson found a pathway between the wall separating the private and public, there might have been a way by which the ethic of other-regard that Jefferson comes to admire in Jesus could have informed public policy. The country might have developed a character in which promoting the good of others lived well with individual rights (Yarbrough, *American Virtues*, 9–21).

183. Burstein notices that the older Jefferson has been ignored by Jefferson scholars until recent new interest in his last years (Burstein, *Jefferson's Secrets*, 6).

14

Contributions of the *LMJN* to the Understanding of Religion in Jefferson

The common approach to the *LMJN* has been to bring known ideas from Jefferson studies to bear on interpreting his Jesus book. In this writing we have reversed the direction of the interpretation and are prepared to ask what the *LMJN* can contribute to Jefferson's view of religion and of Jesus. We have discovered considerable threads of meaning that have not been emphasized in Jefferson scholarship. At this point we will open the dialectic between the established ideas of Jefferson research on religion and the insights the *LMJN* can bring to the conversation. We will follow the list of themes catalogued in Chapter 13.

The Early Critique of Christianity

Concerning Jefferson's early criticism of Christianity, we have little to say directly, as the *LMJN* comes from his mature, postpresidential years. We can note that Jefferson makes many moves in the Jesus book that show he has figured out how to find a respectable, not embarrassing, foundation for the Jesus movement: he knows how to purge most of the problematic themes though his perspicuity criterion and his Enlightenment hermeneutic of explanation. He knows how to find the nuggets of moral wisdom in the dross, and consequently his early anger toward Christianity is quite tamed by the time of the Jesus book. His hermeneutic applies suspicion to any item in the Jesus saga that smells of dogma, and he flushes this material. Thus, any hints that may anticipate the development of Christian doctrine, such as trinitarian thinking and the development of christology, he removes. In addition to finding a way to dispose of such ideas, he simultaneously finds a pleasing marvel at the brilliance of Jesus as a moralist.

So, too, Jefferson's naturalism attacks the traditions of wonders and exorcisms with such confidence that he turns the prodigies into plausible folk exaggerations and tall tales. The fact that the *LMJN* metaphorizes the few hints of wonders that creep into his naturalizing of Jesus' ministry confirms our author's notion that the wonders are really mythicized moral lessons. As we have seen, the *LMJN* allows the parabolic discourse of Jesus to replace the traditions of wonders and exorcisms in the old mythologized saga of Jesus. This displacement and then replacement confirms that Jefferson thinks the moral performances of Jesus' message must substitute for the problematic supernatural features of the saga. Therefore, on his two main, early complaints against Christianity, Jefferson has found a way to make peace. That is, he makes peace with the religion: therefore, *the* LMJN *challenges the views of some scholars who offer completely secular accounts of Jefferson's career under the influence of his early and bitter complaints against Christianity.*

Materialism and Supernaturalism

We have no direct evidence in the *LMJN* to comment positively on Jefferson's materialism. Nonetheless, his removal of most of the hints of supernatural phenomena speaks loudly that he does not have room for a traditional understanding of spirit. We have negative support for his materialism as well, since he eliminates anything traditionally identified with the world of spirit, but there is no claimed support for an ism, much less a theory of a soul or of spiritual reality. Naturally, we slide from the implicit materialism to the critique of supernaturalism. Anything from the saga that hints of the supernature Jefferson leaves out. We do not need to repeat the catalogue. Interestingly, however, the critique does not eliminate God, and thus we see that Jefferson halts the demythologizing of the saga at the point of God. Jefferson implies all kinds of criticism of God concepts, but we seem to have no evidence in the *LMJN* that he ever considers himself an atheist. He simply wants a deity who escapes the critique of supernaturalism: God but no demons! Why Jefferson is not a consistent demythologizer is puzzling. Perhaps he holds to God because of a religious frame that shapes his early years; perhaps he is persuaded by cosmological arguments in his maturity that kept God alive for him. In any case, even if we cannot account for the endurance of God in Jefferson's worldview, two things are clear: First, he norms what is real according to the law-bound, causal nexus of the Newtonian paradigm. When Jefferson has trouble with supernature, it is because he has been such a faithful student of Newton and others in the foundation of modern science. A God concept must participate in that reality or be rejected. Thus, second, Jefferson's only option is to come up with a materialist doctrine of God, as we have seen.

Jefferson is a materialist, and that orientation gets him to favor sense experience and to define reason according to what is materially real and sensible. We see from the pattern of the purging of supernaturalism in the *LMJN* that Jefferson holds out for an Enlightenment style of religion; he has no fear of purging the text of Scripture where it violates those standards of reason.[1] Yet we have to note that the purge of the supernatural is inconsistent or uneven, since he, like many influenced by the deist exception, exempts God from a naturalizing. So, too, he keeps the outlines of the saving historical frame for his gospel, a metahistorical way of reading the Jesus story. In part, perhaps, his incomplete naturalization arises from the fact that Jefferson's materialism values perception and feeling both. And when we deal with primal moral and religious elements, *he recognizes a primal intuitive moment at the foundation of the religious and moral life.* Jefferson insists humans face an undeniable recognition of God when they ponder the order and beauty of nature; it is an a priori, as we know.[2] The *LMJN* works entirely within this uneven natural world that has intuitive room for God and the moral life.

Mysticism

The critique of platonic metaphysic and epistemology follows. Here "mysticism" is of a piece with the other supernatural features of the saga, even as Jesus could not know about Plato. The most telling representation of the way that the critique of the mystical shapes the *LMJN* is in Jefferson's dismissal of nearly all the elements of the religion as we know it. *The vertical dimensions of life and religion all but disappear; the otherworldliness gives way to*

---

1. Recall the famous letter to Peter Carr, August 19, 1785 (Jefferson, *Writings* [Peterson, ed.], 815.

2. The consequence of taking seriously this intuitive moment is that scholars and readers of Jefferson may need to reappraise the image of him as a completely hard-core empirical rationalist. See the point in the Letter to Adams, April 11, 1823 (Jefferson, *Writings* [Peterson, ed.], 1467). Holowchak alerts us to this point and suggests it may press some interpreters to draw back from a hyperrationalist reading of Jefferson (Holowchak, *American Messiah*, 68).

the worldly. In addition to Jefferson's reduction of supernature and spirit, we have his obsession with the practical against the theoretical. Everything about his Jesus is oriented to ethics. Hardly ever does he honor an idea, an abstraction, a theory, a ritual, an issue of holiness in the ministry of Jesus, and almost always he finds a moral demand. Even when he has to mention a wonder or a recent exorcism to get out of an editorial fix, he recovers quickly by finding a related duty and thereby confirms that everything ideational is a cypher to a matter of praxis.

Doctrine

We see Jefferson's distaste for doctrine in the way that the *LMJN* carefully sets up his reduction of the protodogmatic elements in the saga. Naturally, Jefferson allows no Christian doctrine in the saga nor any staging for a doctrine. Actually, his suspicion of doctrine is prophetic of modern biblical criticism; he recognizes, for example, that there is no "higher" christological doctrine in the New Testament or a doctrine of Trinity buried in the Jesus saga. He swims against a theological world that easily found both Nicene and Chalcedonian ideas already in the gospels. Most biblical scholars and theologians discovered Jefferson's insight later in the 1800s, while *he recognizes early that the big doctrines are not in the gospels, and, thereby, he negatively discovers that there is a history to doctrine*, and that doctrine develops (albeit under conditions of corruption).

At this point we see Jefferson's protestant orientation: all developments, including doctrinal ones, represent loss of the primal purity of the founder's wisdom. Already we see traces of his basic stand: that doctrine, at best, is window dressing to the moral heart of religion. Already we see traces of his theory about the corruption of religion: blame it on the priests. The priests, actually any Jewish authorities, are the villains of the *LMJN*, and they play in Jefferson's allegory as the "Cannibal priests" in his struggle with the New England clergy.[3] As for most enlightened thinkers, so for Jefferson the failure of religion can be blamed on the clergy who want power and profit. This criticism is pretty standard fare among the literati of the Enlightenment. But in *a novel twist the* LMJN *enacts an allegorical identification of the Jewish authorities in Jesus' ministry with the blameworthy modern clergy*. Not only does Jefferson transform and project the Jesus Sage onto a battle with the Jewish clerics, but likely he reads that conflict as a cypher to his own

---

3. Letter to Adams, August 22, 1813 (Braden, *"Ye Will Say I Am No Christian,"* 88). Knoles reminds us that Jefferson's scorn for the priests is among his earliest, most critical views on religion (Knoles, "Religious Ideas," 250).

struggles with the New England clergy and others. The trace of ideas leads us to recognize that Jefferson himself plays the part of Jesus in the passion. While the allegorical identification may seem fantastic to some interpreters, the *LMJN* supports it in the way that the end of the gospel demands of Jesus perhaps more than Jefferson is comfortable with on some days.

Private Religion, Subjectification

The idea that religion is a private affair, a very modern idea, finds support in the *LMJN*. Two elements achieve this theme: First, we see Jefferson's pattern of handling both the external and legalistic following of the law by pointing to the real heart of the command with a notion of inner obedience. In this reading any mechanical, legalistic, or showy obedience is superficial unless the faithful recognize the inward expectation for the good life. Over and over Jefferson strips an injunction of its externality and, with Jesus at times, he presses for the inward sense of duty. His point recognizes that the inward escapes hypocrisy or worse, sheer wickedness. Second. Jefferson ethicizes everything in the ritual and holiness traditions. He is completely deaf to things religious, for the central things of religion, since he is so invested in the cultivation of the moral life. If the external is just that, superficial morally, the holy is worse: useless, unless there is a sly way that Jefferson can retrieve a little moral worth out of the holy. Such is *Jefferson's reduction of the Jesus saga to a moral tale*. But so far as he removes Jesus from the ministry that involves him in the nature of Israel, of clean and unclean, of taboo, of ritual purity, of sacrifice, of interpreting Torah and so on, *he actually privatizes the moral life as part of the typical life of the people of Second Temple Judaism*. And then, when he cuts out the wonders and exorcisms, he isolates the moral life from action in a community that needs to be healed. More importantly, Jefferson shows no interest in the ragtag community of those who respond to his message. So, *Jesus is a moral loner*. Remember, he is a "sect of his own."[4]

---

4. Letter to Ezra Stiles Ely, June 25, 1819 (on the *Founders Online* website from the US National Archives, listed in the bibliography; or see Adams and Lester, *Extracts*, 387). One issue of privacy we have not addressed considers the purpose of the *LMJN*. Jefferson's letters are full of suggestions that his *LMJN* is for private use, presumably for his evening meditations. The suggestion rules out an explicit public-religious use or a political use, either in the sense of civic purpose or for political gain. Most scholars have located the private use of the *LMJN* within Jefferson's general concern to keep his religion private, with some speculating about the allegorical application of Jesus' conflicts to the contemporary religious-political battles Jefferson encountered in his political career. Recently, Holowchak has offered an energetic argument to go beyond personal-use theory or occasional allegorical parallels. He sees Jefferson constructing

God

That Jefferson appeals to a natural law and directs all moral injunctions to the universal may reveal some tensions in his understanding of ethics. Can he really pull off a natural-law ethic without a metaphysical umbrella? Jefferson is so allergic to supernature and to Plato, on the one hand, and so wedded to a materialism, on the other, that one wonders how he could deliver on the absolute character of reason and the absolute call of the God he claims. Moreover, we have seen what a strange deity Jefferson worships. Neither has he abandoned completely the old theism, nor does he offer a pure-blood, deist deity. His is a kind of *theistic deism*, since he holds to a deist frame for God even as he insists that this God is involved and caringly providential.[5] Is Jefferson's God at cross-purposes with itself? How can he establish care from God that goes beyond the divinity's establishing and preserving of the natural and moral law? How can his sort of God care and intervene in the world? Jefferson would have to have a theory of how God can act, especially since he flushes the miraculous acts of God. How can divine power be powerful if its power does not extend beyond the ordering of the universe? At some point Jefferson would have to account for a God who acts specially in a Newtonian universe. This tension overlaps with the one appearing earlier

---

in his Jesus a model of the Jeffersonian republican ideal; the *LMJN*'s construction of Jesus is meant for political purposes (with warrant found in the Letter to Kemp, April 25, 1816 [Adams and Lester, *Extracts*, 368–69]). Jesus becomes a Jeffersonian republican (Holowchak, *American Messiah*, 81–84). Jefferson speaks of the vindication of Jesus as a purpose for the *LMJN*; he sometimes wants to reveal or clarify his views among his handful of confidants. He clearly is working out his views of Jesus throughout his three attempts to write about Jesus. And Waldman boldly adds that Jefferson is "to some degree, about justifying his own life and faith" in writing on Jesus (Waldman, *Founding*, 77).

5. We should note that Jefferson interpreters have struggled with and debated how his deism can have a God as involved in creation as he wants. Possibly, Jefferson has not clearly thought through the issues; possibly, his metaphysical and moral commitments and categories are in tension; possibly, he does not care enough about meta-issues to work out a consistent position. We know he does not want an old-fashioned theism, and he seems to want to warm deism. But then, what next? Holowchak reframes the issue by proposing two camps: one he associates with Sanford, and he argues that Jefferson moves in his life from a plainer deism to a more active, superintending God; another position, favored by Holowchak himself, holds that Jefferson consistently commits to a classic deism in which God's care and involvement in the world is woven into the fabric of the Creator's creation (Holowchak, *American Messiah*, 38–44). If an exegesis of the *LMJN* can contribute to this theoretical discussion, we would have to say that the evidence of the *LMJN* favors the warmer change model. But there is one catch to this suggestion: does Jefferson himself credit the suffering and death of the Shepherd-Sage with a transformation of the moral terrain, or does he simply put together inoffensive fragments of the Jesus saga?

in the text: how can Jefferson demythologize the cosmos to eliminate the so-called supernatural and yet leave God mostly untouched by the same, purging hermeneutic?[6] If Jefferson needs a more fulsome way to think of the acts of God, one that does not violate his metaphysical, epistemological, and ethical commitments, he might develop the hints that we find at the end of the *LMJN*. There he seems to be revising his notion of God by way of his portrait of Jesus where the merciful cause of God advances in the suffering and death of the Shepherd-Sage who dies for his wisdom.[7] How far he has come from the young critic, full of vitriol against the so-called wrathful, capricious God of Hebrew Scripture! Indeed, his Jesus project began with a Marcionist caricature of the actual biblical God.

The Afterlife

It is no secret that Jefferson makes a mess of the so-called afterlife. We do not know for sure where he stands and whether he evolves in his thinking. Likely he is an early enthusiast for the immortality of the soul, but comes to have doubts about the doctrine, and perhaps settles on a transcendental necessity of the doctrine for a true moral life.[8] We can assert for sure that

---

6. An even more troubling tension in Jefferson's doctrine of God is his sometime claim that we know nothing about God, while he often glories in the revelation of God in nature and even in Jesus' moral vision: see the Letter to Adams, April 11, 1823 (Adams and Lester, *Extracts*, 411). A charitable reading of the agnostic position is that he declares it in relation to the revelatory confidence of Christians in their traditions and Bible, while he really does believe that nature and the moral life reveals God rightly.

7. At this point Burstein suggests that Jefferson must think Jesus is "maybe divine" (*Inner Jefferson*, 153). The justification for such an un-Jeffersonian idea is the outrageous and daring end to the *LMJN* (Burstein, *Inner Jefferson*, 254).

8. See Gaustad, "Religion," 290–91. Gaustad names Jefferson's position on immortality as "restrained," since the issue of the afterlife cannot be solved by reason. But the transcendental necessity of the afterlife and judgment for the moral life makes the afterlife an attractive bet. Sanford assembled an exhaustive list of suggestive evidence for some kind of belief in an afterlife (Sanford, *Religious Life*, 143–64). Those like Conkin and Gaustad who are confident of an afterlife in Jefferson, and find arguments to support the view, have to face Scherr's daunting critique of their evidentiary work and of their construals of the evidence. See Scherr, "Thomas Jefferson versus the Historians," 71–79. Jefferson scholars will have to work on this battle; my concern is to leave the war at the point of noting the transcendental necessity of a future state of justice for the moral life. The issue is the depth of religion in Jefferson: Was he essentially secularized so that he found Christian faith impossible? Does he warm up to Christianity and Jesus after he learns of a hermeneutic that can clean the corrupt Jesus story? All kinds of things follow in the research according to the way that scholars answer these questions. If Conkin and Gaustad represent the more religious reading, then Scherr represents the criticism of their positions. He offers what is essentially a secular reading of Jefferson

the *LMJN* dumps the resurrection emphatically, even if Jesus and others talk about resurrection. Jefferson does not seem to think that resurrection lives in the apocalyptic and the coming of the Kingdom of God. Rather Easter is summarily deleted. He struggles with the immortality of the soul, first of all, because of his materialist commitments. By the time that he proposes a materialist doctrine of all things, like soul, mind, and God, he may be warming up to some talk of immortality. What is evident in the *LMJN* is his struggle with judgment and the idea that good must be rewarded. He develops the notion that the urgency of the moral life requires a judgment that balances accounts. Does he think that this balancing presupposes the notion of a soul that requires a transhistorical state to secure the immortality of the soul, as Kant does? It is possible, but it is not clear. What is clear is that the *possibility of transhistorical judgment works to support moral seriousness in life*. Jefferson seems to find more transcendental opportunities later in life; in the *LMJN*, for instance, he entertains elements of a day of judgment and apocalyptic scenarios, images, and characters like the Son of Man, not because Jefferson has become an apocalyptic prophet, but because he identifies with the apocalyptic earnestness of Jesus as he faces his undeserved execution. In any case, in his last decade Jefferson seems to move toward ideas unheard of in his early years, but we have to judge that his final position on the afterlife is a solid maybe.[9]

Scripture

The question of Scripture takes us to an obvious theme: Jefferson's enlightened freedom with the Bible is quite evident in the *LMJN*. The technique of cutting and pasting alone would have made the pious wince then. But the hermeneutical question is more intriguing than what he does with a

---

that shapes his politics and his theological judgments (such as of the afterlife). Scherr leaves the question with a denial of the afterlife: he thinks Jefferson flatly rejects it but does not want to say his views publicly (Scherr, "Thomas Jefferson versus the Historians," 71–79). The negative judgment on the afterlife can be found in a telling letter from Francis Van der Kemp, March 24, 1816 (Adams and Lester, *Extracts*, 370–72), where he challenges Jefferson's hopes for a future state, when he can only say such fuzzy things about death, about the material state of the immortal soul, and the resurrected body (Adams and Lester, *Extracts*, 373). Holowchak brings a conclusion to this discussion by declaring that there is no scholarly consensus on Jefferson's view of the afterlife (Holowchak, *American Messiah*, 13).

9. See his Letter to Peter Carr, August 10, 1787 (Jefferson, *Writings* [Peterson, ed.], 903) from the early period or his enthusiastic Letter to George Thacher, January 25, 1824 from the end of his life where he speaks of Jesus' sublime teaching of a "doctrine of a future state of rewards and punishments" (Adams and Lester, *Extracts*, 424).

knife. Jefferson gives no thought to rearranging the gospel materials and to assembling them in clusters drawn from all four gospels. His prejudices and likes in his assemblages point him toward moral nuggets to ponder in a meditative format. We know pretty well what he has to throw out according to his worldview and the epistemological and moral values operative in it. He pays little attention to context and the redactional differences among the biblical gospels. Yet he follows the broadest pattern of the biblical accounts in his story of a moral giant who moves into conflict and comes to his martyr's death. The familiar *heilsgeschichtlich* pattern of gospel writing, evident in both the synoptic gospels and John, moves from the emergence of a precocious lad to deadly conflict with the Jewish authorities to a tragic death.

We conclude that Jefferson was pretty conservative in replicating the basic plot of the Jesus story. Yet within the frame he rearranges and reshapes the emphases of the biblical story in three crucial ways. First, because he puts John's account of the temple at the front of the Jesus story in Judea and conflates the temple conflict involving the Sadducees in Jerusalem with Jesus' controversies over Torah interpretation involving the Pharisees in Galilee, Jefferson displaces the when and where of the gospel in a major way. In so doing he turns the gospel story into a singular conflict account in which Jesus suffers the consequences of his challenge to the morality of the Jewish authorities. The displacement, physical at first, turns into a massive displacement of the themes of the biblical gospels. The displacement turns the Jesus saga entirely into a moral conflict with some nasty Jewish leaders. It eliminates or de-emphasizes a handful of major gospel themes.

Second, Jefferson's director's cut of the gospel eliminates most of the traditions of wonders and exorcisms central to Jesus' ministry. We know why. We also know that he is sometimes inconsistent, and that his effort to demythologize the gospels is incomplete in that he does not attack the metahistorical shaping of the saving history, nor does he go after the God he claims. Oddly, Jefferson is pretty supernaturalist about the God who cares for the world, and pretty supernaturalist about the saving story in which humans live. Nonetheless, *the excising of the supernatural robs the charismatic impulse of Jesus' relationship to the coming Kingdom of God and of his campaign to rebuild Israel's identity in a colonial time.* Jefferson's blunt and unsophisticated hermeneutic simply disposes of Jesus' supernatural actions, for the most part, and robs the story of the charisma that charms some and offends others deeply. The reader wonders how some can become enchanted so quickly and others angered equally so quickly. The application of the *execution criterion* makes it difficult to argue *that Jefferson has provided enough rationale for the execution of Jesus,* especially since the decision to execute him downplays the role of the Romans and puts all blame for the offense on evil Jewish leaders.

Third, Jefferson's method of demythologizing the Jesus story leaves the moral residue in the saga bereft of context. What Jefferson thinks he is rescuing of the real Jesus, in fact, destroys the moral suppositum; the hermeneutic turns the wisdom of Jesus into bland and abstract entries fit for *Poor Richard's Almanac*: generic wisdom, truisms, commonalities that lose the punch of their original contexts. By cutting the moral wisdom from the coming of the Kingdom of God, by separating it from the Mosaic Law and midrashic discussion about Torah, by turning Jesus' vision of Israel into a "commonplace," Jefferson has so displaced the moral genius of Jesus that the ethic no longer can be called historically real. Of course, Jefferson assumes that the moral nuggets can be real, really Jesus' in an acontextual way, as if "Love your enemy" already means the same thing in every place, at every time, and for every audience. However well-meaning are Jefferson's aims, his methods have made him miss finding the real Jesus behind real Christianity, and thus his main goal fails.

The Greeks

The *LMJN* provides us no insight into Jefferson's view of the Greek moral traditions, of course. But as with many things in the study of the *LMJN*, if we walk in the back, apophatic, door, we see more than what appears from the front. We cannot tell much about his comparative interest in ethics and among religions or about his lifelong fascinations, since the task in the *LMJN* turns entirely to mining the Jesus saga.[10] But if we know even a little about his interest in the Greeks, we know how smitten he was by the ethical traditions of Stoicism and Epicureanism when he was young. The young Jefferson praises those traditions when he is departing from his primal involvement in Anglican Christianity during his college years. But in his presidential years and after, when he is planning his *Syllabus* and *Philosophy of Jesus*, we know from his letters that Jefferson enjoys that Jesus has far outstripped the classical sources in his judgments about ethics. As we have seen, he judges Jesus as having unmatched moral insight. He is able to do so primarily because he has been liberated by Joseph Priestley's theory that the religion of Jesus has been corrupted. Jefferson's reaction to Priestley's idea of corruption takes him to see that there is good stuff under the obviously

---

10. Early in Jefferson's thinking about religion, he advocated privately the value of a multiplicity of sects as a protection against the tyranny of an established Church. See Malone's discussion in Malone, *Jefferson*, 4:191.

corrupted. Our point here is that *the classical sources are dropping in Jefferson's pantheon of moral greats, and his early dismissal of Jesus he finds as a mistake.* We know from the letters that he makes a critical judgment about classical ethics: it is brilliant in showing duty in line with reason, but rather weak in the concrete business of caring for people.[11] The classic sources focus on controlling passion and achieving tranquility in external deeds, while Jesus brings charity to all in a focus on purity of thought.[12] Indirectly we can see Jefferson's enthusiasm for Jesus' ethic in the *LMJN* as we watch him conduct the cleaning of the corruptions Priestley never gets to. Note also that Jefferson's developing preference for Jesus' ethic turns on his typical preference for the concrete over the abstract and theoretical.

The Jews

Here we arrive at one of the most painful features in the interpretation of the *LMJN*: Jefferson's hostile attitude toward the Jews. We can find plenty of instances in Jefferson's early writings that suggest he reads the Jews as a people of a wooden and superficial religion. Judaism is a religion in bad need of reformation. His comments about Hebrew Scripture and religious ideas reveal Jefferson to be a completely unsophisticated reader of the sacred texts of Israel, and one who is a victim of certain cultural judgments on the Jewish people. It is the case that Jefferson does not mouth the common stereotypes and complaints about the Jew as in the European world. But he has imbued many of the religious complaints with Judaism that have their explicit home in the writings of Paul, Matthew, and John. Jefferson routinely contrasts Jesus' ethic with the older, tribal, and narrow laws of Moses: the mosaic way focuses on externalities, while Jesus goes for the inner heart of the matter; the mosaic notion aims moral concern for the tribe and the God of Israel, while Jesus brings the moral vision to all humans; the Jews are the originals of moral hypocrisy and it is no wonder that Jesus comes into conflict with Jewish authorities who are "wicked." Jews get lost in superficialities and ritual distractions, while Jesus cuts to the moral heart. The sacrificial system of the Jews is as primitive as their Divine Warrior God. The list could go on. Jefferson's darkest moment is perhaps when he calls Judaism a "depraved religion."[13]

---

11. See the main argument of the *Syllabus* (Jefferson, *Writings* [Peterson, ed.], 1124–25).

12. Letter to Edward Dowse, April 19, 1803, on the *Founders Online* website from the US National Archives, listed in the bibliography.

13. Letter to Short, October 23, 1819 (Jefferson, *Writings* [Peterson, ed.], 1431).

Jesus' ethic contrasts with the religion and morality of Israel at every point. At no point does Jefferson see any serious continuity between Israel's moral traditions and Jesus' Sermon on the Mount, between the Hebrew Scripture and Jesus' parabolic wisdom. There is no continuity, only contrast. We see over and over that Jefferson has no ear for what is already the moral advancement, moral universalism, and moral brilliance on which Jesus stands to make a footnote. In fact, for Jefferson, the Jewish authorities substitute for all the clergy, all the Platonists, all the soothsayers and necromancers Jefferson has denounced in religion since he read Priestley. In his reaction to Priestley's *Socrates and Jesus Compared* and in his famous *Syllabus* of ideas to save in Jesus' story, Jefferson suggests that the religion of the Jews needs to be reformed seriously.[14] And in Jefferson's reading, Jesus corrects the Jewish moral tradition by insisting that God intends all people to be one family.[15]

We have just completed an analysis of the *LMJN*'s treatment of the Jewish authorities and Jesus' opposition to their wicked hypocrisy. The most important point is that the entire biblical account of Jesus has been collapsed into a sustained conflict with the Jewish leaders. Let us review. (1) The Judean story of the Sadducees has been elided into the Galilean conflict accounts with the Pharisees. (2) The *LMJN*'s Jesus intensifies the conflict with the Jews, while other major themes of the gospels get set aside. (3) The Jews get blamed for their moral failure. (4) The Jews get blamed exclusively for the death of Jesus. The list could go on. But the gist of the *LMJN*'s contribution to Jefferson studies rests in the way that its portrait of the Jewish authorities and of the Jews in general suggests a deep anti-Semitic theme in Jefferson's thinking. Problematic references to the Jews in the letters and other places grow into a veritable representation of their moral evil. The Jews of the *LMJN* represent evil in the moral struggle against Jesus. And lest we think Jefferson means only the wicked leadership in the struggle against the moral way, remember that by the time of the passion week, the crowd of "the Jews" has turned against Jesus and cheers for his execution. By blaming the Jews generally for Jesus' death, *Jefferson picks up gospel signals that sacrifice the nation of Israel to absolve the Romans for the death of the Sage.* In taking up the anti-Judaic energy of the biblical gospels in opposition to Jewish wickedness against Jesus, Jefferson takes his long and troubled attitude toward Jews to a painful extreme. *The Jews have become the enemy of the moral life.*

---

14. Gaustad, "Religion," 284.
15. *Syllabus*, Jefferson, *Writings* [Peterson, ed.], 1123–25.

What shall we call Jefferson's act? And how conscious of it is he? Surely, he is anti-Judaic in his religious and moral thinking; surely, he is anti-Judaic and ignorant about the ancient Israelite documents. And we cannot limit his bias to the ancient world, as he uses the word "Jew" to describe an adherent of any religion that needs fixing, a follower of any morality that is wooden, superficial, and spiritless. Is he anti-Semitic? Probably, and probably more anti-Semitic than some others were who swam in the cultural anti-Semitism of Europe then, of which he learned during his years in France.

The Reformer

One of Jefferson's developed notions is that Jesus and Christianity could be purged by a reformer. He seems to get that notion under the influence of Priestley's exposé of the corruption in Christianity. In Jefferson's allegory, the Jesus he recovers from the *LMJN* is the reformer of Judaism even as that Jesus-Jefferson simultaneously acts as the reformer of the Anglican-Calvinist corruption in the US at the beginning of the nineteenth century. And to take the allegory further, the Judaism that needs Jesus' reformation is really the Christianity of Jefferson's America.[16] Surely, he is thinking of the cast of Christian clergymen who accuse him of being an atheist, a deist, and an infidel, and who viciously opposed his election as president in 1800. And when Jefferson picks up his challenge to have Priestley craft the new and real Jesus and does that task himself, we see that Jefferson identifies with the role of Jesus. The allegory continues and Jefferson self-identifies with the part played by Jesus.[17] This Jesus confronts, embarrasses, undermines, ridicules, and traps the Jewish enemies in a deadly struggle, whether by rejecting of the moral limits of Judaism, by breaking free from the corruptive power of Paul and the clergy, or by taking a stand against the Federalists and

---

16. When we consider that Jefferson likely self-identifies with Jesus and that his story of Jesus is an allegory of his political struggles, we should remember that Jefferson has been imbued with the larger national allegory, namely, that the story of America is the enactment of the biblical plotline of redemption. See the suggestion in Sanford, *Religious Life*, 63–64.

17. And in the Jeffersonian allegory, an atopic Palestine becomes the promised land of America; and the enemies of Jesus, the Jewish authorities, become the New England Calvinist preachers and the dreaded Federalists of his lifetime struggles (see Samuelson, "Jefferson," 145). In the anger of the 1800 election his enemies charge him with his infidelity. The presupposition of such a reading of Jefferson's life is that in the 1790s and into the early 1800s *Jefferson has indeed moved beyond his early and harsh criticism of Christian things and Jesus*. He becomes a Christianist of some kind, perhaps with a rational, Unitarian flavor: see the Letter to Waterhouse, June 26, 1822 (Jefferson, *Writings* [Peterson, ed.], 1458).

the New England clergy in 1800. The effect is the same: *moral progress can be found through the sacrificial death of the greatest Sage.*

The causes of the reformer are well-known to us who read the *LMJN* and the letters. We think of simple things, like acting according to what one says; avoiding hypocrisy; avoiding graft and greed for possessions and money; caring for the neighbor; avoiding ostentatious behavior; being modest; and thinking universally about human care and attachment. What we notice about this list of concerns is how generic they are and how far removed they are from religion. Of course, the items in the list are not foreign to religion, but they are not centrally religious in the sense that they cultivate holiness or fulfill one's duties to God. While the virtues are generic and could be drawn into a religious frame, they also function nicely within a secular frame. They exhibit no rootedness in the story of Israel, in God's covenant with the people, or in the Law of Moses. In fact, when Jefferson's Jesus announces, "But I say unto you," he means to replace the Mosaic command with a better one, one not given to superficiality and wooden externality. *The moral past has almost nothing to do with the new commands that refound morality inwardly in the heart.* In truth, Jefferson's Jesus is more of *a founder figure than a reformer*, though Jefferson's project puts quite a bit of stock in the "reformer" term: his Jesus must once again clean house of religion, in this case of the corrupted Christianity that hijacked the message of the founder figure, Jesus. Jesus is perpetually cleaning the house of the religious tendency to turn wisdom into foolishness, newness and insight into layers of obfuscation, pure origins into perversities of profit and power.

Many Jefferson scholars miss how religiously earnest Jefferson is throughout his life. Many see his harsh and indifferent comments as indicating that he is not really religious, not really a Christian, that he has scant connection to the ideas and faith of the Christian salvation story through his own life. And when he goes on his campaign to clean Christianity in the style of Priestley, these scholars think that Jefferson is done with religion, if he has ever had any.[18] But the entire post-Priestley project of Jefferson to clean Christianity and the reputation of Jesus argues against this common view. Paul Conkin is right.[19] Jefferson is earnest about reclaiming the "diamonds" in the Jesus saga, as we see in the *Syllabus*, in the letters from

---

18. Conkin, "Religious Pilgrimage," 23.

19. Conkin's position, against Sanford's and Sheridan's, suggests that the evidence shows that Jefferson's early trouble with Christianity does not end his concern for religion: he retains his seriousness about religion, as his twenty-five-year struggle to make sense of Jesus proves (Conkin, "Religious Pilgrimage," 23). The decision on this issue turns on the question whether Jefferson had a "faith crisis" in his early years, as Malone and others have suggested (Malone, *Jefferson*, 1:107).

the period of the lost *Philosophy of Jesus*, and most powerfully in the *LMJN*. Jesus is transformative for Jefferson, as soon as he can see how the corruption of Jesus' saga works and can begin to retrieve the genuine wisdom of Jesus. *The* LMJN *works powerfully to dispel the notion that Jefferson is not religious, is not interested in Christian materials, and is writing his gospel on a lark or simply exposing the failures of Christianity.* His recovery is genuine, and his effusive claims for Jesus' moral brilliance in the letters are sincere.[20]

So, it is not a surprise that Jefferson is a lifelong member of the Anglican Church, a contributor to his and other local parishes, or that he develops a postcritical faith in the great Sage. A secular vision of Jefferson is unnuanced and likely inaccurate. When we note that he warms up to the Christian religion, we say it with all the critical qualifications that Jefferson puts into his religiousness. It is postcritical and comes through a powerful period of cognitive doubt; it eliminates major features of the doctrinal tradition, as we have seen, and he probably barely tolerates popular Christianity. Jefferson never gives up his points of criticism of Christianity, such as his disgust with the clergy and his views on the mythological features of the gospel. But he never throws out the baby with the bathwater.

Of course, the Christianity Jefferson warms up to has been stripped of many unpleasant and incredible features, but as we have seen, the moral wisdom of Jesus has only to be dusted off. Jefferson thinks it does not need to be purged and certainly not the way he has purged the wonders. Dusting off the moral tradition brings out its universality and ends the accruing tribalism, the externality, the ritualizing of the ethic under the control of priests, ends its selling out to profit and power. Underneath is a simple, magnetic message, the opposite of everything the Jewish leaders stand for. Above all, real religion and real Christianity are simple things. All Jefferson needs from the Jews is enough of their bad behavior to reveal their wickedness so that he can show Jesus' simple and pure message as a welcome contrast.

Public Expression

Finally, scholars of Jefferson and religion usually say something about the way Jefferson wants private religion to enter the public space. We do not see this theme clearly in the *LMJN*, however. Jesus dies quickly and does

20. Here I would side with the researchers who find a rather more religious Jefferson, possibly in his old age, such as Conkin and Gaustad, and against, say, Holowchak's and Scherr's more secular figure, though both these critics pose some powerful criticisms against the religious arguments. But the case I am making in this book does not depend on the victory of one side or another in their holistic interpretations or in particular points.

not seem to have a political theology. Of course, privately moral people will affect the public square in powerful ways. Since *Jefferson lives his life-allegory working with an eye on Jesus and on his contemporary setting*, he can imagine that a Jesus cleaned and simple could bypass the dangers of religion and politics. The thing he worries about most is the dominating intrusion of religious types into the public square, where the religious world and leaders dominate people's lives and thoughts. He wants freedom from a dominating religious establishment, freedom from constraints of every kind. Jefferson is especially concerned about the "power and profit" theme artfully masked by religious rigmarole. He hates the smug, preachy hypocrisy of religious caste. We see the virtues in the *LMJN*, if not their public expressions.[21]

Given these connections between the private and the public, we see in the *LMJN* a powerful allegory of what would have to happen in order to get a good Christianity and a good reformation off the ground. The change would have to begin with a critique of contemporary church/state relationships and stream toward a Jesus-like revision of both culture and church. A Jesus Sage would have to lead a reform of contemporary America and do so with all the plans and risks set out in the *LMJN*.

---

21. When people think of Jefferson, even scholars, they think of a man of reason at the apex of Enlightenment's commitment to a reign of reason. And the shape of this idea is certainly true. But it is incomplete because Jefferson is insistent on the importance of the *primal intuition*, the moral sense, which is independent from the cognitive world and empirical experience. The moral sense shows itself in the innate drive for virtue, which is finally more important than reason. See the discussion of the moral sense in Koch, *Philosophy*, 15–20, where she unpacks the sense in the early Peter Carr Letter of August 1, 1787 (Jefferson, *Writings* [Peterson, ed.], 900–905). She recognizes that Jefferson's moral sense depends on the work of Lord Kames, *Essay on the Principles of Morality and Religion*. The most important point is Kames's notion that the moral sense develops in a social, historical way, and that there is an actual historicizing of the moral sense (Kames, *Essays*, 147–49). If Jefferson follows Kames with a historicized moral sense, he also adds his own utilitarian twist to the moral sense, in which, with reason, persons calculate how to employ their developing moral sense (Koch, *Philosophy*, 20; see also Yarbrough, *American Virtues*, 27).

Bibliography

Adams, Dickinson W., and Ruth W. Lester, eds. *Jefferson's Extracts from the Gospels.* The Papers of Thomas Jefferson. Second Series. Princeton: Princeton University Press, 1983.

Ahlstrom, Sidney E. *A Religious History of the American People.* New Haven: Yale University Press, 1972.

Barton, David. *The Jefferson Lies: Exposing the Myths You've Always Believed about Thomas Jefferson.* Nashville: Nelson, 2012.

———. *The Jefferson Lies.* With an introduction by Glenn Beck. N.p.: WallBuilder, 2012.

Beran, Michael Knox. *Jefferson's Demons: Portrait of a Restless Mind.* New York: Free Press, 2003.

Bernstein, R. B. *Thomas Jefferson.* New York: Oxford University Press, 2003.

Boles, John B., and Randal L. Hall, eds. *Seeing Jefferson Anew: In His Time and Ours.* Charlottesville: University of Virginia Press, 2010.

Bolingbroke, Henry St. John Viscount. *The Philosophical Works 1754–77.* 1754. Reprint, British Philosophers and Theologians of the 17th and 18th Centuries 5. New York: Garland, 1977.

Boorstin, Daniel. *The Lost World of Thomas Jefferson.* 1948. Reprint, Boston: Beacon, 1960.

Braden, Bruce, ed. *"Ye Will Say I Am No Christian": The Thomas Jefferson/John Adams Correspondence on Religion, Morals, and Values.* Amherst, NY: Prometheus, 2006.

Brent, Robert A. "The Jeffersonian Outlook on Religion." *Southern Quarterly* 5 (1967) 417–28.

Brodie, Fawn. *Thomas Jefferson and Sally Hemming: An Intimate History.* New York: Norton, 1974.

Brown, David S. *Thomas Jefferson, A Biographical Companion.* ABC-CLIO Biographical Companion. Santa Barbara, CA: ABC-CLIO, 1999.

Bryan, Susan. "Reauthorizing the Text: Jefferson's Scissor Edit of the Gospels." *Early American Literature* 22 (1987) 19–42.

Buckley, Thomas E. "Placing Thomas Jefferson and Religion in Context, Then and Now." In *Seeing Jefferson Anew: In His Time and Ours,* edited by John B. Boles and Randal L. Hall, 126–51. Charlottesville: University of Virginia Press, 2010.

Burstein, Andrew. *The Inner Jefferson: Portrait of a Grieving Optimist.* Charlottesville: University of Virginia Press, 1995.

———. *Jefferson's Secrets: Death and Desire at Monticello.* New York: Basic Books, 2005.

Cappon, Lester J., ed. *The Adams-Jefferson Letters*. Chapel Hill: University of North Carolina Press, 1988.
Carlson, Peter. "The Bible according to Thomas Jefferson." *Humanist* 72.2 (2012) 19–23.
———. "Resurrecting Jefferson's Bible." *Humanist* (March/April 2012) 19.
Church, F. Forrester. "The Gospel according to Thomas Jefferson." Master's thesis, Harvard Divinity School, 1974.
———. Introduction. In *The Jefferson Bible: The Life and Moral of Jesus of Nazareth*, by Thomas Jefferson, 1–31. With an afterword by Jaroslav Pelikan. Boston: Beacon, 1989.
———. "Politics and Priestcraft: Jefferson's Case against the Clergy." In *Alone Together: Studies in the History of Liberal Religion*, edited by Peter Iver Kaufman and Spencer Lavan, 37–52. Collegium Studies in Liberal Religion. Boston: Beacon, 1978 (1979 printing).
———. "Thomas Jefferson's Bible." In *The Bible and Bibles in America*, edited by Ernest S. Frerichs, 145–61. The Bible in American Culture 1. Atlanta: Scholars, 1988.
Clough, G. Wayne. "Secretary Clough on Jefferson's Bible." Arts and Culture. *Smithsonian* (October, 2011). https://www.smithsonianmag.com/arts-culture/secretary-clough-on-jeffersons-bible-72748111/.
Cogliano, Francis D., ed. *A Companion to Thomas Jefferson*. Blackwell Companions to American History. Chichester, UK: Wiley-Blackwell, 2012.
Colman, John. "Diamonds from Dunghills: Jefferson's Materialism, Free Inquiry, and Religious Reform." *American Political Thought* 6 (2017) 343–70.
Conkin, Paul K. "The Religious Pilgrimage of Thomas Jefferson." In *Jeffersonian Legacies*, edited by Peter S. Onuf, 19–49. Charlottesville: University of Virginia Press, 1993.
Conrad, Edgar W. "From Jefferson's Bible to Judge Moore's Ten Commandments Monument: Secularizing the Bible in the U.S.A." In *Secularism and Biblical Studies*, edited by Roland Boer, 152–77. Bible World. London: Routledge, 2010.
Cooper, Thomas. "The Scriptural Doctrine of Materialism." In *Philosophical Writings of Thomas Cooper*, edited by Udo Thiel, 304–29. Bristol: Thoemmes, 2001.
Crews, Ed. "Jefferson's Secret Bible." *University of Virginia Magazine* (Spring 2012) 38–41. https://uvamagazine.org/articles/jefferson_bible/.
Crossan, John Dominic. *In Parables: The Challenge of the Historical Jesus*. New York: Harper & Row, 1973.
Cunningham, Noble E., Jr. *In Pursuit of Reason: The Life of Thomas Jefferson*. Biography Series. Baton Rouge: Louisiana State University Press, 1987.
Dreisbach, Daniel L. "Mr. Jefferson, a Mammoth Cheese, and the 'Wall of Separation Between Church and State': A Bicentennial Commemoration." *Journal of Church and State* 43 (2001) 725–45.
Edwards, Owen. "How Thomas Jefferson Created His Own Bible." Arts and Culture, *Smithsonian* 42.9 (January 1, 2012) 24. https//www.smithsonianmag.com/arts-culture/how-thomas-jefferson-created-his-own-bible-5659505/.
Ellis, Joseph J. *American Sphinx: The Character of Thomas Jefferson*. New York: Knopf, 1997.
Foote, Henry Wilder. Introduction. In *The Jefferson Bible: With the Annotated Commentaries on the Religion of Thomas Jefferson*, edited by O. I. A. Roche, 115–24. New York: Potter, 1964.
———. *The Religion of Thomas Jefferson*. Boston: Beacon, 1947.

———. *Thomas Jefferson: Champion of Religious Freedom, Advocate of Christian Morals*. Boston: Beacon, 1947.
Frank, Willard C., Jr. "Thomas Jefferson's Religious Journey." *Religious Humanism* 20.1 (1986) 8–17.
Gaustad, Edwin S. "Religion." In *Thomas Jefferson: A Reference Biography*, edited by Merrill D. Peterson, 277–93. New York: Scribner, 1986.
———. *Sworn on the Altar of God: A Religious Biography of Thomas Jefferson*. Library of Religious Biography. Grand Rapids: Eerdmans, 1996.
Glass, Matthew. "Religious Beliefs of Thomas Jefferson." In *Encyclopedia of American Religious History*, edited by Edward L. Queen II et al., 1:353–55. 3 vols. 4th ed. Enhanced Credo ed. Facts on File Library of American History. New York: Facts on File, 2018.
Goodspeed, Edgar J. "Thomas Jefferson and the Bible." *Harvard Theological Review* 40 (1947) 71–76.
Gordon-Reed, Annette. *Thomas Jefferson and Sally Hemings: An American Controversy*. Charlottesville: University Press of Virginia, 1997.
Gould, William D. "The Religious Opinions of Thomas Jefferson." *Mississippi Valley Historical Review* 20 (1933) 191–208.
Hall, J. Leslie. "The Religious Opinions of Thomas Jefferson." *Sewanee Review* 21 (1913) 163–76.
Hamilton, J. G. de Roulhac. "Jefferson and Religion." *Reviewer* 5 (October 1925) 5–15.
Harrington, Donald S. Foreword. In *The Jefferson Bible: With the Annotated Commentaries on Religion of Thomas Jefferson*, edited by O. I. A. Roche, 9–13. New York: Potter, 1964.
Hitchens, Christopher. *Thomas Jefferson: Author of America*. Eminent Lives. New York: HarperCollins, 2005.
Holmes, David L. *The Faiths of the Founding Fathers*. Oxford: Oxford University Press, 2006.
Holowchak, M. Andrew. *American Messiah: The Not-So-Radical Religious Views of Thomas Jefferson*. Tuscaloosa: University of Alabama Press, 2018.
———. *Thomas Jefferson and Philosophy: Essays on the Philosophical Cast of Jefferson's Writings*. Lanham, MD: Lexington, 2014.
———. *Thomas Jefferson, Moralist*. Jefferson, NC: McFarland, 2017.
———. *Thomas Jefferson's Bible: With Introduction and Commentary*. Studies of the Bible and Its Reception. Berlin: de Gruyter, 2019.
———. *Thomas Jefferson: Uncovering His Unique Philosophy and Vision*. Amherst, NY: Prometheus, 2014.
The Holy Bible, Containing the Old and New Covenant, Commonly Called the Old and New Testament. Translated by Charles Thomson. Philadelphia: Jane Aitken, 1808.
Huddleston, Eugene L. *Thomas Jefferson: A Reference Guide*. Reference Guide to Literature. Boston: Hall, 1982.
Huntley, William B. "Jefferson's Public and Private Religion." *South Atlantic Quarterly* 79 (1980) 286–301.
Jefferson, Thomas. *The Autobiography of Thomas Jefferson: 1743–1790*. Edited by Paul Leicester Ford. Philadelphia: University of Pennsylvania Press, 2005.
———. *The Jefferson Bible: The Life and Morals of Jesus of Nazareth*. With an introduction by F. Forrest Church and afterword by Jaroslav Pelikan. Boston: Beacon, 1989.

———. *The Jefferson Bible: With the Annotated Commentaries on Religion of Thomas Jefferson*. Edited by O. I. A. Roche. New York, Potter, 1964.

———. *Jefferson's Literary Commonplace Book*. Edited by Douglas L. Wilson. The Papers of Thomas Jefferson. Second Series. Princeton: Princeton University Press, 1989.

———. *The Life and Morals of Jesus of Nazareth*. Edited and foreword by Douglas E. Lurton. New York: Funk, 1940.

———. *The Life and Morals of Jesus of Nazareth Extracted Textually from the Gospels in Greek, Latin, French & English*. American History (Smithsonian Institution website). http://www.americanhistory.si.edu/JeffersonBible/the-book/.

———. *The Life and Morals of Jesus of Nazareth, Extracted Textually from the Gospels in Greek, Latin, French, and English*. Introduced by Cyrus Adler. Washington, DC: G.P.O. [Government Printing Office], 1904.

———. *The Life and Morals of Jesus of Nazareth, Extracted Textually from the Gospels of Matthew, Mark, Luke, and John*. New York: Eakins, 1968.

———. *The Life and Morals of Jesus of Nazareth, Extracted Textually from the Gospels Together with a Comparison of His Doctrines with Those of Others*. Edited by Henry S. Randall. St. Louis: Thompson, 1902.

———. *Literary Commonplace Book*. Edited by Douglas L. Wilson. Princeton: Princeton University Press, 1989.

———. *The Religious and Moral Wisdom of Thomas Jefferson: An Anthology*. Edited by Allen Jayne. New York: Vantage, 1984.

———. *The Reverse Jefferson Bible: What the President Left Out*. Edited by Carl Haus. N.p.: ClearWords, 2009.

———. *The Thomas Jefferson Bible*. Edited by Henry E. Jackson. New York: Boni & Liveright, 1923.

———. *Thomas Jefferson Papers*. Manuscript Division, Library of Congress. https://www.loc.gov/collections/thomas-jefferson-papers/.

———. *Writings*. Edited by Merrill D. Peterson. The Library of America 17. Distributed by the Viking Press. New York: Literary Classics of the U.S., 1984.

———. *The Writings of Thomas Jefferson*. 20 vols. Edited by Andrew A. Lipscomb and Albert E. Bergh. Washington, DC: The Thomas Jefferson Memorial Association, 1903–4.

Jones, Edgar DeWitt. "Thomas Jefferson and Religion." *Christian Century* 43 (June 17, 1926) 774–75.

Kames, Lord (Henry Home). *Essays on the Principles of Morality and Natural Religion. Several Essays Added Concerning the Proof of a Deity*. Edited by Mary Catherine Moran. 3rd ed., corrected and improved. Natural Law and Enlightenment Classics. Indianapolis: Liberty Fund, 2005.

Kilgo, John C. "Study of Thomas Jefferson's Religious Belief." *Trinity Archive* 13 (1900) 331–46.

Kinsolving, Arthur Barksdale. "The Religious Opinions of Thomas Jefferson." *Historical Magazine of the Protestant Episcopal Church* 20 (1951) 325–27.

Knoles, George Harmon. "The Religious Ideas of Thomas Jefferson." In *Thomas Jefferson. A Profile*, edited by Merrill D. Peterson, 243–60. American Profiles. New York: Hill & Wang, 1967.

Koch, Adrienne. *The Philosophy of Thomas Jefferson*. Columbia Studies in American Culture 14. New York: Columbia University Press, 1943.

Lambert, Frank. "'God—and a Religious President . . . [or] Jefferson and No God': Campaigning for a Voter-Imposed Religious Test in 1800." *Journal of Church and State* 39 (1997) 769–89.
Luebke, Fred C. "The Origins of Thomas Jefferson's Anti-Clericism." *Church History* 32 (1963) 344–56.
Mabee, Charles. "Jefferson's Anti-Clerical Bible." *Historical Magazine of the Protestant Episcopal Church,* 48 (1979) 473–81.
———. *Reading Sacred Texts through American Eyes: Biblical Interpretation as Cultural Critique.* Studies in American Biblical Hermeneutics 7. Macon, GA: Mercer University Press, 1991.
Malone, Dumas. *Jefferson and His Time.* Vol. 1, *Jefferson the Virginian.* 6 vols. Boston: Little, Brown, 1948.
———. *Jefferson and His Time.* Vol. 4, *Jefferson the President, First Term, 1801–1805.* 6 vols. Boston: Little, Brown, 1970.
———. *Jefferson and His Time.* Vol 6, *The Sage of Monticello.* 6 vols. Boston: Little, Brown, 1970.
Manseau, Peter. *The Jefferson Bible: A Biography.* Lives of Great Religious Books Princeton: Princeton University Press, 2020.
———. "Why Thomas Jefferson Created His Own Bible." At the Smithsonian. *Smithsonian Magazine* (September 8, 2020). https://www.smithsonianmag.com/smithonian-insitution/why-thomas-jefferson-created-his-own-bible-180975716/.
McDonald, Forrest. *The Presidency of Thomas Jefferson.* American Presidency Series. Lawrence: University Press of Kansas, 1976.
McGill, Arthur C. *Death and Life: An American Theology.* Edited with an afterword by Charles A. Wilson and Per M. Anderson. Minneapolis: Fortress, 1987.
———. *Death and Life: An American Theology.* Edited with an afterword by Charles A. Wilson and Per M. Anderson. 1987. Reprint, Eugene, OR: Wipf & Stock, 2003.
Meacham, Jon. *Thomas Jefferson: The Art of Power.* New York: Random House, 2012.
Mead, Sidney. "The Nation with the Soul of a Church." *Church History* 36 (1967) 262–83.
Mehta, M. J. "The Religion of Thomas Jefferson." *Indo-Asian Culture* 16 (April 1967) 95–103.
Mellowes, Marilyn. "Thomas Jefferson and His Bible." *From Jesus to Christ.* Frontline (website). https://www.pbs.org/wgbh/pages/frontline/shows/religion/jesus/jefferson.html.
Michaels, J. Ramsey. "Charles Thomson and the First American New Testament." *Harvard Theological Review* 104 (2011) 349–65.
Miller, Charles A. *Jefferson and Nature: An Interpretation.* Baltimore: The Johns Hopkins University Press, 1988.
Neem, Johann N. "A Republican Reformation: Thomas Jefferson's Civil Religion and the Separation of Church from State." In *A Companion to Thomas Jefferson,* edited by Francis D. Cogliano, 91–109. Blackwell Companions to American History. Oxford: Wiley-Blackwell, 2012.
Noll, Mark A., and Nathan O. Hatch. Foreword. In *Sworn on the Altar of God: A Religious Biography of Thomas Jefferson,* by Edwin S. Gaustad, ix–xi. Library of Religious Biography. Grand Rapids: Eerdmans, 1996.
Onuf, Peter. *The Mind of Thomas Jefferson.* Charlottesville: The University of Virginia Press, 2007.

Pelikan, Jaroslav. "Jefferson and His Contemporaries." In *The Jefferson Bible: The Life and Morals of Jesus of Nazareth*, by Thomas Jefferson, 14–67. With an introduction by F. Forrester Church. Boston: Beacon, 1989.

Peterson, Merrill D., ed. *Thomas Jefferson. A Profile*. New York: Hill & Wang, 1967.

———, ed. *Thomas Jefferson: A Reference Biography*. New York: Scribner, 1986.

———. *The Jefferson Image in the American Mind*. New York: Oxford University Press, 1960.

———. "Thomas Jefferson and the Enlightenment: Reflections on Literary Influence." *Lex et Scientia* 11 (1975) 89–127.

Priestley, Joseph. *A Harmony of the Evangelists in Greek: To Which Are Prefixed Critical Dissertations in English*. London: Johnson, 1777.

———. *A History of the Corruptions of Christianity*. Reprinted from Rutt's edition, with notes. London: British and Foreign Unitarian Association, 1871.

———. *Socrates and Jesus Compared*. Early American Imprints. Second Series. Philadelphia: Byrne, 1803.

Prothero, Stephen. *The American Bible—Whose America Is This?* New York: HarperCollins, 2012.

Reimarus, Herman Samuel. *Reimarus: Fragments*. Edited by Charles H. Talbert. Translated by Ralph S. Franzer. Lives of Jesus Series. Philadelphia: Fortress, 1970.

Ricoeur, Paul. *The Conflict of Interpretations*. Northwestern University Studies in Phenomenology & Existential Philosophy. Essays in Hermeneutics 1. Evanston, IL: Northwestern University Press, 1974.

Samuelson, Richard. "Jefferson and Religion: Private Belief, Public Policy." In *The Cambridge Companion to Thomas Jefferson*, edited by Frank Schuffelton, 143–54. Cambridge Companions to American Studies. Cambridge: Cambridge University Press, 2009.

Sanders, E. P. *The Historical Figure of Jesus*. New York: Penguin, 1996.

Sanford, Charles B. *The Religious Life of Thomas Jefferson*. Charlottesville: University Press of Virginia, 1984.

———. "The Religious Life of Thomas Jefferson." In *Religion and Political Culture in Jefferson's Virginia*, edited by Garrett Ward Sheldon and Daniel L. Dreisbach, 61–91. Lanham, MD: Rowman & Littlefield, 2000.

———. *Thomas Jefferson and His Library: A Study of His Literary Interests and of the Religious Attitudes Revealed by Relevant Titles in His Library*. Camden, CT: Archon, 1977.

Scherr, Arthur. "Thomas Jefferson versus the Historians: Christianity, Atheistic Morality, and the Afterlife." *Church History* 83 (2014) 60–109.

Schuffelton, Frank, ed. *Cambridge Companion to Thomas Jefferson*. Cambridge Companions to American Studies. Cambridge: Cambridge University Press, 2005.

Sheldon, Garrett Ward, and Daniel L. Dreisbach, eds. *Religion and Political Culture in Jefferson's Virginia*. Lanham, MD: Rowman & Littlefield, 2000.

Sheldon, Garrett Ward. *The Political Philosophy of Thomas Jefferson*. Baltimore: Johns Hopkins University Press, 1991.

Sheridan, Eugene R. Introduction. In *Jefferson's Extracts from the Gospels*, edited by Dickinson W. Adams and Ruth W. Lester, 3–42. The Papers of Thomas Jefferson. Second Series. Princeton: Princeton University Press, 1983.

———. *Jefferson and Religion*. Monticello Monograph Series. Charlottesville, VA: Thomas Jefferson Memorial Foundation, 1998.

———. *Thomas Jefferson: A Comprehensive, Annotated Bibliography of Writings about Him (1826-1980)*. Garland Reference Library of Social Science 184. New York: Garland, 1983.

———. *Thomas Jefferson, 1981-1990: An Annotated Bibliography*. Garland Reference Library of the Humanities 1217. New York: Garland, 1992.

Sugirtharajah, R. S. *The Bible and Empire: Postcolonial Considerations*. Cambridge: Cambridge University Press, 2005.

Thiry, Paul-Henry, Baron D'Holbach. *Ecce Homo! An Eighteenth Century Life of Jesus*. A critical edition and revision of George Houston's translation from the French. Edited by Andrew Hunwick. History of Religions in Translation 1. Berlin: Mouton de Gruyter, 1995,

Tödt, Heinz Eduard. *The Son of Man in the Synoptic Tradition*. Translated by Dorothea M. Barton. New Testament Library. Philadelphia: Westminster, 1965.

Tucker, David. *Enlightened Republicanism: A Study of Jefferson's Notes on the State of Virginia*. Lanham, MD: Lexington, 2008.

Vicchio, Stephen J. *Jefferson's Religion*. Eugene, OR: Wipf & Stock, 2007.

Virginia Museum of History and Culture. "Thomas Jefferson and the Virginia Statute." https://virginiahistory.org/learn/thomas-jefferson-and-virginia-statute-religious-freedom.

Waldman, Steven. *Founding Faith*. New York: Random House, 2008.

Wettstein, A. Arnold. "Religionless Religion in the Letters and Papers from Monticello." *Religion in Life* 45 (1976) 152–60.

Wilken, Robert L. *The Myth of Christian Beginnings*. Eugene, OR: Wipf & Stock, 2009.

Wills, Garry. "Jefferson's Jesus." *The New York Review of Books* (November 24, 1983). http://www.nybooks.com/articles/1983/11/24/jeffersons-jesus/.

Wilson, Charles A. *Inventing Christic Jesuses: Rules and Warrants for Theology*. Vol. 1, *Method*. Eugene, OR: Cascade, 2017.

———. *Inventing Christic Jesuses: Rules and Warrants for Theology*. Vol. 2, *Christological Recommendations*. Eugene, OR: Cascade, 2018.

Wilson, Douglas L. "Jefferson and Bolingbroke: Some Notes on the Question of Influence." In *Religion and Political Culture in Jefferson's Virginia*, edited by Garrett Ward Sheldon and Daniel L. Dreisbach, 107–18. Lanham, MD: Rowman & Littlefield, 2000.

Wrede, William. *The Messianic Secret*. Translated by J. C. G. Greig. Library of Theological Translations. London: James Clarke, 1971.

Yarbrough, Jean M. *American Virtues: Thomas Jefferson and the Character of a Free People*. American Political Thought. Lawrence: University Press of Kansas, 1998.

Zimmermann, Ruben. *Puzzling the Parable of Jesus: Methods and Interpretation*. Minneapolis: Fortress, 2015.

Zuckert, Michael. *The Natural Rights Republic*. The Frank M. Covey, Jr. Loyola Lectures in Political Analysis. Notre Dame, IN: University of Notre Dame Press, 1998.